Communications
in Computer and Info

Werner Schmidt (Ed.)

# S-BPM ONE - Learning by Doing - Doing by Learning

Third International Conference, S-BPM ONE 2011
Ingolstadt, Germany, September 29-30, 2011
Proceedings

Volume Editor

Werner Schmidt
University of Applied Sciences Ingolstadt
85049 Ingolstadt, Germany
E-mail: werner.schmidt@haw-ingolstadt.de

ISSN 1865-0929  e-ISSN 1865-0937
ISBN 978-3-642-23470-5  e-ISBN 978-3-642-23471-2
DOI 10.1007/978-3-642-23471-2
Springer Heidelberg Dordrecht London New York

Library of Congress Control Number: Applied for

CR Subject Classification (1998): C.2, H.4, D.2, I.2, H.3, H.5

© Springer-Verlag Berlin Heidelberg 2011
This work is subject to copyright. All rights are reserved, whether the whole or part of the material is concerned, specifically the rights of translation, reprinting, re-use of illustrations, recitation, broadcasting, reproduction on microfilms or in any other way, and storage in data banks. Duplication of this publication or parts thereof is permitted only under the provisions of the German Copyright Law of September 9, 1965, in its current version, and permission for use must always be obtained from Springer. Violations are liable to prosecution under the German Copyright Law.
The use of general descriptive names, registered names, trademarks, etc. in this publication does not imply, even in the absence of a specific statement, that such names are exempt from the relevant protective laws and regulations and therefore free for general use.

*Typesetting:* Camera-ready by author, data conversion by Scientific Publishing Services, Chennai, India

Printed on acid-free paper

Springer is part of Springer Science+Business Media (www.springer.com)

# Preface

This volume contains the proceedings of the S-BPM ONE 2011 conference. It was held during September 29-30, 2011 at the Ingolstadt University of Applied Sciences, Germany. As the third conference in the S-BPM series it followed two successful events in Karlsruhe. The series aims to establish a platform for multi- and cross-disciplinary exchange of innovative ideas, concepts, methods, and tools. Besides fundamental issues, applied research is of crucial importance, as the paradigm of Subject-oriented Business Process Management (S-BPM) might affect many of our daily interactions, both in business and in private life.

The intention of this year's event, S-BPM 2011, was to draw the attention of the business process management community to the emerging significant role of stakeholders, communication, and seamless execution of BPM. As S-BPM refers to organizations as socio-technical and socio-economic systems it recognizes current developments in social computing and stakeholder orientation, (re-)aligning human needs and capabilities with artifacts. "Learning by Doing – Doing by Learning" was intended to bring together process-aware stakeholders, educators, and developers. The conference aimed at providing a discussion forum for researchers and practitioners who are interested in working state-of-the-art samples of S-BPM, capturing organizational use cases as well as educational approaches.

According to our objectives of involving both scientists and practitioners, we called for academic contributions and experience reports. All of them were reviewed accordingly. A body of more than 20 international experts from research and industry served both as referees and Program Committee members. They managed to accept most of the contributions in the different categories.

Each of the contributions pushes forward the discussion along various dimensions of S-BPM in particular, and BPM in general. They have been grouped in four areas:

- Part I (Educational Perspectives) introduces novel approaches to learning and teaching (S-)BPM where (new) knowledge and content need to be gained from different sources, structured and represented for various target groups.
- Part II (Methodological Advancements) covers innovative (S-)BPM approaches and methods supporting agility along process management cycles and procedures, as well as specific bundles of BPM activities, such as analysis or optimization.
- Part III (Technological Advancements) addresses two research projects dealing with solutions for inter-organizational business processes and their distributed execution in the future Internet of Services (IoS).
- Part IV (Experience Reports) contains a collection of actual uses cases, approaching BPM in different ways, either utilizing S-BPM or other BPM techniques.

Part I starts with Christian Stary's approach of transferring the concept of evidence-based practice and learning, which is successfully applied in medicine, to the knowledge area of business process management. The major constituents of evidence-based S-BPM education are discussed and exemplified: provision of knowledge and content generation, exploration and consolidation, sharing and distribution.

Stefan Oppl presents a concept for elicitating work-process knowledge in co-located and distributed business settings, using an interactive tabletop interface for modeling and interaction support. The conceptual foundations of both, the elicitation platform, the communication and synchronization mechanism are presented. Finally, implementation details revealing the technical feasibility of the approach are discussed.

Johannes Kröckel and Bernd Hilgarth present their first results and a case study report of the BPM@KMU project. It aims at the efficient implementation of BPM in small- and medium-sized enterprises (SMEs). The authors consider e-Learning as an enabler and tool to overcome barriers for the implementation of BPM in SMEs.

Gregor Back and Klaus Daniel discuss the need for properly designed process training in order to quickly and easily acquire the required process competence (abilities, skills, will, and permission). They suggest a design meeting these requirements and exemplify its benefits in a business case.

In the opener of Part II Matthias Neubauer and Christian Stary look at business process models as means to capture all essential information required for executing business processes in the situational context of agile BPM. They discuss existing concepts of situational context of organizational changes, and exemplify an integrated representation approach enabling situated subject-oriented BPM.

Christian Herrmann and Matthias Kurz present their research on the agility and flexibility of process design particularly for knowledge-intensive processes. They explore the concept of adaptive case management where the knowledge workers themselves take on the responsibility of adapting their processes and IT environment in order to achieve efficient case handling.

The contribution of David Bonaldi, Alexandra Totter and Eva Pinter focuses on the analysis of complex business processes. The authors suggest the contextual design method in combination with subject-oriented BPM to actively foster the consideration of the human elements in complex process environments.

smart4sense2act, approaching systemic performance management, is presented in the concept contribution by Fritz Bastarz and Patrick Halek. The envisioned alignments to S-BPM are subject to ongoing field tests.

Stefan Reinheimer discusses the use of a variety of methods for the manifold activities related to BPM. He contrasts the approach to applying a single comprehensive method.

Hans-Günter Lindner's article presents an applied research project targeting the optimization of processes in residential care services. The author shows how a process model considering subjects allows calculation of the process costs as a result of subject-oriented process simulation.

The contribution by Matthias Kurz, Thomas Schaller, Dominik Reichelt and Michael Ferschl proposes an extension of the Project4Sure methodology and software platform. It provides a process-centric approach to analyzing and realizing business requirements when implementing Microsoft ERP systems (Dynamics NAV, AX, and CRM). The approach utilizes the expertise of the individuals working in operational departments. In this way ERP implementations meeting the requirements of actual business users are facilitated.

In their paper Andreas Hufgard and Eduard Gerhardt recognize a lack of standardization and homogenization of processes, although both are considered as an essential step when consolidating IT systems in the context of mergers and acquisition (M&A) projects. The authors investigate principles and procedures to overcome this deficiency.

The first paper in Part III is the contribution of Nils Meyer, Markus Radmayr, Richard Heininger and Thomas Rothschädl. They revise the existing jCPEX! approach for connecting inter-organizational business processes and present a solution where the jCPEX! platform resolves the problem that workflow engines in most cases are sealed off by a corporate network and thus not reachable from outside without further ado. The solution reveals the jCPEX! platform on a network router that connects the external net with the corporate network of an organization, making a separate demilitarized zone (DMZ) superfluous for this purpose.

Stephan Borgert, Joachim Steinmetz and Max Mühlhäuser present ePASS-IoS, a unified approach to describe processes and service choreographies with well-defined execution and verification semantics. Formulating the well-known workflow and interaction patterns in ePASS-IoS they show that its expressiveness is adequate for S-BPM.

The experience reports in Part IV start with the contribution of Shinji Nakamura, Toshihiro Tan, Takeshi Hirayama, Hiroyuki Kawai, Shota Komiyama, Sadao Hosaka, Minoru Nakamura and Katsuhiro Yuki. They describe how and why the NEC Corporation complemented their traditional BPM development method with a new method called enterprise eco service (EES), based on S-BPM. The authors give a detailed insight into EES and report on the benefits they achieved using its implementation.

Based on many years of BPM experience at AUDI AG, Martin Turinsky reflects on the necessity of consistent terminology, modeling notations, and levels of detail as conditions for allowing different departments in a large organization to develop a common understanding of processes and to learn from each other in their process work. He discusses these aspects with respect to documentation, optimization and control of processes.

Marco Strauss and Siri Lang describe a BPM project carried out in an R&D department in the automotive industry. They explicate the methods they applied in order to successfully set up an agile process management environment with transparent, well-documented processes as well as consistent stakeholder and change management.

Jörg Bindner and Gunther Mayer-Leixner look at BPM both from the perspective of micro enterprises and large corporations. Benefitting from their extensive professional background in process management when working with organizations of different size, they discuss the similarities and differences as a basis for further investigations.

The work of Alexander Gromoff, Valery Chebotarev, Yulia Stavenko and Kristin Evina contains intermediate results of a project aiming at the definition of requirements when developing innovation support in the context of an enterprise content management (ECM) system. Innovation support can be achieved in terms of innovation-process improvements using S-BPM.

Barbara Handy, Max Dirndorfer, Josef Schneeberger and Herbert Fischer present findings of a survey involving several notaries. The survey was one of the initial steps in a project aiming at German notaries' support by implementing a secure electronic communication structure for the various governmental and private parties. The survey provides the first insights into which process modeling techniques could be suitable for this challenging application domain. It guides further investigations and project steps.

The contribution of Patrick Feldbacher, Peter Suppan, Christina Schweiger and Robert Singer concludes Part IV, as the authors interviewed small and medium-sized enterprises (SMEs) in the manufacturing and service sector in Austria to assess their BPM maturity. They come up with significant interpretations of the results impacting future S-BPM developments.

As the editor of these proceedings and as Conference Chair I would like to thank all the members of the Program Committee, the Chairs of all sections and all authors and speakers for their contributions. Thanks also go to the Institute of Innovative Process Management (I2PM, www.i2pm.net), the patron institution of the overall S-BPM ONE conference series. Furthermore, we thank all sponsoring institutions listed in a seperate section here for their financial support, as well as Harald Weinreich, who offered affordable conditions for his ConfTool conference management system.

We owe special gratitude to all helping hands for their support of the local organization (preparation and days of conference), among others: Petra Heckner, Dieter Rohe, Tobias Ochsenkühn, Michael Schneider (Dean's Office at the University of Applied Sciences Ingolstadt, College of Business), Alexandra Kulfanová, Katrin Kindermann and Alexandra Gerrard (Metasonic AG), and Kathrin Ertinger, Marina Völringer and Xiao Xia Chen (student volunteers).

Last but not least, we thank Alfred Hofmann and Leonie Kunz from Springer for their assistance and support in publishing these proceedings.

September 2011                                              Werner Schmidt

# Organization

## Organizing Committee

| | |
|---|---|
| Werner Schmidt (Chair) | University of Applied Sciences Ingolstadt, Germany |
| Christian Stary | Johannes Kepler University Linz, Austria |

## Program Committee

| | |
|---|---|
| Werner Schmidt (Chair) | University of Applied Sciences Ingolstadt, Germany |
| Martin Adam | University of Applied Sciences Kufstein, Austria |
| Thomas Bahlinger | University of Applied Sciences Nuremberg, Germany |
| Freimut Bodendorf | University of Erlangen-Nuremberg, Germany |
| Alexander Gromoff | Moscow National Research University, Higher School of Economics (HSE), Russia |
| Lutz Heuser | AGT Germany GmbH, Germany |
| Hans-Arne Jacobsen | University of Toronto, Canada |
| Bettina Kemme | McGill University Montreal, Canada |
| Klaus Langer | Kulmbacher Group, Germany |
| Stefan Reinheimer | BIK GmbH, Germany |
| Wolfgang Renninger | University of Applied Sciences Amberg-Weiden, Germany |
| Susanne Robra-Bissantz | Technical University of Braunschweig, Germany |
| Gabriele Saueressig | University of Applied Sciences Würzburg, Germany |
| Detlef Seese | Karlsruhe Institute of Technology (KIT), Germany |
| Robert Singer | FH Joanneum University of Applied Sciences, Austria |
| Christian Stary | University of Linz, Austria |
| Alexandra Totter | ByElement GmbH, Switzerland |
| Nikos Vidakis | Technological Educational Institute of Crete, Greece |
| James Weber | St. Cloud State University, USA |
| Cornelia Zehbold | University of Applied Sciences Ingolstadt, Germany |
| Erwin Zinser | FH Joanneum University of Applied Sciences, Austria |

## Major Sponsoring Institutions

Achat Solutions Schrobenhausen, Germany
AUDI AG Ingolstadt, Germany
CISCO Systems GmbH Hallbergmoos, Germany
Ingolstadt University of Applied Sciences, Germany
METASONIC AG Pfaffenhofen-Hettenshausen, Germany
Siemens AG München, Germany
www.web-dienstleister.de Ingolstadt, Germany

# Table of Contents

## Part I: Educational Perspectives

Evidence-Based (S-)BPM Education .............................. 3
   *Christian Stary*

Subject-Oriented Elicitation of Distributed Business Process
Knowledge ..................................................... 16
   *Stefan Oppl*

BPM@KMU – Designing e-Learning for the Introduction of BPM in
Small- and Medium-Sized Enterprises............................ 34
   *Johannes Kröckel and Bernd Hilgarth*

Process Training to Support Change Necessary within the Scope of
Process Implementation ........................................ 48
   *Gregor Back and Klaus Daniel*

## Part II: Methodological Advancements

Situatedness - The Amalgam of Agile (S-)BPM .................... 65
   *Matthias Neubauer and Christian Stary*

Adaptive Case Management: Supporting Knowledge Intensive Processes
with IT Systems ............................................... 80
   *Christian Herrmann and Matthias Kurz*

Towards Contextual S-BPM – Method and Case Study .............. 98
   *David Bonaldi, Alexandra Totter, and Eva Pinter*

smart4sense2act: A Smart Concept for Systemic Performance
Management .................................................... 109
   *Fritz Bastarz and Patrick Halek*

Modeling Needs in the BPM Consulting Process .................. 115
   *Stefan Reinheimer*

Subject Modeling in Residential Care Services ................. 126
   *Hans-Günter Lindner*

Project4Sure X: Accelerating Implementation Projects for the Microsoft
Dynamics Suite with BPM 2.0 .................................... 139
    *Matthias Kurz, Thomas Schaller, Dominik Reichelt, and
Michael Ferschl*

Consolidating Business Processes as Exemplified in SAP ERP
Systems ........................................................ 155
    *Andreas Hufgard and Eduard Gerhardt*

## Part III: Technological Advancements

Platform for Managing and Routing Cross-Organizational Business
Processes on a Network Router ................................... 175
    *Nils Meyer, Markus Radmayr, Richard Heininger,
Thomas Rothschädl, and Albert Fleischmann*

ePASS-IoS 1.1: Enabling Inter-enterprise Business Process Modeling by
S-BPM and the Internet of Services Concept ....................... 190
    *Stephan Borgert, Joachim Steinmetz, and Max Mühlhäuser*

## Part IV: Experience Reports

CGAA/EES at NEC Corporation, Powered by S-BPM:
The Subject-Oriented BPM Development Technique Using
Top-Down Approach ............................................. 215
    *Shinji Nakamura, Toshihiro Tan, Takeshi Hirayama,
Hiroyuki Kawai, Shota Komiyama, Sadao Hosaka,
Minoru Nakamura, and Katsuhiro Yuki*

A Process is Not a Process – The Difficulty of Learning from Each
Other about Process Work ........................................ 232
    *Martin Turinsky*

Agile Process Management in an Industrial R&D Department ......... 246
    *Marco Strauss and Siri Lang*

Differences in Business Process Management between Global Players
and Micro Enterprises – Experiences from Practice .................. 256
    *Jörg Bindner and Gunther Mayer-Leixner*

An Approach to Agility in Enterprise Innovation .................... 271
    *Alexander Gromoff, Valery Chebotarev, Kristin Evina, and
Yulia Stavenko*

Methods of Process Modeling in the Context of Civil Services by the
Example of German Notaries .................................... 281
   *Barbara Handy, Max Dirndorfer, Josef Schneeberger, and
   Herbert Fischer*

Business Process Management: A Survey among Small and Medium
Sized Enterprises ............................................... 296
   *Patrick Feldbacher, Peter Suppan, Christina Schweiger, and
   Robert Singer*

**Author Index** ................................................. 313

# Part I

# Educational Perspectives

# Evidence-Based (S-)BPM Education

Christian Stary

Kepler University Linz
Department of Business Information Systems - Communications Engineering
Competence Center Knowledge Management
Freistädterstraße 315, A-4040 Linz, Austria
Christian.Stary@jku.at

**Abstract.** Establishing new paradigms, such as S-BPM, requires education. In this paper, an educational proposal is developed, not only to help members of existing BPM communities shifting, but also capturing the dynamics of the field itself. The approach is grounded on the concepts of evidence-based practice and learning, stemming from medicine, and epistemological considerations. In the paper the major constituents of evidence-based S-BPM education are discussed and exemplified: provision of knowledge and content generation, exploration and consolidation, sharing and distribution. They can be intertwined and designed in a variety of ways. Of particular interest are stakeholder-specific perspectives and behavior patterns, as the change over time, and require sophisticated features and a corresponding scheme of representing BPM content, information about user-specific content individualization, and social interaction.

## 1 Introduction

Subject-oriented Business Process Management (S-BPM) can help organizations to establish a different, while more effective BPM (cf. [1][6]). However, shifting the focus of BPM from mainly function- or flow-driven representations towards agent-specific communication and information exchange requires substantial re-thinking and significant effort when (re-)engineering business (cf. [4][7]). In this way S-BPM inspires to find deeper meaning in modeling, representation, and organizational development practices.

Creating a sense-AND-response organization [8] requires stakeholder education and qualified stakeholder involvement in organizational development: On one hand, their perspectives need to be captured when BPM-based organizational development is driven by human needs [12][22]. On the other hand the "integration-centric" approach needs to be aligned with the "human-centric" one [13][21]. Consequently, both, high-level support for human-process interaction, and functional knowledge, have to be addressed when developing an educational infrastructure, in particular qualifying for participatory organizational design.

Recalling the initiation of an informed S-BPM community [18] that has led to the S-BPM community platform i2pm (http://www.i2pm.net) a corresponding concept for S-BPM education has been developed and can be implemented using a second generation learning management system. In the following we recapture some background and introduce key concepts as well as requirements (section 2), before we provide epistemological foundations and present implementation details (section 3). In a conclusive summary (section 4), the impact on sustainable BPM literacy is sketched.

## 2 Evidence-Based Practice and Learning

The idea of evidence-based practice and learning has been based on observing doctors being too busy to study relevant information in their disciplines: If we take clinical journals in adult internal medicine reporting studies of direct importance to clinical practice, in 1992 20 of these journals included over 6000 articles. In order to keep up with reflecting relevant developments each specialist in adult internal medicine would have needed to read about 17 articles a day every day of the year [5]. It immediately became evident that (even) experts need education to be kept up-to-date and well informed in their work routines (cf. [20]).

According to Sackett et al. evidence-based medicine is 'about integrating individual clinical expertise and the best external evidence.' [16] Such an understanding seems to be significant for every field characterized by a dynamic development of knowledge. With respect to BPM it means the conscientious, explicit, and judicious use of current best evidence in applying methods, techniques, and tools about the development of particular organizations. Developers of organizations, information and workflow systems should integrate individual BPM expertise with the best available external BPM evidence from systematic research.

Individual expertise addresses the proficiency and judgment that business-process managers acquire through organizational development or BPM experience and respective practice. Increased expertise is reflected in more effective and efficient BPM, in particular in the more thoughtful identification and compassionate use of modeling techniques, as modeling has to be considered the core activity of BPM.

External BPM evidence addresses OL (Organizational Learning) and BPM relevant research, often from the fundamental sciences of Business Informatics, but especially from stakeholder-centered OL/BPM research with respect to the accuracy of developments for organizations. External BPM evidence both questions previously accepted BPM approaches including paradigms, and replaces them with new ones that are more effective and/or efficient (cf. [23]).

Professional developers use individual BPM expertise and the available external evidence in an integrated way. Without BPM expertise, practice risks becoming driven by evidence, for even accurate external evidence may be inapplicable to or inappropriate for an individual case. Without current evidence, practice risks becoming out of date, and risky for organizations [cf. [9]).

Accordingly, evidence-based BPM education requires a bottom up approach that integrates validated external evidence with individual BPM expertise. It should result in a diverse, open, and transparent (rather than cookbook-) style. External BPM evidence should educate and inform. It should trigger individual BPM engagement, whereby external expertise helps to decide whether the external evidence applies to the individual development case at all and, if so, how it should be integrated into a corresponding BPM project. Similarly, any external guideline must be integrated with individual BPM expertise in deciding whether and how it matches the organization's state, and capabilities, and thus whether it should be applied. Guidelines might be framed by concepts and perspectives providing orientation for BPM activities.

In line with Sackett et al.'s observations [15], evidence-based BPM should go beyond randomized applications and meta-analyses. It should involve context-sensitive tracking down external evidence for reflection. Then, it could help to answer organizational development issues. To find out about the accuracy of a validation procedure, we need to find relevant cross-sectional studies of cases of harboring specific BPM elements, not a randomized trial. In particular, for triggering BPM, we need proper follow up studies of organizational developments assembled at a uniform, early point in the procedural course of their development. In this way, BPM procedures, and methods can be challenged.

In some cases evidence will come from the basic sciences, such as computer science or occupational psychology. For instance, it is when asking questions about automation that we should try to avoid bringing in the non-validated modeling approaches, since they might not work. Particularly, for stakeholder involvement - BPM is based on modeling (individual) task procedures - personal engagement has to be addressed while motivating for change.

## 3 Evidence-Based Stakeholder Empowerment

Reflecting the current practice in BPM (cf. [14]) and the development of the field (cf. [19]), research and development are becoming increasingly intertwined. Consequently, the involved roles, such as information producers, learners, and practitioners, also become intermingled. Hence, traditional education processes have to be enriched towards dynamic role understanding and flexible information management. Both elements characterize the field of knowledge management (cf. [11]): Content is generated by informed members of a community. It needs to be structured, represented, validated, reflected and explored to become effective. This type of stringency facilitates continuous knowledge generation and innovation on common grounds.

In the following subsections we detail evidence-based (S)-BPM learning and work practice development along its procedural constituents, grounding the structuring of information on elementary epistemological categories. The latter is of particular importance, as S-BPM requires a communication-oriented perspective on organizations when developing them. Since such a perspective it is not self-evident when applying other BPM approaches, epistemological categories, e.g., paradigms (cf. [10]), provide orientation when reflecting existing and enriching individual knowledge.

### 3.1 Provision of Knowledge and Content Generation

Considering BPM as dynamically evolving field means a variety of knowledge is generated, validated, and explored. This knowledge can be of different flavors. For instance, it can be an add-on to a modeling construct, such as allowing agents to broadcast messages enlarging communication lines from 1:1 to 1:n. It also can be a substantial change in interpreting organizational behavior, as being the case for S-BPM: Subjects represent organizations in terms of communication acts rather than functional units of work and resources for task accomplishment.

From the perspective of theory of science and epistemology, several elements establish a certain field (cf. [2][3]):

- *Underlying assumptions, fundamental concepts, and principles*, such as rationalistic thinking (cf. [24])
- *Procedures, lifecycles, and methods* allowing the application of generated knowledge, and leading to impact on practice, in particular when using engineering techniques
- *Applications and lessons learnt*, as they represent experiences and results from practical work, allowing for reflection and generation of novel concepts and techniques.

Underlying assumptions, fundamental concepts, and principles become visible in S-BPM through

- *modeling and models:* They represent the baseline and focal element for all activities. Hence, we need to understand the principal underpinnings of modeling, in order to understand BPM.
- *conceptualizing organizations:* The organization of work and tasks is represented in models, and can be triggered by various perspectives, such as considering an organizational unit as a black-box and modeling input-output interfaces. It could also be considered as a transparent network of communicating agents, as in S-BPM.
- *process orientation:* BPM tries to bridge the gap between the static and dynamic perspective on organizations. Hence, understanding BPM requires to distinguish between these two perspectives and their intertwining in various models, and phases of development.

Procedures, lifecycles, and methods of BPM need to be considered according to

- *specific contexts and mutual relationships*: For instance, particular procedural frameworks, such as networked communicating actors in S-BPM require communication or interaction analysis methods.
- *the underlying paradigm triggering BPM*: For instance, function trees are not core representations in S-BPM, in contrast to functional approaches, such as ARIS [17].

Applications and lessons learnt require BPM

- *case studies:* They support reflecting field work in a context-sensitive way, and thus, learning.
- *feedback to existing features and suggestions for methodological improvements*, as they trigger further developments in the field.
- *style guides:* They help describing current work practices on a general level, and enriching methodologies.

Hence, education in BPM needs to provide information on all three categories of knowledge and support respective learning processes. Once content of the above mentioned types becomes evident, an educational support system should be able to capture it, including the provision of educational meta data.

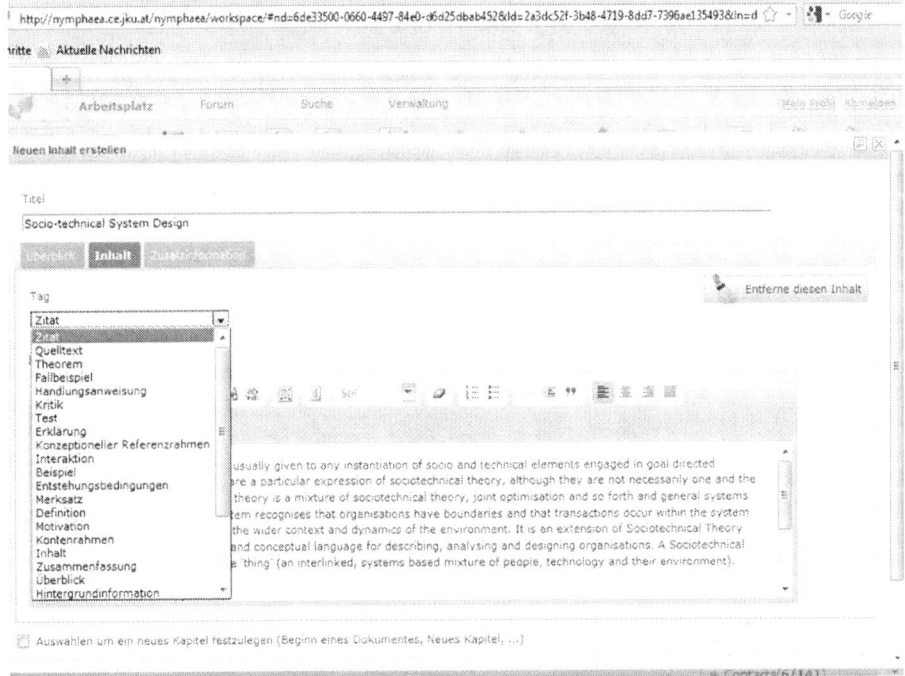

**Fig. 1.** Tagging information with educational meta data when generating content

Figure 1 shows a typical situation of content generation using educational meta data and various levels of detail, using the learning management system nymphaea (http://nymphaea.ce.jku.at). The editor that has to be used requires a repository of consolidated educational meta data, such as background information or explanation. They allow characterizing provided content elements on a level relevant for learning processes.

The screenshot has been taken when editing learning-relevant text on BPM. The learning management system allows the content provider assigning intentional meaning to each piece of information. Typical educational tags are definition, explanation, example, directive, case study etc. as they allow users of that content immediately recognizing its value for learning. The example in the screenshot shows a tagged citation (Zitat). The list of options also contains meta data encoding epistemologically relevant items, such as frame of reference.

After assigning the intended epistemological or didactic meaning to each piece of information the various elements can be arranged in a linear, networked or nested structure. Figure 2 shows a tree structure for an S-BPM introduction on the left side of the screen. The interactive work space shows a behavior diagram enriched with a business object. In the screenshot also two content-management options are displayed in the feature bar on top of the navigation tree, namely 'edit' or 'display' ('Bearbeiten' and 'Betrachten'). Hence, users can switch roles - content provider to learner, and *vice versa* - using those buttons.

### 3.2 Exploration and Consolidation

Once evidence has been structured according to education-relevant categories other members of the community, in our case the (S-)BPM community can access the content. When using a hierarchical structure and a tree view for navigation a particular educational strategy, such as providing conceptual foundations before introducing and comparing particular approaches, can be encoded. Figure 2 shows parts of such an approach in the learning management system.

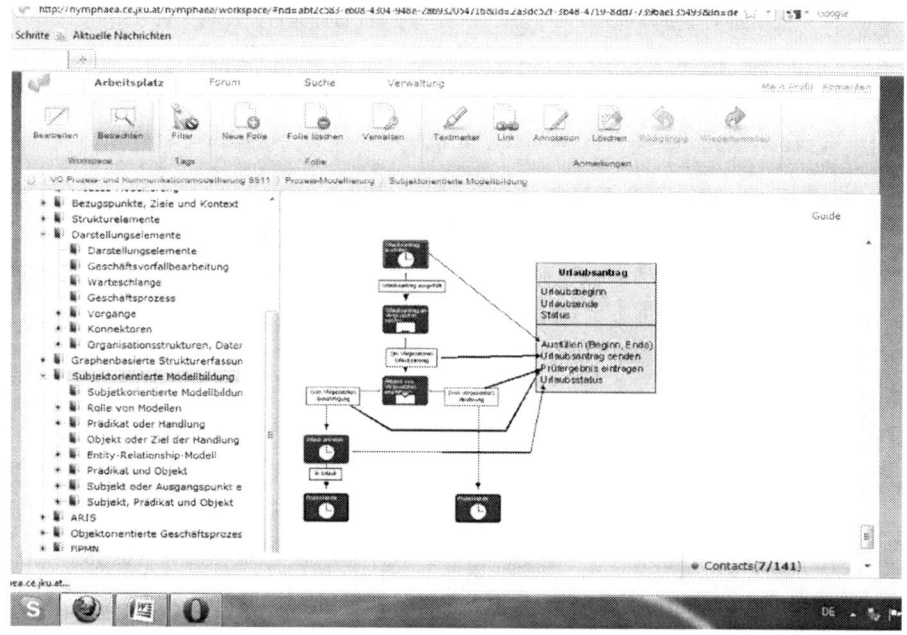

**Fig. 2.** S-BPM content provision based on nested content elements provided by nymphaea

Foundations with respect to modeling constructs are provided, as indicated on the upper part of the navigation tree: Structure and notational elements ('Strukturelemente', 'Darstellungselemente') are introduced. Then, graph-based structuring ('Graphenbasierte Strukturerfassung') is discussed, as it provides a conceptual basis for behavior-oriented approaches, such as S-BPM ('Subjektorientierte Modellbildung'). It is highlighted in the navigation tree, since its content (an enriched Subject Behavior Diagram) is displayed in the workspace of the screen. The S-BPM approach is followed on the top level by ARIS, OOGM (Object-oriented BPM, 'Objektorientierte Geschäftsprozessmodellierung'), and BPMN (Business Process Modeling Notation, www.bpmn.org). Hence, proponents of three conceptually different approaches, and additionally, an integrative standardization effort are tackled with respect to modeling.

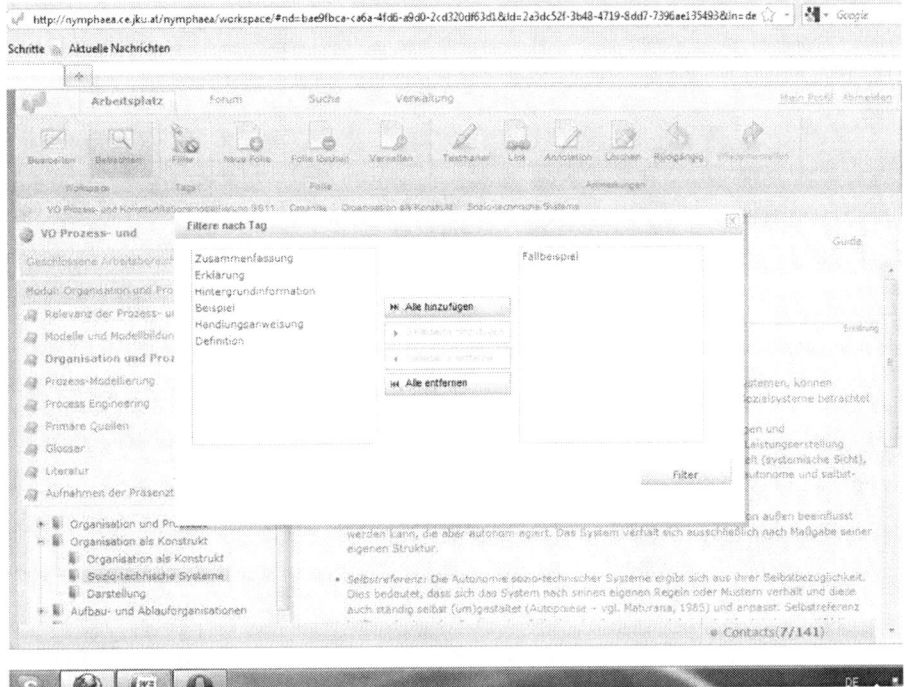

**Fig. 3.** Filtering (= Selecting) evidence according to educational meta data

The represented evidence can be explored in a variety of ways. One effective way is to select those categories of information a user is most interested in. Figure 3 shows the respective feature of the learning management system. In the displayed case the user has selected sample applications ('Fallbeispiel') out of the list of applied educational meta data. In this case, they range from summary ('Zusammenfassung') and explanation ('Erklärung') to definition. After making his/her choice the respective content is displayed in the interactive work space. Those elements that have not been selected cannot be activated (i.e. clicked) in the displayed navigation tree.

Consolidation according to individual and specific organizational learning needs is enabled through annotations. Annotation features allow designing individual information spaces based on already available internal or external evidence, by linking it to various sources of information. Users can also include comments adherent to particular content elements. They can color content items using markers as they are used to with paper-based material and annotation devices (see figure 4 for a certain property of socio-technical systems displayed in the interactive work space).

Typical interactive examples for individualisation are note taking when studying a piece of evidence (e.g., a case study), multimedia attachments to content elements, such as videos referring to content in textual form, links to popular sources of information (e.g., wikipedia), and highlighting text to mark individually relevant items. The linking mechanism is used for information sharing and discussion, as links can also be set to social media, such as forum entries (see next sub section).

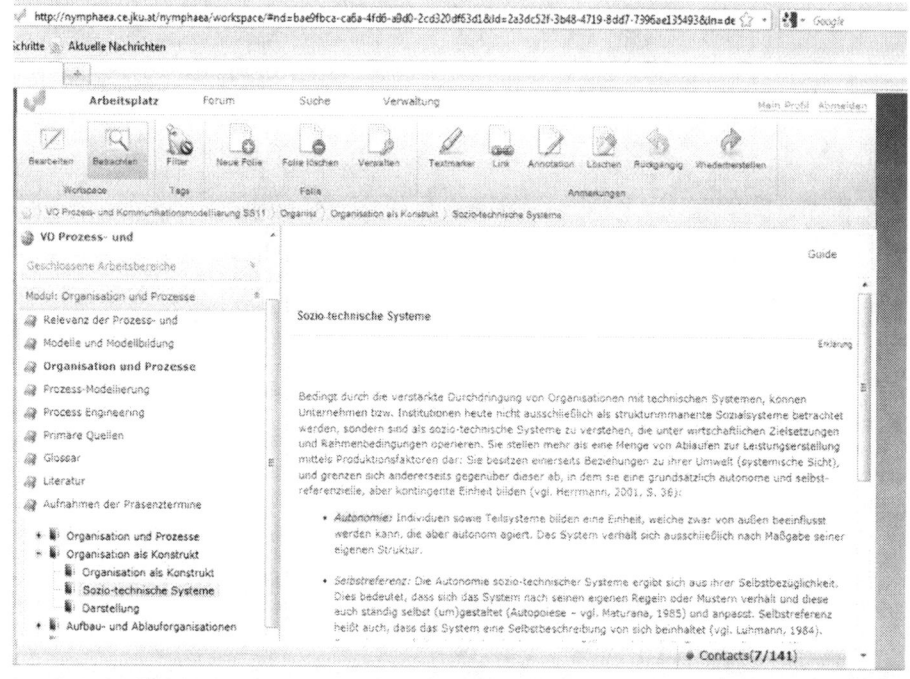

Fig. 4. Consolidation of content through individualization

## 3.3 Sharing and Distribution

As all annotations of individual and external evidence are stored in individual views, not only the content can be shared among users, but also the entire set of annotations. Initially being private users might set their views public, and share them with others by importing them into their work space. As they refer to common content elements, they might even be cascaded, pushing them back and forth among users. In this way, a shared memory of a work groups studying certain topics can evolve. Such a scenario is given, as soon as generated evidence needs to be validated to become part of acknowledged content in the BPM field, e.g., applying a certain construct for modeling. Figure 5 shows the principle of cascading views.

Views are named and can be selected (once becoming available) like the educational meta-data. The name of the currently selected view is displayed on the upper right side of the interactive work space ('Guide' in figure 4). Content providers as well as learners might create and select views. For instance, different user groups, such as S-BPM researchers and practitioners can be addressed explicitly in this way. In addition to the didactically grounded meta-data for domain content representation (definition, explanation, example, case study, business process model etc.) this feature allows for dynamic and target group-specific education.

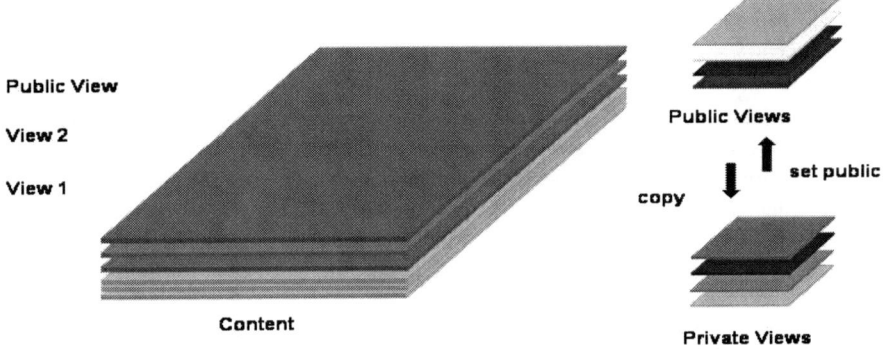

**Fig. 5.** Cascading views

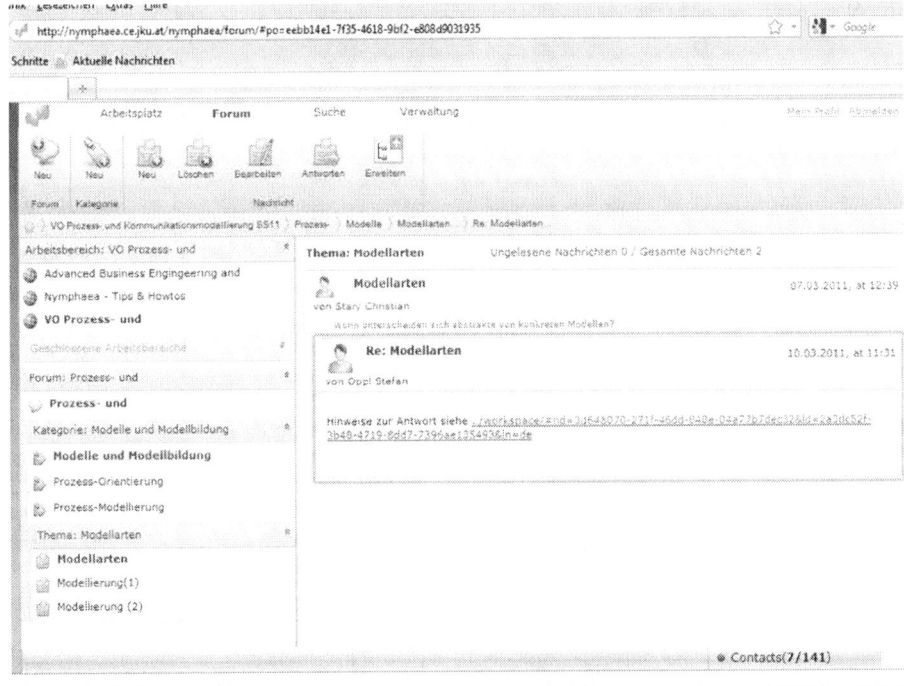

**Fig. 6.** Question answering through direct links of forum entries to relevant content elements

Besides exchanging views users can link social interaction to their interactive content studies. Figure 6 shows one starting point for focused context-sensitive interaction. In the learning management-specific forum a user might raise a question (in this case about categories of models), as displayed in the upper part of the interactive work space. Another user might answer, e.g., an expert. Rather than constructing an own answer or rephrasing the answer according to the provided material, he/she might set a direct link (see highlighted box in the interactive workspace). Clicking on this link allows readers of the forum entry to directly jump to the relevant piece of information in the content part of the learning management system.

Another way of dealing with interactive requests is to enrich views. Figure 7 and 8 demonstrate the use of links in that context. A user might set his/her individual view public in order to achieve focused input, either indicating it directly in the view through a text annotation, or placing a respective forum entry referring to the name of the puble view. Another user picking up the request can add relevant information directly in the view, as shown in figure 7 by providing a link to a wikipedia entry (= external piece of evidence). After adding the link the view contains the link as shown in figure 8.

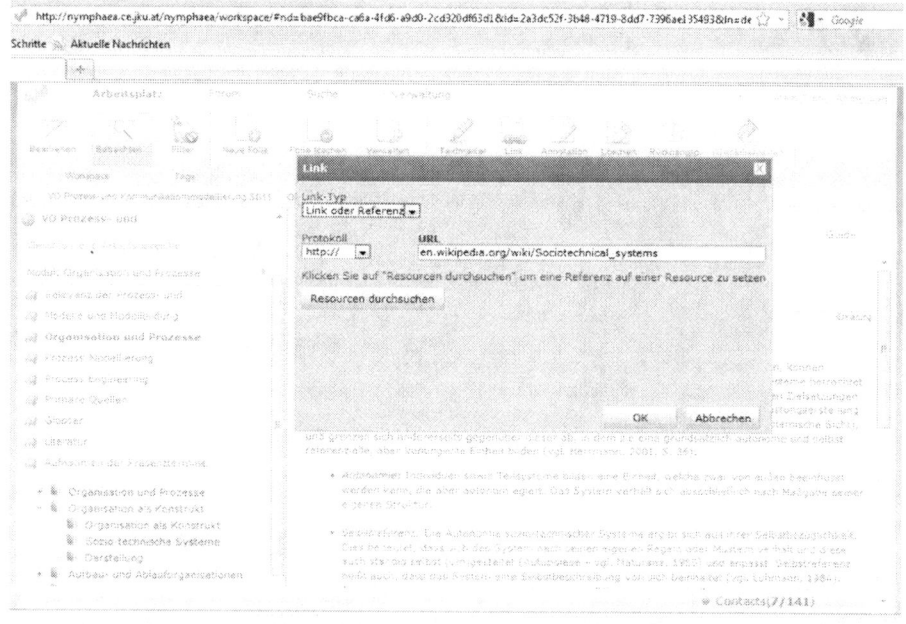

**Fig. 7.** Sharing already shared evidence

In case broadcasts are relevant for an educational setting, e.g., distributing information relevant for a group of users, such as novel S-BPM content elements for S-BPM practitioners, a bulletin board is useful. Such a learning management feature allows asynchronous interaction among users. Entries can be created and edited similar to those of discussion boards. Senders might define the duration of announcements via the board in case of time-sensitive information.

For distributing BPM evidence a learning management system should enable group workspaces besides individual ones, and organizational support when implementing particular qualification schemes. In any case, users should be able to manage their personal data, including personal cards, dedicated work space elements, individual preferences. These features promote the individualization of learning spaces, such as using mobile devices for learning management.

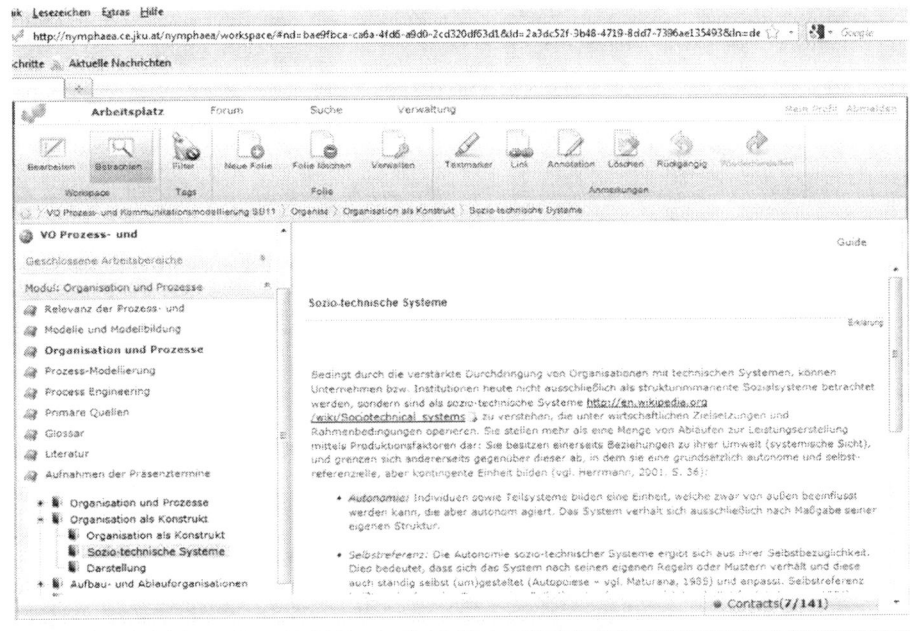

**Fig. 8.** The enriched shared learning space

Individualized work spaces also serve as repository and management facility of further personal data, such as the personal homepage, library, note store, and user-interface adaptation with respect to language, design and communication-feature access. It could also contain a set of media and links to specific BPM evidence, such as self tests according to various levels of (S-)BPM competence. Creating a personal look and feel users might also define the visibility of their data, as they are used to in other social networks.

For class or course management, dedicated views might be defined in order to prepare content for target groups, and an instant messaging system might be configured according to the characteristics of a specific learning process.

## 4 Conclusive Summary

S-BPM can be considered as a novel BPM paradigm, as its models are centered on communication acts rather than work tasks. In order to empower organizations and to facilitate shifting from other approaches to S-BPM, an evidence-driven educational design has been proposed and implemented. It does not only allow recognizing recent research efforts, such as coupling process models from different organizations at run time, but also organization-specific applications and case studies. The approach is grounded on the concepts of evidence-based practice and learning, and has been enriched with concepts from theory of science and knowledge management.

A structured procedure has been proposed allowing keeping up with the dynamics of the field. The educational setting distinguishes several phases of knowledge generation and use: provision of knowledge and content generation, exploration and consolidation, sharing and distribution. These phases are intertwined and allow various stakeholders accessing information in different roles, e.g., either as knowledge provider or learner. In this way, specific perspectives and behavior patterns can be changed and traced, in particular when changing over time.

Technical key enablers are a meta data-based content management system, annotation features for individualization, and social media-based sharing capabilities that allow focusing interaction. They lay ground for a more sophisticated education management, as they trigger self-organized learning and meta-cognitive capability development, such as the reflected switching between BPM approaches. The latter will be investigated in the context of BPM-literacy development.

## References

1. Buchwald, H., Fleischmann, A., Seese, D., Stary, C. (eds.): S-BPM ONE– Setting the Stage for Subject-Oriented Business Process Management 2009. CCIS, vol. 85. Springer, Heidelberg (2010)
2. Carnap, R.: An Introduction to the Philosophy of Science. Basic Books, New York (1994)
3. Chalmers, A.: Science and Its Fabrication. Minnesota Press, Minnesota (1990)
4. Chakraborthy, D.: Extending the Reach of Business Processes. IEEE Computer 37(4), 78–80 (2004)
5. Davidoff, F., Haynes, B., Sackett, D., Smith, R.: Evidence based Medicine: A new Journal to Help Doctors Identify the Information they Need. BMJ 310, 1085–1086 (1995), http://ebm.bmj.com
6. Fleischmann, A., Stary, C.: Whom to Talk to? A Stakeholder Perspective on Business Process Development. Universal Access in the Information Society 11(2) (2011)
7. Fleischmann, A., Schmidt, W., Stary, C., Obermeier, S., Börger, E.: Subjektorientiertes Prozessmanagement. Mitarbeiter einbinden, Motivation und Prozessakzeptanz steigern. Hanser, München (2011)
8. Haeckel, S.S.: Adaptive Enterprise: Creating and Leading Sense-AND-Respond Organizations. Harvard Business School Press, Cambridge (1999)
9. Havey, M.: Essential Business Process Modeling. O'Reilly, Beijing (2005)
10. Kuhn, T.: The Structure of Scientific Revolutions. University of Chicago Press, Chicago (1962)
11. Laudon, K.-C., Laudon, J.P.: Essentials of Management Information Systems: Managing the Digital Firm, 6th edn. Pearson, Upper Saddle River (2005)
12. Lewis, M., Young, B., Mathiassen, L., Rai, A., Welke, R.: Business Process Innovation based on Stakeholder Perceptions. Information Knowledge Systems Management 6, 7–17 (2007)
13. Neubauer, M., Oppl, S., Stary, C.: Towards Intuitive Modeling of Business Processes: Prospects for Flow- and Natural-Language Orientation. In: England, D., Palanque, P., Vanderdonckt, J., Wild, P.J. (eds.) TAMODIA 2009. LNCS, vol. 5963, pp. 15–27. Springer, Heidelberg (2010)
14. Rouse, W.B. (ed.): Enterprise Transformation: Understanding and enabling Fundamental Change. Wiley, Hoboken (2006)
15. Sackett, D.L., Rosenberg, W.M.C., Gray, J.A.M., Haynes, R.B., Richardson, W.S.: Evidence based Medicine: What it Is and What it Isn't (1996), http://ebm.bmj.com

16. Sackett, D.L., Straus, S.E., Richardson, W.S., Rosenberg, W., Haynes, R.B.: Evidence-based Medicine: How to Practice and Teach EBM. Churchill Livingstone, New York (2000)
17. Scheer, A.-W.: ARIS - Modellierungsmethoden, Metamodelle, Anwendungen, 4th edn. Springer, Berlin (2001)
18. Schmidt, W., Stary, C.: Establishing an Informed S-BPM Community. In: Buchwald, et al. pp. 34–47 (2010)
19. S-Cube Consortium: Survey on Business Process Management (2008), http://www.s-cube-network.eu
20. Sebbens, D., Kaufmann, J., Straka, K.L., Houck, P.R.: Evidence-Based Education. The Use of a DVD to Educate Parents on the Care of a Central Venous Catheter. ICAN: Infant, Child, & Adolescent Nutrition 1(6), 316–324 (2009)
21. Spurway, K.: The State of BPM: Perspective of an Industry Insider, http://www.bpm.com (download April 5, 2011)
22. Stary, C.: Quo Vadis S-BPM? The First World Café on S-BPM Developments. In: Buchwald, et al. pp. 136–147 (2010)
23. Thomas, G., Pring, R.: Evidence-based Practice in Education. Open University Press, Maidenhead (2004)
24. Winograd, T., Flores, F.: Understanding Computers and Cognition: A New Foundation for Design. Addison-Wesley, New York (1986)

# Subject-Oriented Elicitation of Distributed Business Process Knowledge

Stefan Oppl

Kepler University Linz
Department of Business Information Systems – Communications Engineering,
Freistaedterstrasse 315, A-4040 Linz, Austria
stefan.oppl@jku.at

**Abstract.** Subject-oriented business process modeling enables people to represent their knowledge about their individual ways of performing parts of a cooperative work process and to collaboratively specify the interfaces with their co-workers. How this knowledge can be captured and represented by stakeholders themselves has hardly been addressed. This paper presents an individual-centered approach to cooperative elicitation of work process knowledge in co-located and distributed business settings. An interactive tabletop interface is used for modeling and interaction support. Interactions among subjects are derived from how people cooperate using the interface. For cross-organizational use, several tabletop interfaces can be linked and used for synchronous, distributed modeling. The conceptual foundations of both, the elicitation platform and the communication and synchronization mechanism are presented and their technical feasibility is shown.

**Keywords:** subject oriented business process modeling, knowledge elicitation, tabletop interfaces, distributed systems.

## 1 Introduction

Subject-oriented Business Process Management (S-BPM) enables organizations to model and support their business processes along the flow communication among subjects (entities in an organization) rather than focusing on the global control flow like in traditional approaches (e.g. ARIS [1]). Considering subjects as the main building blocks of an organization changes the way people see and act in their organizations [2]: Business processes are considered a set of messages that trigger individual behavior rather than a strictly predetermined way of enacting given steps towards reaching a business goal. Consequently, subject-oriented business process models decouple the description of the flow of work on an organizational level and the description of individual work practices within these flows of work.

People can thus describe their actual ways of performing tasks and only need to be aware of and be able to describe their interfaces to other subjects. The ability to individualize the work practices within a business process and the possibility of starting modeling from a local rather than a global point of view are the core properties that distinguish subject-oriented business process modeling from other approaches that focus on the sequence of activities rather than the flow of communication.

The *subject-oriented elicitation of work process knowledge*, however, has hardly been addressed methodologically and technically so far. Following the individual-centered philosophy of S-BPM, *work process knowledge should be captured and reflected upon by the individuals involved in the current work process.*

Work processes are not necessarily executed solely within the borders of one organization, but can span across organizational borders. Knowledge elicitation thus potentially has to be performed in spatially distributed settings, where the involved people are not able to interact directly with each other.

People that are involved in a work process on an operational level often are hardly able to abstract from and reflect upon their daily routines [3]. Elicitation of knowledge then requires methods and tools to support these people in externalizing their view of their work processes.

In this paper, an approach for subject-oriented knowledge elicitation is presented that explicitly addresses these requirements. In chapter 2, a methodology and tool for work knowledge elicitation is presented that is founded upon an approach to describe cooperative work processes focusing on the involved individuals. Chapter 3 reviews the specific requirements on tool support for distributed elicitation of subject oriented work process knowledge and proposed possible solutions. Chapters 4 and 5 finally describe the technical implementation of the support platform and provide an outlook of how the system can be deployed in real world settings. The paper closes with an account on needs for further research, especially in terms of empirical evaluation of the presented approach.

## 2 Human-Centered Business-Process Knowledge Elicitation

In order to support working and learning in complex organizational settings, information about

- what worker do when accomplishing tasks in an organization
- how they perform tasks, and
- in which context their work is situated

has to be available [3]. Hence, this area addresses capturing individuals' knowledge about their work and transforming it to representation usable by interactive support systems for knowledge communication and elicitation.

Information on how organizations work can stem from various sources. Basically all organizational resources can be utilized, ranging from process documentations via organizational handbooks and business rules to human actors. The richest source of information is the human part of work processes. Not only that humans can provide information about what has to be done and how it is accomplished, but also why a certain activity is performed in a certain way [4].

Asking people about their work entails subjective and selective perceptions. While in the context of capturing knowledge this is an intended effect, support for organizational development not only requires information about the individual work contributions but also information about the global goals and modes of operation and collaboration in the work system [5]. The process of finding or defining a global, common view on cooperative work is an act of negotiation carried out by individuals, who are responsible for, involved in or affected by the respective work system.

A work knowledge elicitation process thus requires both, individual knowledge, and commonly agreed information on how to cooperate. Finding this common understanding in turn is an integral part of the negotiation process, and has to be considered by any infrastructure aiming to support interactive knowledge elicitation. In inter-organizational work scenarios, cooperation of individuals during elicitation of work process knowledge not only has to be supported in traditional workshop settings, where all participants are co-located. Support is even more important in situations, where the involved individuals are spatially distributed and do not have the opportunity of interacting directly with each other.

Introspection and personal views on performed work by means of externalization is a prerequisite for the development of common view on work and organizational improvement, respectively. Theories originating in cognitive sciences offer an explanatory approach on how individual perceptions and pictures and (organizational) reality influence mutually.

## 2.1 Individual Models of Work in Business Processes

A widely adopted theory to explain individual actions in a certain situation (such as being involved in the enactment of a business process) is that of "mental models" [6]. "Mental models" as a construct explains the foundation of thought processes. Whenever individuals are confronted with situations in which they should act, they create an explanatory model in their mind. The contents of this model are based on individual perception of the situation, previous experiences and personal values.

In organizational settings, mental models also guide an individual's way of interacting with others. It includes decisions on when to explicitly cooperate, with whom to cooperate in which way, when to expect input from others and when to deliver results to others.

In order to interact successfully, individual mental models have to fit each other in the aspects that are concerned during cooperation. Mental models are purely cognitive constructs and are per definition not accessible to others. In order to align mental models, the involved individuals first have to make their mental models visible to others. In many situations, pure verbal expression may be sufficient to create sufficient visibility for successful alignment. When the work setting is perceived to be complex or when unexpected contingencies arise, more explicit representations of mental models are required. Explicit representations of mental models are called "externalizations".

In collaborative work, externalization is necessary to provide stakeholders with a common ground when negotiating individual perspectives and sharing information. Developing shared views trigger changing individual mental models and enabling the emergence of a common understanding while interacting. Externalizations also provide the foundations for computer support of the respective work process, e.g. for the configuration of collaboration support systems or workflow engines.

Externalization can be supported methodologically in a variety of ways [7] and by several tools [8]. Structure-elaboration techniques are sophisticated approaches with respect to the specification of both, the methodology and the instruments to be used. They use physical representations of relevant concepts, which are put into mutual relationship. Their suitability for the externalization of mental models has already been evaluated empirically [7, 9]. Some researchers, such as Dann [5], suggest adapting structure elaboration techniques to the situation at hand, either in terms of modeling elements or methodology. For elicitation of distributed work process knowledge, using a subject-oriented form of concept representation is reasonable, because of its explicit separation of interaction activities form internal, individual work behaviors. Chapter 3 of this paper is dedicated to elaborate on how structure elaboration techniques can be tailored for representation of distributed work knowledge using subject-oriented concepts. The next section presents an interactive platform for supporting knowledge communication and elicitation using structure elaboration techniques.

## 2.2 Tool Support for Elicitation

The tool used for elicitation is based on a digitally augmented tabletop system (cf. Figure 1). It uses a variant of structure elaboration techniques that is implemented with graspable modeling blocks [10]. The persons engaged in modeling physically put together and connect these blocks to form the model.

The hands-on-experience of building a representation physically facilitates modeling and provides anchors for reflection of the modeled phenomenon [11]. The articulated knowledge is made persistent by synchronously capturing the information using a digital version of the model. It becomes available for later processing or communication.

**Fig. 1.** Interactive modeling surface implemented using a tabletop interface

The tabletop TUI described here has been developed to enable cooperative modeling in arbitrary modeling languages as a means to elicit and communicate knowledge about work processes. In the specific use case described in this paper, the system is configured to support subject-oriented modeling of work process knowledge. The system allows for collaborative physical construction of meshed networks of modeling elements, each representing an element of the problem domain using subject-oriented concepts (messages, states, etc.). Elements are put into mutual relation, thus defining the semantic associations among them.

All interaction between the users and the system occurs on the table surface to enable simultaneous manipulation of the concept map. The table surface and an auxiliary traditional display are used for visual information output.

The modeling elements used for representing concepts are available in different shapes. Each shape represents a subject-oriented concept type (messages, states, etc.). To create associations between modeling elements, the representing tokens have to be briefly brought in close proximity to each other (cf. Figure 2, left). Any participant can name established connections and concepts using a wireless keyboard. Removal of associations is realized using a physical eraser that allows for erase operations analogous to the real world.

Modeling elements are built as containers (cf. Figure 2, right). Digital business objects can be bound to an embeddable element by placing the token in a dedicated area of the surface and selecting the business object in a pop-up dialogue window on the auxiliary screen. The business object then can be attached to a message element by putting the embeddable token briefly next to an open message container token, and simply placing it inside afterwards. A tokens placed inside a container significantly adds weight and also produces audible feedback when grasping the container. In this way, physical indicators of additional available information become available.

The system provides history and reconstruction support to facilitate exploration and experimentation. It automatically tracks the creation history of the subject-oriented model and allows for navigation along a time line (similar to the concept of design history [12]). The reconstruction of former states of the model (as, for instance required for ad-hoc changes) is supported by the system. In this case, users are directed using visual clues when re-constructing the former model state (like removal signs or arrows pointing to the new position of an element).

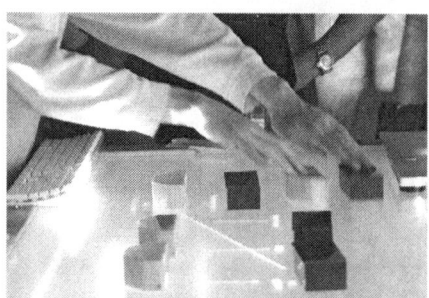
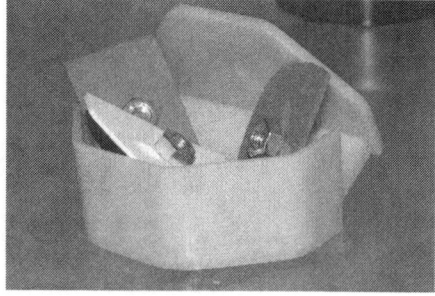

**Fig. 2.** Creation of connections between elements (left), elements used as containers (right)

The system has been designed to be controllable by several users simultaneously. They group themselves around the table, which is about 110 cm in height. Letting users stand instead of sit has been chosen deliberately to foster interaction and active involvement in the modeling process.

## 3 Elicitation of Distributed Process Knowledge

Knowledge about work processes is distributed within and across organizations. In order to elicit well-founded models of organizational work, this knowledge has to be collected from where it actually resides – from the people involved in the respective work processes [13].

Subject-oriented modeling explicitly distinguishes between knowledge on how to orchestrate organizational work (interaction) and on how to actually conduct one's personal contribution to these work processes (internal behavior). Consequently, elicitation has to be carried out on two layers of modeling:

- modeling of interaction among subjects
- modeling of internal behavior of subjects

The division of concerns makes S-BPM well suited for an individual-centered approach to work knowledge elicitation as described in chapter 2. Other modeling approaches like ARIS [1] or BPMN [14] assume the existence of a top-level view on the whole work process. ARIS EPCs can only be modeled from a control-flow perspective and do not focus on individual contributions to a work process (elements representing *who* performs or contributes to an activity can only be integrated in an extended EPC and interaction is only modeled implicitly). BPMN inherently considers interaction among actors in a process (using the construct of swimlanes and pools adopted from UML Activity Diagrams [15]) and provides means to model both the flow of control and the flow of communication. However, this distinction and the explicit modeling of communication flows is largely driven by technical factors [14] (e.g. separation of technical systems for workflow support), rather than being motivated from a conceptual point of view.

Integrating the concepts of S-BPM with the individual work knowledge approach described above and the requirement of spatially co-located and distributed elicitation of this knowledge leads to several use cases for the required support system:

- modeling of interaction
    o co-located modeling of interaction
    o distributed modeling of interaction
- modeling of internal behavior
    o individual modeling of a certain internal behavior
    o co-located modeling of more than one closely related internal behaviors
    o distributed modeling of a certain internal behavior

The following sections describe these use-cases in detail, review their specific requirements and constraints and show how they can be supported by an interactive modeling system.

### 3.1 Co-Located Modeling of Interaction

In S-BPM, modeling of interaction is based upon identification of the relevant subjects and the messages they exchange in the course of performing their collaborative work process. In scenarios where representatives for all involved subjects are available on-site, the elicitation of interactions in a certain work process can be performed using a methodology similar to storytelling [16]. The involved individuals assemble around the surface of the support system (cf. Figure 3), each representing one subject. A part of the surface is assigned to each subject.

The involved people agree upon a scenario that serves as an example for the work process to be modeled. They then start to collaboratively describe their roles and activities in the work process and their interactions with each other.

For each interaction, a physical message element is placed on the table surface (cf. Figure 3). These message elements are named and additional information can be assigned. Assignment is performed using the elements as containers and putting inside physical representations of digital information (business objects). The message elements are then passed to the representative of the receiving subject. The receiver continues to act according to the received information. In cases where different messages can be passed from one subject to another (e.g. depending on a decision of the sending subject), these cases are acted out one after another. As incoming messages stay on the surface in the area of the receiving subject as long as they are unhandled, messages cannot get lost or be overlooked. For each outgoing or incoming message, the representatives can take (digital) notes of what activities triggered the message or are triggered by the message. This information is used to provide context for modeling internal behavior later on.

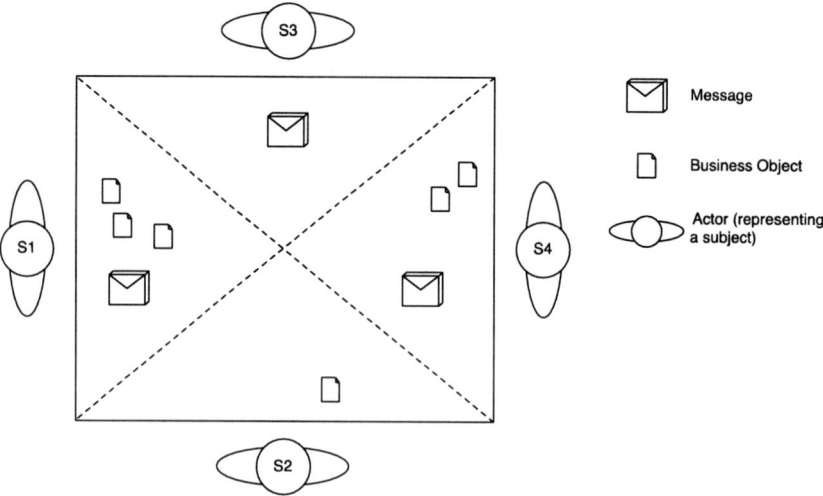

**Fig. 3.** Co-located creation of interaction models on a shared surface

The support system tracks the interactions in the background. Without any additional user interaction, it extracts a subject-oriented representation of the interaction (cf. section 4.2). This representation is shown on the auxiliary display and serves as both, an additional way to keep track of the modeling process and an approach to convey subject oriented modeling concepts to people unfamiliar with S-BPM. Direct interactions from within a work process are simultaneously translated to a subject-oriented model, allowing people to follow this step of abstraction without being initially able to perform it themselves.

## 3.2 Individual Modeling of Internal Behavior

After modeling their collective view on interaction, the representatives of the subjects have to model their internal behaviors to react upon the incoming messages.

The involved individuals use the interactive support system to model their behavior one after another, handling one or several incoming messages at a time. The main building blocks for modeling internal behavior are states. States are visualized using physical building blocks and can represent functions (i.e. activities, which create some result) or message handling (receiving and sending states). While state elements are generic before they are placed on the surface, they take one specific role (function, sending, receiving) as soon as they are used. The modeling surface shows messaging ports to all other subjects at its borders when modeling internal behavior (cf. Figure 4). The ports display all incoming and outgoing messages for the respective subject, visually marking those that are still unhandled. Placing the state element on an incoming message and dragging it to its position creates a receiving state. Temporarily dragging a state element to a messaging port (and putting it back into place again afterwards) creates a sending state.

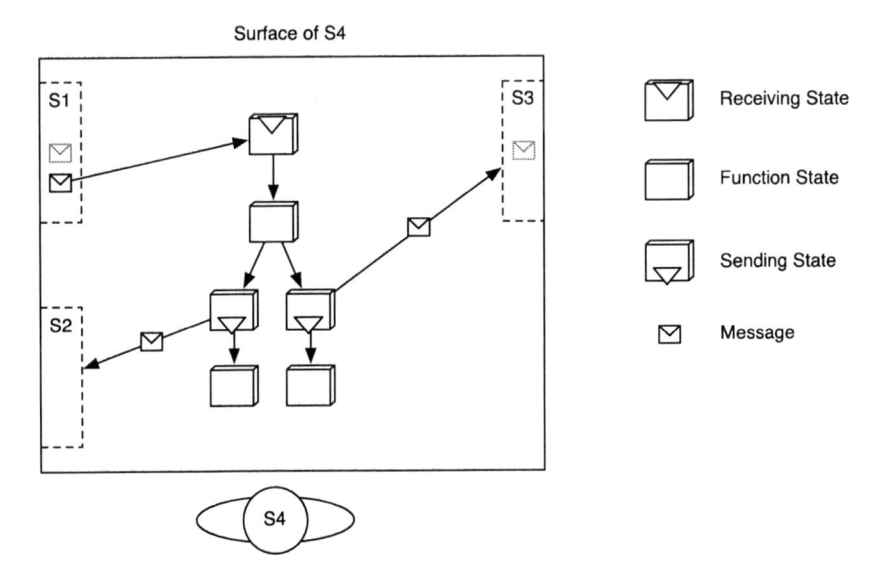

**Fig. 4.** Modeling of internal behavior on an interactive surface

Placing a state element without any interaction at the borders of the surface creates a function state, which then can be described textually. The control flow of the internal behavior can be established by associating the elements with one another.

Displaying the incoming and outgoing messages provides the global context for a subject, even across several models of internal behavior. Information that was captured during modeling the interaction among subjects (e.g. notes about what happens when a certain message is received) is additionally provided during modeling. The representatives of the subjects in this way can focus on internal behavior without loosing the big picture provided in the interaction model. The resulting models can be mapped directly onto an S-BPM representation without any further steps of interpretation.

### 3.3 Spatially Distributed Modeling of Interaction and Internal Behavior

The former modes of modeling support are tailored to co-located settings, where all representatives of the involved subjects are gathered at the same place at the same time (although modeling of internal behavior can be performed asynchronously, too). These settings can be conducted with only one interactive support platform.

In scenarios, where elicitation has to be performed in a spatially distributed setting, several interactive support platforms can be connected and used to elicit subject-oriented process representations in one single step (the use of several support platforms at the same site would also allow single-step elicitation in a co-located scenarios). The ensemble of platforms for four subjects is visualized in Figure 5.

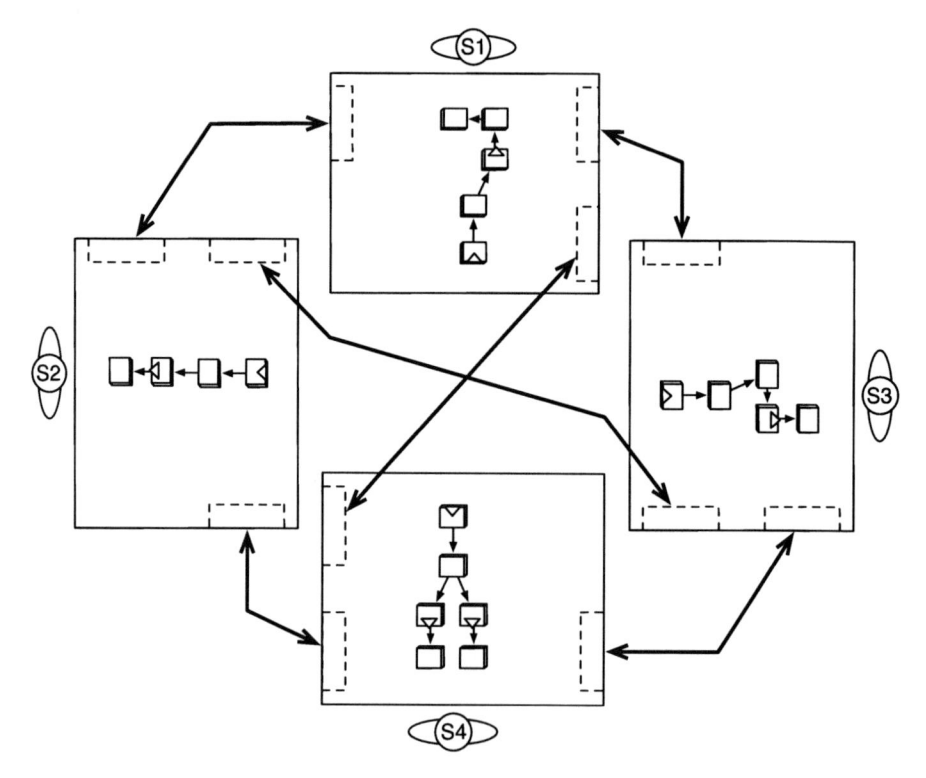

**Fig. 5.** Multi-surface setup for distributed modeling of subject-oriented models (bold arrows indicate linked messaging ports)

Each support platform acts as a modeling environment for the internal behavior and interaction of one subject in the work process. For the individuals representing the subjects, the modeling experience is similar to modeling individual behavior in the co-located setting. The major difference is that the messaging ports of two subjects (allowing mutual communication) are connected directly and synchronized live.

During operation, a sent message from one subject appears as an incoming message at the receiving subject's side without any noticeable delay and is ready to be handled. Using this mechanism, the work process can be acted out, as in the real world.

Moving a state element to a messaging port generates an outgoing message. Additional information can be attached to the message using the element as a container (as described in section 3.1). Incoming messages are visualized differently depending on whether they have already been handled or not. In this way, users can easily distinguish messages that require additional modeling activities, from those that have already been used in another model of internal behavior for the same subject.

In cases of partial co-location of subject representatives, the support surface can also be used in a split-pane view (cf. Figure 6). In this case, the respective subjects share a common messaging port, while ports to the distant subjects remain replicated.

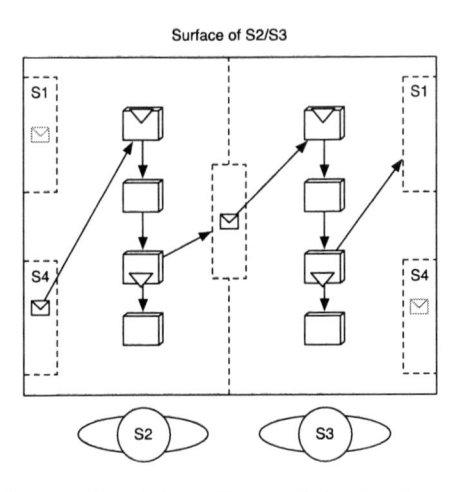

**Fig. 6.** Co-located modeling of internal behavior of two subjects

The S-BPM model representations evolve over time when using the system in a spatially distributed setting. Models of internal behavior are created independently from each other. The model of interaction among subjects is derived from actual interaction among the modeling surfaces. State elements are again generic and are assigned their role (sending, receiving, function) dynamically during modeling. Models of individual behavior can thus even be temporarily decoupled for the remaining models, using function states as placeholders for sending or receiving states to be assigned to messages at a later point in time.

The state of the model (i.e. all interactions among all subjects and all their internal behaviors) is distributed to all support platforms, so that users can access the full modeling context on demand (using a visualization of the S-BPM model on the auxiliary display).

### 3.4 Spatially Distributed Modeling of Internal Behavior

Spatial distribution has only been considered on subject granularity within a work process in the former settings. The behavior of one subject was completely modeled on one interactive support platform (whereas one support platform could be used to model the behavior of several subjects).

A scenario, in which the representatives of one subject are spatially distributed, poses further requirements on modeling support. The basic mechanisms of modeling internal behavior remain unchanged. Models of internal behavior, however, have to be kept in sync across several modeling support platforms. Changes in a model (adding, moving or removing a state element, establishment of a connection as well as sending or receiving a message) have to be propagated to all other platforms involved in the modeling of the respective internal behavior.

Modifications of a model are not applied automatically by the system. They are rather kept in a queue for incoming changes and have to be reconstructed by users manually with the support of the system. The decision for manual reproduction of changes is grounded in two reasons. First, automatic application of changes is not possible consistently for all model elements on the physical interaction platform. Physical parts of the model (i.e. the state elements) cannot be moved by the system, whereas digital information (such as connections, captions and messages) can be changed by the system autonomously. Second, manual reproduction of the current model state raises awareness for changes and thus enables distant users to comprehend the creation history of a model and the specific design decisions.

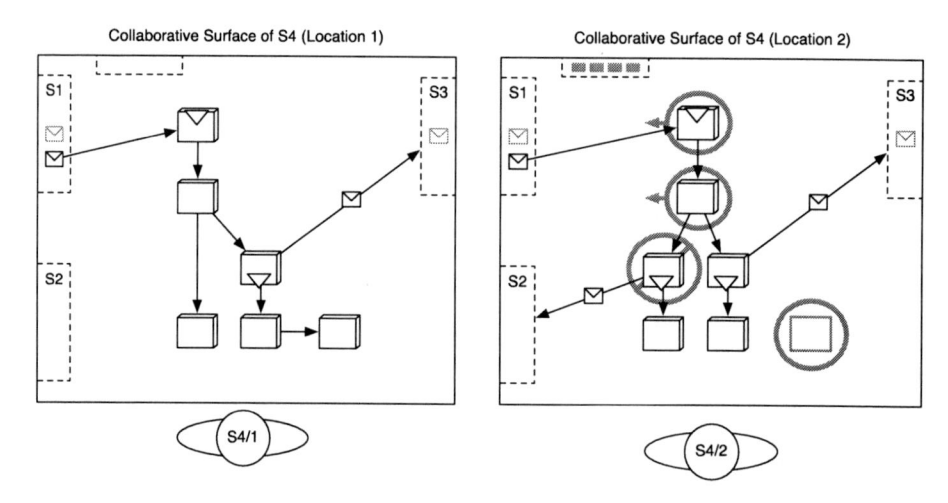

**Fig. 7.** Synchronization of spatially distributed interactive modeling surfaces (location 1 on the left showing the current model state; location 2 on the right showing the original, outdated model state; changes from location 1 queued at location 2)

Whenever a change occurs on one modeling surface, the change is sent to and queued on all other connected surfaces. As shown in Figure 7, a waiting change is indicated visually in an additional port on the surface (used as an input queue – waiting changes are represented by a dot each) as well as using a marker at the changed element (to make obsolete model parts immediately visible). In order to avoid inconsistencies, changes to elements already marked obsolete are ignored. As soon as a certain change has been reconstructed on a distant surface, the respective element can be changed there again. The queues of further surfaces, which still might contain the initial change, are modified to contain the most recent state of the changed element. Consequently, there can only be one waiting change for a model element on a certain surface at a time. Users can thus freely choose the sequence of reconstructing changes.

Awareness about what is happing on the other modeling surfaces is a central aspect in this scenario. The physical nature of the interactive support system does not allow for locking of model parts, which are currently manipulated elsewhere. While sequential modifications cannot lead to inconsistencies in the model state (as described above), concurrent modifications could basically occur and lead to an inconsistent model. Conceptually, a first-come-first-serve algorithm solves this problem. The modification that was started first is propagated to all other clients, while the second modification is ignored. Visual indicators on the surface provide awareness information about a currently ongoing modification on a distant surface.

Besides the synchronization of model states, additional means of communication provide awareness about what is happening at distant sites. A text chat is provided for persistent note taking. Additionally, textual notifications about ongoing changes are also filed there. A streaming media channel (audio and/or video) enables direct, synchronous communication among the participants to discuss or clarify modeling issues.

### 3.5 Combined Mode of Operation

All information about a modeling session can be stored persistently in a central repository and locally (in each of the participating support platforms). The different modes of operation (co-located or spatially distributed, explicit or implicit modeling of interaction) can be combined or even switched between during modeling time.

Interaction thus could be modeled in a co-located setting (as described in section 3.1), while individual behavior then could be modeled afterwards spatially distributed (as described in section 3.2). When process interfaces among two or more subjects need clarification, the respective interactive support systems could be dynamically linked together (as described in section 3.3). For alignment of work procedures in spatially distributed organizational units (e.g. for local sales representatives), multiple interactive surfaces could additionally be linked for negotiation of a common view on internal behavior (as described in section 3.4).

## 4 Implementation

This section outlines the implementation of the interactive support systems and shows, how the features described above are realized technically.

### 4.1 Elicitation Platform

The elicitation platform is based on an interactive tabletop interface with tangible modeling elements. The table surface is used to present digital information that augments the physical elements of the model that is created by the user(s). Digital information is back-projected onto the table surface from underneath. A camera identifies and tracks the physical elements using fiducials (visual codes that uniquely identify an element). The ReacTIVision-Framework [17] is used to extract element information from the video stream of the camera. The JHotDraw-Framework [18] is used for information visualization on the table surface. An auxiliary display visualizes additional information about the model (such as alternative forms of representation) or the modeling process (such as the creation history of the model).

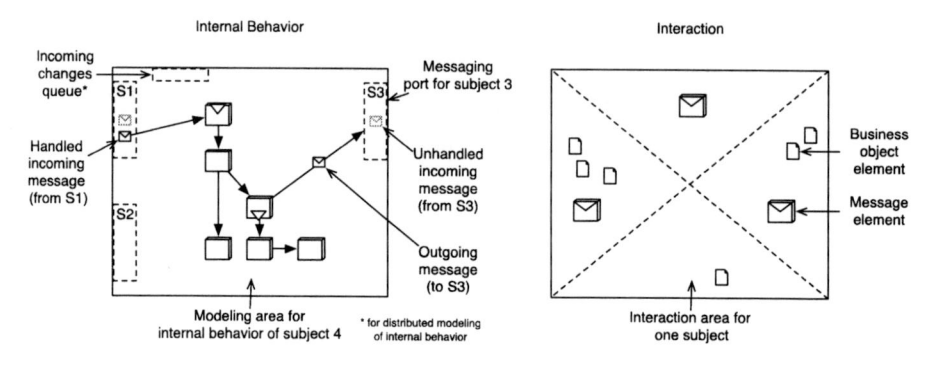

**Fig. 8.** Interactive surface layouts (left: internal behavior, right: interaction)

The elicitation platform does not predetermine the modeling approach to be used for knowledge representation (cf. section 2.2). In its current configuration for supporting subject-oriented modeling, the modeling surface is used in two layouts (cf. Figure 8). The primary layout is used for modeling internal behavior and interaction in spatially distributed settings (cf. Figure 8, left). For modeling interaction among subjects in co-located settings, the layout on the right in Figure 8 is used. Both layouts are conceptually based upon the design approach for interactive surfaces specified by Ullmer & Ishii [19]. The main interaction elements are physical *tokens* (elements) that can be manipulated by users and are used to represent the system's state. Additionally, certain areas of the surface are defined to act as *trays*, i.e. triggering a specific action, as soon as a token is places inside them. The messaging ports on the "internal behavior" layout and the interaction areas on the "interaction" layout are examples for trays.

The use of trays always represents interaction among subjects in the application presented here. In order to integrate explicitly represented parts of the model and the implicitly modeled aspects (interactions) an additional software component, the interaction interpreter, is required.

## 4.2 Interaction Interpreter

In contrast to traditional modeling tools, the elicitation platform proposed here does not use model visualizations that can be directly mapped to its model representations. Parts of the model representation have to be extracted from user interaction with the modeling elements during the process of modeling. An "interaction interpreter" component is used in each participating support platform to extract the meaning of user actions. The "interaction interpreter" is configured to recognize user actions targeting on sending or receiving messages on the interaction layer of an S-BPM-based model representation (cf. Figure 9).

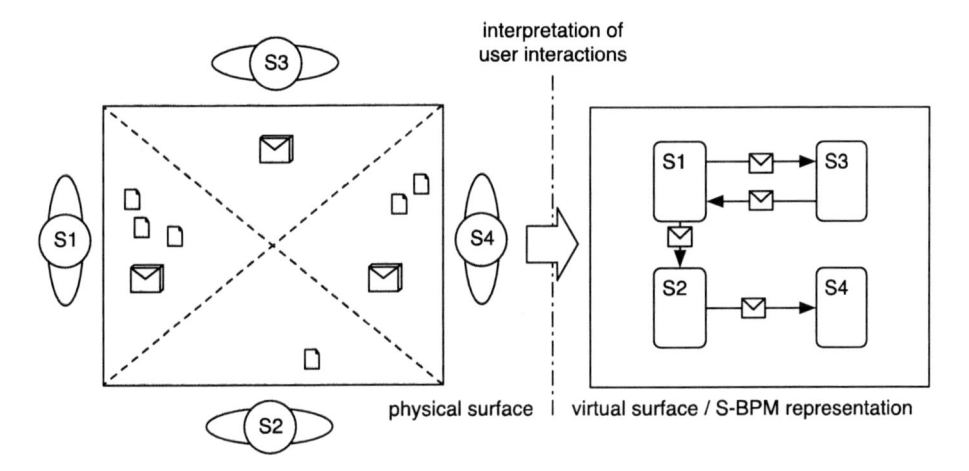

**Fig. 9.** Interpretation of interactions on a shared tabletop interface

Fig. 9 shows the result of information extraction during co-located modeling of interaction. Interaction interpretation, however, is also needed when modeling individual behavior. User actions involving the messaging ports to other subjects basically hold the same semantics as direct exchange of messages in the co-located setting.

Interaction interpretation is performed locally and integrated immediately in the subject-oriented model representation. In spatially distributed settings, only information contained in the representation (i.e. only already interpreted information) is communicated to other connected platforms. The technical implementation of communication and synchronization among platforms is described in the following section.

### 4.3 Distributed Communication and Synchronization of Models

Communication among and synchronization of the interactive support platforms is performed using bidirectional messaging based upon XMPP (eXtensible Messaging and Presence Protocol) [20]. XMPP is a flexible XML-based messaging service and provides a number of standardized services (such as text messaging, file transfer or A/V-session signaling). Services can be extended arbitrarily depending on their use cases. Its design allows for dynamic and extensible configuration of the distributed modeling environment.

For communication between parts of the model (i.e. internal behavior of different subjects), text messages are sent from the initiating support environment to the affected others (i.e. if a message is sent from subject 1 to subject 3, the platforms used to model the internal behavior of subject 2 and subject 4 would not receive a message) using the XMPP instant messaging service (unicast). For synchronization of model states (in the case of concurrent modification of internal behavior at two or more support platforms), messages are broadcasted to all involved support platforms using the XMPP multi-user chat service (multicast). Communication sessions are managed using an "interaction event dispatcher" component, that allows for joining already ongoing sessions and logging of events.

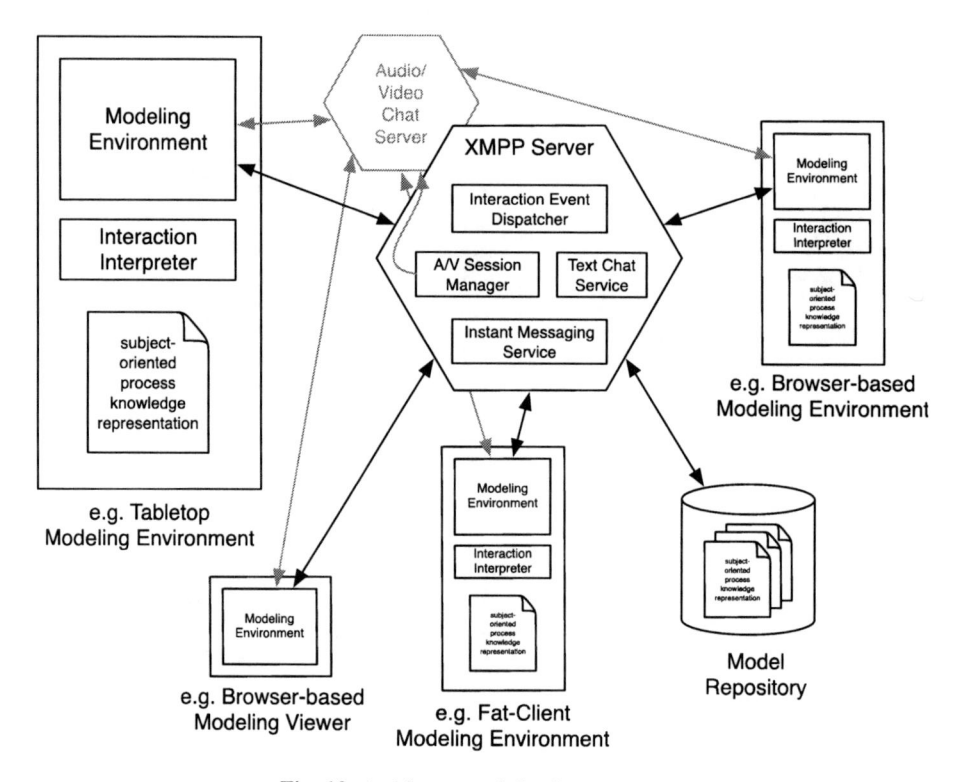

**Fig. 10.** Architecture of distributed system

Awareness features among distant surfaces are enabled using the multi-user chat service to propagate information about ongoing modifications. The XMPP server can additionally be used to establish an audio or video stream between the support platforms. While media streaming itself is not part of the XMPP specification and requires an additional server (e.g. Redfire, http://code.google.com/p/redfire), session initiation and management is performed using XMPP.

The client components connecting the support platforms to the XMPP-server (e.g. OpenFire (http://www.igniterealtime.org/projects/openfire, cf. Figure 10) are implemented in a platform-independent way that allows connection of clients other than the tabletop interface described above. In this way, computer-based support environments (e.g. using a fat client or a browser-based client) can be used to join a modeling session. Plain viewers (without modeling capabilities) can also be realized.

The central repository component also is connected using the XMPP service and can be used to store and retrieve model representations from the support platforms. Storage and retrieval uses the same mechanisms that are used to let support platforms join already ongoing modeling sessions. The "interaction event dispatcher" pushes the full set of changes describing the transition from an empty surface to the current model state to the repository (for storage) or the loading support platforms (for retrieval).

## 5 Sample Deployment Scenario

The sample deployment scenario described here is situated in a business setting in the automotive sector. An OEM (Original Equipment Manufacturer) has to setup its work process with a supplier for ordering and delivery of motor parts. People involved in this process include the stock manager and a production planner of the OEM as well as the CEO of the supplier and a key account manager of the involved logistic services provider. The supplier manager of the OEM supervises the setup of the process. The four people directly involved in the work process meet at a workshop at the OEM's site, which is moderated by the supplier manager. They use an interactive support platform to run through the interactions necessary to perform the ordering and delivery process of the motor parts and get a common view of the global parts of the process.

Back at their organizations, the CEO of the supplier and the logistics provider each model their internal behavior using their own support platform based upon the messages they agreed upon in the workshop. The logistics provider at a certain point in time discovers some missing information needed from the supplier to be able to guarantee the necessary quality of service for just-in-time delivery to the OEM. The logistics provider and the supplier thus link their support platform and interactively revise their internal behaviors and interaction to find a suitable process. Concurrently, the stock manager and the production planner of the OEM have cooperatively used their support platform to model and align their internal behaviors.

The OEM-based participants in the work process finally link their platform with the platforms of the supplier and the logistics provider to reflect upon the overall process. The OEM's supplier manager joins the modeling session as a viewer directly from her desktop computer (without being able to directly intervene in the modeling process but being involved via the A/V-channel). They agree on the overall process but identify potential for optimization at the stock manager's internal behavior and his handling of deliveries from the logistics provider. The key account manager of the logistics provider and the stock manager thus subsequently link their platforms to cooperatively optimize the internal stock management process for incoming deliveries. The whole process is then stored to the S-BPM repository of the OEM and deployed to the workflow management instances of all involved parties.

## 6 Conclusions

In this paper, the conceptual foundations of distributed elicitation platform for subject-oriented business process knowledge has been presented. The conceptual foundations of the approach have been presented and its technical feasibility has been shown.

The system proposed here is based upon the assumption, that work process knowledge should be captured where it actually is generated and used – from the people actually involved in the work process. Literature [4, 21] shows that people inexperienced with modeling are able to externalize their knowledge in diagrammatic, formalized models when they receive appropriate support. The system presented here aims at providing this kind of support. It supports the externalization of individual views on work processes with physical modeling elements. It allows for interactive, scenario-based elicitation of interaction among the involved subjects and provides means to conduct elicitation in co-located as well as spatially distributed settings.

Future research will focus on end user studies to evaluate the effectiveness of the proposed approach. Effectiveness here addresses the *possibility* to create sound S-BPM-models as well as the *ability* of workers to use the system in the intended way. Further empirical evidence will be required to be able to compare the elicitation approach proposed in this paper to already established means of S-BPM-based process knowledge elicitation in terms of their outcome.

## References

1. Scheer, A.W.: ARIS – Business Process Modeling, 3rd edn. Springer, Heidelberg (2003)
2. Sachs, P.: Transforming work: collaboration, learning, and design. Communications of the ACM 38(9), 36–44 (1995)
3. Ulich, E.: Arbeitspsychologie. Poeschl, Stuttgart (1991)
4. Dann, H.D.: Variation von Lege-Strukturen zur Wissensrepräsentation. In: Scheele, B. (ed.) Struktur-Lege-Verfahren als Dialog-Konsens-Methodik., Arbeiten zur sozialwissenschaftlichen Psychologie, vol. 25, pp. 2–41. Aschendorff (1992)
5. Firestone, J., McElroy, M.: Key Issues in the new Knowledge Management. Butterworth-Heinemann, Butterworths (2003)
6. Johnson-Laird, P.N.: Mental models in cognitive science. Cognitive Science 4(1), 71–115 (1981)
7. Ifenthaler, D.: Diagnose lernabhängiger Veränderung mentaler Modelle. Ph.D. thesis, University of Freiburg (2006)
8. Pirnay-Dummer, P.N.: Expertise und Modellbildung - MITOCAR. Ph.D. thesis, University of Freiburg (2006)
9. Groeben, N., Scheele, B.: Dialog-Konsens-Methodik im Forschungsprogramm Subjektive Theorien. Forum Qualitative Sozialforschung 1(2) (2000)
10. Oppl, S., Stary, C.: Tabletop concept mapping. In: Proceedings of the 3rd International Conference on Tangible and Embedded Interaction (TEI 2009). ACM Press, New York (2009)
11. Hornecker, E.: Tangible User Interfaces als kooperationsunterstützendes Medium. Phd-Thesis, University of Bremen. Dept. of Computing (2004)
12. Klemmer, S., Thomsen, M., Phelps-Goodman, E., Lee, R., Landay, J.: Where do web sites come from? capturing and interacting with design history. Human Factors in Computing Systems, CHI Letters 4(1) (2002)
13. Jørgensen, H.: Interactive Process Models. Ph.D. thesis, Department of Computer and Information Sciences, Norwegian University of Science and Technology Trondheim (2004)
14. White, S., Miers, D.: BPMN Modeling and Reference Guide: Understanding and Using BPMN. Future Strategies Inc. (2008)
15. Dumas, M., ter Hofstede, A.: UML activity diagrams as a workflow specification language. In: Gogolla, M., Kobryn, C. (eds.) UML 2001. LNCS, vol. 2185, pp. 76–90. Springer, Heidelberg (2001)
16. Swap, W., Leonard, D., Shields, M., Abrahams, L.: Using mentoring and storytelling to transfer knowledge in the workplace. Journal of Management Information Systems 18(1), 95–114 (2001)

17. Kaltenbrunner, M., Bencina, R.: ReacTIVision: a computer-vision framework for table-based tangible interaction. In: TEI 2007: Proceedings of the 1st International Conference on Tangible and Embedded Interaction, pp. 69–74. ACM Press, New York (2007)
18. Gamma, E., Eggenschwiler, T.: The JHotDraw-Framework (1996), http://www.jhotdraw.org/
19. Ullmer, B., Ishii, H.: The metaDESK: models and prototypes for tangible user interfaces. In: Proceedings of the 10th Annual ACM Symposium on User Interface Software and Technology, pp. 223–232. ACM Press, New York (1997)
20. Saint-Andre, P., et al.: Extensible messaging and presence protocol (XMPP): Core. RFC 3920, W3C (2004)
21. Herrmann, T., Hoffmann, M., Loser, K., Moysich, K.: Semistructured models are surprisingly useful for user-centered design. In: Dieng, R., Giboin, A., Karsenty, L., De Michelis, G. (eds.) Proceedings of COOP 2000. Designing Cooperative Systems, pp. 159–174. IOS Press, Amsterdam (2000)

# BPM@KMU –
# Designing e-Learning for the Introduction of BPM in Small- and Medium-Sized Enterprises

Johannes Kröckel[1] and Bernd Hilgarth[2]

[1] Institute of Information Systems, University of Erlangen-Nuremberg
Johannes.Kroeckel@wiso.uni-erlangen.de
[2] Department of Computer Science and Information Systems, University of Jyväskylä
bernd.hilgarth@jyu.fi

**Abstract.** Business Process Management (BPM) becomes more and more relevant also for small- and medium-sized companies (SME's). Today's strategies and approaches for the implementation of BPM rely on methods and tools mainly developed by and focused on large enterprises but less on the needs of small- and mid-sized organisations. With the BPM@KMU project the Institute of Information Systems of a Bavarian university conducts together with the Virtual University of Bavaria (VHB) and a set of SMEs a project which aims on an efficient implementation of BPM in such organisations. Considering e-Learning as an enabler or tool which matches existing barriers for the implementation of Business Process Management, this paper offers a case study report on the observations when designing and implementing the BPM@KMU e-Learning program guided by the *Cybernetic e-Learning Management Model*. The paper considers first project results and shows, that e-Learning can address the heterogeneous maturity and previous knowledge about BPM by an adequate set of instructional as well as technological strategies and concepts.

**Keywords:** Business Process Management, e-Learning, BPM@KMU, Case Study, Case Adaption.

## 1 Introduction

Business Process Management (BPM) encompasses and integrates a variety of concepts and methods for strategic alignment and operational improvement of business processes in enterprises. Since the implementation of comprehensive BPM is associated with high costs, especially large companies rely on BPM concepts. Besides missing means, these concepts are rarely considered by SMEs due to a lack of knowledge and experience. For that reason, a knowledge transfer project for SMEs funded by the European Union and the Free State of Bavaria is set up. Coordination is carried out by the Virtual University of Bavaria and the Institute of Information Systems of a Bavarian university.

The project BPM@KMU aims to convey an adapted, practice-oriented concept for Business Process Management in small- and medium-sized companies. Therefore, theoretical knowledge from academia and companies' best practice experiences are combined. For instance, following the IfM [14] statistics for existing SMEs in Germany, a number of nearly 3.7 million companies exist which can be reached best by media-driven learning resources like e-Learning. Therefore, knowledge transfer will be carried out as a modular e-Learning course using a Moodle-based learning platform. This enables participants to access predefined resources as well as to develop and discuss new resources collaboratively. Thereby, theoretical and practical content will be offered as a basis for company- and sector-specific adaptations.

Existing drawbacks of e-Learning such as its anonymous instructional design and lack of socio-interactive elements (in sense of *Change Management*) will be compensated by a variety of instructional design approaches e.g. blended learning concepts [15], the use of collaborative learning concepts or social-media (e.g. discussion boards or videoconferencing) [16] as well as by other facilitating concepts like individual coaching.

The paper at hand aims to give an overview of experiences made throughout the first steps of the project. Therefore, the research design and the case setup are described, firstly (section two). Subsequently, an overview about hurdles and barriers being faced during the introduction of Business Process Management in small- and medium-sized companies is given (section three). Afterwards, the framework being used during the conception of the e-Learning program is introduced and adapted to the characteristics of the BPM@KMU project (section four). Last, a report on the recent results of the project is given (section 5).

## 2 Research Method and Design

This work shows a case study report. The instruments for data gathering within the case study are participatory observation, face-to-face meetings and interviews. In this context that means, that the project is observed during its first stages providing first experiences and results.

The project "BPM@KMU - Business Process Management for Small and Medium-Sized Enterprises" was accepted as a partial project for the 2010 funding round of the European Social Fond. The call for proposals addressed projects that support knowledge transfer between SMEs and academia. For Bavaria the lead partnership was transferred to the Virtual University of Bavaria (VHB) which is a merger of all Bavarian universities sharing e-Learning courses for a large variety of topics. A special focus was placed on SMEs with locations in less developed areas of Bavaria.

The proposal for BPM@KMU was submitted by a Bavarian university along with three Bavarian SMEs. One of them is a regional provider of asphalt concrete materials located in the north of Bavaria near the Czech boarder. The heads of the about 15 man in size company are very interested in testing the opportunities of BPM to analyze and improve internal processes. A second company based nearby Erlangen develops customized solutions and professional services related to IT. The third company is a manufacturer for all kinds of cables with about 20 employees located in Reichenbach, Upper Franconia. Both the IT service provider and the cable manufacturer have less experience in using Business Process Management and are interested in extending their knowledge.

Besides business intelligence and service science, BPM is one of the core competences of the Institute of Information Systems. The Institute has gathered years of experience with it especially during inter-university projects like forFLEX as well as cooperation with providers for process management solutions.

Meanwhile a professor from the University of Applied Sciences, Amberg-Weiden as well as two further SMEs joined the project. One of them is a Pfaffenhofen based enterprise developing and providing BPM software with a special focus on subject-oriented BPM (S-BPM). The other one is a company operating in the fields of service engineering, software development processes and process maturity models located in Erlangen. Both companies have deep knowledge and experience in implementing and conducting Business Process Management. They are interested in working together with SMEs to see how they may improve their service offers.

## 3 Business Process Management for SME's

As described by Hammer and Champy [1] as well as Treacy and Wiersema [2] Business Process Management (BPM) is a structured method for organisations to get transparency on their own business for further improvements and optimizations. The fields of activities within the BPM approach are among others described by Hilgarth et al [12] and depicted in Fig. 1.

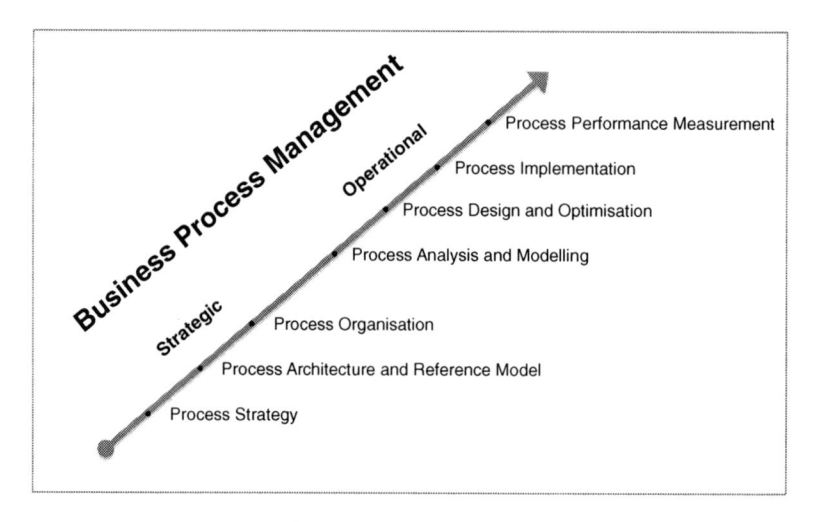

**Fig. 1.** BPM activity model

In large companies the activities and benefits of Business Process Management are perceived for some years. This also goes along with the understanding for *process-oriented management* in these organisations [7]. Besides the awareness of BPM numerous approaches for the implementation and operation of it have been developed over the years (e.g. KAIZEN, BPR, Lean Management, Total Quality Management – TQM). In addition to generic concepts companies like Siemens AG developed their own maturity and capability methods (e.g. CMMI [6]) for increasing the degree of

BPM professionalism for all of their different business units. In contrast, BPM has rarely been considered or implemented in small and medium-sized enterprises. This leads to questions like whether there is a minimum entry requirement or size for Business Process Management or whether advantages could also be achieved by SMEs. From the authors' point of view and experience BPM is also adequate for smaller organisations with a lower degree of professionalism. Especially when it comes to rising requirements given by cross-linked value chains in the markets (e.g. in Tier-2 mechanical engineering in automotive industry) and the needs for quality assurance and management certifications BPM can be an instrument for SMEs that meets existing requirements by balancing efforts and benefits. Regarding the statements listed in Fig. 1, in the area of strategic BPM the *Process Strategy* and *Architecture* might be considered as highly relevant; focusing on operational BPM all topics are important for SMEs. Besides, there are no limitations regarding size or characteristics given by the existing concepts of Business Process Management. As the authors experienced, BPM in SMEs shows basically the same character as in large-sized companies with exception that flat hierarchy structures allows fast decisions by the management while implementing it. Rather the limited knowledge about and the perception of BPM are the main reasons why BPM is not adopted by such organisations [8].

In addition Chong [8] describes some more constraints for the implementation of BPM in the area of SME (see Table 1).

**Table 1.** Barriers in SME for BPM implementation

| # | Factor |
|---|---|
| 1 | Lack of financial resources |
| 2 | Lack of time |
| 3 | Lack of support from senior management |
| 4 | Lack of information technology expertise |
| 5 | Poor knowledge of process-oriented approaches |

While most business process concepts include a great variety of steps to be conducted by a company even during the implementation process they don't consider limited time and financial resources. Besides, due to the lack of business process experts and persons responsible for introducing and maintaining a business process implementation seems not to be feasible. Therefore, a lightweight variation of Business Process Management regarding the limited time and financial resources as well as the limited knowledge of employees has to be created.

Addressing the issues mentioned by Chong [8] four working hypotheses are stated:

1) An increased understanding of the benefits of BPM will support a successful implementation of Business Process Management (also) in small- and medium-sized organisations. Therefore, adequate information exchange and training about the *knowledge of process-oriented approaches* is required.
2) Besides a comprehensive understanding of Business Process Management respecting the circumstances of *time* and *financial resources* in SMEs is a crucial factor. Therefore, adapted concepts and technology-support for information and knowledge exchange have to be provided.

3) Stakeholder-specific reporting is important for achieving acceptance at hierarchical levels. For instance, the s*enior management* might be addressed with a kind of *SME executive summary for BPM* which is transported by technology-driven knowledge and training material.
4) Using matured information technology is an important success factor for the implementation of Business Process Management. This means, that the introduction of Business Process Management should be accompanied by an adaption and optimization of the prevalent information technology infrastructure.

As a result of the four working hypothesis e-Learning or *Technology-Enhanced Learning* shows an adequate approach to address most of the existing barriers in an efficiently way. It should not be expected that a set of e-Learning modules summed up in a course may solve the entire existing issues that deter SMEs from implementing BPM. But it might be expected as one central concept for a structured information and communication policy while implementing and conducting BPM in SMEs. An adequate employee training program with e-Learning will show following benefits:

1) Using a web-based platform for providing the e-Learning contents enables designated employees of SMEs to access the BPM training program.
2) Module-oriented curriculum implementation allows target-specific learning paths, e.g. senior executive vs. employee-oriented curriculum.
3) By using an online available learning management system the inter-company exchange of BPM related information and collaboration for example through training exercises is possible.
4) Innovative e-Learning software tools (e.g. lecture-on-demand) help to address different types of learners (e.g. *visual* vs. *auditory*) and enables individual learning reflection.

Considering the barriers for SMEs as well as the opportunities provided by e-Learning, the project BPM@KMU was initiated a Bavarian university and the Virtual University of Bavaria (VHB) in association with local SMEs.

## 4 Adaption of the *Cybernetic e-Learning Management Model*

Using e-Learning for this specific subject of BPM in SMEs shows the need for structured and coordinated activities for the design, implementation and production of it. Beforehand describing the specific results of the BPM@KMU e-Learning solution in Ch. 5, this section aims on the description of the in Fig. 2 depicted *Cybernetic e-Learning Management Model (CeLMM)* as a descriptive framework [10] helps to identify and respect necessary and critical steps and influencing factors in the preparation phase.

The *Cybernetic e-Learning Management Model* covers a framework for the management of e-Learning in organisations, mainly for internationally acting ones. It aims for transparency of typical e-Learning *phases & processes* [11], *success domains*, *success paths* as well as the needed management methods and instruments for e-Learning [10]. The model bases on a long-termed study and matches the need for professional e-Learning management in different situations.

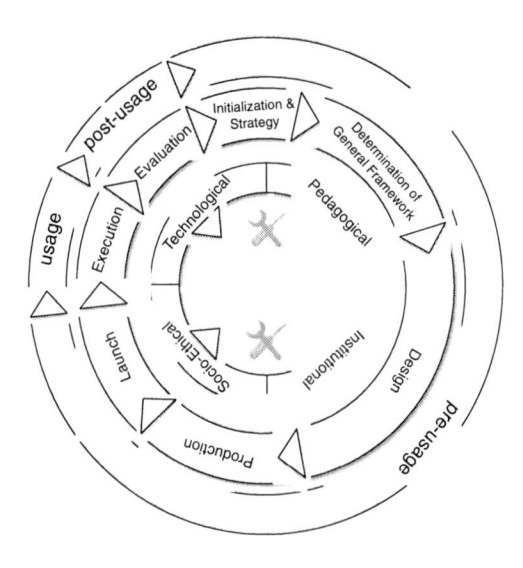

**Fig. 2.** Overview *Cybernetic e-Learning Management Model*

Using the presented model helps the BPM@KMU project team to address relevant issues for *initialization, determination of the general framework* and *design* of the BPM e-Learning course. It shows a holistically bias by respecting issues for e-Learning in different *success domains* (e.g. *institutional, socio-ethical, pedagogical* and *technological*). During the phases of initiating, determining and designing of the e-Learning program, the e-Learning critical success factors listed in Table 2 should be considered. Therefore a learning path considering the critical success factors as well as the barriers of SMEs has to be developed.

**Table 2.** Typical e-Learning Critical Success Factors in Initiation, Determination and Design referring to Hilgarth [10]

| e-Learning Critical Success Factor |
| --- |
| • Professional e-Learning project management |
| • Respecting language differential in international target group |
| • Support cooperative and collaborative learning settings |
| • Respect direct communication to and feedback from target group |
| • Do comprehending audience analysis |
| • Involve powerful organisational instances in e-Learning process/project |
| • Make high-quality learning material available by adequate ICT |
| • Assure continuously management of content up-to-datedness as well as of communication and marketing for the e-Learning course |
| • Do content analysis with subject matter experts |
| • Respect in general cultural diversity in target group |

In the succeeding sections a closer looking is taken on the different critical success factors considering the BPM@KMU project clustered after its regarding *success domain*:

- *Project management and organisational setting – institutional domain*
One important issue is a professional management of the e-Learning project similar to other organisational or IS projects. Another success driver for e-Learning – still existing in SMEs setting – is the consideration and involvement of powerful organisational instances like the senior management. This also includes the determination of clear responsibilities and roles within the project as well as recording a project and status report. Besides responsibilities for the initial project the role and organisational setting for continuously content update and management have to be determined.

- *Respecting cultural and language diversity – socio-ethical domain*
E-Learning is often proposed for international target groups. For this, *language differences*, *content representation*, *content selection* and *adaptation processes* as well as *differences in educational and school background* and *learning style* might be respected in the early stages. For the BPM@KMU project in a first release German SMEs are addressed. Hence, no intercultural differences have to be addressed yet. Nevertheless, expanding especially for internationally operating companies should be considered. Besides, the different point of views of organisations of different branches, sizes and levels of experience have to be considered. This issue is regarded as one of the most critical success factors of the e-Learning program.

- *Instructional settings and design – pedagogical domain*
One important way of interaction between students and advisors is the direct communication as well as direct feedback to actions performed by the participants. This type of communication provides a fast way of interaction which allows participants to get customized answers to their questions. A second way is the interaction between the participants. Previous research on e-Learning success in organisations shows the positive influence of collaborative aspects. Therefore, a platform allowing participants to communicate and work collaboratively is needed. Using such a platform enables participants to learn, discuss and develop their own adapted contents. This is especially important for the BPM@KMU project. While other e-Learning programs mostly focus on learning of facts the named project focuses on the creation of adapted way to introduces Business Process Management. Therefore, it is important for every participant to think about the best way for introducing BPM in his or her own company environment. On the on hand this requires to think about the characteristics of the own company. On the other hand it is especially important to share the experiences and ideas from different company environments for building up a company adapted best practice.

- *Audience analysis and curriculum – institutional and socio-ethical domain*
The target group of the BPM@KMU e-Learning program are *senior executives* as well as *regular employees*. This is due to the fact that in smaller companies the senior management is much more involved in the implementation of Business Process Management than in larger enterprises. Besides, tasks are not well-defined in SMEs.

That means employees have to fulfill a variety of strategic and operational tasks at the same time. Another issue is the companies structure itself. SMEs can show heterogeneously characters concerning the number of employees, its revenue structure as well as its business subjects. They act as profit organisations at local markets as well as within globalized partner networks (e.g. supply-chain networks with Asia-Pacific contractors). The internal organisational structures vary between flat hierarchy and highly functional structures. These facts should be considered while setting up the e-Learning program. Therefore it is important to create a program covering generic facts as well as an SME adapted way of implementing and conducting Business Process Management. The BPM@KMU project tries to address these issues by building up an e-Learning program allowing participants to enter the course contents where they experienced lacks of knowledge and where they find guidance to their problems. This means that not all contents of the course will be considered by all participants. Rather, the participants will be guided through their own learning paths by their needs.

- *Content analysis and design – pedagogical domain*

The central subject of the e-Learning course is the introduction of Business Process Management. For this, the BPM activity model like the one illustrated in Ch. 3 offer a good general structure for the curriculum. The development of the content might respect the heterogeneous BPM experience in the target audience. A BPM subject expert with experience in small- and medium-sized organisations (e.g. a business consultant or a team consisting of BPM researchers and experienced BPM users/employees coming from a SME) might guide the content development process. Use cases and exercises should respect the mind-set and experience of the target group. In addition, a special focus should be set on the time restrictions named in Ch. 3. That means, the duration of the chapters should not exceed the participants time resources. Content has to be provided in a modular structure. This enables the participant to decide which chapters have a higher priority and which ones could be neglected. Contents should be provided in different formats. Besides textual contents visual and auditory ones have to be considered, too. A combination of all of them might result in a more varied course and therefore in a higher acceptance by the participants.

- *Technology analysis and tool design – technological domain*

Because of the fact, that SMEs are not able to introduce their own learning management system (LMS) without any limitations of budget, time and knowledge, the e-Learning program should be operated at a hosted learning environment. Therefore, each organisation or specific learner has to have an internet access through a computer. The learning environment should be accessible outside a SME's local network. This allows employees to use the program from any place they want (e.g. at home after regular working time). This also means, that the e-Learning program should be usable in an easy way to reduce time being spent learning how to use the e-Learning platform and its various tools.

For focusing the relevant aspects during the creation phase Table 3 shows a checklist was developed respecting the above-mentioned barriers for BPM introduction in SMEs. The checklist is structured after the typical e-Learning phases and processes which are mapped to the relevant activities and roles (responsible or involved). It aims as a structured guideline for the project team.

**Table 3.** Instantiated e-learning management checklist for BPM@KMU

| Item | Process | Regarding sub-processes | Activities | Owner | Process Manager | Process Performer | Involved |
|---|---|---|---|---|---|---|---|
| 1 | e-Learning Initialisation and Strategy | 1.1 Initialisation<br>1.2 Identifying e-Learning Stakeholder<br>1.3 Defining e-Learning strategy and goal-setting<br>1.4 Analysing e-Learning requirements | 1. Checking of participants and stakeholders in SME.<br>2. Writing a ESF request for BPM@KMU describing strategy and goal.<br>3. Write a first outline for the BPM contents.<br>4. Outlining of IT-technical e-Learning requirements. | SME Management | University Erlangen-Nuremberg/Wi2 | e-Learning Analyst | BPM Expert |
| 2 | Analyzation and determination of the General Framework | 2.1 Analysing external context<br>2.2 Analysing personal resources<br>2.3 Analysing e-Learning target group<br>2.4 Analysing of institutional context<br>2.5 Analysing e-Learning equipement<br>2.6. Determining project timeline and budget | 1. Identification, description and validation of external (law, economical, social, trends and policy of education) issues affecting eLearning and will be affected through eLearning.<br>2. Analysing (identification and description) of personnel resources (roles, competencies, skills, formal qualification and availability) are given in as-is situation and affected by eLearning or will affect eLearning concept.<br>3. Analysing of eLearning target group respecting socio-cultural and social factors, individual attitudes, motivation for using of eLearning, skills and previous knowledge, self-efficacy and role.<br>4. Analysing Organisational structures, process organisation, business model, internal politics and cultural issues, learning culture and significance of education and learning in eLearning target Organisation.<br>5. Analyzing the technical as well as infrastructural conditions are affected through or will affect the use of eLearning.<br>6. Conducting project planning for the eLearning project respecting the issues of time, financial budgets and contracting with vendors. | SME Management | University Erlangen-Nuremberg/Wi2 | e-Learning Analyst | SME Management<br>SME employees<br>SME IT Management |
| 3. | Designing e-Learning | 3.1 Designing e-Learning targets<br>3.2 Designing content<br>3.3 Define didactical/methodological concept<br>3.4 Definition of e-Learning roles and responsibilities<br>3.5 Define Organisational design<br>3.6 Define technological design (request for proposal - RFP)<br>3.7 Define media and interaction design<br>3.8 Define application of media<br>3.9 Define e-Learning communication concept<br>3.10 Define test and examination concept<br>3.11 Define technical and maintenance and operation concept | 1. Definition of BPM training targets and competency model.<br>2. Definition of BPM content including topics/courses, length and depth.<br>3. Selection and combination of didactical concepts, selection of adequate methodological concept. This includes instructional models, curriculum, learning scenarios as well as social interaction and collaboration methods for SMEs.<br>4. Definition of Organisational framework are relevant for educational processes. Includes components learning/teaching destination, time for learning as well as overall program length.<br>5. Definition and description of technical concept respectively of requirements for eLearning software, interfaces as well as definition of the involvement of given IT infrastructures of SMEs.<br>6. Definition of the design concept. These are media design, layout, color schemata as well as screen design.<br>7. Definition of media and its usage, functionalities, target group, learning targets, learning contents, rules and standards. Criteria for the usage of media are:<br>  a. presentation and distribution of information;<br>  b. collecting and filtering of information;<br>  c. processing of information and interaction;<br>  d. constructive illustration of learner-own results;<br>  e. performance too-set;<br>  f. communication.<br>Methods are: effect analysis, working and learning place analysis.<br>8. Definition of communication and interaction concept for inter-company exchange. | SME Management | University Erlangen-Nuremberg/Wi2 | Content Author Content/Media | BPM Expert<br>SME IT Expert |

## 5  BPM@KMU – From the Analysis to the E-Learning Solution

This section describes the first results of the e-Learning program BPM@KMU. The report is structured after the three areas; the *institutional* issues by describing the project setup and determination of the organisational issues (1); the *pedagogical and technological* issues by illustrating the instructional design and the set of tools chosen for the program (2); and the *socio-ethical* issues addressing the heterogeneous setting of target group in SMEs by development of specific BPM curriculum (3).

**(1)  BPM@KMU – the organisational and project setup**
Starting in January 2011 the project comprises a total duration of two years containing a start-up phase as well as two course terms divided by a course improvement phase. Last, an evaluation phase for analyzing the final outcomes is added. Especially the start-up phase requires a strong interaction between the university and the SMEs for building up an optimized learning program for the SMEs' needs.

At the preparation time of this paper a first meeting between representatives of all enterprises and the university has taken place. The meeting has shown that due to different demands of the SMEs a common understanding of Business Process Management and the course's goals has to be created first. Therefore, all parties agreed that the individual modules of the course are created under the leadership of the Institute of Information Systems and are subsequently discussed by the SMEs.

**(2)  Lecture-on-demand, exercises, face-to-face meetings and forum and chats**
The e-Learning course is provided on a Moodle-based learning management platform containing a variety of resources and possibilities of collaborative cooperation. One of them are lecture-on-demand packages. For that, a player implemented by the Institute of Information Systems and tested during several semesters is deployed. It offers a synchronized combination of slides, lecturer video and table of contents. This enables users to navigate through the recording targeting specific topics. The player will be used as the main technology for the transfer of theoretical knowledge. Besides, the entire content will be provided as text documents and slide collections which allow the participants to print out the contents and take them away or write down their own notices on paper. While theoretical backgrounds will be kept as short as possible case studies are used to show participants the relevance of the learned topics. Therefore, case studies are applied to guide participants from the theoretical foundations to an adapted solution for their own company. The discussion of case studies will be carried out by a set of collaborative tools such as chats, real-time text editors and video conferences. Especially the basics of Business Process Management have to be understood clearly. Consequently a review of learned knowledge is in some parts of the e-Learning course mandatory. For this reason, checking of knowledge can be carried out by short-time online exercises. Proven free tools like Hot Potatoes are easily implementable and provide a wide range of exercise types. Following illustration provides an overview over the chosen pedagogical and technological e-Learning components.

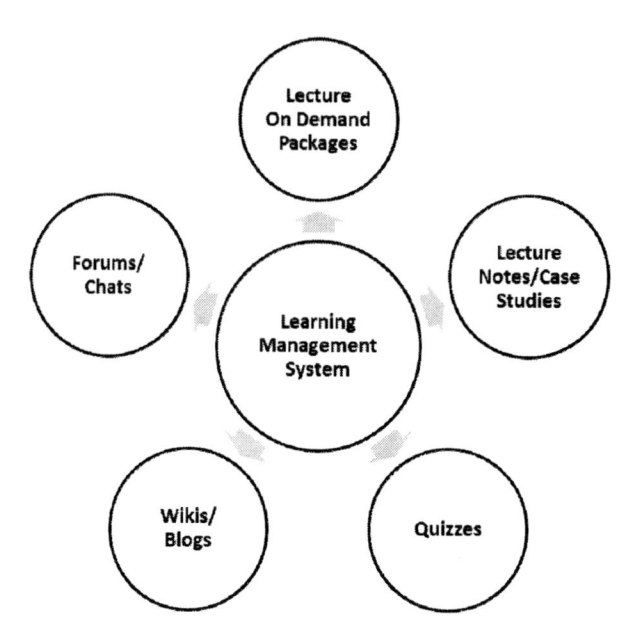

Fig. 3. Instructional-technological elements of BPM@KMU e-Learning

**(3) Curriculum – BPM contents and target-specific entries**
The learning program is separated into nine sections. The sections are depicted in Fig. 5.

The first section is an introductory chapter that imparts basic knowledge about Business Process Management. The section is especially suitable for participants having only less knowledge about BPM. After conducting a survey about the company's BPM readiness including the positioning of the company (section two), section three aims to provide participants information about the process architecture. Therefore, a clear understanding of the processes in the considered company as well as their structure is important. As a result of this section, a process map should be achievable. The section "process organisation" covers topics like the assignment of responsibilities and the selection of modeling methods and conventions. After working through this section a process manual containing information about the introduction of BPM can be created. Process modeling (section five) deals with the modeling and optimization of business processes. Therefore, relevant processes have to be identified and the methods for analyzing and optimizing business processes have to be applied. During the organisational implementation (section six) the newly modeled business processes have to be implemented in the company. This implies identifying the stakeholders and setting up a change management project. Subsequently, IT support for selected business processes has to be implemented (section seven). Hence, suitable automation approaches have to be chosen and the levels of automation must be determined. The section performance measurement will guide the participants during developing a small performance measurement that will help them to keep an eye on relevant business processes by continuous monitoring. Finally, a last section is set up, that sums up the learned content and gives a comprehensive overview on Business Process Management.

## Overview Curriculum

**Introduction**
Questions
- Why should we conduct business process management at all?
- How interact our corporate strategy and Business Process Management?

Approach
- Development of a basic understanding of process management and its benefits

→ Basic understanding

**Survey**
Questions
- What is the status of our business?
- What are our goals?

Approach
- Management Workshops

→ Positioning

**Process architecture**
Questions
- What are our key processes and what structure do they have?

Approach
- Analysis of the business organization as a basis for structuring the key processes

→ Process map

**Organizational implementation**
Questions
- How can we implement the improved business processes in our enterprise?

Approach
- Identification of stakeholders
- Conception and conduct of a change management project

→ Change management project

**Process modeling**
Questions
- How can we model and improve our business processes?

Approach
- Selection of relevant business processes
- Usage of simple modeling methods and tools for analyzing and improving business processes

→ Process models

**Process organization**
Questions
- What are organizational requirements for process management?

Approach
- Assignment of responsibilities
- Establishment of modeling methods and conventions
- Training of process owners

→ Process documentation guide

**IT support**
Questions
- How can we automate our business processes and what are the benefits?

Approach
- Selection of appropriate processes
- Provision of appropriate support/automation levels
- Selection of IT systems

→ IT support map

**Performance measurement**
Questions
- How can we measure and control the performance of our processes?

Approach
- Definition of indicators and metrics
- Extraction and aggregation of indicators

→ Process reports/Controlling cockpit

**Outlook**
Questions
- How should we adjust our BPM if the company continues to grow?

Approach
- Introduction to maturity models
- Consideration of BPM implementations of larger companies

→ Instructions for further actions

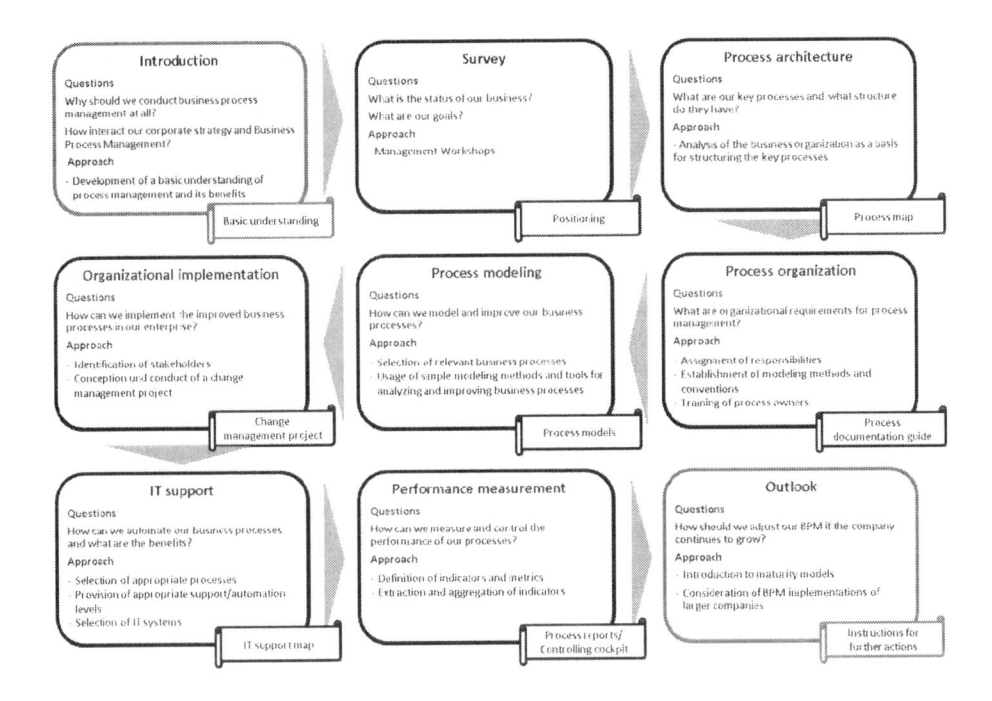

**Fig. 4.** Overview curriculum

At this point should be noted, that the recommended curriculum developed during the first phase of the BPM@KMU project might be observed regarding its adequateness and completeness for the specific target group of SME's. If improvement potential is detected, the curriculum will be adjusted accordingly in subsequent phases.

## 6 Conclusion and Further Research

BPM comprises not only for large enterprises but also for SMEs a relevant set of methods and management instruments for the improvement of their business structure. Therefore, existing barriers for the implementation of BPM in small- and medium-sized enterprises need to be addressed by innovative approaches. This paper has shown how these issues might be addressed during the initiation, planning and design of an e-Learning program for BPM in SMEs. Regarding the current phase of the project a first reflection of the proposed four working hypotheses can be done:

1) E-Learning programs like BPM@KMU offer the space for an adequate information exchange and training about the knowledge of process-oriented approaches.

2) With the creation of centralized e-Learning solutions financial and time constraints for the implementation of BPM in small- and medium-sized

organisations can be lessened. Learning about BPM therefore can happen in a flexible way and mostly independent from timely restrictions or shortfalls through time consuming of face-to-face training sessions.

3) Especially during the planning and designing stage the need for target specific information transfer to the senior management of SMEs is a crucial factor. This is addressed by the programs different levels of detail. Role specific entries into the learning path as well as flexible technology like the lecture-on-demand are possible solutions for this.

4) A flexible and module-like design of the curriculum allows the inclusion and exclusion of specific topics like contents regarding information technology and its link to Business Process Management.

The illustrated *Cybernetic e-Learning Management Model* offers a pragmatic framework for the planning, designing and implementation of similar projects. On the one hand it provides a descriptive structure for the implementation of an e-Learning program. On the other hand typical success factors for e-Learning in heterogeneous target groups like the of the BPM@KMU project are provided. The use of supporting instruments like checklists facilitates the project team with its work.

In future research the effects of BPM@KMU should be observed via a mid-termed study of the management and learner experience as well as the change of the BPM maturity in the participated organisations. On the other hand some specific issues have to be observed in the project and might be improved in future releases of the BPM@KMU e-Learning program (e.g. the in Ch. 5 mentioned adequateness and completeness of the curriculum). The long-term duration of BPM@KMU provides possibilities for these investigations.

# References

1. Hammer, M., Champy, J.: Business Reengineering: Die Radikalkur für das Unternehmen. München (1998)
2. Treacy, M., Wiersema, F.: The Discipline of Market Leaders (1997)
3. Keen, P.G.W.: The Process Edge – Creating value where it counts. Havard (1997)
4. Porter, M.E.: Competitive Advantage: Creating and Sustaining Superior Performance, New York, London (1985)
5. Rosemann, M.: Die Grundsätze ordnungsmäßiger Modellierung. Intention, Entwicklung, Architektur und Multiperspektivität. In: Maicher, M., Scheruhn, H.J. (eds.) Informationsmodellierung. Referenzmodelle und Werkzeuge, Wiesbaden, pp. 1–21 (1998)
6. Feldmayer, J., Seidenschwarz, W.: Marktorientiertes Prozessmanagement – Wie Process Mass Customization Kundenorientierung und Prozessstandardisierung integriert, München (2005)
7. Baker, G., Maddux, H.: Enhancing organisational performance: facilitating the critical transition to a process view management. S.A.M Advanced Management Journal 7(4), 30–60 (2005)
8. Chong, S.: Business Process Management for SME's: an exploratory study of implementation factors for the Australian wine industry. Journal of Information Systems and Small Business 1(1-2), 41–58 (2007)
9. Riley, M.J., Brown, D.C.: Case study of the application of BPR in an SME contractor. Knowledge and Process Management 8(1), 17–28 (2001)

10. Hilgarth, B.: E-Learning Success in Action! From Case Study Research to the creation of the Cybernetic e-Learning Management Model. International Journal of Computer Information Systems and Industrial Management Applications 3 (in Press, 2011)
11. DIN: PAS 1032-1: Aus- und Weiterbildung unter besonderer Berücksichtigung von e-Learning - Teil 1: Referenzmodell für Qualitätsmanagement und Qualitätssicherung - Planung, Entwicklung, Durchführung und Evaluation von Bildungsprozessen und Bildungsangeboten (2004), `http://www.beuth.de`
12. Hilgarth, B., Purucker, J., Mayer, H., Göldner, F.: ProcessSharePoint® - ein Praxisbericht zur Lösung des Last-Mile-Problems in der Prozessimplementierung. In: HMD – Praxis der Wirtschaftsinformatik, Vol. 266, pp. 90–99 (2009)
13. Rossi, M., et al.: Action Design Research. MIS Quaterly 35(1), 37–56 (2011)
14. Institut für Mittelstandsforschung Bonn (IfM Bonn) (2011), `http://www.ifm-bonn.org/index.php?id=590`
15. Sauter, A., Sauter, W.: Blended Learning. Effiziente Integration von E-Learning und Präsenztraining. Luchterhand, Neuwied (2002)
16. Weinberger, A., Ertl, B., Fischer, F., Mandl, H.: Cooperation Scripts for Learning via Web-based Discussion Boards and Videoconferencing. EARLI SIM (2004)

# Process Training to Support Change Necessary within the Scope of Process Implementation

Gregor Back[1] and Klaus Daniel[2]

[1] Deutsche Telekom AG, T-Online-Allee 1, 64295 Darmstadt, Germany
g.back@telekom.de
[2] Scio GmbH, Henkestrasse 91, 91052 Erlangen, Germany
klaus.daniel@scio.eu

**Abstract.** Introducing new or modified business processes is a change task that so far has played only a minor role within the discussion of business process management. Process training – if properly designed – can contribute significantly to ensure that all parties involved can quickly and easily acquire the required process competence (knowledge, skills, will and permission). They are therefore effective tools of change management. In this paper we will draft the requirements of process training and will highlight the proposed approach using an actual case study. In addition to technical and organizational aspects we consider process competence (the "human factor") as a third important criterion in successful Business Process Management (BPM).

**Keywords:** Process implementation, change management, process competence, process training.

## 1 Introduction

The introduction of new or modified business processes is often done in the context of a planned change. Such a planned change can be the result of, for example, strategy planning, the implementing of new business models within the scope of cost reduction programs, or M&A activities.

One of the central management tasks – besides (re-)designing business processes – is to appropriately assist the necessary change from the actual situation to the target situations. This requirement is based on a simple observation of business practices: a desired target situation is never reached by itself but only by active intervention. According to the basic idea of the S-BPM approach, however, the individual should be the center of attention, not the technical and organizational aspects of the process.

Hence, in the following we would like to present first the importance of a change management for a successful implementation of business processes. Next we will focus on how process training can help to master the necessary change successfully.

## 2 Change Management in the Context of Process Implementations

Implementing a process can be the result of an introduction of a new process or the modification of an existing process. Both cases constitute a change, whose success will depend not only on its technical and organizational implementation, but above all on a change in the minds of the people affected. A process implementation can fail because the parties involved do not have the necessary process competence. This is the case when the knowledge and the skills required are not sufficiently developed, the motivation to implement the necessary changes *(the will)* is lacking, or the leadership has yet to establish the necessary general conditions *(the permission)*.

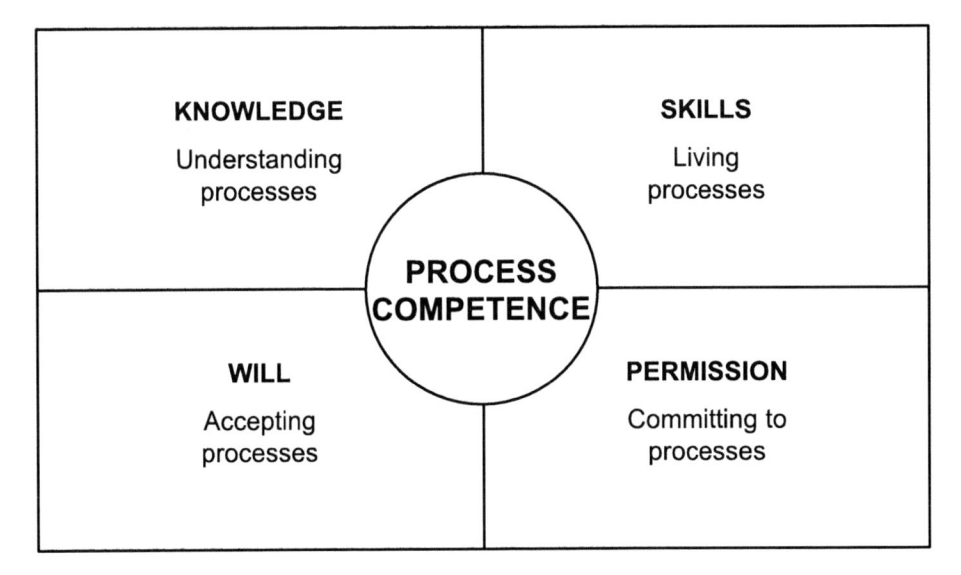

**Fig. 1.** Dimensions of process competence

For the following we assume that a process-related change will be particularly successful if the development of the necessary process competence is consciously organized for all those involved. We see change management as a specialized management approach that can help fulfill this task of the business process management in a professional manner.

The various attempts at defining change management show how closely related the two concepts of business process management and change management are in terms of content. According to Claßen, change management comprises "the active, guided monitoring of change processes with the aim of achieving business objectives and company performances." [1] In this respect, change management can be understood as a meta competence that contributes to the effective introduction and establishing of business processes.

The study "Change Management 2010" by Capgemini Consulting lists ten starting points for successfully managing change projects: [2]

- Ensuring mobilization and commitment
- Analyzing and understanding both situation and environment
- Promoting guidance
- Comprehending and designing both organization and processes
- Identifying and consolidating successes

- Performing target group-specific qualification and development
- Driving orientation and alignment
- Developing and establishing structures and monitoring
- Avoiding or reducing conflicts and resistance
- Refining corporate culture

According to this estimation, the success of implementing a process is based primarily on "bringing the people aboard". This is not only about communicating the desired target situation once the process has been implemented; it is rather about involving already at an early stage all the people affected by the change. The situation should be examined together with them to find out how the process implementation affects the company in general and their jobs in particular. [3] In this respect, the previously outlined list can serve as a starting point for identifying appropriate change measures. We consider it important to note that the approaches mentioned above should not be applied individually but preferably in combination.

## 3 Process Training

As far as our article is concerned, the previously outlined considerations on change management require any process training to go beyond merely conveying the relevant abilities and skills. Moreover, it should establish a high degree of motivation and clear outline the individual accountability of all parties involved. The question of what level of process competence to develop can, of course, be answered only individually. However, when defining the training targets and non-targets, one should strive for a minimum level of standardization in the process work. [4] The four proficiency levels by O'Connor and Seymour offer a useful conceptual model: [5]

- Stage 1: Unconscious incompetence
- Stage 2: Conscious incompetence
- Stage 3: Conscious competence
- Stage 4: Unconscious competence

The stages of learning – as derived from the learning theory – can be well applied to the process implementation case at hand. The initial situation, i.e. the time before the new or changed processes is implemented, can be described as state of "unconscious incompetent" (stage 1). The parties involved in the process are not yet aware that they will soon need a change process competence. Such a problem awareness, however, is not yet necessary at that stage.

The parties reach the state of "conscious incompetence" (stage 2) once they learn of the planned change (whether intentionally or not) but still lack the process competence necessary to actually "live" the target process.

This is where the process training picks up, with the goal of quickly bringing all those affected by the change to the state of "conscious competence" (stage 3). This is achieved when knowledge, skills, will and permission of all parties involved have been developed in a way that makes it possible to work effectively and efficiently in the target process.

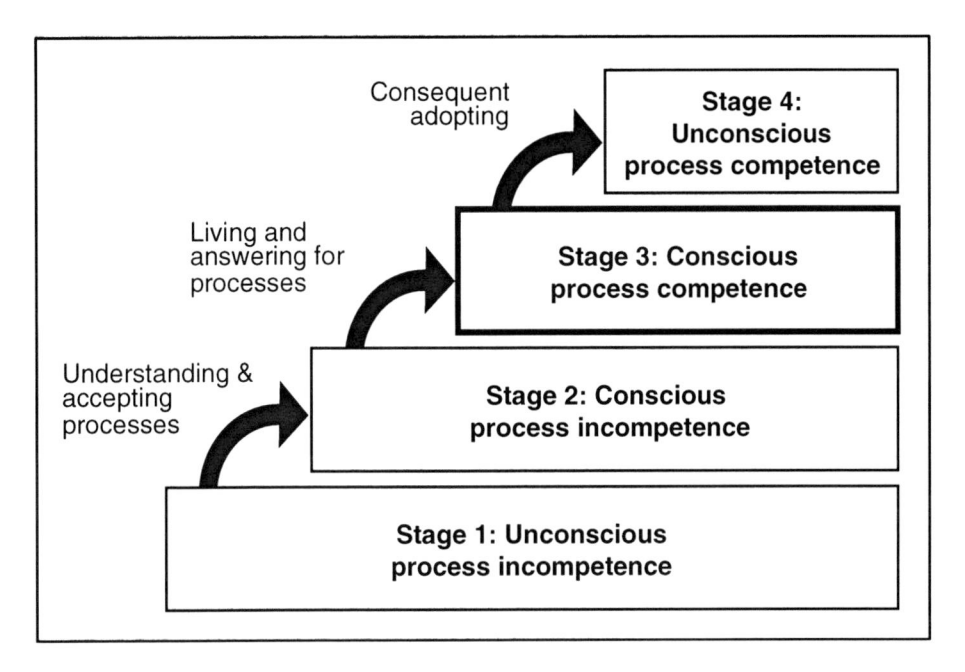

**Fig. 2.** Conceptual model of the process competence "stages"

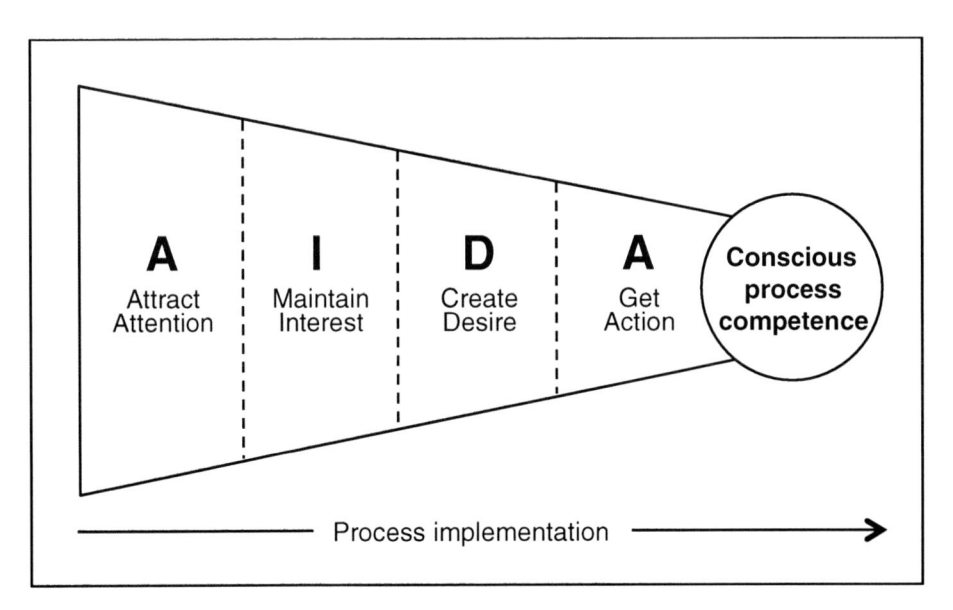

**Fig. 3.** Use of the AIDA principle to achieve conscious process competence

The state of "unconscious competence" (stage 4) is achieved once the process-related abilities and skills have become "second nature" for all those involved in the process. This, for example, would be the case if all parties involved work together so harmoniously that process control is no longer necessary because everybody knows intuitively what to do. As desirable as this state may be, it is rarely achieved. After a certain time, fluctuation and process adjustments, for example, can cause the parties involved in the process to "fall back" into a state of "unconscious incompetence" (stage 1); the development of process competence will begin anew.

Process training should strive to achieve the state of "conscious competence" (stage 3) to all those involved. How can the parties involved leave the current state and reach the target state? The so-called AIDA principle could be a helpful conceptual model for answering this question. Although originally part of the advertising impact research, it is nonetheless suitable for the situation at hand.

In order to achieve "conscious competence", the first step is to obtain the necessary attention (Attract Attention) among the involved parties. This can be done through communication: in form of announcements in the Intranet or information in the regular meetings. This communication is aimed at creating awareness for both the upcoming changes and for the fact that the active participation by affected people is desired – and "mission critical".

The second step is to keep the involved parties interested (Maintain Interest), to create appreciation and to promote support. It should be made clear why the process is implemented, what this means for the company, the divisions, and the individuals, and what the upcoming steps are.

The third step aims to instill in all those affected the wish to participate and be involved (Create Desire). This may, for instance, include collecting proposals on how to implement the desired change from the perspective of those involved, specifically for their workplace. All in all, it has to be the frequently quoted recommendation: make partners of those affected.

The fourth step is a matter of implementing the target process in the business reality and adapting the behavior of the parties involved accordingly (Get Action). From the perspective of change management, there are several options for this: staff meetings, negotiations, and specialized coaching. It is important to let those involved soon experience the promised benefits of the process implementation, and to quickly remove obstacles, which typically arise during the implementation process, in a straightforward way.

When designing and implementing process training, the considerations outlined above – the process competence model, the proficiency-level manager, and the AIDA principle – need to be considered simultaneously, if possible. In short, the goal of process training should be the development of the process competence (knowledge, skills, will and permission) of all parties involved in order to quickly reach the state of "conscious competence" and to "bringing aboard" all those affected. This results in a clear "commitment" as to the new processes; the people affected realize that their participation in reaching the target state is both required and desired.

For the practical design of a process training, these requirements can be deduced:

- The process training should be specifically designed and carried out for each target group. This ensures that different competence requirements are adequately addressed according to the functions (e.g., product management, engineering, controlling, etc.) and hierarchical levels (e.g., top management, middle management, implementation level).

- In terms of content, the focus of the process training should be on the business perspective; the methods of process modeling, however, should not be the focus of the training. Complicated process notations (e.g., EPC models) should be avoided as far as possible and should be "translated" to a language appropriate for the participants.
- The training participants will recognize their future role, the associated competence requirements and the necessary collaboration with the other involved parties. By the end of the training, they will have understood their personal responsibilities in such a way that their workplace practices are complied with the process.
- If possible, the "new" types of collaboration should be tried out already during the process training. The spectrum of possibilities ranges from a deliberately heterogeneous groups of participants to simulating collaboration in the process training. The "key learning" that the participants should, by all means, receive in the process training is which rules and standards of collaboration will be apply in the future. Ideally, they will have compiled the rules and standards together.
- The "human factor" is at the center of the process training. While all process aids and tools should be included in the training events to realistically reproduce reality, they should not be given too much weight.
- Process training should take place at a time when the design of future operational and organizational structure has been resolved as far as possible. The degrees of freedom for designing the future process organization should exist until then to allow the integration of participatory elements (such as collecting and processing feedback as to process content and process sequences) into the training process.
- Controversial views and discussions should not be seen as disruptive, but as an enrichment to a process training. From the principal's point of view there are usually unbeatable factual arguments in favor of a training process that make an implementation of change a desirable objective; in contrast, trainees are often unsure whether the "right thing" is happening here from a business and/or personal perspective. Hence, the objective should be to establish a "fair process" culture [6] within the process training. This can be done, for example, by marketing changes and associated personal consequences not only positive (value propositions), but by also stating clearly which "cornerstone" apply from the perspective of management, and where they expect the participants to shape the process (challenges). Such a transparent and fair approach creates the desired motivation for all parties involved.
- In addition to conveying relevant process knowledge, it would also be desirable to include and work with concrete case studies in terms of action learning [7] in the process training. This approach allows turning theoretical process knowledge into practical skills. The precondition is that the training participants have the opportunity to submit their specific case studies in the preparatory phase.

On the basis of a case study, the following section examines the existing theoretical models in detail, which have been outlined above and highlights their practical use.

## 4 Case Study: Process Training as a Significant Factor within the Implementation of a New Operating Model at Deutsche Telekom AG

With almost 200 million customers, Deutsche Telekom AG is one of the world's leading telecommunications and IT service companies [8]. It employs about 252,000 people worldwide, 79,000 of these in Germany [9]. Since the privatization of the company in 1996, Deutsche Telekom AG, a formerly state-owned monopoly, is in a constant process of transformation, adapting to new market trends, keeping up with technological development and becoming more and more an innovative, customer-oriented and competitive service company.

As part of the implementation of a new group structure in June 2006, the Internet service provider T-Online AG was reintegrated into Deutsche Telekom AG. The formerly independent business unit was merged with the fixed network carrier T-Com. Shortly after the appointment of Rene Obermann as CEO a new transformation began and another business unit "Products and Innovation (P&I)" was founded in 2007. Emerging from former T-Online, P&I became responsible for innovation and the international development of new products. For the German domestic market, the broadband and fixed-line network business (BBFN) was consolidated under the brand "T-Home".

To define responsibilities and describe the different ways of collaboration between P&I and T-Home, a new operating model was designed – the "Operating Model Germany". The preceding organizational changes, which came in rapid succession and involved more than one business unit, also required a cultural change within the company. All in all, this entire change process had to be well planned and designed as one coherent change program. From the beginning, the Operating Model Germany and the training sessions for its redesigned product development process became one key component of this program.

The basic concept was initially developed by one of the leading consulting firms and then handed over to a project team for the actual rollout. Goals of the project were to empower the employees to work within the new organizational environment, to give orientation and point out which problems might arise, what the reasons could be and how possible solutions might look like. Furthermore, it should build acceptance for the new structures as well as the reassigned tasks and responsibilities.

With the help of a practical example, an approach for the implementation of a new operating model should be outlined. Especially the role of process training as an important factor of organizational change as well as the development of process competence as an important factor for BPM should be pointed out in the following.

## 5 Training Approach

Once the concept of the Operating Model Germany was handed over to the project, the implementation of the new processes could be roughly divided into five overlapping phases. The first one was the elaboration of the process on an operational level. In parallel the second phase was about the development of a training concept. The third phase, the involvement of senior management was the inception of a series of training sessions, starting with a workshop for the top and middle management. The initial training sessions for the operative level constitute the fourth phase. Finally during the fifth phase, which again overlaps the preceding one, the project is transferred into continuous process management.

These five phases of a process implementation at Deutsche Telekom AG will be explained more in detail on the following pages. Some action items will be highlighted and evaluated on the basis of the theoretical models, which were outlined above.

# 6 Elaboration of the Process on an Operational Level (1$^{st}$ Phase)

In this first phase of process implementation, the process was elaborated by defining the tasks and assigning clear responsibility for every process step. A recommendable procedure was the participation of process users and experts from involved roles and business units.

One important part of the newly defined operating model was the definition of a new product development process, based on a classical stage/gate approach, including two decision bodies and three responsible roles. The operating model sets the standards of collaboration between all involved business units and the three responsible roles: Product Manager (product development), Commercial Manager (marketing & sales) and Service Launch Manager (IT-integration and customer related processes). But the process itself still had to be detailed on an operational level, then coordinated with all involved roles and stakeholders and finally implemented into the organization.

Therefore representatives and experts from involved business units were invited to a series of workshop sessions. They brought in the necessary operational know-how and coordinated the intermediate and final results with their business units. Having them aboard at such an early stage also increased the acceptance of the new processes and the change program in general.

# 7 Development of a Training Concept (2$^{nd}$ Phase)

To ensure that all involved parties have the necessary process competencies (knowledge, skills, will and permission) a holistic training and communication concept is needed. Employees have to be enabled to take over their new tasks and responsibilities.

Besides the process training the communication concept involved staff-meetings, publications in employee newspapers and newsletters, intranet communication, cross-functional workshops, etc. The goals of the process training were set as follows:

- Create a profound understanding of the new „Operating Model Germany" and find the necessary support for it.
- Achieve a high level of competency as well as motivation to accept and live the new process.

- Conduct spatially inclusive and comprehensive training sessions for all key-responsible roles (approximately 250 employees) and achieve a comparable state of knowledge between all roles and stakeholders.

Both, the AIDA principle and the conceptual model of the process competence "stages", as described beforehand, have been considered equally for the design and execution of the training sessions.

The active participation by effected people at an early stage of the entire change process accompanied by a regular and broad communication of project status created attention and maintained interest. Thus having the possibility to be involved in shaping the own future tasks and responsibilities increased the willingness to participate (create desire) and to support the implementation (get action), although there was a strong initial resistance.

Looking at the conceptual model of the process competence "stages", several measures were taken in order to achieve or after new changes to get back onto at least the third level of proficiency, the „conscious competence". Those measures, like setting up a process team, or providing support tools via the internet, etc. will be briefly explained in a later chapter.

The next two chapters will show the target group-specific structure and content of the training sessions for the planed process implementation. Except for the communication and coordination with the top management level, all training sessions have a strong focus on active involvement of the participants to let them evaluate and experience the promised benefits of the "Operating Model Germany" by themselves.

# 8 Involvement of Senior Management (3$^{rd}$ Phase)

For several reasons the involvement of senior management level is also a key success factor not only in change management, but also for process training sessions. The official approval from top management and its direct involvement into the communication made it a lot easier for people to accept their new roles and responsibilities and to support the change in general.

Apart from increasing the acceptance, the involvement of the senior management constitutes acceptance and understanding at leadership level and motivates executive managers to support their teams in their work within the new operating model and the new processes. Therefore a special 2 hour workshop for approximately 60 executive managers was set up. The tree responsible senior vice presidents invited to this event to communicate the key messages in person, what showed the importance of this change program.

The aim of this event was to point out the interrelation of the strategic business objectives and the "Operating Model Germany". Furthermore the executive managers were asked to figure out, how they could contribute personally to the success of the new operating model and how they want to support their fellow employees in the adherence of the new processes. These ideas were documented and every participant symbolically had to sign a pledge to enforce commitment. For the execution of this workshop the following training methods were applied:

- professional inputs
- moderated panel discussion (with the senior vice presidents)

- group work,
- networking session
- marketplace (poster exhibition)

For the workshops it was also important, that all contend was explicitly related to the leadership role, that no basic knowledge was imparted and that no one considered the topics covered in the workshop as optional.

## 9 Process Training on an Operative Level (4$^{th}$ Phase)

The implementation of process training was already predefined to a great extent by setting up the training concept. Compared to the workshop for executive managers the focus of these training sessions lies on the shift of tasks, the demand for new competencies and the (re-)assignment of responsibility. The basic targets of the training were set as follows:

- Changes and challenges of the Operating Model Germany (OMG) are understood
- All participants have applicable and specific process competence
- Rules and standards of cooperation are generally accepted

Fig. 4. "Role play - working in teams"

Furthermore the training was designed to promote acceptance of the change and identification with the new forms of cooperation within the company. The training structure shows three essential parts, which use different training methods each. The first part is a theoretical introduction into „how to work successfully in project or process teams". In case the participants don't have any special topics, which they want to discuss, the theoretical part can be completed by a role play to demonstrate the difficulties of cooperation and task sharing in a project.

The second part consists of a general introduction into the basic principles of the new operating model. In this part of the training a responsible process manager explains the background as well as the chances and challenges of the "Operating Model Germany". As in the first part the focus topics depend on the individual needs and interests of the participants.

The central and also most time-consuming part of the training is the elaboration of the process in small groups. Accompanied by the trainer and an expert the trainees should compile the rules and standards of collaboration within the new operating model by themselves. Having a set of posters showing all phases of the process with the key activities of each role, the participants can walk around and discuss their individual questions and topics.

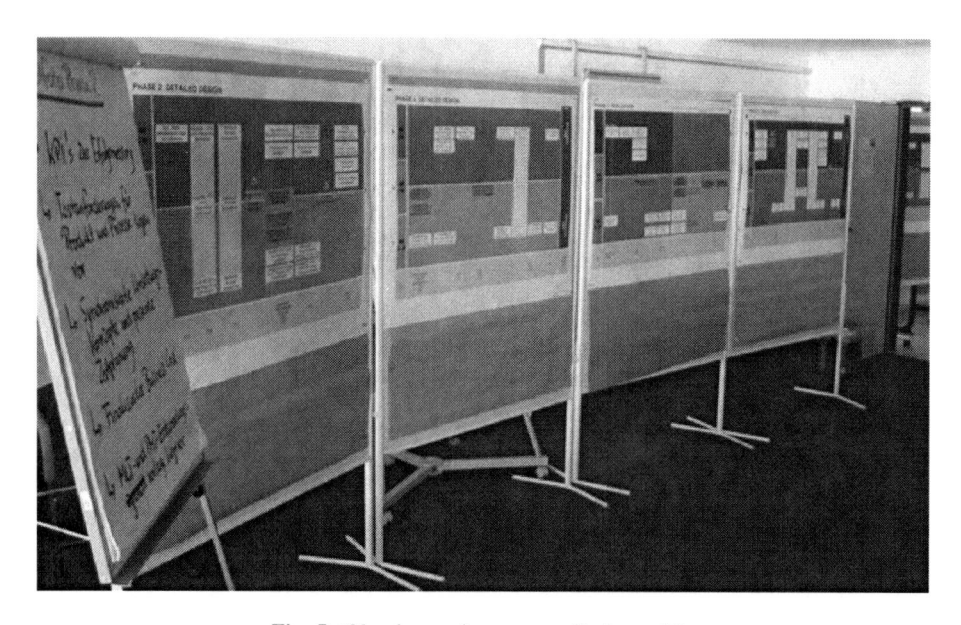

Fig. 5. "Vernissage / process walk-through"

After each phase of the process they present their findings of the "walk-through" to the class. Gaps in understanding or other things which might be interesting for everyone are collected on post-its and discussed in front of class. This way the participants can bring in their own expertise and know how and the process managers get valuable feedback, which they can use for process optimization. Further Feedback concerning the needs, requirements und suggestions for improvements is collected by the trainer at the end of each session. Therefore he asks three central questions:

- What can I/ what do I want to do personally for the success of the Operating Model Germany?
- What can we as a team/ what do we as a team (CM, PM, SLM) want to do for the success of the Operating Model Germany?
- What can/ what should the company do for the success of the Operating Model Germany?

Like in the preceding chapters about training design and the involvement of senior management, also in training for this target group the „human factor" stands in the centre of interest. The focus is on the involvement of process users to create a good understanding of the own tasks and responsibilities as well as the ones of the other roles. Participants should develop their individual abilities and skills at the one hand, at the other hand they should identify with their new role, tasks and responsibility.

## 10  Transfer Project Into a Continuous Process Management (5$^{th}$ Phase)

To achieve a sustainable change and to guarantee ongoing support for the process execution the project was transferred into a permanent team of process managers and several measures for continuous process optimization were implemented. Not only during the project phase, but also after implementation all involved roles were offered a range of options to reshape and optimize the processes. Furthermore the training sessions became part of the regular company training catalogue.

Moreover apart from process training other measures were necessary to stabilize and optimize the new processes. In the case of coordination problems between departments a special team-coaching was offered as well as other forms of direct project support. Another measure was to establish a communication platform to publish the latest process documentation, training work books, information about changes in the process or responsibly, a Q&A-List, etc. For the continuous process improvement a steering team was established to collect, coordinate, implement and communicate necessary changes. Also the feedback from regular training sessions still helps to identify possible improvements.

Referring again to the learning theory, all those measure are used to shorten the time, when fellow employees fall back to a lower competence level and have to improve their skills and competence again to achieve the third level of proficiency, the "conscious competence". Reasons for falling back could be new changes in the process or other changing factors (e.g., a modification of an IT-Tool).

## 11  Lessons Learned

In the final chapter of this article the key findings of this process training within the framework of the implementation of a new operating model at Deutsche Telekom AG are summarized.

The advantages identified by the authors in this training case match very close the conclusions of the theoretical approach presented in the first part of this article. Most findings can be generalized and transferred on other training programs. The authors are of the opinion that the following aspects had a positive effect on the process training and at the same time helped to make the change program successful and sustainable:

- **Commitment of Top Management** – the explicit statement from top management that they will support the implementation and even more will demand the adherence of the „Operating Model Germany" definitively was an important success factor to the process implementation. The personal attendance and participation of top management showed the importance of the change program and thus supported the acceptance.
- **Commitment of the responsible process managers** – the participation of at least one responsible process manager at every training session did not only show commitment but also increased the acceptance of the change and the willingness to support the accompanying measures. Participants also were engaged in giving feedback or bringing in their knowledge.
- **Individual and target group-specific training** - the training was set up to achieve a comparable state of knowledge between all roles and stakeholders. That for a personal coaching in small groups by one professional trainer with the support of experts and responsible process managers was considered more effective than a training concept using multipliers, i.e. train only the team leaders and let them communicate the changes within their teams.
- **Training sessions with cross-functional assignment of participants** – To support networking and exchange across business units the participants were put together according to their role and function. This also helped to understand the tasks and responsibilities of other parties involved in the process.
- **Training sessions with flexible agenda and focus topics** – controversial views and discussions should be allowed and even welcome. Since the groups are heterogeneous, trainees could help each other to understand the process as they would have to explain their requirements to other involved parties during a product development project. Further more this way the training course could be adapted to the individual needs of the participants.
- **Interactive communication during a „Process Vernissage"** – By imparting their knowledge the participants get a better understanding of each others role. At the same time all questions and discussion points are collected on post-its to be discussed and solved in front of all participants.
- **Direct feedback for process optimization** – By using the method of a "process vernissage" the responsible process managers receive a lot of direct Feedback on quality of the process. Furthermore they also get information about problems und suggestions for process optimization.

As those points show, the training design was mainly based on „bringing the people aboard". According to this approach effected people should be involved as early as possible into the implementation of the change.

Moreover the training should create acceptance for the new operating model and create a common understanding of the assigned tasks and responsibilities. Employees should be motivated to accompany and support the process-related as well as the organizational changes. Even though not mentioned explicitly technical and organizational changes which are equally imported were considered inherent but not explicitly referred to within this article.

## 12 Conclusion

It is not surprising that the "human factor" plays a significant role in (re-)design of business processes. Unfortunately this factor often gets underestimated or only considered incidental. This article shows that there are other effective instruments besides the technical and organizational ones, which also do effect change positively and help to achieve faster, better and more sustainable results.

Process training – if appropriately designed – can be a central component of successful change management and can contribute to the successful establishing of new or modified business processes. The special importance of the "human factor" in this connection thus makes process training particularly interesting for the S-BPM approach.

## References

1. Claßen, M.: Change Management aktiv gestalten, p. 39. Luchterhand, Cologne (2008)
2. Capgemini Consulting: Change Management Studie, pp. 20–23 (2010)
3. Hansmann, H., Becker, J., et al.: Prozessmanagement. Ein Leitfaden zur prozessorientierten Organisationsgestaltung, p. 270. Springer, Berlin (2000)
4. Daniel, K.: Managementprozesse und Performance, pp. 138–148. Gabler, Wiesbaden (2008)
5. O'Connor, J., Seymour, J.: Neurolinguistisches Programmieren – Gelungene Kommunikation und persönliche Entfaltung, pp. 31–32. VAK, Kirchzarten bei Freiburg (2002)
6. Limberg, T.: Examining Innovation Management from a Fair Process Perspective, pp. 81–85. Gabler, Wiesbaden (2008)
7. Meynhardt, T., et al.: Werkzeugkiste. Action Learning. Organisations Entwicklung 26, 84–87 (2011)
8. Deutsche Telekom AG, Deutsche Telekom AG at a glance, http://www.telekom.com/dtag/cms/content/dt/en/13588
9. Deutsche Telekom AG, Konzernabschluss, p. 193 (2010)

# Part II

# Methodological Advancements

# Situatedness - The Amalgam of Agile (S-)BPM

Matthias Neubauer and Christian Stary

Kepler University Linz,
Department of Business Information Systems–Communications Engineering,
Freistädterstraße 315, A-4040 Linz, Austria
{Matthias.Neubauer,Christian.Stary}@jku.at

**Abstract.** Process development has become vital for enterprises operating in an increasingly dynamic business environment. As business process models represent boundary objects between technology and business operations they need not only be able to capture all essential information required for executing business processes, but also for the situational context of agile Business Process Management (BPM). Of particular interest are aspects such as: What is triggering changes? What are the targets of an organizational move? Which impact could it have on the business operation? Although several categories of BPM approaches have been established, the situational context of organizational change has only been tackled rudimentary on the level of representational requirements. In this contribution we discuss existing concepts to represent situations and their capability to support the modification of business operations on-the-fly. Furthermore, we exemplify an integrated representation approach enabling situated subject-oriented BPM.

**Keywords:** Situation Theory, Situation awareness, Subject-oriented Business Process Management (S-BPM).

## 1 Introduction

The competitiveness of organizations can be challenged by a variety of ways: merger or acquisition, changes of markets or customer profiles, unexpected events, such as catastrophes, network restructuring or partnership rearrangements. They can occur any time, and effect a variety of (organizational) elements, as the recent maximum credible accident in Japan demonstrates. Organizations started to address continuous, sometimes disruptive changes by means of informational and structural flexibility aiming for a high degree of velocity (cf. [19]). However, achieving 'sense-AND-respond' organizations [9] might require fundamental changes and transformations [17].

Although many organizations regard information as a specific asset (cf. [1]), most of them are not able to manage this asset maximizing the value of information. There is still a lack of effective methods and techniques for capturing, storing, using and disposal of the information in a situation-aware way, in particular addressing strategic decisions and business operations [16]. Although organizations invest in so-called knowledge repositories (cf. [12]) and meta capabilities (cf. [2], [15]), so far, even fine-grain models of organizational change referring to business processes as carrier of change and their organizational context, such as the 3-tier approach by Firestone [7], do not take into account situational context explicitly.

In this paper, we explore concepts of situations and situation awareness to enhance agile (S-)BPM in terms of representational assets. Consequently, business process models could capture the dynamics of change in the respective situation of change. Section 2 introduces theories of situation and the concept of situational awareness. Section 3 addresses essential S-BPM concepts and the representation of situation-specific information in that context, targeting to increase the capabilities of S-BPM with respect to agility support. Section 4 concludes the paper summarizing and reflecting the achievements.

## 2  Situation Awareness and Situation Theory

In this section we review situation awareness as concept spanning across different disciplines, before detailing Situation Theory and its representational capabilities.

### 2.1  Situation Awareness

Situation awareness has gained attention in different research communities. Research efforts can be classified by the object that performs situations awareness. For instance, Endsley et al. [5] investigate the design of user interfaces in order to support a human operator to achieve situation awareness in a timely fashion. In this context situation awareness is performed in the mind of an operator and understood as *"the perception of the elements in the environment within a volume of time and space, the comprehension of their meaning, and the projection of their status in the near future"* (Endsley, cited in [10]). Consequently, situation awareness can be considered as the mental model of the dynamic environment that, when combined with more static system and procedural knowledge, allows decision makers to function [5].

The authors propose a generic model of situation awareness (i.e. a model that can be applied across many different dynamic task environments) with three levels of situation awareness [10]:

1. Level 1 – *Perception* – concerns stakeholder's ability to perceive elements in the current situation.

2. Level 2 – *Comprehension* – integrates information concerning the current process state derived at Level 1 into the overall comprehension of the current situation.

3. Level 3 – *Projection* – concerns the projection of the current process state into the near future. The importance of this future projection is that a stakeholder must assess now if the anticipated future process state is perceived as disparate with operational goals and plan mitigating actions accordingly.

Following, the given levels of situation awareness are depicted in figure 1. It shows the model for situation awareness in dynamic decision making proposed by Endsley [4].

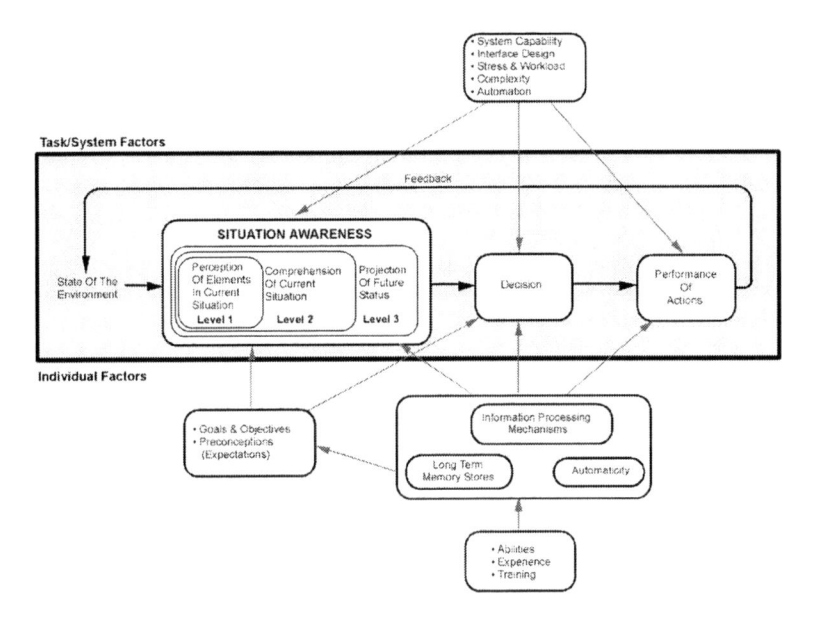

**Fig. 1.** Model of Situation Awareness in Dynamic Decision Making [4]

The model presented in figure 1 basically consists of three interdependent elements: (i) situation awareness, (ii) decision and (iii) performance of actions. Situations are constantly changing. Thus, situation awareness is dynamic and also needs to be constantly changed by an operator. Based on the awareness in a given situation operators take decisions, whereas individual and task/system factors influence both – situation awareness and the process of decision making. The performance of actions is based on taken decisions triggering the change of the environment. Performing actions feeds back to the state of the environment and triggers new situations. For instance, when executing a business process the business process manager recognizes that some modeling decisions are not suitable for the case at hand. This triggers a new situation where he/she re-designs the business process model based on the perceived results.

The dynamic dimension of situation awareness is also given through behavior diversity: Depending on the situation, users might behave differently (cf. [5], [8]). Computer support might only be perceived as such, in case all three different levels of situation awareness can be handled adequately by software systems. The latter means that for organizational development systems, the history of the (group) work processes as well as the projection of the future ones have to be reflected and processed by software in order to provide context-sensitive support.

The notion of situation awareness in social sciences, as revealed so far, and the notion of workspace awareness in CSCW (Computer-Supported Co-operative Work) have similar meanings. Workspace awareness in CSCW includes dedicated information about the workspace, such as information about other users of the shared workspace and the artifacts being part of that space. The notion of situation in social sciences has a larger scope, and can be understood to be a general one, as can be shown with respect to the perception of elements of the environment (cf. Level 1 in figure 1). In the social science literature the elements are traditionally not detailed any further—for instance, it is not specified whether the element is an artifact or another person. However, for organizational development support this type of information needs to be identified and assigned to functional or non-functional requirements. Following [13] situation awareness is highly determined by the field of view and the adequacy of the presentation of information. Provision of explicit projections into the future of collaborative activities leads to increased understanding of individual behavior of group members, and allows sound revision of individual expectations.

Besides "human-centered" investigations of situation awareness, alternative research efforts consider computational support as object performing and supporting situation awareness. In this context, a major object of investigation is the identification of situations [21]. Situation identification includes

- Representation of situations – Which entities are used to depict situations?
- Specification of situations – How can situations be discovered?
- Reasoning based on situations – How can projection be supported?

This decomposition of situation identification is in line with the three levels defined by Endsley – Representation relates Perception (Level 1), Specification matches Comprehension (Level 2) and Reasoning aims to support Projection (Level 3). The decomposition of situation identification shows that representing situations is fundamental for comprehension and projection. The formal representation of situations has been investigated by various approaches and frameworks. However, the basic concepts of Barwise and Perry's generic Situation Theory are incorporated in most of these frameworks [14]. Therefore, Situation Theory is explored in the following section as basis for enabling situated business process model development in the course of organizational change.

## 2.2 Situation Theory

Situation Theory originated from the work of Jon Barwise and John Perry in the early nineteen eighties [3]. This theory provides a formalism to describe limited parts of reality, namely situations persons perceive, reason about, and live in. *"Barwise and Perry began with the assumption that people use language in limited parts of the world to talk about (i.e., exchange information about) other limited parts of the world. They call those limited parts of the world situations. Events and episodes are situations in time, scenes are visually perceived situations, changes are sequences of situations, and facts are situations enriched (or polluted) by language*" (Barwise and Perry cited in [14]). Thus, situations represent context-dependent meaning of information items.

Situation Theory is a generic framework and uses several fundamental elements to represent limited parts of the perceived reality [3]:

- **Situations** are top level constructs of Situation Theory. Infons are used to describe situations in terms of information items. The relationship between situations and infons is defined by the "supports" relation (formally written as |=).

- **Infons** express information about a situation by defining an n-place relation of objects. Infons are of the form <<R, $a_1$, ..., $a_n$, p>>. R defines the n-ary relation of a certain type. The objects in the relation are $a_1$,..., $a_n$ which can be of different type. p represents the polarity of an Infon and indicates whether the objects $a_1$...$a_n$ are part of the relation R (p=1) or not (p=0).

    *Example:* <<isAuthorOf, John Doe, ProcessX, 1>> represents an Infon identifying John Doe as the author of ProcessX. Within a concrete modeling situation S' the given infon can be supported or not. Alternatively, John could not be the author in S'. In this case S' |= <<isAuthorOf, John Doa, ProcessX, 0>> would be valid.

- **Types** capture different aspects of the perceived world. They allow decomposing situations into manageable pieces. This enables intelligent behavior in terms of type recognition. Situation Theory defines different types, e.g., situation-, relation-, object- or location types, in order to describe similar situational aspects.

Following, the basic types defined by Barwise and Perry are described.

## Basic Types defined in Situation theory [3]

**TYP** is the top-level class in order to represent different types in Situation Theory. Basically, two basic kinds of types are provided: ***Situation types*** (**SIT**) and ***Object types***. Situation-types enable classifying situations according to their internal structure, namely supported infons, types, etc. The basic object types defined by Situation Theory represent:

- Temporal Location (**TIM**) represents a single moment in time, or some time interval.

- Spatial Location (**LOC**) depicts a point in space or spatial region.

- Individual (**IND**) represents types of individuals in situations, e.g., persons, documents. The notion of individual corresponds to objects and entities. Individuals need not necessarily to be atomic, they can be further decomposed, e.g., by using parameter types and specific relation types.

- Relation type (**REL$^n$**) specifies the type of an n-place relation within an infon.
- Polarity (**POL**): The polarity (0 or 1) specifies whether objects at hand, e.g., individual or location, stand in an infon or not.
- Infon type (**INF**) specifies the type of an infon, e.g., whether an infon is elementary or compound.
- Parameter type (**PAR**) – the type of a parameter. Parameters are not individuated (in any direct sense), they are theoretical constructs which allow to model types on anontological level. Parameters are place-holders for specific entities and provide a mechanism (anchors) to link them to actual entities, such as individuals or locations.

The constructs so far describe generic elements requiring a domain-specific alignment to enable domain-specific situational support (cf. section 3.2). Additional conceptual constructs enable comprehension, and the projection of domain-specific situations.

**Advanced features for modeling situations**
Besides the basic constructs of Situation Theory advanced features can be used to describe relationships between situations. According to [21] these advanced features include:

- **Generalization:** Situations can be more general than other situations, e.g., "Modeling business processes" is more specific than "Modeling".
- **Composition:** Situation can be decomposed into smaller situations, e.g., "Modeling business processes in a subject-oriented way" could be decomposed in "Modeling subjects", "Modeling message flow between subjects", and "Modeling internal behavior of subjects".
- **Dependence:** Situations might depend on other situations, e.g., model validation requires an already created model.
- **Contradiction:** Situations can be mutually exclusive in case they cannot co-occur in the same place involving the same subject. For instance, a modeler cannot model and validate a business process model at the same time.
- **Temporal Sequence:** Situations naturally occur in a timely fashion. They can occur before or after other situation, but can also be interleaving. For example, modeling a business process needs to be accomplished before validating a certain model.

# 3 Towards Situated S-BPM

In this section we present a situated S-BPM approach addressing the previously introduced situation concepts. We discuss the situated S-BPM approach in terms of representational assets along the S-BPM cycle.

## 3.1 S-BPM

### 3.1.1 S-BPM Cycle

The subject-oriented business process modeling approach defines a S-BPM Cycle structuring organizational activities in the course of change. Major phases of the cycle are according to [18]:

- Analysis
- Modeling
- Validation
- Optimization
- Organization-specific implementation
- IT-Implementation
- Monitoring

A first step in the S-BPM Cycle is usually the *analysis* of a certain process and its context. It also includes the decomposition of the process. On one hand, concrete objects of interest are derived from the strategy of an organization or the implemented S-BPM strategy. On the other hand, feedback from other phases of the life cycle, especially from monitoring, trigger analysis such as error detection or improvement of process performance. Subsequent to the analysis is the creation of a business process model (*modeling*). Modeling in S-BPM uses the notation presented in the following subsection. S-BPM tool support enables the immediate *validation* of modeling results. Within the validation phase the effectiveness of a process is tested. Following validation, process efficiency is optimized using simulation within the *optimization* phase. After optimizing a process it is implemented in organizational structures and routines (*organizational implementation*) as well as in the IT-Infrastructure (*IT-Implementation*). The last phase of the cycle is the *monitoring* phase in which data gained from executed business processes are collected and compared to target values. Tool support enables target-group specific reporting of the monitored data and triggers (further) changes [18].

### 3.1.2 Modeling Approach

In S-BPM a process is considered to be a structured interaction of subjects (e.g., between users or even systems) [6]. Subjects transfer information and coordinate their work by exchanging messages. Messages can be exchanged synchronously, asynchronously or in a combined form. The synchronization type can be specified depending on the message type and the sending subject. Each subject has an input pool as a mail box for incoming messages. The synchronization type is defined by attributes of the input pool.

The following figures show the subjects and messages exchanged along a simple vacation application process. It exemplifies the behavior of a subject Employee. The state ´work´ is the initial state of the subject. Figure 3 reveals the interaction between an employee and the management. Each subject sends and receives messages and accomplishes some tasks without interaction. The definition and the behavior of a subject depend on the order of sent and received messages, tasks being accomplished and the way how it influences the behavior.

If a subject sends a message the information transferred with that message is derived from user inputs or computed by some applications. These 'send' functions are executed before a message is sent. Vice versa, if a subject accepts a message a corresponding function is executed. The information received through the message is used as input for that function. This type of receive and send functions represent so-called refinements of a subject. They constitute the interface of a subject to the applications used by a subject.

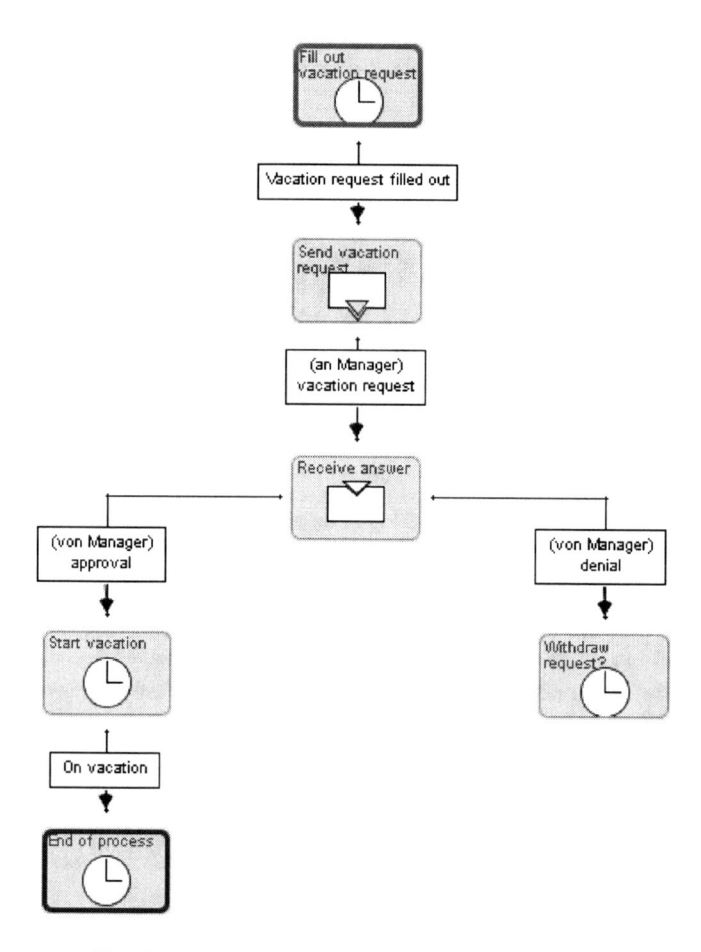

**Fig. 2.** Applying for holidays for the subject Employee

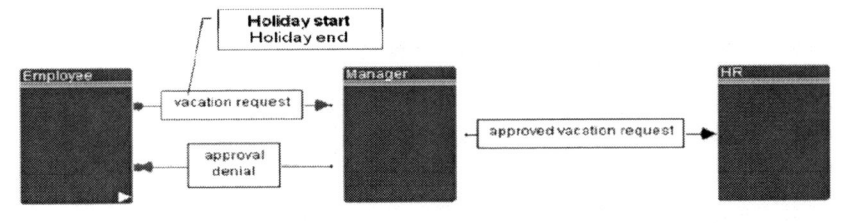

Fig. 3. Message exchange between the subject Employee and Management Level

The flow of control in a networked subject-driven environment is illustrated with the vacation process example. The behavior of the manager is complementary to the employee's. The messages sent by employee are received by the manager and vice versa. Figure 4 shows the behavior of the manager. The manager is on hold for the holiday application of the employee. Upon receipt the holiday application is checked (state). This check can either result in an approval or a rejection, leading to either state, informing the employee. In case the holiday application is approved, the HR department is informed about the successful application.

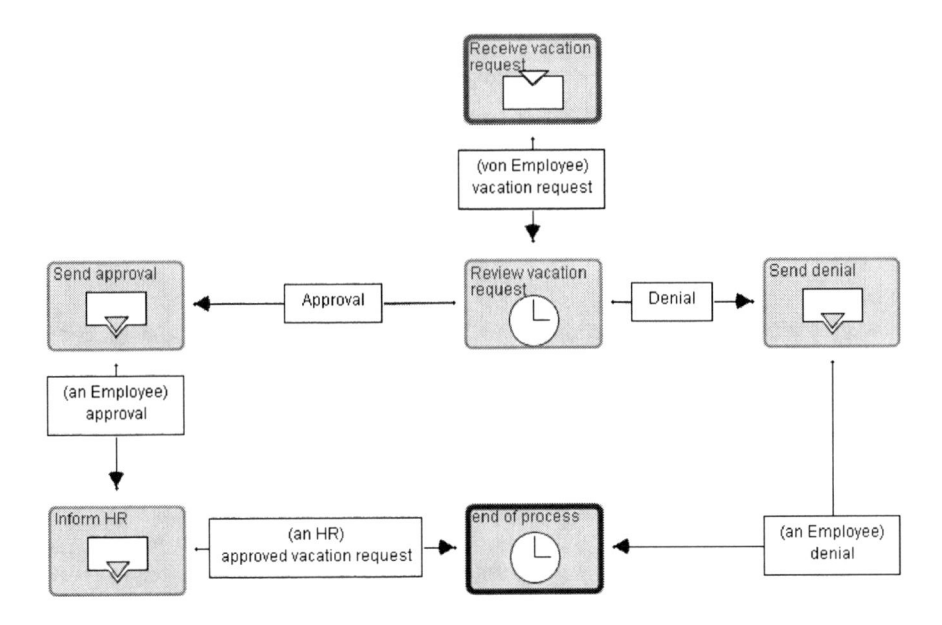

Fig. 4. Managers behavior in holiday application process

Finally, the behavior of the HR department has to be detailed. It receives the approved holiday application and puts it to the employee's days-off record, without further activities (process completion).

The description of a subject defines the sequence of sending and receiving messages, or the processing of internal functions, respectively. In this way, a subject specification contains the pushing sequence of functions, so-called services (as an abstraction from implementation). These services can be the standard ones like 'send' or predicates dealing with specific objects, such as required when an employee fills a holiday application form (vacation request in Figure 3). Consequently, each node (state) and transition has to be assigned an operation. The implementation of that operation does not matter at that stage, since it can be handled by object specifications, as shown in the implementation section.

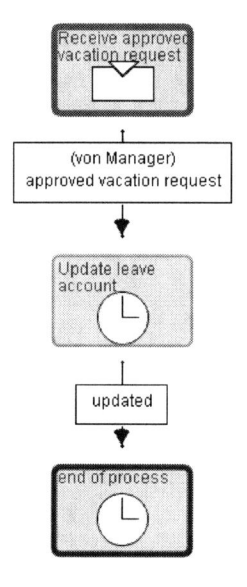

**Fig. 5.** HR department behavior to process vacation requests

A service is assigned to an internal functional node. If this state is reached, the assigned service is triggered and processed. The end conditions correspond to links leaving the internal functional node. Each result link of a sending node (state) is assigned to a named service. Before sending this service is triggered to identify the content or parameter of a message. The service determines the values of the message parameters transferred by the message. Analogously, each output link of a receiving node (state) is also assigned to a named service. When accepting a message in this state that service is triggered to identify the parameter of the received message. The service determines the values of the parameters transferred by the message and provides them for further processing.

These services are used to assign a certain meaning to each step in a subject. Services allow defining the functions used in a subject. All of those are triggered in a synchronous way, i.e. a subject only reaches its subsequent state once all triggered services have been completed. Figure 6 shows how the functions of a subject are defined by means of objects. In this way, a process specification is completed for automated execution.

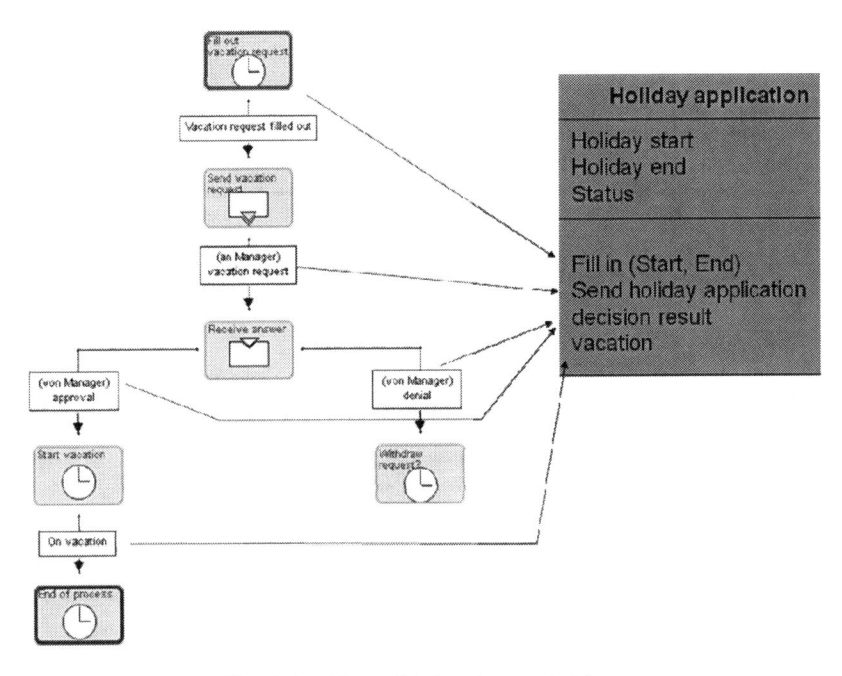

**Fig. 6.** A subject with functions and objects

## 3.2 Situated S-BPM

After investigating concepts of situation awareness, Situation Theory, and S-BPM we present an integrated representation approach enabling situated S-BPM. The following representation uses a layered approach which consists of three layers:

- Concepts of Situation Theory (Meta-Meta Layer)
- Situated (S-)BPM ontology (Meta-Layer)
- Concrete Situation (Instance Layer)

The top layer includes the given concepts of Situation Theory (compare section 2.2) and provides the conceptual basis for describing situations in different domains. The middle layer contains ontologies for situated BPM, e.g. situated S-BPM, and the bottom layer represents concrete situations occurring in the course of organizational change (e.g., analysis-situation, modeling-situation or implementation). Within the middle layer application-specific information (aviation, education, medicine, etc.) as well as approach-specific information(S-BPM, BPMN, etc.) for various situations is represented. Relationships between the given layers are described using "type-instance" relations. Thus, meta-data considering the structure of an application context and the actually applied approach (e.g., education and situated S-BPM) enable supporting situations of change (e.g., indicating validation after modeling).

Following, parts of the representation for situated S-BPM are illustrated using the vacation application case presented in section 3.1.2. The representation for situated S-BPM is structured through the S-BPM cycle presented in section 3.1.1. Figure 7 illustrates that the concrete analysis situation "analyze holiday application" is triggered by the organizational unit "HR department" and a "monitored processing time" at a certain point of time ("Processing time exceeded – 2011-1-1-12:00"). The given analysis situation triggers further situations considering organizational change, such as modeling (cf. figure 8), validating or implementing.

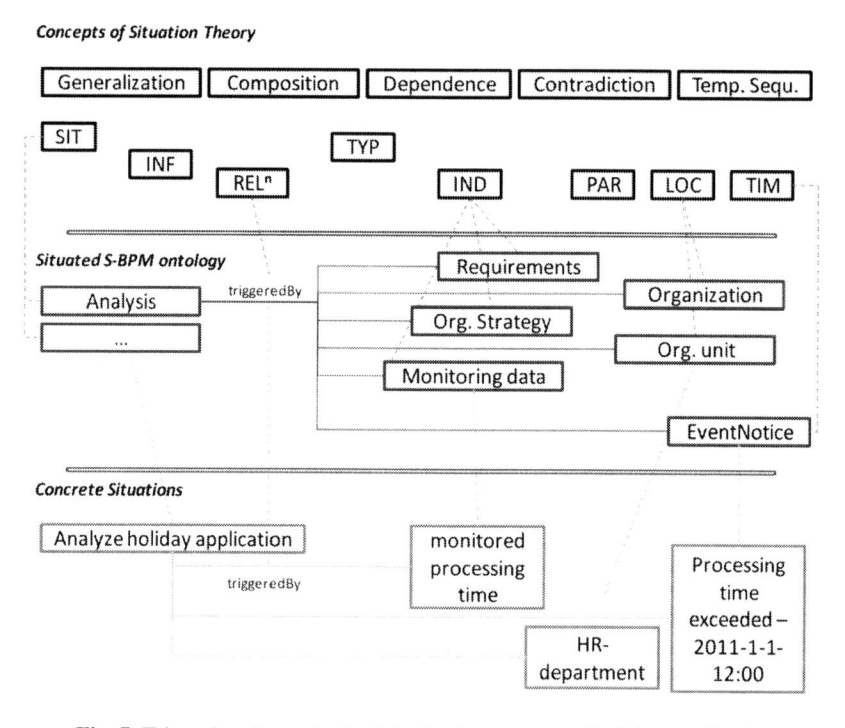

**Fig. 7.** Triggering the analysis of the business process "holiday application"

Figure 8 depicts a concrete modeling situation triggered by the analysis of the vacation application process. Within the middle layer of the respective representation different dependencies between situation types are shown:

- temporal dependence of "analysis" and "modeling"
- decomposition of "modeling" in "modeling message flow" and "modeling subject behavior".
- Interleaving of "modeling message flow" and "modeling subject behavior".

These dependencies can be used in order to support the process of change in the course of the S-BPM cycle. Besides, modeling constructs of S-BPM, such as "Subject" and "Message" (or even complete models), as well as responsible modeler types can be represented in the middle layer.

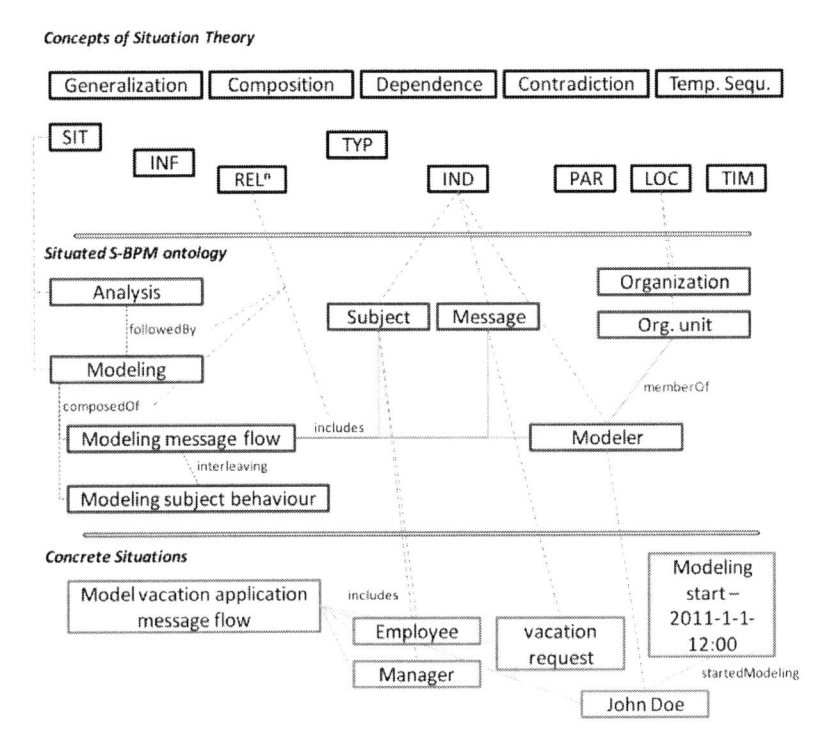

**Fig. 8.** Modeling "vacation application"

Within the concrete situation "Model vacation application flow" "Jon Doe" models the subjects "Employee" and "Manager". Furthermore, "Jon Doe" models the "vacation request" between the given subjects. He starts modeling at "2011-1-1-12:00". A following or interleaving situation could be "Model Employee behavior" or "Model Manager behavior". The given situation in figure 8 is depicted in Situation theory by two infons

- << includes, Employee, Manager, vacation request, John Doe, 1>>
- <<startedModeling, John Doe, Modeling start – 2011-1-1-12:00, 1>>

supported by the situation $SIT_{\text{Model vacation application message flow}}$.

### 3.3 Benefits

In the previous subsection we have presented an integrated representation approach utilizing concepts of Situation Theory, in order to enable situated (S-)BPM. The examples illustrate how situation specific information can be represented in the course of organizational change when following the S-BPM approach. The main contributions to (S-)BPM are:

- The given representation supports storing situation-specific attributes with respect to organizational change, such as triggers of change, involved

organizational members, sequences of situations which are traversed when responding to changing environmental demands, and dependencies between situations of change.
- The approach can be adapted for different application contexts and modeling approaches.
- The situated approach can be used on different levels of granularity, e.g., situation-specific information considering a model or even model elements.
- The additional situation-specific information enables reflecting processes of organizational change, e.g., through a "replay traversed situations" feature.
- Situated (S-)BPM ontologies enable situational support of stakeholders when implementing organizational change, in the course of analysis, modeling, or validation.
- Information gathered in concrete Situations can be used to refine and adapt situated (S-)BPM ontologies.

Upcoming work considers the refinement and complete representation of the situated S-BPM ontology. However, the situated S-BPM ontology still needs to be empirically validated. For validation a corresponding computational representation scheme needs to be implemented. Following an ontology-based approach to situation awareness like [14], Topic Maps [11] are used, as they are a standardized means for representation.

## 4 Conclusion

Organizations act within volatile and rapidly changing business environments. Several key factors determine business operations, such as increasing global competition, short-term changes of organizations, and the reliable availability of resources. Organizations need to respond to turbulences accordingly to remain competitive and be successful on the market [20]. In that context business process development has become crucial, as the underlying technology allows effective and efficient changes of the organization of work. Business process models represent boundary objects between technology and business operations. Enriched with situational context they are likely to facilitate business process management (BPM) as BPM utilizes business process models in various contexts, such as process analysis, given by the different phases of organizational change [18]. The more developers can be informed through explicit representations of a situation, the more informed they can handle business process models and BPM activities.

So far, the situational context of organizational change has only been tackled rudimentary on the level of representational requirements. Therefore, we have investigated concepts of situation awareness and Situation Theory to enhance (S-)BPM. Based on our investigations we have developed a layered representation approach towards situational S-BPM that allows (i) the flexible definition and storage of situations specific attributes, (ii) the adaptation according to different application contexts and modeling approaches, (iii) the reflection of processes considering organizational change as well as (iv) the development of situational modeling support.

# References

1. Abdul Karim, N.S., Hussein, R.: Manager' Perception of Information Management and the Role of Information and Knowledge Managers: The Malaysian perspectives. International Journal of Information Management 28(2), 114–127 (2008)
2. Day, Y.G.: The Capabilities of Market-driven Organizations. Journal of Marketing 58, 37–52 (1994)
3. Devlin, K.: Situation Theory and Situation Semantics. In: Handbook of the History of Logic, vol. 7, pp. 601–664. Elsevier, Amsterdam (2006)
4. Endsley, M.R.: A taxonomy of situation awareness errors. In: Fuller, R., Johnston, N., McDonals, N. (eds.) Human Factors in Aviation Operations, pp. 287–292. Ashgate Publishing Ltd., Aldershot (1995)
5. Endsley, M.R., Garland, D.J. (eds.): Situation Awareness Analysis and Measurement: Analysis and Measurement. Lawrence Erlbaum, Mahwah (2000)
6. Fleischmann, A., Schmidt, W., Stary, C., Obermeier, S.: Subjektorientiertes Geschäftsprozessmanagement. Hanser München (2011)
7. Firestone, J.M.: On Doing Knowledge Management. Knowledge Management Research & Practice 6, 13–22 (2008)
8. Graham, J., Schneider, M., Bauer, A., Bessiere, K., Gonzalez, C.: Shared Mental Models in Military Command and Control Organisations: Effect of Social Network Distance. In: Proceedings of the Human Factors and Ergonomics Society 48th Annual Meeting - HFS 2004, September 20-24. ACM Press, New York (2004)
9. Haeckel, S.S.: Adaptive enterprise: Creating and leading sense-AND-respond organizations. Harvard Business School Press, Cambridge (1999)
10. Hogg, D.N., Folleso, K., Strand-Volden, F.: Development of a Situation Awareness Measure to Evaluate Advanced Alarm Systems in Nuclear Power Plant Control Rooms. Ergonomics 38(11), 2394–2412 (1995)
11. ISO/IEC SC34/WG3 Topic Maps ISO Standard, http://www.isotopicmaps.org/ (retrieved April 11, 2011)
12. Gallup, S.D., Dattero, R., Hicks, R.C.: The Enterprise Knowledge Directory. Knowledge Management Research & Practice 1, 95–101 (2003)
13. Gross, T., Stary, C., Totter, A.: User-Centered Awareness in Computer-Supported Cooperative Work-Systems: Structured Embedding of Findings from Social Sciences. International Journal of Human-Computer Interaction 18(3), 323–360 (2005)
14. Kokar, M., Matheus, C.J., Baclawski, K.: Ontology-based situation awareness. Information Fusion 10, 83–98 (2009)
15. Liedtka, J.: Linking Competitive Advantage with Communities of Practice. Journal of Management Inquiry 8(1), 5–16 (1999)
16. Ladley, J.: Making Enterprise Information Management (EIM) Work for Business: A Guide to Understanding Information as an Asset. Elsevier Science & Technology, Amsterdam (2010)
17. Rouse, W.B. (ed.): Enterprise transformation: Understanding and enabling fundamental change. Wiley, Hoboken (2006)
18. Schmidt, W., Fleischmann, A., Gilbert, O.: Subjektorientiertes Geschäftsprozessmanagement. HMD – Praxis der Wirtschaftsinformatik, Heft 266,S. 52–62 (2009)
19. Stephenson, S.V., Sage, A.: Architecting for Enterprise Resource Planning. Information Knowledge Systems Management 6, 81–121 (2007)
20. Westkämper, E., Zahn, E.: Wandlungsfähige Produktionsunternehmen: Das Stuttgarter Unternehmensmodell. Springer, Heidelberg (2009)
21. Ye, J., Dobson, S., McKeever, S.: Situation identification techniques in pervasive computing: A review. Pervasive and Mobile Computing (2011); doi. 10.10.16/j.pmcj.2011.01.004

# Adaptive Case Management: Supporting Knowledge Intensive Processes with IT Systems

Christian Herrmann[1] and Matthias Kurz[2]

[1] Accenture GmbH, Anni-Albers-Straße 11, 80807 Munich, Germany
[2] University of Erlangen-Nuremberg, Information Systems II, Lange Gasse 20, 90403 Nuremberg, Germany

**Abstract.** As the transition to the knowledge society is steadily proceeding in industrialized countries, increasing knowledge workers' productivity in businesses becomes crucial. However, current business process management approaches and systems are unable to satisfy the high requirements of flexibility in knowledge intensive processes. Adaptive Case Management (ACM) is an emerging yet still immature approach in the business process management field that promises to bridge this gap. This contribution substantiates ACM by presenting a corresponding procedure model along with a software system. Applying the concepts of empowerment, the knowledge worker takes on the responsibility to adapt "his" IT environment in order to achieve efficient case handling. The validation by expert interviews critically examines the feasibility both of the concept as well as the software system.

**Keywords:** Adaptive Case Management, Business Process Management, Case Management, Enterprise 2.0.

## 1 Introduction

The transition to the knowledge society proceeds steadily in the industrialized countries [1], which emphasizes the importance of knowledge workers' ability of being productive.

Business process management (BPM) and workflow management systems (WfMS) are well-established instruments that increase businesses' productivity [2]. Thereby, it is crucial for BPM and WfMS that the process has to be defined before it can be implemented and executed. Thus, these approaches are only suitable for repeatable and predictable routine processes [3].

Knowledge work fundamentally differs from routine processes. Knowledge work and knowledge intensive processes are significantly less structured [4]. It is not possible to define the exact activity flow before the process has been executed [3]. Supporting such processes with traditional WfMS has little prospect of success.

This contribution presents the new BPM concept Adaptive Case Management (ACM), which aims to flexibly support these knowledge intensive, less structured business processes, along with a corresponding software system.

In order to illustrate the approach, we will use the development project of an electronic car as an example of a knowledge intensive process. The process underlying this example project exhibits the characteristics of knowledge intensive processes defined by [4], as research and development processes in general can be characterized as weakly structured, highly complex and knowledge intensive. Furthermore, the process participants are supposed to be well educated in their specialized field and are granted a broad leeway in decision making when pursuing their profession [5].

The article is structured as follows: In chapter two, current BPM approaches are examined with regard to their support of process flexibility. In chapter three, the new BPM concept ACM is introduced as well as a suitable procedure model. This concept has been implemented through a software prototype, which is presented in chapter four. Chapter five summarizes the performed validation of the concept as well as the system.

## 2 Flexibility and BPM

### 2.1 Flexibility-to-Use vs. Flexibility-to-Change

In the context of information systems (IS), [6] based on [7] distinguishes between flexibility-to-use and flexibility-to-change.

Flexibility-to-use of an IS describes, whether the system is able to cover new business requirements without a major change. In case of an electronic procurement system, the flexibility-to-use includes for example the different built-in procurement processes. In contrast, flexibility-to-change of an IS measures how much investment is needed to change, upgrade or expand the IS after its initial implementation. For example, the effort required for introducing a new procurement process to an existing IT system depends on the flexibility-to-change of the respective IT system [6].

When applied to BPM, flexibility-to-use measures the ability of an implemented business process to adapt to new business requirements without a major change while flexibility-to-change summarizes the efforts to change a process if new process requirements cannot be covered by its flexibility-to-use.

To be able to distinguish between flexibility-to-use and flexibility-to-change, it is important to define what a major change constitutes. In BPM environments, we define a major change as a process adjustment that requires organizational change management or code based development efforts in IT systems.

### 2.2 BPM and BPM 2.0

BPM systems are based on the principles of scientific management invented by [8]. This is reflected in the temporal and personal separation between process design and execution.

The flexibility-to-use of processes in BPM is very limited. Following the classic BPM methodology, the process is first designed, then implemented, afterwards executed and finally controlled [9]. Due to this temporal separation, effort is needed to capture the process including all of its variants and possible exceptions in the design phase. Forgotten variants will not be implemented and therefore are not available during process execution, thereby limiting the flexibility-to-use of processes in BPM to a minimum.

The flexibility-to-change of processes in BPM is very limited as well. [2] distinguishes between two approaches to improve business processes in order to align them to new business requirements: Business process improvement (BPI) and business process renewal (BPR). Both approaches assume that the processes will be executed frequently under constant parameters. BPI needs a multitude of finished process instances to come up with links for future improvement. In BPR, the huge investments for the process adaptations need to be compensated by efficiency gains in future process executions [10]. As the parameters in today's business environments become increasingly dynamic [11], the practicability of those approaches decreases. The use of alternative sources for process improvements, like the know-how of the employees in the operating departments, is limited in the BPM methodologies inspired by tailorism [10].

Therefore, [10] introduces the concept of BPM 2.0, which aims at increasing the flexibility-to-change of business processes by empowering employees to design "their" processes. It utilizes Web 2.0 technologies to overcome employees' inhibitions in participating in the process improvement discussions [10]. With the inclusion of all relevant process stakeholders – also including the IT-department – BPM 2.0 leverages the process know-how in the operating departments, guarantees the practicability of the process in the implementation phase, lowers the risks of the process roll out [12], and therefore increases the flexibility-to-change of a business process. Nevertheless, BPM 2.0 is not able to increase the flexibility-to-use of a business process as it keeps the temporal separation between process design and execution.

Fig. 1 pictures the presented BPM approaches in the context of their provided process flexibility:

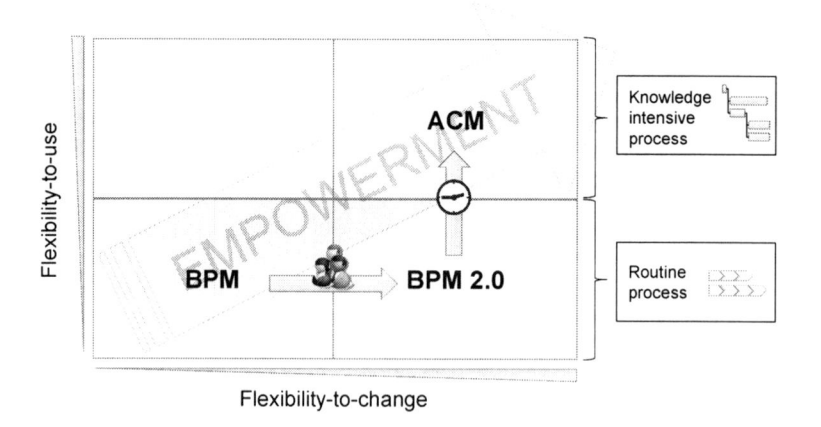

**Fig. 1.** BPM approaches and their process flexibility

With its low flexibility-to-use, BPM and BPM 2.0 focus on supporting routine processes. Both approaches are inappropriate to support our proposed example process of developing an electric car. The temporal separation between process design and execution would deny the engineers to flexibly respond to unforeseen development results. To support knowledge intensive processes, one will have to give up this temporal separation and additionally empower the knowledge workers to change the process during execution. In the next chapter, we will introduce ACM as a possible solution to bridge this gap.

## 3 Adaptive Case Management

Adaptive Case Management (ACM) is a new trend in the field of BPM research [13] that focuses on the IT support of knowledge intensive and therefore weakly structured business processes. It has been founded in 2009 during a meeting of BPM specialists. These founders agreed on the fact that classic BPM tools like WfMS cannot satisfy the requirements of today's knowledge workers [14].

As consequence, they introduced ACM and define it as *"Systems that are able to support decision making and data capture while providing the freedom for knowledge workers to apply their own understanding and subject matter expertise to respond to unique or changing circumstances within the business environment"* [14]. Although, the experts could agree on this definition describing the overall goal of ACM, they have not been able to reach a consensus on how this goal should be achieved [14].

In the next chapter, we provide a general overview of the ACM principles. Afterwards, we present our proposal for an ACM procedure model, which combines these principles with the BPM 2.0 idea of empowering employees to increase BPM flexibility.

### 3.1 Central Principles

The central entity in ACM is the case, which encapsulates a knowledge intensive process as its case process. Therefore, the case template and accordingly the case instance can be seen as the equivalent of a process model or process instance in BPM. Analyzing the available contributions with regard to ACM in the miscellany [15], we identified the common principles of ACM. Fig. 2 gives an overview of these elements grouped in the categories organization, case handling and adaption.

**Organization**
In ACM exists no predefined control flow like in BPM. As knowledge work is not predictable, the flow of activities emerges during case handling being aligned to the case's goals. All activities during case handling are performed in order to achieve these goals [16].

An ACM system is organized data-centric. In contrast to a BPM system, ACM puts the case data at the center of consideration instead of the case process. The case data is known before the case process is defined. The case process is then derived from the case data in a goal-oriented way [13].

With the goal of developing an electric car, the flow between research or development tasks would emerge during case handling. This process evolution is mainly driven by the available case information.

Fig. 2. ACM principles

**Case handling**
Knowledge intensive processes are highly collaborative. A multitude of knowledge workers with various educational backgrounds participate in these processes and need to communicate, coordinate and cooperate with each other [4]. Therefore, one goal of ACM is to remove the barriers between case management, BPM and collaboration [17].

In dynamic environments, transparency is required particularly to ensure efficient case handling. In general, the case worker needs to know what tasks he or she has to perform, their time constraints and which information and functionality is available to complete this task in the most efficient way. After task completion, the system has to capture who performed which action at which time with what result [18]. Furthermore, the progress of a case should be available to all case participants as well as the management [16].

Efficient case handling also requires the integration of all relevant resources. Besides of internal and external persons, all knowledge workers should have access to the organization's knowledge base and the intermediate results of the case [18].

As research and development processes, e. g. the process of developing an electronic car, include various stakeholders [5], these process participants have to be coordinated to ensure they work hand in hand towards the project's goal. Transparency and the integration of all required resources becomes crucial to avoid project inefficiencies like missed deadlines or duplication of work.

**Adaption**
The most characteristic component of ACM is the idea of adaption. Thereby, the knowledge worker adapts the system to the individual requirements of the case in the short term and to the organization's needs in the long term. In our ACM understanding, the employee is empowered to perform these changes on his own. We distinguish two levels of adaption.

On the first level, the *case-specific adaption*, the system adapts to the specific requirements of one individual case during its execution. At any time, the knowledge worker, triggered by external events or case related findings, can customize the case instance to fit to these new requirements [18, 19]. Business rules are used to structure the solution space and hence guarantee efficient, goal-oriented case handling [20]. Thus, ACM provides a high level of flexibility-to-use by empowering its case participants to change the case environment on the fly.

On the second level, ACM uses the knowledge, which it has gained during previous case execution, to adapt the ACM framework to the organization's and its employees' needs and thus pursues continuous improvement [18]. Therefore, the knowledge workers can save recurring patterns in the case execution and reuse them in future cases [19]. We call this kind of emergent system design *cross-case adaption*, which increases the flexibility-to-change of the ACM system by empowering the case participants again.

In the example scenario, the process participants can use the case-specific adaption to adjust the development process to changing project circumstances like material innovations or unforeseen design problems. In the next step, the cross-case adaption can be used to save best practices, like proven methods for carrying out a feasibility study, to be re-used in future development projects.

### 3.2 Related Concepts

BPM 2.0 applies empowerment to increase the flexibility-to-change of the traditional BPM. ACM expands the idea of process flexibility through empowerment by further enabling the knowledge worker to change the case process during execution and thereby increases the flexibility-to-use of present BPM approaches.

ACM also adopts concepts of Computer Supported Collaborative Work (CSCW) [14], Case Management (CM) and Enterprise Content Management (ECM) [21]. CSCW influenced ACM with its idea of increasing the effectiveness and efficiency of group work through IT systems [22]. CM represents a professional support and provision management that organizes a goal-oriented system facilitating the collaboration of the various stakeholders in the healthcare field [23]. ACM builds on the idea of goal-oriented collaboration and extends the traditional CM understanding by both overcoming CM's integration deficits and by introducing the concept of system adaption. Most case management systems are suffering from the missing integration between process and knowledge on a conceptual level, as well as, technical lacks regarding the integration of data, functionality and external services on one platform [24]. In contrast, the key principle of ACM is integrating all case relevant resources and functionality on one platform. Furthermore, the idea of system adaption has not been focused in the traditional CM. Ultimately, ACM integrates ECM's information management methods for setting up and optimizing the information infrastructure for the support of business processes [25].

While the previously mentioned approaches focus on improving the flexibility-to-change of business processes exhibiting a low degree of automation, other concepts attempt to bring this kind of flexibility to highly automated business processes by leveraging the principle of loose coupling that comes with service-oriented architectures [26]. By making components (services) easier to replace or by providing means for dynamically "plugging" them into existing business processes, knowledge-intensive business processes are easier to support. Such changes, however, can have unintended consequences for processes spanning multiple organizational units. [27] suggests a framework for that assists in preventing such semantic incompatibilities. Once such components are provided by the cloud, the need for sufficient service availability arises. [28] provides an event-based architecture that considers the formally described service level agreements when integrating new components in a business process. [29] tackles the challenge of integrating automated components into business processes by defining an agent-based architecture.

### 3.3 Procedure Model

This chapter introduces an appropriate procedure model which is based on the BPM 2.0 model presented by [10]. It integrates the adaptive properties of ACM while satisfying the high flexibility requirements of knowledge work. Therefore, the phases of design, implementation and execution have been merged to the case-specific adaption. Furthermore, the cross-case adaption has been added after the control phase (cf. fig. 3).

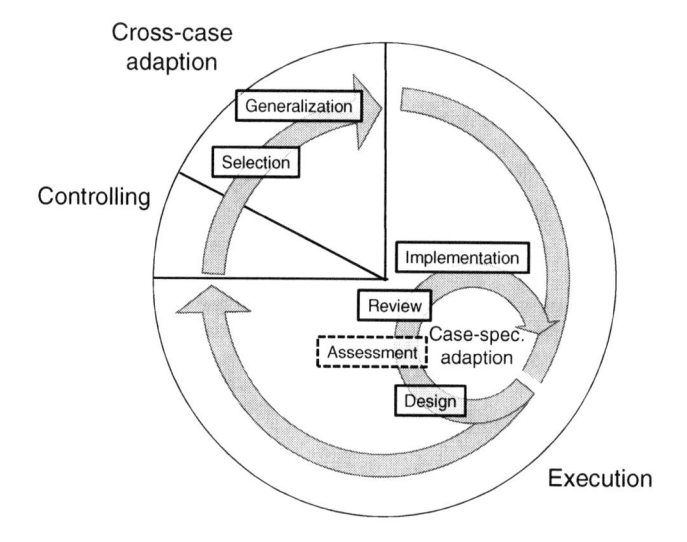

**Fig. 3.** ACM procedure model

**Execution and case-specific adaption**
In the beginning, the case responsible instantiates the most appropriate case template, e. g. a general research and development template, and defines the goals of that case instance. Afterwards, the instance can be adapted to the individual requirements of the case by passing through one or more iteration loops of the case-specific adaption at any time during case execution. In the example scenario, the generic research and development tasks have to be detailed in order to meet the characteristics of the electronic car development project.

This iterative approach has been adopted from the software development field. In this discipline, iterative development models are used within dynamic environments with changing software requirements [30]. These surrounding conditions are similar to those in knowledge intensive work environments, where external events or new findings can swiftly change the requirements of knowledge workers with regard to the supporting IT systems [18]. The following advantages can be gained of this iterative approach [30]:

- Changing requirements and surrounding conditions can be handled during process execution.
- By limiting the amount of change of single iterations, changes can be implemented more swiftly.
- This accelerated fulfillment of user requirements increases the users' system acceptance.

The case-specific adaption cycle is geared to the BPM 2.0 model [10]:

1. Similar to BPM 2.0, the knowledge workers create or collaboratively develop a case innovation. Within a web based platform, the employees can discuss these innovations in bulletin boards, document them in wikis and – depending on the complexity of the innovation – can implement them on the fly in the case instance. As a simple case innovation, an engineer could add the steps to carry out the feasibility study to analyze the performance of electric engines. A more complex innovation would be the proposal for a new workflow to query component prices at the procurement department.
2. In the next step, the draft will optionally be evaluated and then reviewed. In case of complex modifications, a collaborative assessment by the employees can help to identify the most promising proposals. Afterwards, the case owner reviews and decides about the remaining drafts. For simple modifications, the adaptations require no review by the case owner.
3. With the acceptance of the modification, the innovation's implementation will be triggered. In case of simple innovations, like the creation of the simple user tasks to carry out the feasibility study, the required modifications can be carried out automatically. Otherwise, e. g. if complex workflow functionality has to be implemented, further specialists have to be included.

Furthermore, key performance indicators (KPIs) will be collected during case execution. In the electronic car scenario, the number of design mistakes discovered in the later development process can exemplarily be named as a KPI.

**Control and cross-case adaption**
After the case has been closed, the achievement of its objectives and the case handling efficiency can be assessed using the collected KPIs. This includes an evaluation of the implemented case innovations.

As soon as a sufficient number of starting points for the improvement of a case template exists, the cross-case adaption can be started. In this phase, the modifications in the case instances are at first analyzed in view of their usefulness in future cases. For example, the workflow innovation for the price request at the procurement department can be useful in future research and development projects. In the next step, promising innovations will be selected, generalized for a broader intended use and saved either into entire case templates or modular case components. These entities are saved in libraries, which are made available for future case handling.

## 4 Software Platform

In this chapter, we present a software prototype, which implements the ACM principles along with the proposed procedure model.

### 4.1 Design

The case workspace unites all related entities of a single case instance and is based on a template that is stored in the template library. Each case workspace aims to achieve multiple goals and consists of the components *case process*, *information* and *workflows*. Predefined elements for these components are available in the component library and organized through hierarchical structures as well as social tagging (cf. fig. 4).

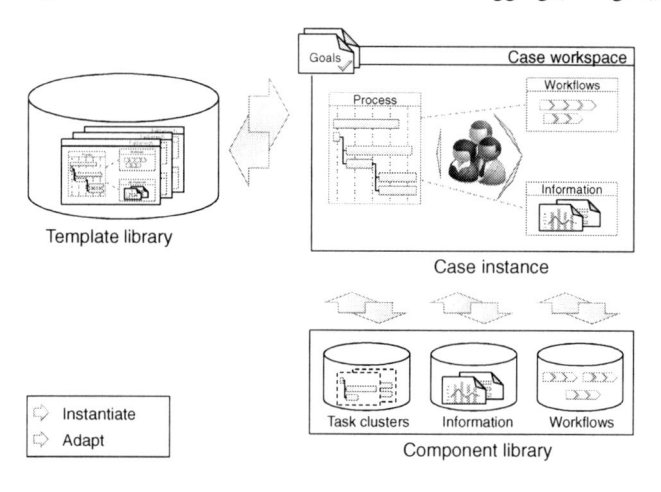

**Fig. 4.** System design

**Process**
The case process is the central steering instrument within the case instance. In contrast to BPM, this process is not defined ex ante, but emerges during case execution.

In literature exist different paradigms for process control. Our proposed approach for ACM combines the activity based control type, where activities are connected to create a control flow, with the artifact based paradigm, which links the process control to the artifacts produced by the process [31].

The initial idea of this approach has been introduced by [32] and has been revitalized during the ongoing ACM discussion [19]. The concept is built on a simple task list, where each task is carrying its planned start as well as finish date and can be skipped or redone [32]. As tasks can be started at any time, the process is not controlled by a predefined control flow, but by the case, its data and its objectives. Nevertheless, the control flow, which emerges during case handling, can be analyzed later for improvement purposes.

This approach provides the following advantages [32]:

- The sequence of the tasks can be easily modified.
- The possibility to skip, redo or parallelize activities increases process flexibility.
- The case progress and the remaining effort are transparent.

As a one-level task list seems to be inappropriate for complex cases, we substitute this simple task list with a complex work breakdown structure like it is used in the project management field (cf. fig. 5).

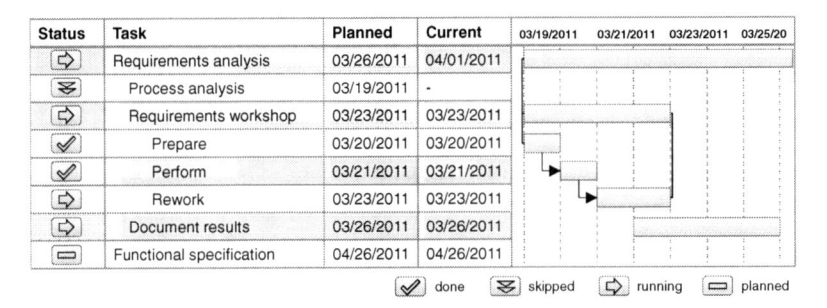

| Status | Task | Planned | Current |
|---|---|---|---|
| ⇨ | Requirements analysis | 03/26/2011 | 04/01/2011 |
| ⩾ | Process analysis | 03/19/2011 | - |
| ⇨ | Requirements workshop | 03/23/2011 | 03/23/2011 |
| ✓ | Prepare | 03/20/2011 | 03/20/2011 |
| ✓ | Perform | 03/21/2011 | 03/21/2011 |
| ⇨ | Rework | 03/23/2011 | 03/23/2011 |
| ⇨ | Document results | 03/26/2011 | 03/26/2011 |
| ▭ | Functional specification | 04/26/2011 | 04/26/2011 |

✓ done   ⩾ skipped   ⇨ running   ▭ planned

**Fig. 5.** Process control approach (cf. [32])

Adapting the concepts of project management, the knowledge worker is now able to break down the case scope into manageable work packages. Moreover, he can define a control flow between these work packages using constraints [33]. The temporal task sequence and the mutual dependencies between these tasks can be visualized through a gantt chart.

For the case process, the component library holds predefined hierarchical task clusters for instantiation during case handling. An example for such a task cluster would be the "requirements workshop" with its sub-work packages as displayed in fig. 5.

**Information**
In knowledge intensive processes like those addressed by ACM, information plays a central role [4]. In the ACM system, we distinguish between working results and knowledge.

Working results capture intermediate or final results of a case instance. For this type of information, the system provides wikis, structured lists or document sharing functionality.

The knowledge components represent the organization's knowledge. The component library stores this knowledge within documents. Therefore, the component library acts as the organization's knowledge base within the ACM system.

**Workflows**
Even in flexible environments like in ACM exist structured, conventional activity sequences (e. g. a feedback process) [34]. Therefore, the system provides basic workflow functionality allowing to instantiate a static workflow within the dynamic ACM environment.

Predefined workflow components are stored in the component library and can be added to a case if necessary.

**Adaption**

Case templates as well as case components can be adapted to new business requirements. In the case-specific adaption, the knowledge workers can adjust the case workspace according to their needs. Thus, they can add new elements to the case process, information and workflows by importing elements from the component library, by creating new elements or by changing existing elements. For all these operations, the system provides suitable Enterprise 2.0 tools to lower the inhibition threshold of the employees to participate:

- Bulletin boards to discuss new case innovations.
- Wikis to document the knowledge regarding these innovations.
- An editor for real-time collaborative document editing.
- A web based workflow modeler for formalizing workflow innovations.
- Social tagging to structure the system's entities in a non-hierarchical way.

According to [35], these web 2.0 tools are easy to use, require no additional software installations and therefore qualify in particular for incidental contributions [10].

All changes in the case workspace require the approval of the case responsible. This guarantees that all modifications within the case workspace are aligned to the case objectives.

For the cross-case adaption, the system provides a special workspace, where the knowledge workers can analyze case instances of one case template in order to identify recurring patterns. Based on these findings, the employee can modify the components in the library and the new case template. In both cases, one can decide, whether to update existing entities or to create new specialized versions.

## 4.2 Prototype

The ACM prototype is built on Microsoft SharePoint and implements the ACM procedure model as well as the design elements of the last chapter. In the following, we will demonstrate the prototype's functionality alongside the life cycle of a case.

In order to start a new case, the case responsible can select the most appropriate case template in the library and instantiate it. Afterwards, he can define the case's objectives and add further participants, who can start to adapt the workspace to the case's needs. The case workspace holds a page for each component type: the case's process, information and workflows. Furthermore, the case responsible can add additional collaborative elements like discussion boards, wikis or surveys.

Fig. 6 pictures the website for the case process. It displays the workbench structure for the case process and its visualization as a Gantt chart.

All case members can adapt the case process by adding or modifying tasks and defining constraints between them. Furthermore they can start, stop, skip or redo these tasks if necessary. If the carrying out of a task requires special knowledge or workflow functionality, the knowledge workers can add these elements to the case workspace and link them with the applicable tasks.

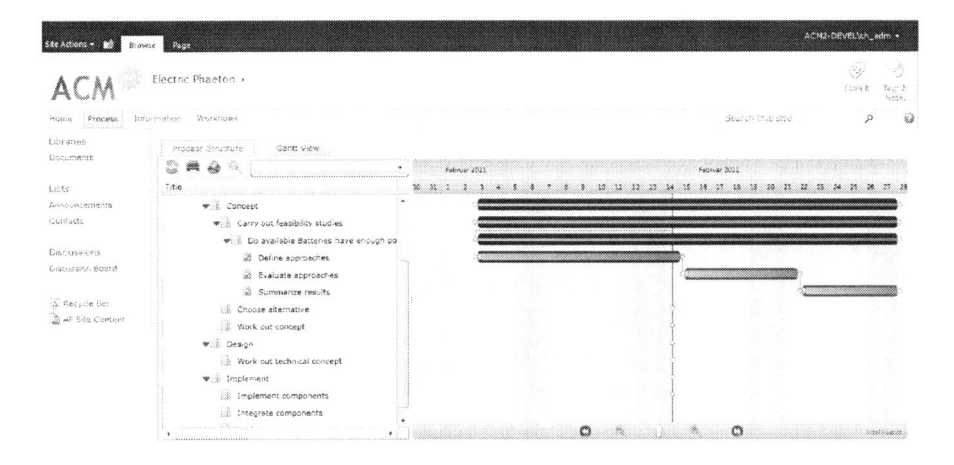

**Fig. 6.** Gantt view of the case process

Using the component library, the knowledge worker can add pre-built task clusters to the case process (e. g. the task structure for performing a requirements analysis), knowledge pieces as case information (e. g. documentation about requirements gathering techniques) or pre-implemented workflows (e. g. an approval workflow). The dialog for adding new elements to the case process is pictured in fig. 7.

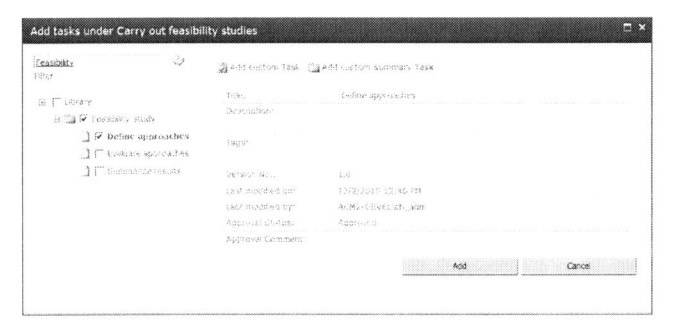

**Fig. 7.** Component library

On the left, the component library is displayed in a hierarchical tree view. On top of the tree view, the knowledge worker can filter the component library using tags. If the employee finds no fitting pre-built component, he can create his own, custom components. Adding information or workflow elements to the case process is similar to the addition of tasks.

After having finished the case, the cross-case adaption for the case template can be started. For this adaption, the system creates a special workspace, where a cockpit for each component type is provided (cf. fig. 8 for adapting process-related components).

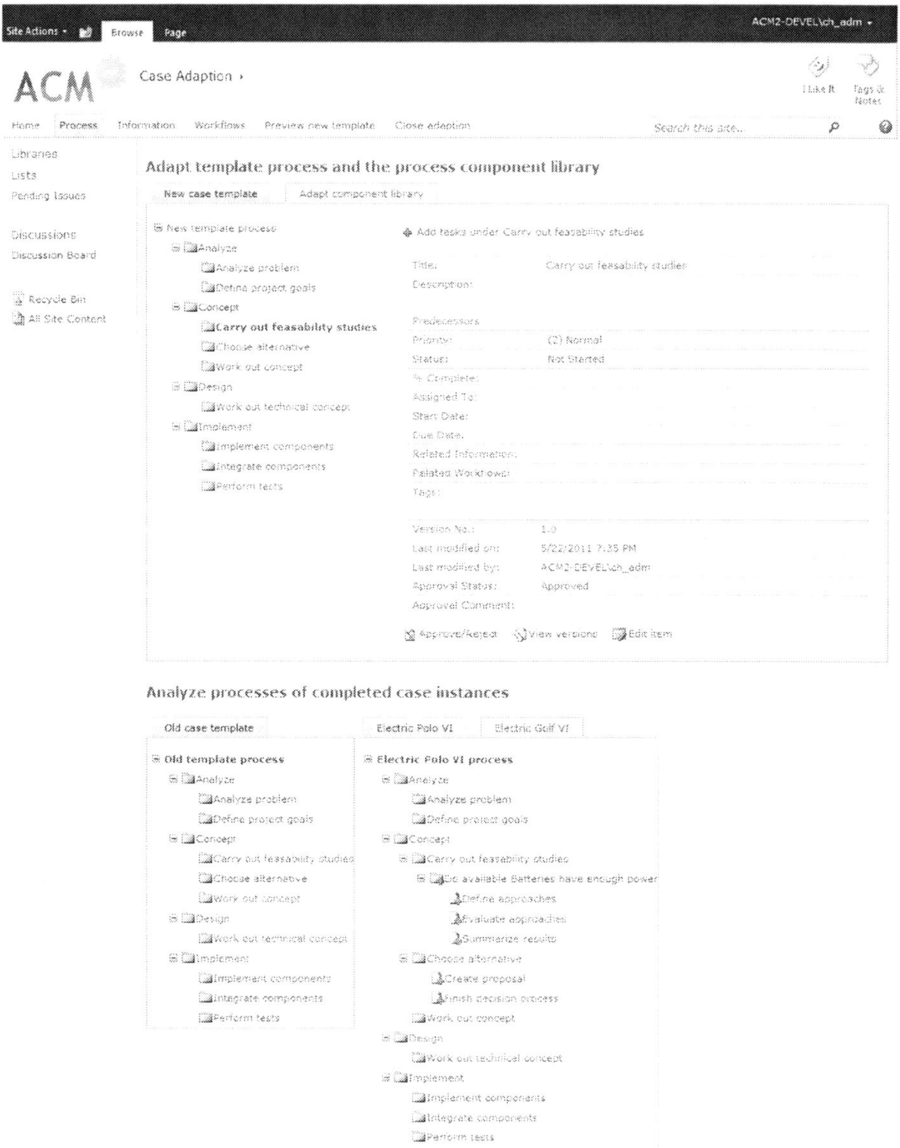

**Fig. 8.** Cross-case adaption of the case process

On the bottom of the cockpit, the processes of the old case template and of the completed case instances are visualized. By selecting a process task in the old template, the employee can track the changes that have been made to this element in the completed instances. In return, the selection of an instance task compares the element with its original version in the old template and the component library.

Having identified patterns throughout the different instances, the knowledge worker can start to adapt the process of the new case template as well as the component library.

As soon as all stakeholders are satisfied with the new version of the template, it can be added to the template library and is available for future cases.

## 5 Validation

In order to validate the proposed ACM concept and system, five qualitative expert interviews with one expert each have been conducted.

### 5.1 Interview Design

The interview objectives were to evaluate...

- the relevance of knowledge intensive processes and therefore the potential impact of ACM in today's business environments,
- the proposed procedure model and
- the implemented prototype.

Each interview was based on the same interview guideline and a demonstration of the prototype. The questions are grouped in three blocks (cf. table 1). The prototype demonstration included a complete round-trip through the ACM procedure model.

Table 1. Interview guideline

| ACM relevance |
| --- |
| 1. How many processes are too unstructured to capture them in a process model or support them by a WfMS?<br>2. How have these unstructured processes been supported by IT systems of your company so far?<br>3. Which gaps can you identify regarding this IT support? |
| ACM concept |
| 4. How do you assess the ACM procedure model?<br>5. How do you assess the use of empowerment within this model? |
| ACM prototype |
| 6. Which percentage of your company's unstructured processes can be addressed by the demonstrated prototype?<br>7. What further prototype improvements or extensions could you envision? |

The central selection criterion to qualify for an interview was the BPM experience of the candidate. Additional knowledge in the ACM field was an aspect in the expert's favor but could not have been set as obligatory criterion because of ACM's novelty. Five experts met the requirements (cf. table 2):

**Table 2.** Interviewed experts

| Expert | BPM experience (years) | Related positions |
|---|---|---|
| A | 2 | Consultant for the technical conversion of processes |
| B | 3 | Consultant for the technical conversion of processes |
| C | 5 | Consultant for the technical conversion of processes |
| D | 5 | Responsible for the BPM methodology in a multi-national enterprise |
| E | 16 | Working on an educational concept for BPM at an university chair; Managing director of a BPM consultancy |

## 5.2 Findings

**ACM relevance**

The relevance of weakly structured processes and therefore ACM, in particular in modern organizations, could be confirmed. Current concepts for supporting such processes with IT systems combine information centric approaches like document management systems (DMS) with WfMS.

Within the interviews, we could identify various gaps in the present IT support of such processes. Firstly, one of the biggest challenges is to satisfy the huge flexibility requirements of such processes. In practice, it is nearly impossible to detect all exceptions at the design time of the processes. Therefore, employees get frustrated as mostly deployed IT solutions offer insufficient flexibility in execution. Secondly, currently used systems like DMS or expert systems do not provide an appropriate way to support the whole lifecycle of a case, like instantiating a case. The two experts possessing the highest level of experience in the group (expert D and E) further pointed out that current systems are lacking functionality to build up and reuse pools for methods or procedures (e. g. established methods for business consulting).

**ACM concept**

The ACM procedure model has been rated positively by all experts. In particular, the cross-case adaption and the idea of continuous improvement through empowerment of the employees as well as linking the in-case improvements to the case's objectives through an approval process appealed the experts. All experts agreed that in highly qualified environments like ACM, the empowerment of the employees should be obligatory.

Nevertheless, implementing this procedure model comes with two major challenges. Firstly, as all knowledge workers are able and invited to create new case innovations, the number of entities in the libraries could grow fast. Therefore, adequate mechanisms have to be provided that enable the knowledge worker to easy find and retrieve the required entity. Secondly, a successful implementation of this empowerment driven ACM concept requires BPM trained employees as modifying the case workspace, for example the case process, calls for advanced knowledge in the BPM field.

**ACM prototype**
The experts rated the ACM prototype positive as well. The majority of the interviewed persons could imagine that the system would be able to support all knowledge intensive processes. Experts D and E emphasized that the ACM system is able to support both highly flexible processes and – by using the system's workflow components – structured routine processes.

The most promising suggestions for the prototype improvement include a task routing system, further mechanisms for managing the complexity of the library and extended controlling and monitoring functionality.

## 6 Conclusion

This contribution demonstrates how empowerment can be used to satisfy the high flexibility requirements of knowledge intensive processes for their IT support. Our proposed empowerment-driven ACM understanding has the ability to increase both the flexibility-to-use as well as the flexibility-to-change of business processes. Applying the concepts of BPM 2.0 to the new BPM approach Adaptive Case Management, we presented a procedure model that structures the various adaptive concepts of ACM while considering the flexibility driven aspects of knowledge work.

In a software prototype, we demonstrated how this concept could be implemented by using several Enterprise 2.0 tools. The validation by expert interviews confirmed the relevance of ACM in modern organizations as well as the feasibility of both the proposed ACM concept and the prototype.

As next step, we suggest to evaluate the concept and system within a case study.

## References

1. Schmidt, K.: Gestaltungsfeld Arbeit und Innovation. Perspektiven und Best Practices aus dem Bereich Personal und Innovation Haufe, Freiburg (2009)
2. Schmelzer, H.J., Sesselmann, W. (eds.): Geschäftsprozessmanagement in der Praxis. Kunden zufrieden stellen, Produktivität steigern, Wert erhöhen Hanser, München (2008)
3. Swenson, K.D.: The Nature of Knowledge Work. In: Swenson, K.D. (ed.) Mastering the Unpredictable. How Adaptive Case Management Will Revolutionize The Way That Knowledge Workers Get Things Done, pp. 5–27. Meghan-Kiffer Press, Tampa (2010)
4. Remus, U.: Prozeßorientiertes Wissensmanagement. Konzepte und Modellierung Regensburg (2002)
5. Bürgel, H.D., Haller, C., Binder, M.: F-&-E-Management Vahlen, München (1996)
6. Gebauer, J., Schober, F.: Information System Flexibility and the Cost Efficiency of Business Processes. Journal of the Association for Information Systems 7, 122–147 (2006)
7. Hanseth, O., Monteiro, E., Hatling, M.: Developing Information Infrastructure: The Tension Between Standardization and Flexibility. Science, Technology, & Human Values 21, 407–426 (1996)
8. Taylor, F.W.: The Principles of Scientific Management. Dover, Mineola (1998)
9. Allweyer, T.: Geschäftsprozessmanagement. Strategie, Entwurf, Implementierung, Controlling W3L, Herdecke (2005)

10. Kurz, M.: Kollaborative Gestaltung von Geschäftsprozessen. In: Schumann, M., Kolbe, L.M., Breitner, M.H., Frerichs, A. (eds.) Multikonferenz Wirtschaftsinformatik 2010, February 23 - 25, pp. 729–740. Universitätsverlag Göttingen, Göttingen (2010)
11. Picot, A., Reichwald, R., Wigand, R.T.: Die grenzenlose Unternehmung. Information, Organisation und Management Gabler, Wiesbaden (2003)
12. Kurz, M.: BPM 2.0. Organisation, Selbstorganisation und Kollaboration im Geschäftsprozessmanagement Bamberg, Erlangen-Nürnberg, Regensburg (2009)
13. Swenson, K.D.: Historical Perspective. In: Swenson, K.D. (ed.) Mastering the Unpredictable. How Adaptive Case Management Will Revolutionize The Way That Knowledge Workers Get Things Done, pp. 293–302. Meghan-Kiffer Press, Tampa (2010)
14. Palmer, N.: Introduction. In: Swenson, K.D. (ed.) Mastering the Unpredictable. How Adaptive Case Management Will Revolutionize The Way That Knowledge Workers Get Things Done, pp. 1–4. Meghan-Kiffer Press, Tampa (2010)
15. Swenson, K.D. (ed.): Mastering the Unpredictable. How Adaptive Case Management Will Revolutionize The Way That Knowledge Workers Get Things Done. Meghan-Kiffer Press, Tampa (2010)
16. Kraft, F.M.: Improving Knowledge Work. In: Swenson, K.D. (ed.) Mastering the Unpredictable. How Adaptive Case Management Will Revolutionize The Way That Knowledge Workers Get Things Done, pp. 181–209. Meghan-Kiffer Press, Tampa (2010)
17. Pucher, M.J.: The Elements of Adaptive Case Management. In: Swenson, K.D. (ed.) Mastering the Unpredictable. How Adaptive Case Management Will Revolutionize The Way That Knowledge Workers Get Things Done, pp. 89–134. Meghan-Kiffer Press, Tampa (2010)
18. McCauley, D.: Achieving Agility. In: Swenson, K.D. (ed.) Mastering the Unpredictable. How Adaptive Case Management Will Revolutionize The Way That Knowledge Workers Get Things Done, pp. 257–276. Meghan-Kiffer Press, Tampa (2010)
19. Khoyi, D., Swenson, K.D.: Templates, Not Programs. In: Swenson, K.D. (ed.) Mastering the Unpredictable. How Adaptive Case Management Will Revolutionize The Way That Knowledge Workers Get Things Done, pp. 145–162. Meghan-Kiffer Press, Tampa (2010)
20. Shepherd, T.: Moving from Anticipation to Adaptation. In: Swenson, K.D. (ed.) Mastering the Unpredictable. How Adaptive Case Management Will Revolutionize The Way That Knowledge Workers Get Things Done, pp. 41–62. Meghan-Kiffer Press, Tampa (2010)
21. Moore, C.: Foreword. In: Swenson, K.D. (ed.) Mastering the Unpredictable. How Adaptive Case Management Will Revolutionize The Way That Knowledge Workers Get Things Done, pp. VII–X. Meghan-Kiffer Press, Tampa (2010)
22. Teufel, S., Sauter, C., Mühlherr, T., Bauknecht, K.: Computerunterstützung für die Gruppenarbeit. Addison-Wesley, Bonn (1995)
23. Wendt, W.R.: Case Management im Sozial- und Gesundheitswesen. Eine Einführung Lambertus, Freiburg im Breisgau (2008)
24. Matthias, J.T.: Technology for Case Management. In: Swenson, K.D. (ed.) Mastering the Unpredictable. How Adaptive Case Management Will Revolutionize The Way That Knowledge Workers Get Things Done, pp. 63–88. Meghan-Kiffer Press, Tampa (2010)
25. Reich, S., Behrendt, W.: Technologien und Trends für Wissensarbeit und Wissensmangement. In: Fröschle, H.-P., Reich, S. (eds.) Enterprise Content Management, pp. 6–15. dpunkt, Heidelberg (2007)
26. Stähler, D., Meier, I., Scheuch, R., Schmülling, C., Somssich, D.: Enterprise Architecture, BPM und SOA für Business-Analysten. Hanser, München (2009)

27. Yooon, Y., Ye, C., Jacobsen, H.A.: A Distributed Framework for Reliable and Efficient Service Choreographies. In: 20th International World Wide Web Conference, Bangalore (2011)
28. Muthusamy, V., Jacobsen, H.A.: BPM in Cloud Architectures. Business Process Management with SLAs and Events. In: 8th International Conference on Business Process Management, Hoboken (2011)
29. Li, G., Muthusamy, V., Jacobsen, H.A.: A Distributed Service-Oriented Architecture for Business Process Execution. ACM Transactions on the Web 4(1) (2011)
30. Gernert, C.: Agiles Projektmanagement. Risikogesteuerte Softwareentwicklung Hanser, München (2003)
31. Manolescu, D.A.: Micro-Workflow: A Workflow Architecture Supporting Compositional Object-Oriented Software Development Urbana-Champaign (2000)
32. Swenson, K.D.: Workflow for the Information Worker. In: Fischer, L. (ed.) Workflow Handbook 2001, Future Strategies, Lighthouse Point, pp. 39–49 (2000)
33. Schwarze, J.: Projektmanagement mit Netzplantechnik NWB, Herne (2010)
34. Schwarz, S., Abecker, A., Maus, H., Sintek, M.: Anforderungen an die Workflow-Unterstützung für wissensintensive Geschäftsprozesse. In: Deutsches Forschungszentrum für Künstliche Intelligenz GmbH (ed.) Workshop 'Geschäftsprozessorientiertes Wissensmanagement' auf der WM 2001, Baden-Baden (2001)
35. O'Reilly, T.: What Is Web 2.0. Design Patterns and Business Models for the Next Generation of Software,
    http://oreilly.com/web2/archive/what-is-web-20.html

# Towards Contextual S-BPM:
# Method and Case Study

David Bonaldi[1], Alexandra Totter[1], and Eva Pinter[2]

[1] ByElement GmbH, Schönheimstr. 14, 8902 Urdorf, Switzerland
{bonaldi,totter}@byelement.com
[2] RBA Technologies GmbH, Schachenstrasse 59, 4562 Biberist, Switzerland
epinter@rbapplications.eu

**Abstract.** This paper makes the case for using Contextual Design and Subject-oriented Business Process Management (S-BPM) for analyzing complex business processes in ways that not only support, but in fact actively foster the consideration of the human elements within them. Specifically, the paper provides an outline of the defining characteristics of Contextual Design and S-BPM, following which it presents an outline of an ongoing case study. The presentation of the latter focuses on the lessons learnt and benefits derived from the proposed approach. Overall, Contextual Design allows including in a systematic way the work, usability and technology requirements for the S-BPM method. The combined methodology connects efficient business process management with appropriate contextual design in the workplace. The case study shows that this approach has a high potential for complex business process with specific contextual challenges and for the improvement of business processes with the employment of mobile electronic communication and information technology.

**Keywords:** Case study, Method, Contextual Design, Business process management method.

## 1 Introduction

To people who work on business processes and socio-technical system design it seems obvious that humans are central to the development and management of business processes [1]. Yet, today, projects in this domain often focus purely on business and IT related objectives and the applied methodologies move rapidly to a system-specific functional analysis and implementation. Users and employees as actors and subjects of a business process are often neglected. Their involvement is limited to identifying and describing the required business data and functions for the development and management of business processes.

As a result of the above, there is often the tendency in such projects to rush or skip considerations of the work environment and user needs; instead, the typical concern is usually with arriving at a system centered and business goal-directed information system deployment [2]. This procedure can be successful where the problem and business requirements are well defined, or already well known and experienced from former similar business cases and environments. However, applying such procedures in highly dynamic, real-time and individual business environments can prove quite detrimental.

In this paper we introduce a novel approach that aims to overcome these deficiencies while taking into account highly dynamic environments. In particular, the said approach demonstrates the benefits of combining the participatory and customer-centered method of Contextual Design (for the definition of work, usability and technology requirements) with Subject-oriented Business Process Management (S-BPM) as a business process management method. The application of the proposed approach is shown in a case study that took place as part of a project. The project was initiated with the aim of evaluating and designing a modern information system for maintenance management and daily planning and dispatching of buses. We present the first results of the case study and conclude with lessons learnt.

## 2 Combining Contextual Design and S-BPM

Our approach is based on the idea of mutual broadening and cross-fertilization between Contextual Design and S-BPM. In this context, S-BPM modeling supports the identification and design of organizational and business processes. Contextual Design, on the other hand, provides accurate information and models about the respective environment and context. The two, combined, connect efficient business process management with effective human-centered design.

### 2.1 Contextual Design

"Contextual Design is an approach to defining [...] systems that collects multiple customer-centered techniques into an integrated design process (p. 3)" [3]. The principle of context implies observing how the work unfolds, directly at the workplace. This allows gathering ongoing experience about the peoples' work, how business processes are managed and systems are used, rather than relying on abstract information. Contextual Design focuses on the usability and usefulness of a design, as determined by personal, group, organizational and environmental contexts of use.

The core Contextual Design techniques can be summarized as follows [4] [5]:

- *Contextual Inquiry* is conducted with users in their workplace while they work, observing and inquiring into the structure of the users' own work practice. Data is collected through observations and interviews and is validated through team interpretation sessions.
- *Work Modeling*: Five work models capture the work of individuals and organizations in diagrams. Each model provides a different perspective on how the work is done.
- *Consolidation* refers to the process of defining a common pattern and structure without losing individual variation.
- *Work Redesign* uses the consolidated data to focus the conversation on how technology can help people accomplish their tasks. The redesigned work is captured in scenarios embodied and elaborated upon in storyboards.

- *User Environment Design* captures the "floor plan" of a new system, how each part of the system supports the users' work – along with what functions are available in it – and how to access each of these parts.
- *Mockup and Prototype Testing* are important to system development in ensuring functionality and usability. Furthermore, continuous iterations of prototyping and testing have the potential to bring incremental improvement to the system and drive detailed design.

In itself, Contextual Design is an approach to designing products; in combination with S-BPM, it can be broadened up to organizational system design, allowing a human- and organization-centered approach to the development / implementation of standard information systems (such as Enterprise Resource Planning systems (ERP), see also [6]).

## 2.2 Subject-Oriented Business Process Management (S-BPM)

S-BPM is, according to [7], "… a BPM approach which focuses on the acting elements in a business process, i.e. the subjects" (p. 90). The subjects are active elements and abstract resources which execute defined actions on objects. They synchronize their activities by exchanging messages. When process models with subjects are employed within organizations, organizational units are assigned to subjects, which are the starting point of activities. Therefore, S-BPM shifts the focus towards communication and information exchange [8].

S-BPM is intended to be an optimal way of managing the dialectic between subjective, organizational problem inquiry and bridging the gap to a goal directed process and technical solution design [2].

S-BPM modeling offers an easy way of describing and illustrating the processes in place, using interaction diagrams to identify the subjects and their interactional relationships, i.e. the messages and business objects exchanged between them. The S-BPM approach for modeling business processes consists of several steps [7, 9]:

- Identification of business processes and creation of a specific process network
- Identification of subjects
- Identification of exchanged messages between the subjects
- Identification of the payload of the messages
- Definition of the behavior of each subject
- Embedding the model in the respective environment and context.

The S-BPM modeling language is similar to the grammar of natural languages and of object-oriented programming, and is extended with additional pragmatic elements.

The S-BPM approach focuses on direct interactions between people supported by information technology during execution time, rather than ex post or ex ante interaction.

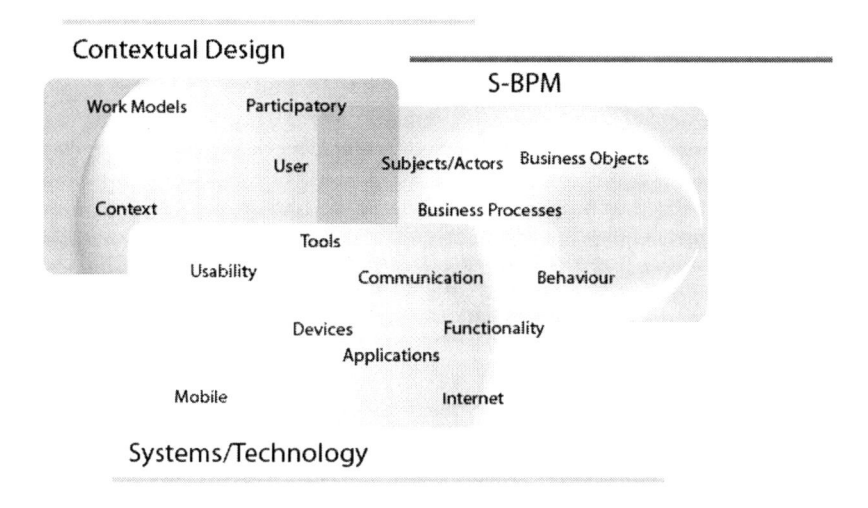

Fig. 1. Combining Contextual Design and S-BPM for system assessment and design

To better illustrate the main points of the combination of Contextual Design and S-BPM we will first look at a case study of applying this approach. Following that, we will return to the theoretic elements and further elaborate on them.

## 3 Case Study: Maintenance Management, Daily Planning and Dispatching of Buses

The largest operator of transport services in Zurich (Switzerland) provides the city and surrounding regions with high-quality municipal public transport services, 365 days a year, at least 20 hours a day. The company operates daily over 300 rail vehicles and about the same number of buses for 80 bus lines. These services require three shifts for operations and planning. The planning of the daily routes is a top priority for the public transport company, with punctuality and availability being the primary goals.

The above create a highly dynamic work environment. The communication and decisions regarding parking locations of incoming buses, required repairs and maintenance as well as the assignments of outgoing buses to specific routes for the next shift have to be handled in real-time. These tasks become very challenging during peak times. When buses drive out or in at the bus parking, the planner needs to act very quickly to prevent traffic jam and difficult parking situations. As the planners also check the entering buses onsite regarding damages and required repairs, they are constantly in motion. The planners' effective working space is the whole parking area. Therefore, the used planning and dispatching tools and information have to be easily accessible at all times.

A project has been initiated that aims at evaluating and designing a modern information and communication system for maintenance management and daily planning and dispatching of the buses. This information and communication system should optimize the planning activities, while ensuring a reliable level of control over daily operations. The first objectives of the project are to examine and analyze how the information and communication flow can be streamlined: how labor-intensive, time-consuming manual processes using specific tools, documents, paper maps and boards for planning and dispatching can be replaced by a more automated and integrated system.

Particular attention has to be paid to the users' acceptance of the system. For this dynamic work environment and critical tasks, an information and communication system must support and facilitate the planners' daily planning and dispatching work, with an emphasis on user experience and system usability.

To sum up, the following specific challenges have to be taken into consideration for an appropriate system design and development:

- Time-criticality: During peak times over 100 vehicles drive in and need to be assessed and dispatched within one hour.
- Difficult planning: Daily irregularities and unforeseeable traffic events make it difficult to standardize the planning (e.g. different entry sequence and parking logic, unforeseen damages and problems with buses requiring immediate repairs and replacements).
- Requirements coming from the maintenance department and quality management: These may necessitate suitable alignments in, among other things, an integration to the backend system (e.g. SAP).

**REAL TIME DECISION SUPPORT**
**Planning and Dispatching**

- Ensuring schedules of lines
- Optimization of Parking facilities and order
- Quality assessments

**BUSINESS PROCESS SUPPORT**
**Maintenance and Repair Management**

- Business Processes and SAP integration
- Maintenance and Repair Processes/Cycles
- Spare Parts Logistics
- Quality Management

**SYSTEM ACCEPTANCE**

- Work Environment
- Usability at the point-of-action
- Performance and provided support

**Fig. 2.** Important aspects and challenges of the system assessment and design

## 3 Procedure

As already outlined in the introduction the main objectives of the maintenance management project are to examine and analyze how the information and communication flow can be streamlined. The aim is to analyze whether and how labor-intensive, time-consuming manual processes using specific tools, documents, paper maps and boards for planning and dispatching can be replaced by a more automated and integrated system. Which work, usability and technology requirements can be identified and have to be considered ensuring high user acceptance?

The procedure of the combined Contextual Design and S-BPM is described below. Note that steps 1 to 4 address assessment activities, whereas steps 5 to 7 can be seen as design and development activities. In this paper we will only present results addressing steps 1 to 4:

1. Contextual Inquiry: Field observation and interviews with employees of all three shifts to capture the 24 hours maintenance and planning process have been performed using observation and interview protocols.
2. Contextual Design work models and S-BPM modeling: Based on the data derived from the field observations and interviews, several work models have been developed (flow model, sequence model, artifact model, physical model), as well as the S-BPM model.
3. Consolidation with the team: The work models and the S-BPM model have been validated with employees and consolidated with the project team.
4. Combining S-BPM and Contextual Design to identify work, usability and technology requirements.
5. Re-Design and development of an enriched contextual business model (taking into account new and/or adapted business processes and technology choices)
6. Acceptance Test of the business process model and/or system prototype
7. Deployment and Roll-out

The Contextual Inquiry techniques for the data collection have been very well accepted by the employees. Further, for the employees it was easy to understand and validate the presented work and S-BPM models.

## 4 Results

The following section highlights what Contextual Design and S-BPM can contribute to each other, and outlines the actual findings from the case study.

### 4.1 Contributions of S-BPM

**Adding business orientation.** One of the strengths of S-BPM is the focus of the subject-interaction diagram on the exchange of business objects between the subjects. This systematic business modelling helps to clarify where communication related to business processes takes place, who launches business objects and who receives them. It refines the more generic work models of Contextual Design and filters and structures the communication with relevance to business processes.

Within the project, the subject-interaction diagram draws a complete picture of the complex and many-sided business activities and communications of the planners. It offers a bird's-eye view of any set of distributed data exchanges critical to the planners' work. The subject-interaction diagram helps to structure and separate the complex processes linked to the planning and dispatching of buses, and to cluster all the business functions and processes to be performed. It clearly distinguishes three main business processes, where the planners are involved:

1. Repair and maintenance management,
2. Planning and dispatching and
3. Quality management.

The visualization of the identified three different business processes and their current intersections are depicted in Figure 3.

Further, the subject interaction diagram also shows that several types of documents currently used hold the same business information content (repair report, repair planning drive-in, new repairs) among the three shifts. These different documents lead to a quite complex and redundant information flow with respect to repair management.

Additionally, the bus planning process and its dependency on repair planning is not clearly defined. The subject interaction diagram shows only one interfacing business object – a lot of request and business coordination happens in an informal way between the three shifts and the repair management.

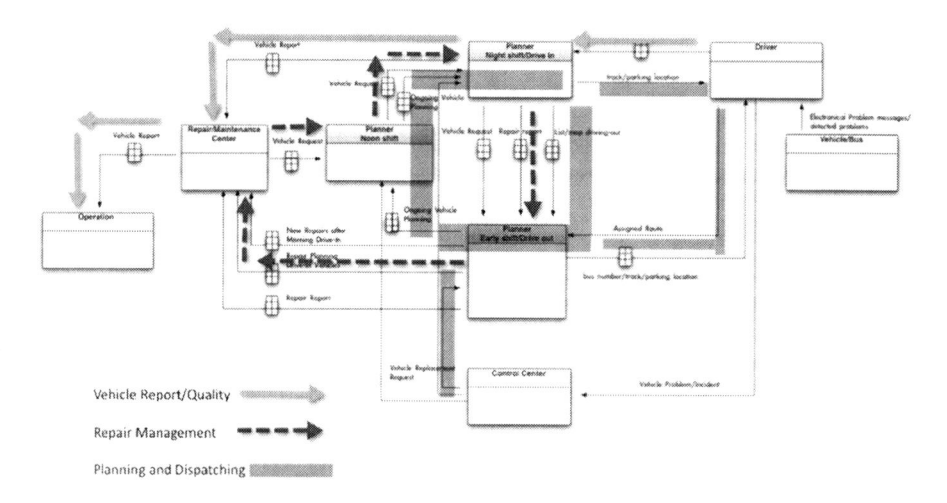

**Fig. 3.** Subject-Interaction Diagram for the three shifts and the main business processes

**High subject-orientation - clarification of involved subjects.** The subject-oriented view automatically considers and includes all the relevant business processes for the subjects.

This integrated view shows, at a glance, where planning related communication takes place and at what stage the repair management processes are triggered.

The subject-oriented approach also helps to identify the different functions and tasks of the three shifts. Although every planner has the same job description, the analysis shows clearly that, within the three shifts, they have to be treated as separate acting elements of the business scenario; therefore, each shift is represented as a subject on its own that interacts and exchanges different business information and objects.

Approaches to process modelling with a function-, object-, or data-orientation would probably miss or even attempt to integrate the three shifts into one role, which could lead to misinterpretations and high complex solutions.

**Supporting a participatory approach and efficient project management.** The subject interaction diagram of S-BPM has proven to be an easy to use tool, and has fostered discussions and joint design activities with the planners over the business processes and the data exchange, as well as over the very specific planning procedure applied for the bus scheduling.

The close link of S-BPM modelling and natural language with the basic building blocks (subject, predicate and object) makes it easy to identify important subjects and relationships together with the system's stakeholders. S-BPM thus supports and fits well to the participatory approach of Contextual Design.

### 4.2 Contribution of Contextual Design

A complete business process model can be created together with an artefact model and a physical model to derive a comprehensive / holistic view of complex business processes. The combination of Contextual Design and S-BPM leads to a clearer picture as to how the business objects are designed, and in which circumstances the interactions and message exchanges occur.

The artefact model illustrates in detail the layout, structure and content of the business objects and the required interactions of the subjects. In the project under discussion we linked the subject interaction diagram with the artefact model, by indicating the artefacts as business objects.

The physical model is very helpful in clarifying the requirements regarding the technology choices and the workplace – it is possible to determine in which situation the user needs to act physically and what time restrictions should be considered.

In the presented project the physical model shows that the three shifts have very different needs regarding mobile access to information and also very different time constraints. For the technology choices and system acceptance such considerations are very crucial and need to be thoroughly considered.

The combination of the physical model with the S-BPM model set the requirements for a potential system design as a supporting tool.

The sequence model enriches S-BPM as follows. In S-BPM the modeller refines the subjects by describing their behaviour as a sequential series of activities and interactions with the help of states and transitions. The sequence model clearly shows how the work tasks are ordered as a sequence of actions and what the triggers that kick off these actions are. In addition to the subject behaviour diagram, it labels problems and difficulties that can affect and interfere with the process execution. Among the strengths of the sequence model are, that it can be studied easily, and at any level of detail from high-level tasks, all the way to the detailed action steps for a specific task. Especially its ease of use for illustrating the overall work structure, supports and completes the detailed modelling of the subject behaviour model of S-BPM.

Overall, Contextual Design allows including and considering in a systematic way the work, usability and technology requirements for the S-BPM method. The combined methodology connects efficient business process management with appropriate contextual design in the workplace.

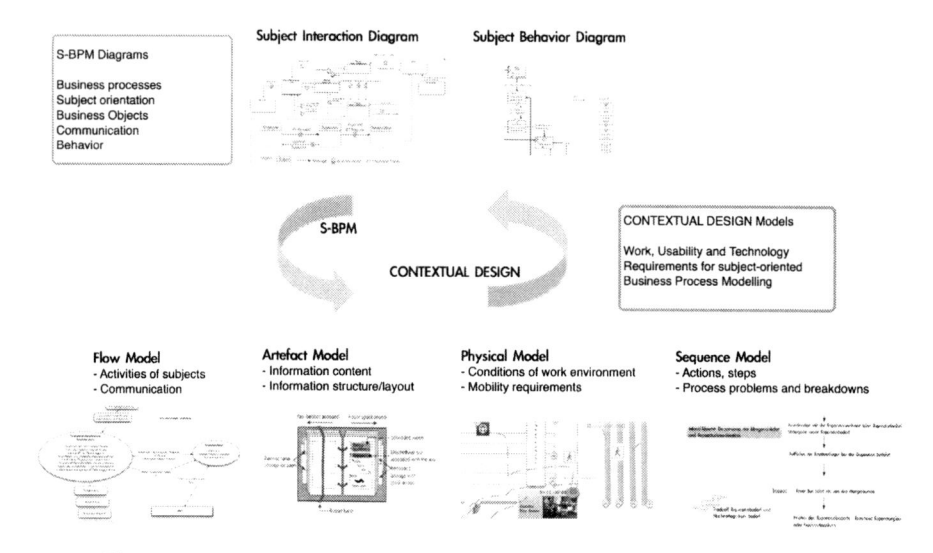

**Fig. 4.** Contextual Design and S-BPM: Providing complementary information

The combination of Contextual Design and S-BPM gives the decision maker a new approach to determining what technology and / or systems need to be developed or acquired, as it answers the following questions:

a. Mobility: By establishing the information needs of the actors during their movement in the workplace, the decision about the mobility can easily be justified.
b. Ease of use: Contextual Design allows defining the quantity and the pertinence of the information immediately available to the actor. This element being a major factor for user acceptance, the development methodology used in this case starts from the design of the human interface, adding later the required functionality. The ability to create an acceptable human interface will be a criterion for the choice of the system.
c. Communication flows: S-BPM defines the information flow between the different actors. From the system point of view, it is necessary to determine which communication flows need to be automated, as well as the impact of that automation on humans: For instance, if information that was transmitted orally must be keyed into the system, the work may be slowed down, but it may support follow-up processes. Further, as actors may also be other systems, there will be a higher global complexity for each communication flow between systems. As an analogy to the S-BPM interaction diagram, the system interaction diagram can also be defined as basis for system choice.

d.  Functionality: Once the three points cited before are determined, it is possible to define the functionality. It will be far more than the functionality defined only knowing the business processes, as we may have extra functionality in order to fulfil the requirements of mobility, ease of use and communication flows.

**Advantages of this approach:** In many IT-projects, the work done by the end-user is rarely taken as the basis for decision. Therefore, it is often necessary to apply change management methods to the companies to support a change that is not wanted by the users and where the user needs are rarely satisfied. With this combined approach, the user is in the center of all decisions taken related to the human-machine interface. His/her word has an effect on the chosen technology and he/she can also bring proposals for enhancement of the business processes and the daily tasks. The probability of a better efficiency is higher than in traditional projects.

On the other hand, this approach does not support the implementation of standard systems with standard business processes, as for such systems, the man-machine interface is already defined.

## 5 Conclusions

In this case study, the combined use of Contextual Design and S-BPM has demonstrated that S-BPM is not only applicable for business processes referring to traditional office work and business functions. The proposed combined use of the two is also very suitable where standard business processes are not obvious and very specific interactions, process flows and communication activities have to be considered. Typically, such specific business areas are not yet fully supported by standard ERP or workflow systems, due to very idiosyncratic environmental and contextual restrictions.

Nevertheless and in view of the growing new possibilities of mobile technology such specific business cases are getting increasingly important for business process management. The combined S-BPM and Contextual Design approach has a huge potential for:

- Specific business processes with specific contextual challenges and
- the introduction of new, mobile technology developments.

## References

1. Swenson, K., Farris, J.: Human-Centered Business Process Management. Fujitsu Scientific & Technical Journal 45(2), 160–170 (2009)
2. Gasson, S.: Human-Centered vs. User-Centered Approaches to Information System Design. Journal of Information Technology and Application (JITTA) 5(2), 29–46 (2003)
3. Beyer, H., Holtzblatt, K.: Contextual Design. Defining Customer-Centered Systems. Morgan Kaufmann Publishers, San Francisco (1998)

4. Holtzblatt, K., Burns Wendell, J., Wood, S.: Rapid Contextual Design. A How-to Guide to Key Techniques for User-Centered Design. Morgan Kaufmann Publishers, San Francisco (2005)
5. Holtzblatt, K.: Contextual Design: Experience in Real Life. Mensch & Computer. B.G. Teuber, Stuttgart (2001)
6. Vilpola, I., Väänänen-Vainio-Mattila, K., Salmimaa, T.: Applying contextual design to ERP system implementation. In: CHI 2006 Extended Abstracts on Human Factors in Computing Systems, pp. 147–152. ACM, Canada (2006)
7. Fleischmann, A.: What is S-BPM? In: Buchwald, H., Fleischmann, A., Seese, D., Stary, C. (eds.) S-BPM ONE 2009. Communications in Computer and Information Science, vol. 85, pp. 85–106. Springer, Heidelberg (2010)
8. Stary, C.: Quo vadis, S-BPM? The first world-café on S-BPM developments. In: Buchwald, H., Fleischmann, A., Seese, D., Stary, C. (eds.) S-BPM ONE 2009. Communications in Computer and Information Science, vol. 85, pp. 136–147. Springer, Heidelberg (2010)
9. Schmidt, W., Fleischmann, A., Gilbert, O.: Subject-Oriented Business Process Management. In: HDM-Praxis der Wirtschaftsinformatik, vol. 266, pp. 52–62 (2009)

# smart4sense2act:
# A Smart Concept for Systemic Performance Management

Fritz Bastarz and Patrick Halek

Infomedia Services GmbH, Rosenbursenstraße 4, 1010 Vienna, Austria
{fritz.bastarz,patrick.halek}@infomedia.at

**Abstract.** smart4sense2act (read: smart for sense to act) is a technology-supported solution for systemic performance management and corporate governance. Be it strategic planning, organisational development or project mangement, smart4sense2act offers one method and one web-based tool for different tasks. By means of integrated information and subject-oriented process-management, processes can be created and evaluated quickly and directly as well as integrated into every-day-business on the grounds of actual needs. Therefore, smart4sense2act is barrier-free as well as quick and easy to use. The principle of smart4sense2act is a stakeholder based systemic and structured seizing, analysing and arranging of tasks. This is assured by considering all relevant stakeholders and factors of influence and the possibility of the quick and direct implementation of results within assessable processes ready for implementation within the organisation. The goal of smart4sense2act is to obtain a holistic understanding of tasks and processes through bridging the gap between theory and operation. This approach supports organisations in gaining a more solid and sustainable performance management.

**Keywords:** Complexity, Corporate Governance, Holistic Management, Lateral Thinking, Performance Management, Stakeholders, Systemic Thinking.

## 1 Basic Thoughts about Performance Management

We know that the circumstances in our society and economy are far more complex and interconnected today than they were years ago [1]. But quite a few among us still think challenges of today and tomorrow can be met with the knowledge and the methods of yesterday [2]. This is understandable from the human point of view, because it is convenient. But it is getting dangerous because the new challenges of today need new methods and new tools. For many of our traditional ways of thinking and acting are based on linear and hierarchical approaches they are not suitable for solving modern, complex and multidimensional tasks successfully today [3]. In other words: on the one hand we have already been flying to the moon but on the other hand we still don't want to give the flintstone away.

In recent years critical conditions have changed dramatically. The rules of the game have been redefined [4]. The knowledge society is creating a lot of new opportunities but also forcefully calls for new patterns of thinking and acting [5]. The usual homogeneity is getting replaced by heterogeneity and complexity increasingly.

Thereby, the transparency of social and economic processes increases apparently. But just apparently. The truth is it's the complexity of these processes which dramatically increases. Conclusion: We can see more but we understand less and less. Therefore, it is increasingly difficult to understand coherences and to predict or shape trends [6]. By the usual, ancient way of thinking, complex coherences can no longer be dealt with in every-day-business. The Big Picture is getting lost more and more and we seek refuge in details. This creates a downward spiral. The problem is that this danger creeps up almost unnoticed and then suddenly and inevitably breaks open. At that time an effective response in many cases is not possible anymore. So, the all-important question is: How can we remain competitive in such an environment at all – and most important: in a sustainable way [7]?

Therefore, companies and their performance management are challenged increasingly. Because they want to remain competitive, they need to abandon ways of thinking and managing they have practised for decades. The message is that companies today must obey and take into account much more than it was the case until now. Companies have to balance a turbulent environment, heterogeneous markets, different stakeholders, new social rules and new patterns of thinking and behaviour [8]. Dealing with knowledge and information is the crucial basis for managing businesses and the resource for their competitive position. Though, it is still widely ignored that not moving figures and managing databases, but creating and managing a sustainable competitive perspective is the essential discipline of entrepreneurship [9]. Therefore, performance management is about managing an ongoing creative process focussing on a sustainable competitive position. But how is this supposed to work?

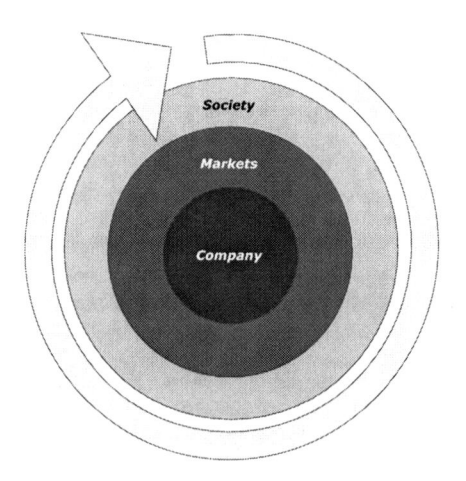

**Fig. 1.** Interdependence of company, markets and society

The linear, mostly one-dimensional thinking we have been taught is standing in our way, because it results in methods and tools that cannot meet the multi-dimensional requirements we have to deal with today. A conclusion we have been aware of for several years [10]. Newer approaches, such as Lateral Thinking and Systemic Thinking introduce enormous potential, because they can develop unknown dimensions of high quality solutions in a very pragmatic way. But the point is that humans have limited capabilities in dealing with abstract thinking [11]. Therefore, we need a barrier-free tool to be able to manage capturing, analysing and designing complex tasks pragmaticaly, building the basis of a focused and sustainable development. Organisational development means improving both the effectiveness and the efficiency in managing clearly defined tasks [12]. This requires clarity, agility, transparency and compliance which leads to more effectiveness and efficiency. Therefore, the goals must be the following:

- improving the quality of decisions
- improving both the effectiveness and efficiency of communication
- saving the setup of actions
- accelerating of task-implementation
- adapting of new circumstances more flexibly

But how can a solution look like, that can actually be used in every-day-business?

## 2  smart4sense2act

Multidimensional tasks which are subject to the principles of networking and complexity cannot be solved with the tools of a hierarchically structured and linear world anymore [13]. That's why smart4sense2act was created. It was developed based on the findings that the knowledge society cannot be implemented with previously lived patterns of thinking and acting [14]. It is a novel method development providing a specific approach and a web-based tool for networks and complex environments, not only to meet complexity and enable knowledge-orientation, but especially to facilitate organisational changes and managing systemic performance in every-day-business.

smart4sense2act ensures bridging the gap between theory and operation, as it works in a context-sensitive (systemic) while focussed way based on subject-oriented and semantic process-modelling. The question smart4sense2act answers is: "Who or what is related to whom or what in which way?" Therefore, it takes into account only elements that can be implemented in every-day-business, as they lay ground to competitive advantages [15]. smart4sense2act allows not only responding to new challenges, but also creating networks, and recognising complex environments as knowledge pool quickly and without barriers. Therefore, the key to define processes is to focus on the stakeholders and their stakes involved [16]. Organisations are not only driven by formal structures and processes, but also strongly by informal processes, values and the implicit knowledge of the people who are in touch with these organisations [17]. The latter allow discovering and developing organisational potential.

Since every theory is only as good as effectively it can be implemented, smart4sense2act offers a specific IT-supported tool to implement the method presented quickly and without the need of special skills. The focus of the development is on barrier-free accessibility and integration into every-day-business because the needs of today demand a proper procedure. Therefore, processes are not only designed in specifically defined procedures. They can be designed as a part of daily business and adapted quickly and flexibly from time to time to meet new requirements – without the need of opening the "entire package" again. In doing so, smart4sense2act helps creating a long term flow. This means there are no obstacles that usually could make it difficult to adapt processes to new challenges - obstacles that often stand in the way of the future and a sustainable perspective.

The term smart was created by the 1st letters of the following expressions:

- *SYSTEMIC*: holistic, in order to allow the basical understanding of a situation and recongnising of principles, patterns and dependencies.
- *MODEL-DRIVEN*: a structured description / interpretation of relevant realities.
- *ACHIEVABLE*: really feasible, thus to be implemented effectively.
- *RELATED*: not only linear hirarchies but relations and their impacts are part of success. Not only the formal, certified processes are considered, but also the informal and human motives of relevant stakeholders that determine success or failure.
- *TIMELY*: up to date and meeting today's requirements. Everywhere we hear of creating networks, even across company boundaries. But how to deal with

Following these definitions, the focus is on the terms "sense" and "act", which clearly express that all states from capturing the situation to executing the solution are considered and integrated.

***sense***: *SENSING* means the capturing, perceiving and recognising of important events and factors – it means to feel and to interpret. In the corporate meaning it is like putting out the feelers in order to understand the environment, their own company and its relevant stakeholders and to properly interpret their actions [18].

***act***: *ACTING* means acting as a result of a need for action that arises from different perceptions (sensing) and calls for clearly defined and structured activities. The quality of action depends on the players' abilities and the functionality of the chosen tools.

## 3   The 5 Pillars of smart4sense2act

Since *smart4sense2act* was created to bridge the gap between theory and operation, a solution was designed in order to follow the concept of a barrier-free and ready to use tool based on a clear and structured method. *smart4sense2act* has 5 pillars:

**Web-based:** The tool *smart4sense2act* uses is web-based. This creates the opportunity for different users to work on the same task at different places.

**Semantic:** No special process-language is needed. *smart4sense2act* is based on free semantic modelling. Processes are created on the basis of our natural language, which means the language we speak.

**Subject-oriented:** The focus of modelling is on the subject and its clearly defined realtions. The question *smart4sense2act* answers is not "What has to follow what?", it is "Who or what is related to whom or what in which way?"

**Interconnected:** Modellig can be done on various and different levels which can be linked through just a mouse click. This way, the Big Picture never gets lost even when modelling details.

**Multi-usable:** Be it strategic planning, organisational development or one single project – *smart4sense2act* offers one tool for different tasks. Modelling different tasks can be done and linked to eachother as well as to documents and websites barrier-free.

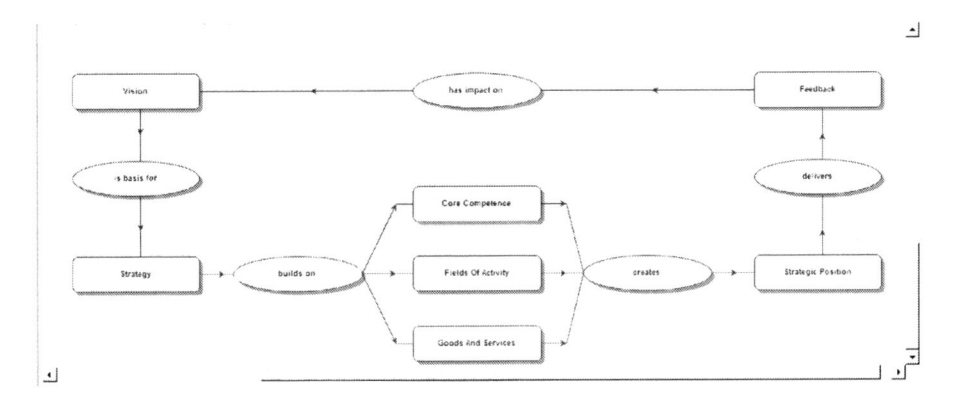

**Fig. 2.** smart4sense2act: What is related to what in which way? (a case; screen shot)

## 4 Summative Conclusions

*smart4sense2act* offers a method and a web-based tool to display and understand complex environments, tasks and situations. Based on subject-oriented and semantic modelling, it enables individuals and organisations to recognise interconnected elements in order to use so far unseen potentials. *smart4sense2act* is quick and ready to use as well as multi-usable for different kinds of tasks which can be linked to each other. These features and attributes support catering to a more systemic and sustainable performance management.

## References

1. Vester, F.: he Art of Interconnected Thinking. Ideas and Tools for tackling complexity. MCB-Verlag, Munich (2007)
2. Williams, B.A.O.: Descartes: Das Vorhaben der reinen philosophischen Untersuchung. Beltz Athenäum, Weinheim (1996)
3. Heftberger, S., Stary, C.: Partizipatives organisationales Lernen; Ein prozessbasierter Ansatz. GWV-Fachverlag, Wiesbaden (2004)

4. Anthony, S.D.: The Silver Lining: An Innovation Playbook for Uncertain Times. Harvard Business Press, Boston (2009)
5. Halek, P., Nyiri, A.: Das Heartbeat-Modell. Der Brückenschlag zwischen strategischem Marketing und Wissensmanagement. Gabler, Wiesbaden (2002)
6. Senge, P.: The Fifth Discipline: The Art & Practice of The Learning Organization, rev. edn. Crown Business, New York (2006)
7. Kiessling, W., Bable, F.: Corporate Identity. Strategie nachhaltiger Unternehmensführung (2007) Ziel- Zentrum F. Interdis, Solothurn
8. Haas, B., Oetinger, R., Ritter, A., Thul, M.: Nachhaltige Unternehmensführung. Verknüpfung wirtschaftlicher, sozialer und gesellschaftlicher Forderungen. Hanser, Munich (2007)
9. Nyiri, A.: Corporate Performance Management. Ein ganzheitlicher Ansatz der Unternehmenssteuerung. Facultas.wuv, Vienna (2007)
10. Ossimitz, G.: Entwicklung systemischen Denkens. Theoretische Konzepte und empirische Untersuchungen. Profil Verlag, Munich (2000)
11. Glasersfeld, V.E.: Wege des Wissens. Konstruktivistische Erkundungen durch unser Denken. Carl-Auer-Verlag, Heidelberg (1997)
12. Grimberger, G.: The High-IQ Company: The Development of the Organisational IQ. VDM Verlag, Saarbrücken (2009)
13. Pullen, A., Beech, N., Sims, D.: Exploring Identity: Concepts and Methods. Palgrave Macmillan, Basingstoke (2007)
14. Yeo, R.K.: Organisational Development in the 21st Century: Learning for Success - Lessons from Singapore's Learning Organisations. VDM-Verlag, Saarbrücken (2009)
15. Varela, F., Thompson, E., Rosch, E.: Der mittlere Weg der Erkenntnis: die Beziehung von Ich und Welt in der Kognitionswissenschaft - der Brückenschlag zwischen wissenschaftlicher Theorie und menschlicher Erfahrung. Goldmann Wilhelm, Munich (1995)
16. Nel, R.: Puppets Or People: People And Organisational Development: An Integrated Approach. Juta Academic, Claremont (2008)
17. Allee, V.: The Future of Knowledge: Increasing Prosperity through Value Networks. Butterworth-Heinemann, Burlington (2003)
18. Halek, P.: Die Marke lebt! Das All-Brand-Concept. Die Marke als Kern nachhaltiger Organisationsführung. Facultas.wuv, Vienna (2009)

# Modeling Needs in the BPM Consulting Process

Stefan Reinheimer

BIK GmbH
Aeußere Sulzbacher Str. 16
90489 Nuremberg
sr@bik.biz

**Abstract.** Business Process Management is a complex assembly of activities with the need for various methodologies in order to achieve the relevant goals. Different approaches and visualization requirements have to be taken into account to fulfill the demand of the roles involved. It is the consultant´s choice, which methods to choose. The article pledges for a variety of methods instead of only one single-sided view at the challenge. Subject orientation is only one approach to support BPM.

**Keywords:** business consulting, process modeling, process documentation, BPM, BPM consulting.

## 1 Introduction

For business consultants one of the reasons to be in business is their methodological portfolio. Thus, trends in BPM are of major importance for consultancies that earn their income with BPM. Versioning as used in software release history has been a way to attract attention for major changes. So BPM 2.0 [1] needs to be looked at closely – does it really deserve a new major release denomination? Does S-BPM revolutionize daily BPM consulting business?

### 1.1 Subject Orientation in BPM

Subject orientation in BPM claims to be THE new methodology to bring more efficiency into business process modeling, to bridge the gap between documented business processes and IT implementations and to allow for easy measurability of process efficiency (see [1]).

Like sentences in natural language process steps can be described by subject (who or what is in charge?), object (what or who is the target or are the means?) and predicate (what is the activity?). Subject orientation in BPM puts the subject in the center of interest (see [2]).

In BPM like in natural language, the question arises, which of the elements is the most important one to take the lead – is it the subject, the predicate or the object? As in real life, an appropriate answer could very well be: "it depends". This is what shall be proved in the following chapters.

## 1.2 BPM Consulting – Clarifying the Scope

From a BPM consulting view, one of the first tasks in client presentations is to communicate what BPM really is. A central misunderstanding needs to be dealt with right at the beginning: BPM does not stand for Business Process Modeling, but for Business Process Management. Actively managing business processes implies – on a very generic level – to plan, implement and control processes.

**Operational BPM**

- **Process Monitoring**: Definition of KPIs and implementation of systems for monitoring the processes
- **Process Execution**: Supporting the operational process execution and monitoring the rollout of changed / new business processes
- **Process Implementation**: Implementing new organizational structures and/or IT solutions
- **Design of target processes**: Design of target processes and planning of activites for realization of optimization potentials
- **Process Analysis**: Identification of weak points and room for improvement in the current process landscape
- **Collection of as-is-processes**: Structuring and documentation of current processes based on (e)EPC, BPMN, SCOR, UML etc.
- **Rules & Regulations**: Specification of methodology and conventions for process modelling and for the process documentation

(Process Modelling spans from Collection of as-is-processes to Design of target processes)

**Strategic BPM**

- **Process Organization**: Definition of roles for the rollout, execution and continuous improvement of the processes
- **Process Architecture**: Identification of identity, priority, background and compulsion processes and presentation in a process house
- **Process Strategy**: Adopting the process strategy from the corporate strategy and definition of activities for process standardization / harmonization

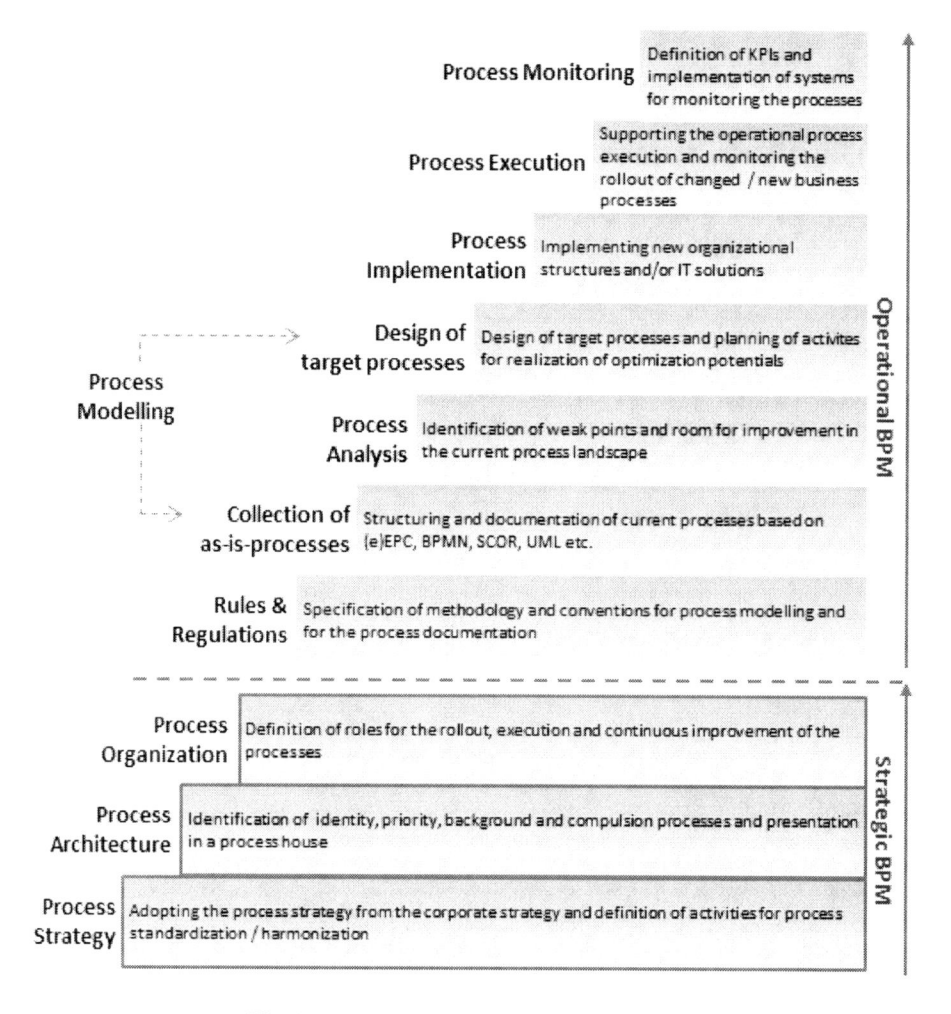

**Fig. 1.** Blocks and activities in BPM consulting

As part of an operational planning task, process documentation is one step; process improvement requiring remodeling the processes is another step. Both are of major importance, but can never represent BPM as a whole. This general understanding is vital for the correct setup of a corporate BPM.

In business consulting various activities converge to a service bundle that results into a client's benefit. In the following an approach is chosen that distinguishes between strategic and operational BPM and divides these two activity blocks into smaller elements (see 11).

To determine the relevant services according to the needs is step one in the interaction between consultant and client.

This understanding of BPM services paves the way for a closer look at the methodology and raises the question of how to actually consult companies in BPM.

The intention of the upcoming chapters of this article is to prove that a multitude of methodologies is needed to fulfill the needs of the relevant views. Like in most languages' grammars all three main parts of a sentence need to be taken into account: subject, predicate and object.

## 2 Models and Target Groups

The various steps visualized in 11 require different consulting approaches. In the execution of these steps, different target groups need to be dealt with, each group having its own expectation as far as result types and results are concerned.

### 2.1 Strategic BPM

Following the general understanding of the strategic aspects of business (e.g. [3]), strategic BPM comprises the activities that need to be executed in order to provide a general direction, define top level goals and establish a basic organization in the setup of a corporate BPM.

**Process Strategy and Process Architecture**
This first phase of BPM focuses on the effectiveness of processes – to identify the processes that are relevant for a company to fulfill their corporate goals and to support the company's strategy. The relevant questions to be answered in this stage are[1]:

- "What processes are we actually executing?"
- "Are these processes relevant for our strategy?"
- "If not, can we apply standardized processes or even outsource them?"
- "If they are relevant for our strategy, are we good at these core processes or do we need to reengineer them?"

The target group for a process strategy is usually upper and top management. Their basic interest in this part of BPM is to ensure that the organization provides the appropriate process environment to be successful. They will not care about who is executing the processes, nor are they expecting deeper knowledge on the objects of the processes. Hence, a predicate-oriented representation like in a process architecture is the relevant result type (see Fig. 2). The process architecture is the big picture for the organization's process world. It identifies the main processes on the highest abstraction level.

---

[1] For further information on process strategy see [4], [5].

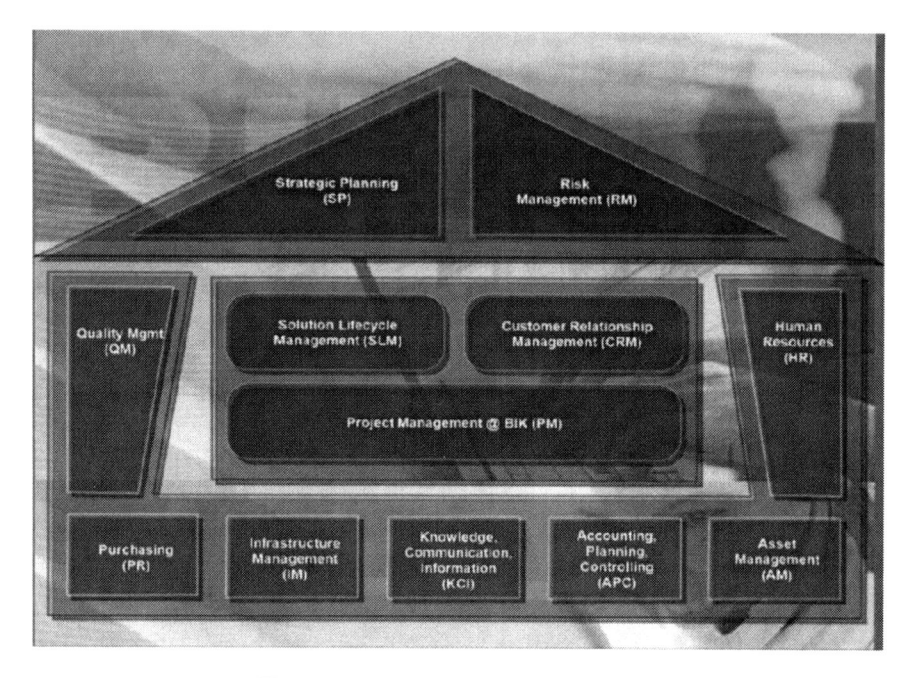

Fig. 2. Example for a process architecture

**Process Organization**
Every organization requires a definition of its roles, boards, committees and their related tasks. This is also true for a process organization. Modeling in the sense of visualizing this organization can be done in a simple org-chart or a table-oriented way

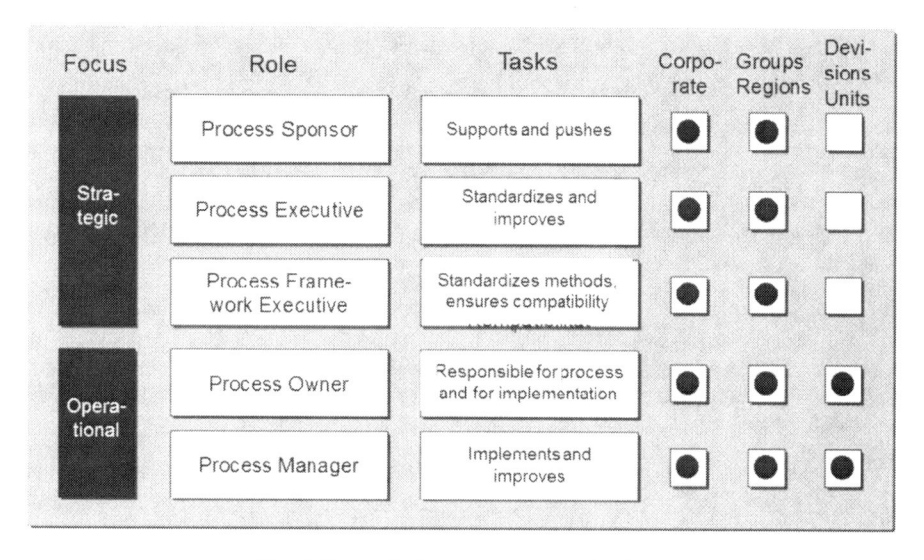

Fig. 3. Example for a process organization

of displaying subject and predicate information with the subject orientation clearly in the lead (see Fig. 3). Object-related enhancements of the process organization are usually only documented in roll descriptions or committee charters.

## 2.2 Operational BPM

The operational part of BPM focuses on everyday handling of processes on a practical level destined for process efficiency.

**Rules and Regulations**
Based on the strategic measures, rules and regulations operationalize the defined principles for processes. It contains the modeling methods and the special guidelines for establishing fixed modeling standards. The importance increases with the complexity of the organization and with the number of people involved. All process models must fit into the given process architecture.

Here is where the decision is announced what methodology has to be applied for what occasion and how the result types have to look like.

Since these rules and regulations usually resemble a hand book, its orientation (subject, predicate, and object) is not relevant.

**As-is-Processes and Process Analysis**
The as-is-processes draw the picture of the present. Manager in charge need these documentations to identify what steps are executed in what order. The owner of the respective activity is only important at a second glance. Even less important are required inputs, expected outputs, related rules and regulations as well as the tools employed. Taking this into account, a subject orientation at this stage of BPM does not make sense. Predicate-orientation is to be chosen as seen in Fig. 4, where an EPC[2] is applied.

Based on the documented as-is-processes, the analyst searches for improvement opportunities, e.g.

- sequential procedures where parallel execution could save time without threatening a proper result,
- redundant process steps or
- too complex tasks that should be split up in separate tasks.

Here again, the predicate-orientation prevails.

When looking at alternations of roles in charge, a more subject-orientated model would definitely help to visualize the improvement options. In practice a change from a straight EPC to a table-oriented EPC is chosen frequently.

---

[2] EPC = Event driven Process Chain.

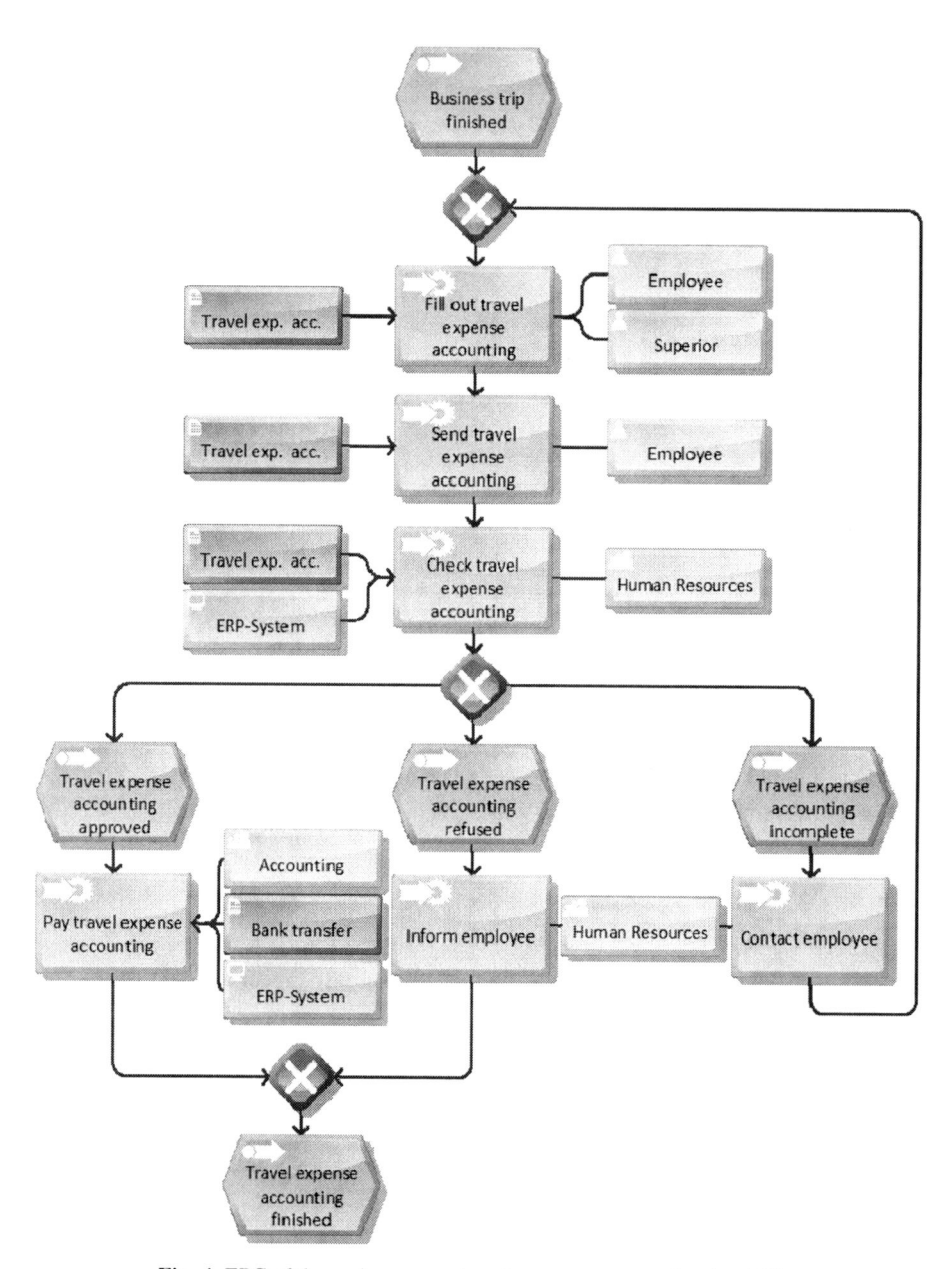

**Fig. 4.** EPC of the as-is-process travel expense accounting (see [6])

## Design of Target Processes
Based on the as-is-processes and the findings of the analysis, the target processes can be derived. In most cases the method of choice is a predicate-oriented visualization like EPC (or eEPC[3]) or Activity Diagrams out of the UML[4] family.

In case an IT implementation is very likely to follow the process optimization, for example as part of a portal solution, a slight subject-orientation might be added to the predicate-orientation by applying a BPMN[5] (compare [2]). The swim lanes help to identify the human or electronic roles involved (see Fig. 5).

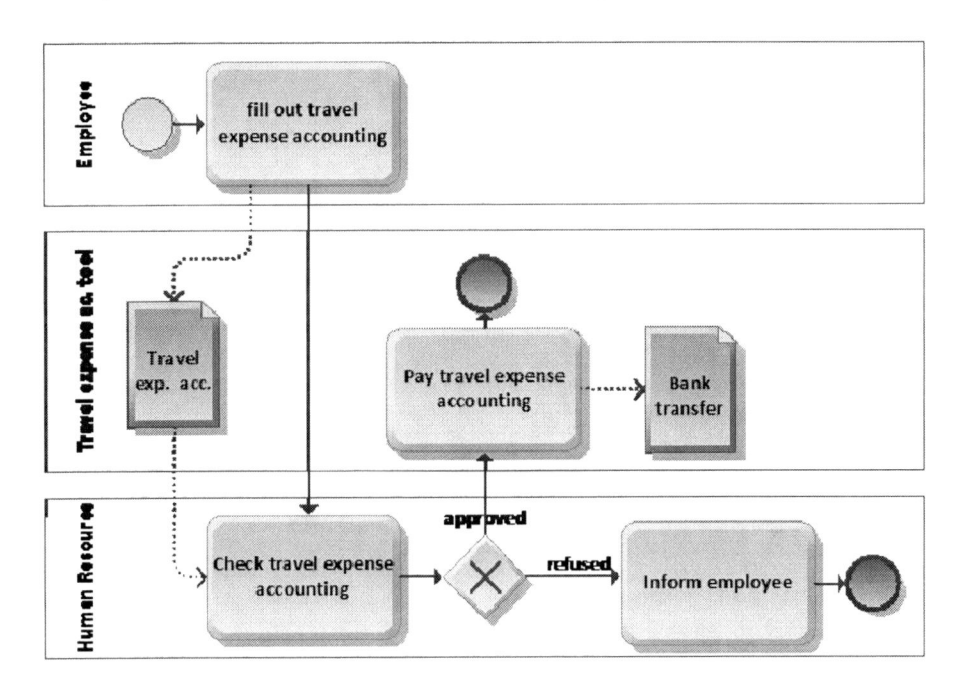

**Fig. 5.** BPMN of the Target Process travel expense accounting (see [6])

In practice even BPMN seems to bring business managers to the edge of their capabilities when asked to verify and sign off the respective models. EPCs or similar models depicting nothing more than just functions and statuses is the only content that can easily be grasped and evaluated by people in deciding positions. So even if there were models that would pave the way for easier implementation, their lack of acceptance would probably prevent them from becoming the new standard.

## Process Implementation and Execution
Process implementation is probably the most complex task and absolutely mission critical for companies. Unless the newly designed and optimized processes are in

---
[3] eEPC = enhanced Event driven Process Chain.
[4] UML = Unified Modeling Language.
[5] BPMN = Business Process Modeling and Notation (for details see [7]).

place and working, all earlier efforts are wasted. It is important to understand that IT solutions are only one means to implement processes. There is also the possibility of implementing organizational solutions to bring processes to life, e.g. through the adaptation of organizational structures or the publishing of rules to be obeyed. In most cases, though, IT solutions do support new processes. For this to be effectively done, S-BPM (see Fig. 6) can be a good support for object-oriented and functional specifications [8].

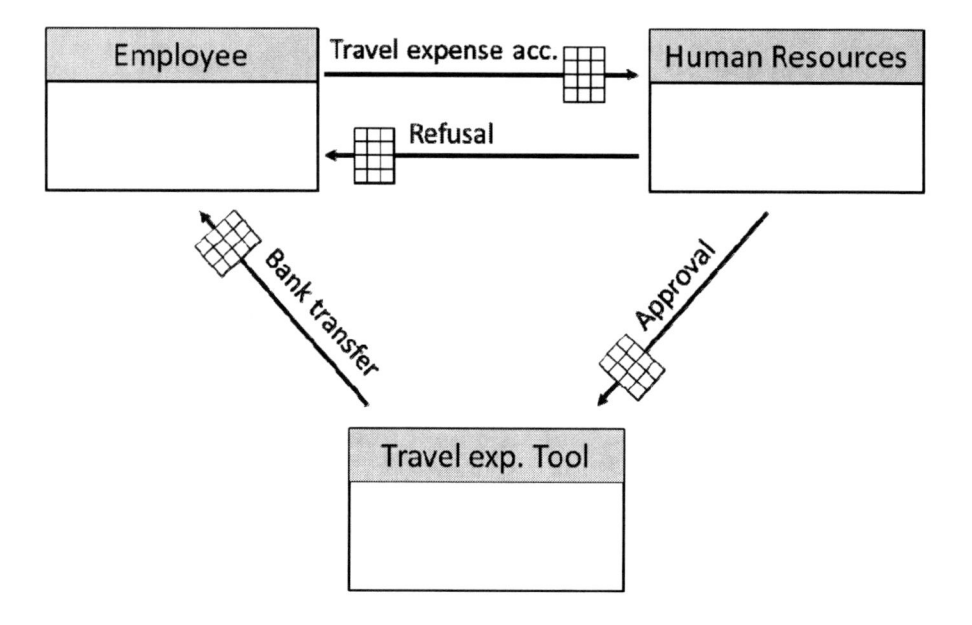

**Fig. 6.** Subject Interaction Diagram (SID) for the process travel expense accounting

In this step typically object-oriented software modeling methods are used, like for example UML state charts, ERM[6] or specific SOA[7]-related models (e.g. component diagrams, message diagrams).

**Process Execution**
In process execution usually no modeling is necessary. Process-oriented implementations relate all activities, status information, meetings and results (files) to the underlying process step and trigger escalation when the timeline attached to the process-instance (= project) is not matched by reality any more.

An example for a process-oriented Microsoft SharePoint solution can be seen in Fig. 7.

---

[6] ERM = Entity Relationship Model.
[7] SOA = Service Oriented Architecture.

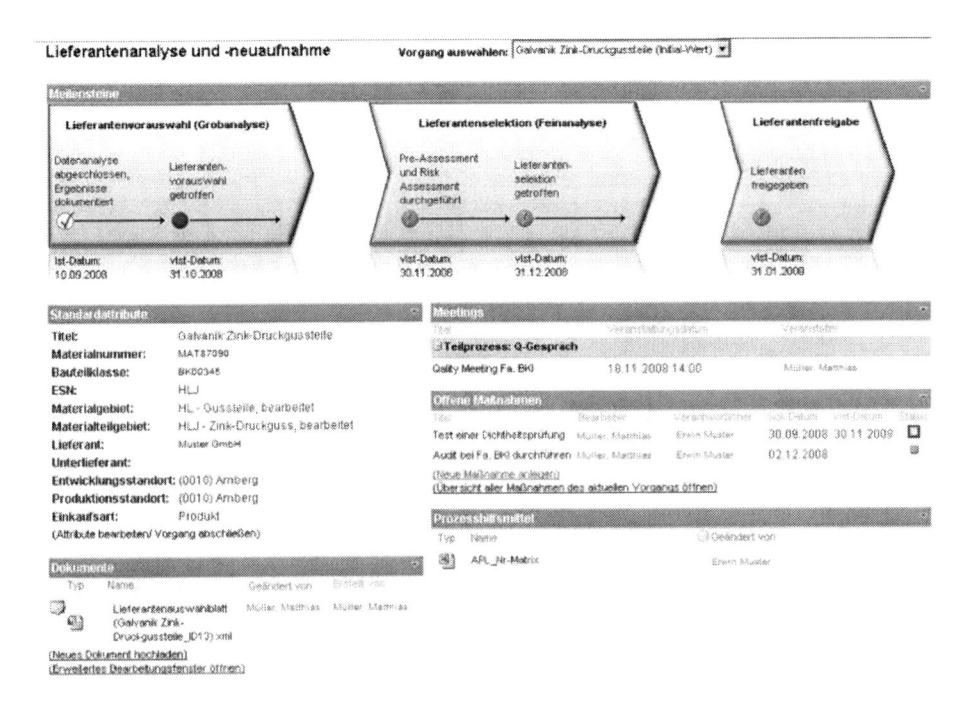

**Fig. 7.** MS SharePoint-based process implementation [9]

**Process Monitoring**

Developing KPI[8] to determine efficiency of process instance executions is usually part of the business process modeling. In some companies processes cannot be officially released without the KPI being defined and modeled.

In the ARIS-world measure points can be modeled into the EPC (see [10]), thus being part of a functional or predicate-oriented model. Alternatively, a more object-oriented KPI-model was developed in [11] to describe relationships of KPIs in a process performance metrics structure.

## 3 Challenges for a Coherent Modeling Environment

As shown in the first chapters of the article, BPM requires numerous modeling capabilities in order to visualize the relevant matters for the relevant people or roles. This leads to the necessity to change the view accordingly. Pure subject-orientation is an attempt to shortcut the way from process definition to executable IT solutions. But losing the decider´s acceptance on the transfer from as-is business statuses to IT-requirements is not an option to streamline a proper support of task execution on a company. In most organizations with no or few engineering orientation, more complex models than EPC or eEPC[9] are not bearable for everyday requirement definition.

---

[8] KPI = Key Performance Indicator.
[9] eEPC = enhanced EPC (functions and events are enriched by inputs, outputs, roles, rules, tools, etc.).

The challenges for the next years will be to define paths through the jungle of methods to coherently connect strategic business issues all the way through the stages of BPM as shown in 11. Transferring EPCs into BPMN is already state of the art, although with the large number of objects defined in BPMN and lots of subsets defined in the BPMN modeling tools, it still cannot be called a standardized interface. From BPMN it is only a small step to BPEL[10] definitions, allowing the direct execution of workflows in most modern workflow engines. Still, we will need ERM to define normalized and optimized data bases and less standardized methods in early stages of strategic BPM, e.g. to visualize a corporate process strategy.

The reason for different models is also the reason why there will hardly be a perfect interface path through all the relevant models. Every visualization has got a key strength, a reason, why it actually exists. Naturally, interfacing into a method or out of it into another method leads to a lack or a loss of information. Nevertheless it is our challenge to minimize these losses to be as integrated as possible. Looking at the ARIS house and the long time that this method collection has been around, it becomes obvious that even within one single tool environment not all models can be compatible with each other and that the transit from one model to another cannot be lossless.

## 4 Summary

From a consultant´s perspective it is important to bring across that BPM is not a mere documentation of processes and that it cannot be the only reason for BPM to provide an efficient way of bringing business requirements into IT solutions. A proper fit where methods and their visualizations meet the expectations of the ones to cope with the results must dominate the goal to develop software easily. BPM is a means to deal with processes as an organizational necessity as a whole and is not intended to replace CASE-tools!

From my perspective EPCs will for a long time lead the pool of methodologies to visualize processes in the documentation and optimization phases. Other methods need to be able to accept EPCs as an input and transfer EPC information into their own needs. The challenge will thus be to find more or less seamless interfaces connecting to EPCs.

## References

1. Fleischmann, A.: What Is S-BPM? In: Buchwald, H., Fleischmann, A., Seese, D., Stary, C., et al. (eds.) S-BPM ONE 2009. Communications in Computer and Information Science, vol. 85, pp. 85–106. Springer, Heidelberg (2010)
2. Schmidt, W., Fleischmann, A., Gilbert, O.: Subjektorientiertes Geschäftsprozessmanagement. In: Fröschle, H.-P., Reinheimer, S. (eds.) HMD266 – Geschäftsprozessmanagement, pp. 52–62. dpunkt, Heidelberg (2009)
3. Hungenberg, H.: Strategisches Management in Unternehmen. Gabler, Wiesbaden (2010)

---

[10] BPEL = Business Process Execution Language.

4. Porter, M.E.: What is strategy? Harvard Business Review, 1–20 (November-December 1996)
5. Keen, P.G.W.: The Process Edge – Creating value where it counts. Mcgraw-Hill Professional, New York (1997)
6. ARIS Express, http://www.ariscommunity.com/ (accessed April 4, 2011)
7. OMG, http://www.omg.org/spec/BPMN/2.0/PDF/ (accessed April 4, 2011)
8. Fischer, H., et al.: Subjektorientierte Modellierung und automatische Codegenerierung bei ERP-Prozessen. ERP Management 1, 22–24 (2005)
9. Hilgarth, B., et al.: ProcessSharePoint – ein Praxisbericht zur Lösung des Last-Mile-Problems in der Prozessimplementierung. In: Fröschle, H.-P., Reinheimer, S. (eds.) HMD266 – Geschäftsprozessmanagement, pp. 90–99. dpunkt, Heidelberg (2009)
10. Kronz, A.: Management von Prozesskennzahlen im Rahmen der ARIS-Methodik. In: Scheer, A.-W., et al. Corporate Performance Management, Berlin, pp. 31–44 (2005)
11. Strauch, S.: Entwicklung eines Modellierungswerkzeugs für Prozesskennzahlen. Master Thesis. University of Stuttgart (2008)

# Subject Modeling in Residential Care Services

Hans-Günter Lindner

Cologne University of Applied Sciences, Claudiusstr. 1, 50678 Cologne
hans-guenter.lindner@fh-koeln.de

**Abstract.** Residential Care Services operate under high pressure: Raising quality requirements collide with time and legally defined cost constraints. Different from other service branches, prices are not dependant on realized costs and services for patients' care. Residential care service employees' real activities and cognitive workloads were not taken into account. A detailed process model including subject modeling is overdue. The described process model is the first approach in Germany with the goal to optimize structures and processes in residential care services. Empirical values by an experience group are used to optimize the services and enable change management by building models and simulations. The article shows two parts of the reference model: The initial reception and the billing process. An example of a subject model in the initial reception process shows the usage in a standard tool for modeling and simulation. The results already changed the processes of participating companies of the experience group.

**Keywords:** residential care services, process modeling, optimization, simulation, adaptive feedback systems, change management, activity based costing, process costs, subject-oriented modeling.

## 1 Introduction

Residential care services cannot adjust their prices according to quality and performance. In Germany, prices for residential care services are regulated. They are not dependant on realized costs and services for patients' care. Quality requirements collide with needs for reducing time and costs. New legal standards do not consider financial impacts but cost rates are defined by health care service providers and more competition is supported by the German nursing insurance law. Residential care services suffer from inadequate financing and extended liquidity cycles. In negations for compensation no cost analyses for pricing are used regarding SGB V and SGB XI[1]. Actually, the practical discussions focus only costs and time. Parameters like cognitive workload and qualifications are not included but they are relevant for a real use of process optimization with respect to quality.

If prices are fixed, internal structures of care companies have to be adapted. One key to fill the gap between quality and profitability is process optimization. Therefore, Alexander Falkenberg, PMG-NRW GmbH and Hans-Günter Lindner, Cologne

---
[1] SGB = Sozialgesetzbuch (German social security statute book).

University of Applied Sciences started a cooperation to improve performance in residential care services [1]. The first milestone was a reference model of complex activities in care processes to fulfill legal requirements in daily operations. It is the first approach in Germany, maybe because these processes were wrongfully assumed as fairly simple in the past.

Empirical data is collected from participants of an experience group and hereafter estimated by experts to allow proper simulation scenarios. The models include activities, subjects and their parameters. There are two advantages of the model. Firstly, care services may learn to improve their performance and quality individually. Secondly, care services and associations will take advantage in negotiations to fill the gap between effort and compensation.

Current approaches to model residential care processes result in descriptions of common life cycles. Business cases address practitioners and mention emotionally influenced details like "help for dressing, washing body, defecation makes 19 minutes, wearing compression stockings 5 minutes, travelling time 6 minutes". No descriptions can be found for customer reception, internal accounting and billing. Although, a newer expert report from the University Witten-Herdecke outlines more common conclusions concerning costs: "…for essential services longer durations and higher compensations according to performance are necessary" [2], the data found during an investigation are not sufficient for a simulation model[2]. On the one hand, current research in process optimization mainly addresses services in hospitals [3] but this is totally different to residential care services, though both areas use the name care services. On the other hand, research for residential care services mainly addresses medicinal content. There is no literature that covers the field of process modeling, simulation and optimization in residential care services with respect to economical issues. Only one expertise deals with the initial reception of customers and [4] one advertising publications can be found, e.g. from Guidon Performance Solutions [5] about process optimization in health insurance billing. Though billing service providers offer solutions for care services, they do not cover internal process improvements and efforts for private care service companies.

Therefore, students of the Cologne University of Applied Sciences launched a survey on health care service providers in Germany but received no answers. The necessity for a detailed process model was given. Meanwhile, the opta data group in Essen, Germany, joined the project to support further studies. Together with opta data, the project members and participants of an experience group collect data about process behavior and qualifications. The first results for Germany will be presented at the "Experten Forum Pflege" in Mallorca in June 2011.

## 2 Process Optimization and Simulation

The approach adjusts parameters of residential care services to increase sustainable performance. In this project, parameters are costs, time, use of resources, human qualifications and cognitive workload. Optimization does not mean costs cutting at all because an increase of costs may lead to higher qualification, more effective cost relocation and better workforce management. It is not only dependent on time and

---

[2] The information is based on a conversation with the University Witten-Herdecke.

money! Optimization in residential care services is not a technical issue that allows algorithms to change parameters in processes like in a production process. The care service is a mainly people driven process.

The optimization mechanism is based on the model of adaptive feedback systems without model comparison [6] with two cascades depicted in Fig 1. The core feedback system consists of the individual care service company's goals, a comparator, care service management, care service employees, their output (actions and information) and the inner loop. The comparison of employees' output and goals lead to perceived differences by the management that acts like a regulator to achieve minimal disparities by the right instruction to employees. The outer loop system compares the individual company's results to legal constraints including the obligatory quality measurement system. These constraints depend on the German state where the service company is located. Associations, health insurance and politics are the regulators in the outer system. Only if there is an optimized reference model, these instances can be influenced in a longer period which is a long time goal and not part of the optimization explained is this article.

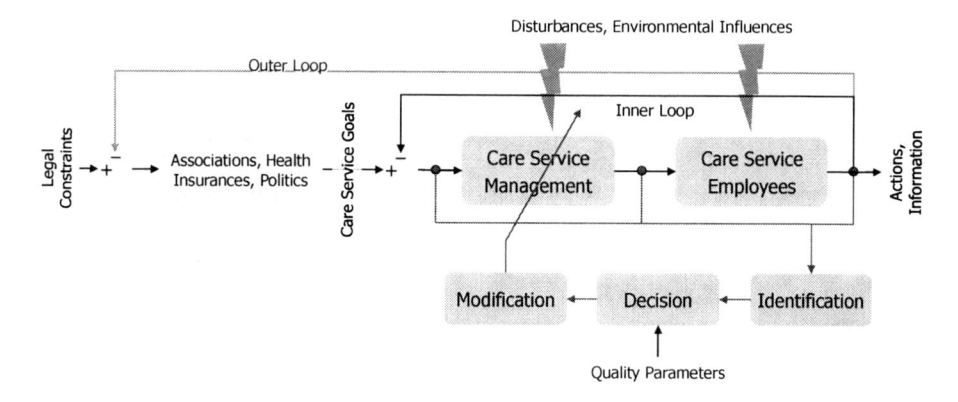

**Fig. 1.** Collecting data for simulation

Though, there is feedback in the two loops, learning is not included because the actors internal structures, i.e. cognitive models, are not changed. Actors do not change their behavior and organizational structures because they think their cognitive models are complete. The loops only cover operative feedback. Only change management and the variation of structures and processes happen if the actors and especially the management as a regulator changes its overall behavior. The potential function for change is depicted by the diagonal arrow over care service management. But this change only happens if an adaptive system is added to the regular feedback system. The adaptive supplement contains the three stages identification, decision and modification. The identification collects inputs and outputs of acting persons and fills the process models as a part of this stage. Depending on quality parameters, the assumed decisions from the actors show consequences by using simulation. The derived results lead to modifications that influence care service management. As a consequence, the adaptive supplement changes the decision makers' cognitive models because it makes the changes explicit. A prerequisite for an overall optimization is a shared common model that is the reference model.

From theories of change management like Peter Senge's fifth disciplines [7] and the SECI-model of Nonaka/Takeuchi [8] the core dimensions for changing residential care service can be derived. Senge's model demands personal mastery, mental models, team learning, shared vision and as a central element systems thinking. Nonaka and Takeuchi assume the cycle of socialization, externalization, combination and internalization for information creation and innovating companies. This leads to the necessity of a systemic view for care services that can be achieved by externalizing the implicit behavior using process models. Modeling and the consecutive discussion of resulting models with heterogeneous participants in this domain leads to a broader mental model of care service management and team learning. The precondition of the willingness for personal mastery and a shared vision is given for experience groups that are moderated by the project members because all participants want an efficient organization and are intrinsically motivated that is proven by their participation. The process models give them a systemic view that is only implicit before participating in a modeling workshop. During the workshop the knowledge is explicitly collected by metaplan technique and drawing process models with Bonapart. Then, the models are simulated and show all participants the consequences of their knowledge. This method contains the three steps of the adaptive supplement. Here, simulation is our method to analyze the dynamic systems of residential care services based on process models.

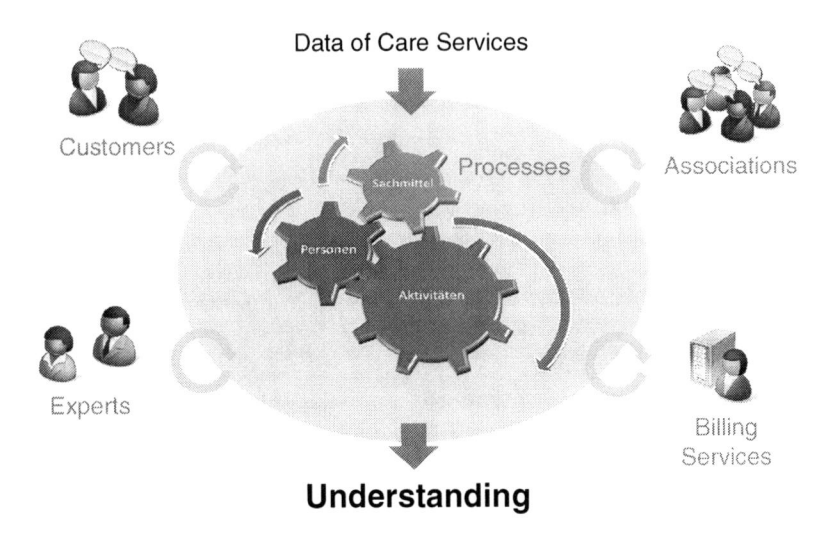

**Fig. 2.** Collecting data for a distributed cognitive model

As a result, systems thinking is individually implemented to enable further organizational change. This is why figure 2 is so important: The optimization is based on a common understanding of a unified distributed cognitive model that is filled with values given by experts, customers, health care associations and billing services.

Results from experience groups in modeling workshops show that people that are not well educated in business science and even worse in process modeling directly understand economic constraints after discovering dynamic process models. The participants are able to define their process very quickly and perceive a unified model by structured discussions, starting from individual cognitive distributed models. Behavioral changes appeared between two workshops and improvements are reflected by the other participants. Our simulation results lead to an externalization resp. visualization of behavior, resource constraints and distributions of costs and time. When individual data derived from individual experiences and the reference model is compared, benchmarking can be done. This continuous work leads to an optimized model of residential care services and is finalized in our common reference model. A resulting experience is that process models and the optimization itself is no longer the focus of discussions and will not perceived as a part of the problem that appears when processes are only drafted.

## 3 The Reference Model

The reference model is based on a generalized organizational structure and the four core processes initial reception, planning, care and billing. In this article only the two processes initial reception and billing are described. The initial reception process serves as an entry to advise new customers and to collect customer master data. This leads to the planning process that coordinates all activities under influence of relatives. All services have to be integrated in a route and a staff plan. The care process follows. Beside care services and quality regulations, it includes transfers to and from patients. Finally, the billing process collects all services and divides them in several modules according type and number of service providers. This process requires continuous documentation in the form of performance records that have to be signed by patients and nurses.

The model was built in BTC's Bonapart, a process modeling tool with simulation mechanisms based on colored level three petri nets [9]. In this article, the two processes initial reception and billing are repainted in diagrams that combine KSA [10, 11] and BPMN [12] together with swimlanes. The author found out that this combination is easy understandable for practitioners. KSA models processes are free of redundancy and show the use of info containers resp. storage and resources. BPMN helps to explain the process structure with slightly better semantics, but some icons have to be redesigned for better acceptance and meaning.

### 3.1 The Organizational Structure

The organigram maps the legal minimum requirements and is easy applicable in practice (Fig. 3). The management division is staffed by the owner. The operative management, the so called PDL (Pflegedienstleitung i.e. head of nursing services) is commonly done by the owner. The PDL coordinates and controls administration, care

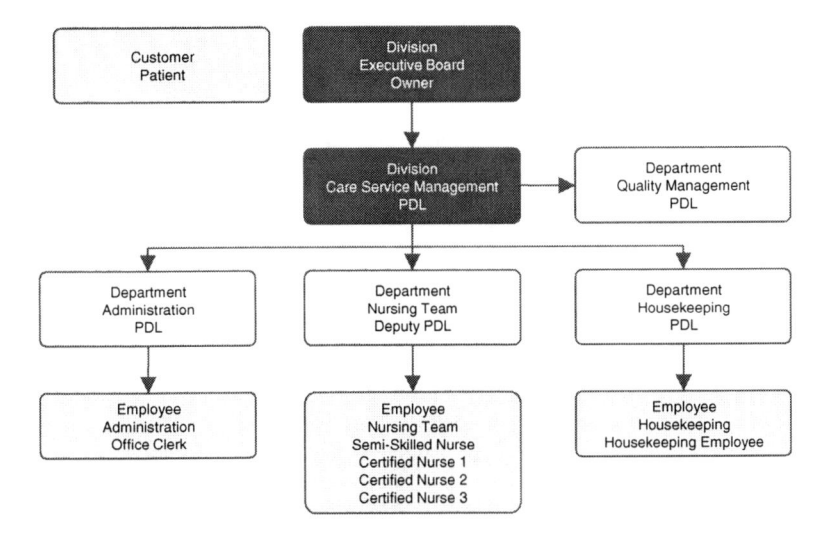

Fig. 3. Reference organigram of residential care services

operations and housekeeping and is responsible for care, tour and roster plans. A typical problem is the PDL's conflict between management and operative responsibilities. The deputy PDL plans and organizes invoicing, contracts, documentation and partially customer support. Responsibilities are administration of customer and personnel records, master data management, correspondence and further organizational tasks. The PDL controls the deputy's results and therefore the PDL controls partially itself.

The quality management is located under the PDL, mostly as a staff department that is staffed by the PDL itself. Quality management has to be done in addition to care service that leads to conflicts, especially if it is the PDL. The care team consists of three certified nurses and one semi-skilled nurse for operational care service plus the PDL because five persons are legally required. One office clerk and one person for housekeeping complement the care team.

## 3.2 The Initial Reception Process

The so called initial reception process is the initial reception of customers combined with initial reception (Fig 4). Normally, the customer calls the service, eventually the customer in on-site and arranges an appointment. The PDL drives to the customers within 10 minutes on average. An interview with the patient and relatives of 60 minutes on average follows. The admission is recorded in paper form or directly in a mobile computer. The PDL returns from the customer or directly drives to the next patient. Returning home, an offer is worked out using PC, price list and printer. Then, the offer is sent by the office clerk.

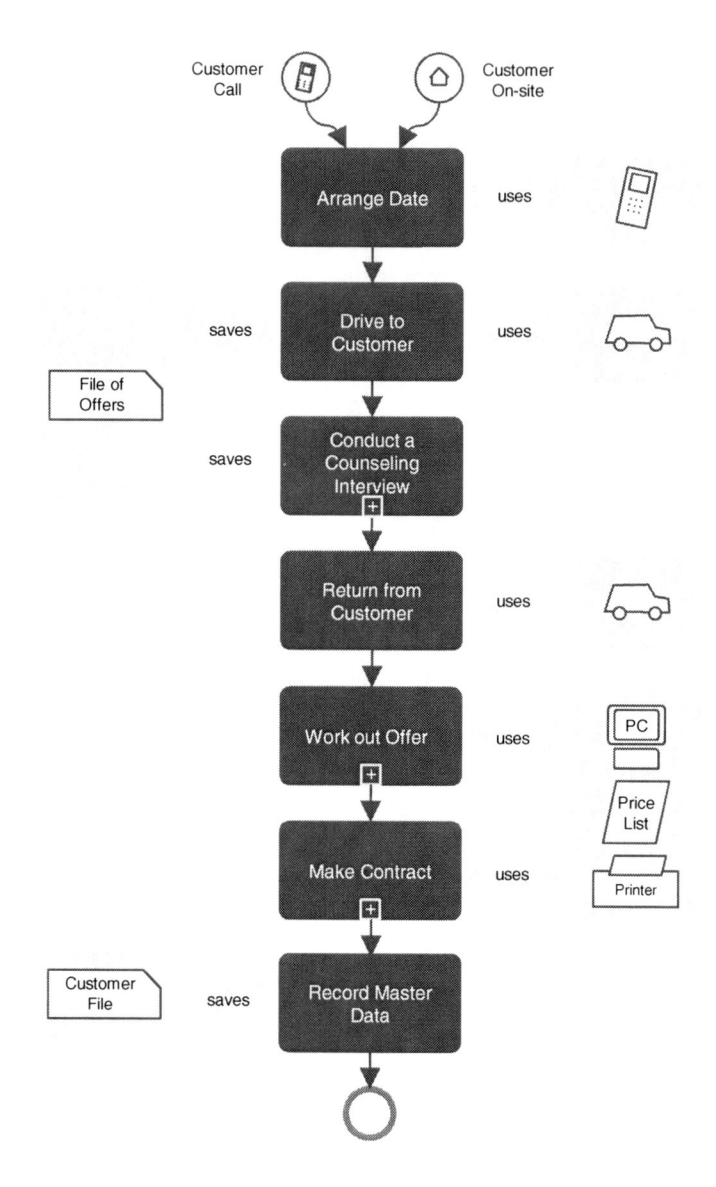

**Fig. 4.** The initial reception process

If the offer is accepted by the customer, the PDL records the patient's master data, the office clerk finalizes the contract which will be handed out to the patient personally for signing. The interview, contract and offer preparation includes further processes and activities. Contracts may be refused if the profitability is too low or the service cannot be fulfilled adequately.

Exemplary entries of one participant in the experience groups for modeling system in the initial reception process are partially shown in table 1. The values in this table do not cover the whole range of observations from all participants. To cover practical experience, we take all samples, derive mean, standard deviation and measures for asymmetry. Since Bonapart handles different types of distributions, the simulation is more realistic. For each activity the designer has to decide the kind of distribution with appropriate parameters. Additionally, we directly use the sample data for an input. Experiences with the experience group show that it is necessary to discuss the distribution of data with the participants that increases the understanding of the model.

**Table 1.** Modeling parameter example of the initial reception process

| Activity | Position | Time (min.) | Physical resources | Physical resources costs (€) | Personnel costs (€) |
|---|---|---|---|---|---|
| Customer calls, arrange date | Office clerk | 8 | Phone, PC | 0,7 | 13,65 |
| Drive to customer | PDL | 10 | Car | 10 | 18,85 |
| Cuonduct a counseling interview | PDL | 60 | Phone, PC, paper | 3 | 18,85 |
| Return from customer | PDL | 10 | Car | 10 | 18,85 |
| Work out offer | PDL | 5 | PC, printer | 0,5 | 18,85 |
| Send offer | Office clerk | 2 | Envelope, postage | 0,6 | 13,65 |
| Make contract | Office clerk | 10 | PC, printer | 0,5 | 13,65 |
| Make contract | PDL | 5 | PC, printer | 0,5 | 18,85 |
| Bring contract to customer | Nurse | 20 | Car | 10 | 15,08 |
| Record master data | PDL | 10 | PC, printer, price list | 0,5 | 18,85 |

It is not necessary to capture all parameters for each care service. Only main deviations are important because other parameters are already included in the reference model. This is an advantage because only parts have to be adapted and a simulation can quickly run to show results.

### 3.3 The Billing Process

The billing process starts at the end of a month. The condition is a valid medical ordinance that was sent from the service provider to the care service. Required documents are completed duplicated resp. divided for specific health care service providers. The bill is worked out. All activities below are done by the PDL. The office clerk only prepares documents like making the ordinance available or packaging the postal items that is relevant in subordinate processes.

A part of the billing process starts again if returns have to be handled again. The reasons of refusal and the bills' attachments are analyzed as well as errors are corrected. The correct bills are accepted form the health insurance and invoice receipts can be booked. Incoming transfers are received online and the final step is accomplished.

Figure 5 shows the billing process without underlying processes. The first layer looks quite easy but is complex in practice. The separation of partial bills is very complex and forecasts cannot be made. Therefore the simulation helps to calculate different scenarios under various conditions.

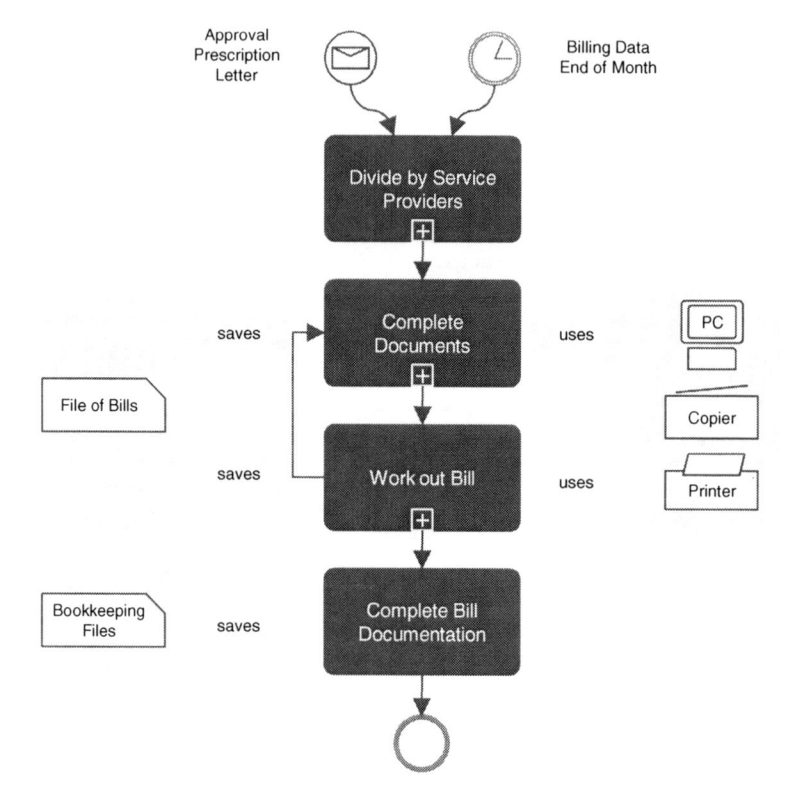

**Fig. 5.** The billing process

## 4 Subject Modeling

The critical issue in modeling residential care systems is to model acting persons, the subjects. Explicit activities normally perceived by process owners can be executed in given time with given rules. As could be seen in the past negotiations for care services, thinking about services does not include humans' implicit processes and their interaction. This is one of the reasons why costs rates are inadequate, personnel development is underdeveloped or resources are used wrongly. Especially the care process shows underlying processes that are implicit because they are located inside persons. The time to medicate and to nurse does not only depend on technical tools and perceivable tasks. Good care services cover emphatic relationships with patients. The empathic conversation needs resources that have to be used parallel to medicinal tasks. Therefore, medication and patient-based communication needs higher concentration, more resources and more time.

This approach tries to model implicit cognitive processes. Process borders do not stop at the human interface. They extend explicit perceivable activities with internal activities of subjects. Classical process modeling software systems do not cover subject modeling as a feature. Some players in the market only address subjects but have no functions to provide human modeling. A typical way to model subjects is to parameterize holders of positions in an organigram or to use swimlanes for subjects. But this is only one side of the medal: Parts of the cognitive structures have to modeled, too.

In a first step we had to model the organigram and the acting subjects (Fig. 3). As an example, simulation results in figure 6 show the timely workload for departments and their staff. The upper right windows shows the waiting jobs over time (x-axis) for the care team. The lower right windows illustrates a high capacity during the period of billing.

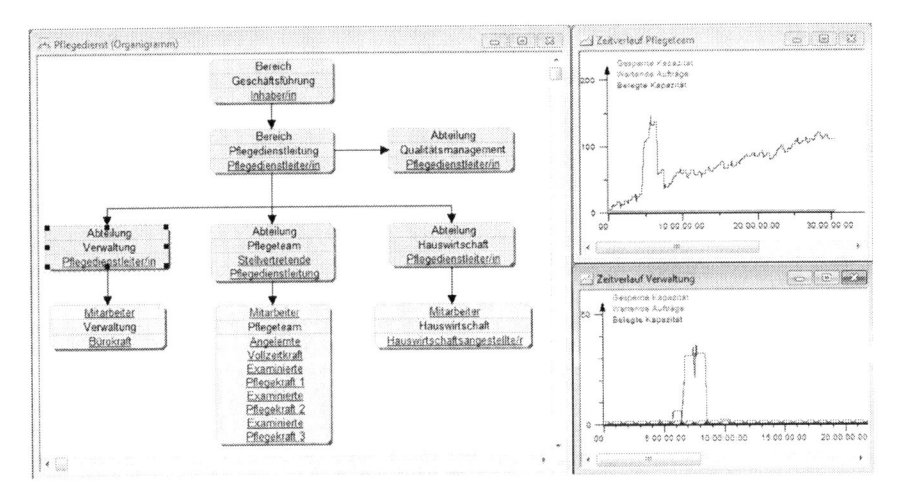

**Fig. 6.** Simulation results of departments and staff

Job holders can be included with assigned tasks for a later consistency analysis (Fig. 7) but for simulation, normally only costs and time are relevant.

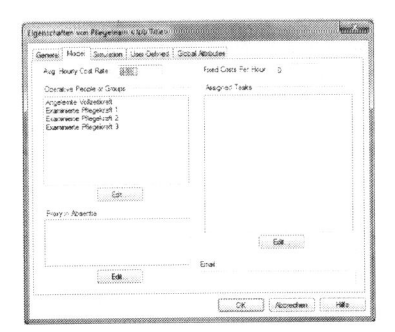

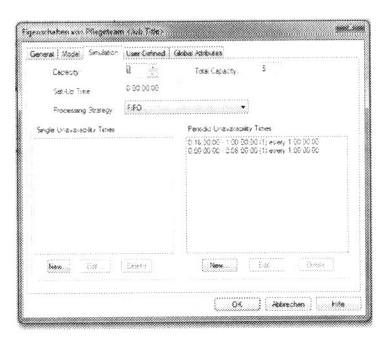

**Fig. 7.** Modeling parameters in Bonapart

In Bonapart, values for costs, time and capacity can be used for dynamic simulation but subjects' properties only for static reasons. This needs a new usage of standard elements for subject modeling that will be shown below.

Based on the idea that processes do not end at the human interface, the processes have to be overlapping. Therefore, internal processes of subjects must be modeled as an extension of explicit processes and standard elements are used to reflect subject properties.

Figure 8 shows the nurse subject model for the communication with a patient. After arriving at the patient, a reception takes place that gives information to the patient. Then, a presentation of the service follows. The next step is the recording of the patient's model. An info container is the patient model, a resource the communication skill. The subject processes need further input like questions to be asked because the initial simulation token is the visit of a customer. The output condition is of type "information based" and not a normal one that mirrors the probability of an output. After the patient modeling, an offer is outlined and coordinated. Figure 8 depicts the process and the workload to build the patient model and the patient activities. On the left hand side, the process is shown and on the right hand side the simulation results for building an patient model and the communication during the process. The x-axes show time, the y-axes the number of waiting jobs in red and the active jobs in blue color.

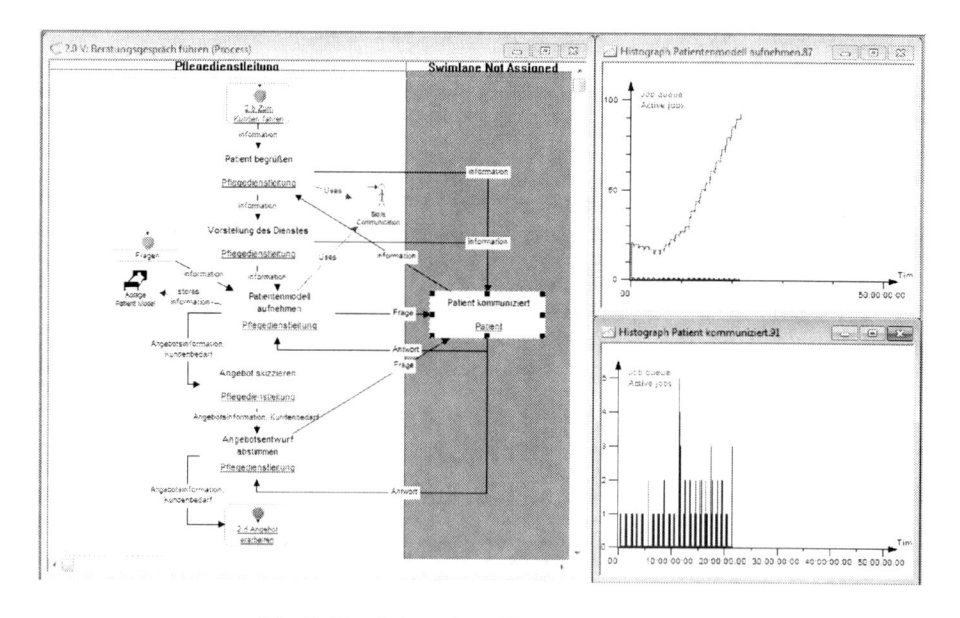

**Fig. 8.** Simulation of a subject-based process

The simulation outlines a gradually increasing workload (the upper right window) that normally would not be taken into account. The lower right windows shows the communication workload that lasts nearly the whole simulation period. This is only the first step to model human partners but exemplifies the possibilities that a standard simulation software like Bonapart is able to manage subject modeling. Mainly important is as new thinking of processes when subjects are modeled: Processes do not stop at the human interface and need cognitive modeling.

The subjects' part of the simulation model may not only lead to the conclusion that employees are inadequately paid, what is only partially true. High cognitive workload may be an indicator for inefficient operations. In the case of long communication time, a qualification course in patient's conversation may be appropriate. Alternatively, the process has to be restructured, e.g. a well structured questionnaire in the initial reception process helps to reduce time.

## 5 Conclusions

Residential care services have to optimize their work since legal constraints and economic developments will threaten their survival. Fix costs remain because head count cannot be reduced and quality is legally required. There is a shift from cost cutting to smart optimization of the residential care companies structure, processes and qualifications. For optimization, a reference model is required as the main part of an adaptive feedback system.

Change management was introduced based on general theories. The optimization process is done in cooperation with experience groups which share their cognitive models to build a common reference model to improve their companies and built better argumentation in negotiations with health insurance and service providers. Subject modeling is appreciated from the group because subject oriented simulation leads to a deeper understanding that influences more parameters than normally taken into account. The primary results of an optimization should be a redesign of organizational structures, processes and behavior which as a consequence affect cost and time.

Since the effort of two processes initial reception and billing contains underestimated costs and side effects, the reference model started to analyze them together with an experience group. All samples are statistically evaluated and transformed in the reference model for a simulation that is highly related to practical issues. Together with workshops the reference model gives the chance to orientate on best practices. The proven results from the experience group will be published exclusively in a conference in June 2011.

The main advantage of the model and the modeling process is the creation of awareness. The understanding of complex processes and their dynamics leads to a surprising effect and new insights for an intrinsic motivated change of economic behavior. Subject-oriented models help process owners feel understood. Without understanding, process optimization whether subject-oriented or not, process optimization is only a piece of paper.

## References

1. Lindner, H.-G., Falkenberg, A.: Transparente Prozesse – Mit optimierten Unternehmensabläufen die Leistungsfähigkeit ambulanter Dienste steigern. Häusliche Pflege, 20–26 (March 2011)
2. CAREkonkret, Nr. 48, (December 3, 2010)

3. Blonksi, H., Strausberg, M. (eds.): Prozessmanagement in Pflegeorganisationen. Schlütersche, Hannover (2003)
4. Görres, S., Zimmermann, M., Schmitt, S.: Grundlagen zur Bemessung des Erstgesprächs / Erstbesuchs in der ambulanten Pflege, bpa, Berlin (2011)
5. Guidon Performance Solutions (2011), http://www.guidonps.com/default/assets/File/Process_Optimization_Health_Insurance_Case_Study.pdf
6. Unbehauen, H.: Regelungstechnik, Bd. III - Identifikation, Adaption, Optimierung, pp. 133, Braunschweig et al (1988)
7. Senge, P.: The Fifth Discipline: The Art & Practice of The Learning Organization. Crown Business, New York (2006)
8. Nonaka, I., Takeuchi, H.: The Knowledge-Creating Company: How Japanese Companies Create the Dynamics of Innovation. Oxford University Press, New York (1995)
9. http://www.btc-ag.com/de/bonapart.htm
10. http://bonapart.btc-ag.com/pdf/BTC_Factsheet_KSA_Methode_200090806.pdf
11. Krallmann, H., Schönher, M., Trier, M. (eds.): Systemanalyse im Unternehmen - Prozessorientierte Methoden der Wirtschaftsinformatik, Oldenbourg, München, Wien, p. 115 (2007)
12. http://www.omg.org/spec/BPMN/2.0/PDF/

# Project4Sure X: Accelerating Implementation Projects for the Microsoft Dynamics Suite with BPM 2.0

Matthias Kurz[1], Thomas Schaller[2], Dominik Reichelt[2], and Michael Ferschl[3]

[1] Lehrstuhl Wirtschaftsinformatik II, Universität Erlangen-Nürnberg,
Lange Gasse 20, 90403 Nürnberg
matthias.kurz@wiso.uni-erlangen.de
[2] Institut für Informationssysteme, Hochschule Hof,
Alfons-Goppel-Platz 1, 95028 Hof
{thomas.schaller,dominik.reichelt}@iisys.de
[3] impuls Informations management GmbH, Deutschherrnstr. 15-19,
90429 Nürnberg
michael.ferschl@impuls-nbg.de

**Abstract.** Implementation projects for the Microsoft Dynamics NAV, AX, and CRM family are typically conducted according to the Sure Step methodology. The Project4Sure approach extends this methodology with a software solution that assists in managing and controlling large implementation projects. This contribution proposes an extension to the Project4Sure methodology and software platform that provides a process centric approach to analyzing and realizing business requirements for projects implementing the above-mentioned ERP systems. While classical ERP implementation approaches tend to focus on the requirements laid out by managers and the IT department, the new approach integrates concepts of BPM 2.0. By utilizing the expertise of the individuals in the operational departments, it can be ensured that ERP implementations match the requirements of the actual business users.

**Keywords:** Microsoft NAV, ERP, Implementation, Project4Sure, Sure Step, BPM 2.0.

## 1 Introduction

Business software systems are often compared to the nervous system of animals. Within such applications, the actions of one (or more companies) are coordinated using information exchange. So – if not properly planned – the modification of a business software system can be an operation running a high risk of leading to system malfunctions.

According to [1] and the 2009 Standish Group "Chaos Report" [2], there is a significant rate of software projects failing or running out of time and budget (Fig. 1). The Chaos Report mentions a list of failures typically made before or within the project such as:

- Unclear objectives of the project and incomplete requirements
- Lacking know-how about the business processes

- Resource shortages
- Technology illiteracy
- Improper planning and project management

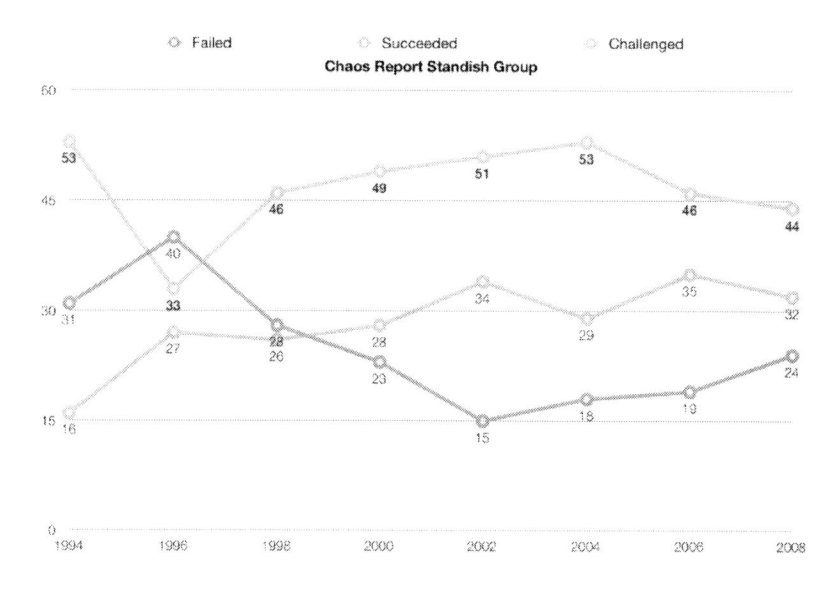

**Fig. 1.** Failed, challenged and succeeded IT projects [2]

In order to address these problems, the use of a proper process model accompanied by an appropriate project management approach is often proposed. As the number of succeeded projects is a crucial quality metric that is directly affecting the sales of ERP products such as Microsoft Navision, Microsoft proposed the *Sure Step* software project management method in 2007 for its partners. Beside project management issues, the field of requirements engineering plays a central role in the Microsoft approach.

In the following we will describe Sure Step shortly and give a brief overview over Project4Sure, the software incarnation of Sure Step provided by Nuremberg based impuls GmbH. After that we will focus on the BPM 2.0 approach and suggest how Project4Sure (and Sure Step) can be extended with concepts and tools this approach has to offer. The article concludes with the presentation of a prototype and a critical discussion of the actual findings.

## 2 Sure Step

### 2.1 Intention and Structure

Sure Step [12] is Microsoft's official project management method for implementing MS Dynamics NAV, AX and CRM projects. Sure Step started in 2001 as a project named *OnTarget* and evolved to *Sure Step 2010* passing several intermediate versions.

The method offers a large quantity of tools, best practices and documentation templates with a strong focus on the implementation of ERP systems. In parallel to the classic waterfall model, an ERP project is divided into the objectives, diagnosis, analysis, design, development, operation, and maintenance phases. During all steps, the client and the business partner have to fulfill different roles prescribed by the framework. In the following we will give some insights into these steps.

During the *objectives* step, the scope of the project has to be determined. Besides the definition of these objectives, an infrastructure assessment, a first estimation of the fits and gaps of the software, a rough calculation of the budget, and a high level project plan are results.

The classical requirements engineering is done in the *analysis* stage. At this point in the project, the business process models have to be defined. It is important to know that the method dictates no specific process modeling method like the widespread event driven process chain. Consequently, the partner is free to choose a preferred method. The single activities of a process are described using functional requirements documents (FRDs). In parallel, a data migration plan is developed. These documents are used for the refinement of the gap-fit analysis, the budget estimation, and the project plan.

Within the *design* stage, the configuration of the target software platform and the solution design related to gaps have to be developed. Concerning the functional requirements and the data migration needs, a set of solution design documents (in case of a fit), a set of technical design documents (in case of a gap) and a set of test case documents have to be developed. At the end of this step, the business partner is able to communicate a fixed price to the client.

In the *development* step, the system modifications and the data migration functionalities are coded and tested using both unit and system tests. In addition, the technical and end user documentation has to be written.

During the deployment phase, the client system environment has to be finalized. Moreover, the end user trainings are set up and carried out. This step ends with the final data migration and the *go live* of the system.

Within the *operations* phase, the post go live support starts. The phase comprises the handling of bugs and change requests, both resulting in the modification of technical as well as end user documentation.

The linear steps presented above are supported by so-called cross phase processes that focus on the organization, the solution and technology management.

## 2.2 Potentials and Limits

The employment of the Sure Step methodology opens up significant potentials for the accomplishment of software projects to come, independent from the final product and on a constantly high level of quality. The basis for this successful outcome is formed by the standardized process models and templates provided by the methodology. Additional potentials emerge from the acceptance of the methodology by more than 8.000 IT service providers and the synergetic effects resulting from this wide acceptance. As an example, bottlenecks that occur during the allocation of resources can be balanced quickly and efficiently by adding resources of other companies. Due to the standardized processes, an often-laborious training effort can be omitted. As a consequence of the well-defined roles within the Sure Step methodology, responsibilities are accurately and clearly assigned. This immensely alleviates the risk of tasks not being executed because of unclear responsibility scopes. The wide range of adoption of the Sure Step methodology throughout the whole landscape of Microsoft partners yields immense additional synergies for its continuous improvement. Based on the experience of the individual companies with the methodology, every revision of Sure Step makes it more efficient and effective, without adversely affecting established standards.

No matter how important theoretical standards and their methodical employment are, they approach their limits whenever their practical execution is concerned. In such situations, the fact that Sure Step is essentially a theoretical model of an approach – complemented by various templates – comes to notice.

## 3 Project4Sure

### 3.1 Overview

Project4Sure (P4S) represents the concrete embodiment of the Sure Step project management approach on the basis of a Microsoft Office SharePoint Server 2007 based environment.

Consequently, it represents a collaboration platform that accompanies consultants as well as customers throughout all phases of the Sure Step methodology. The aim of this implementation is to provide a clear and orderly execution of the introduction of the ERP system. The main objective is to provide clarity and transparency about the implementation project to all stakeholders.

Due to its origin in the Sure Step methodology, the structure of the platform reflects the principal steps of that approach (cf. Fig. 2).

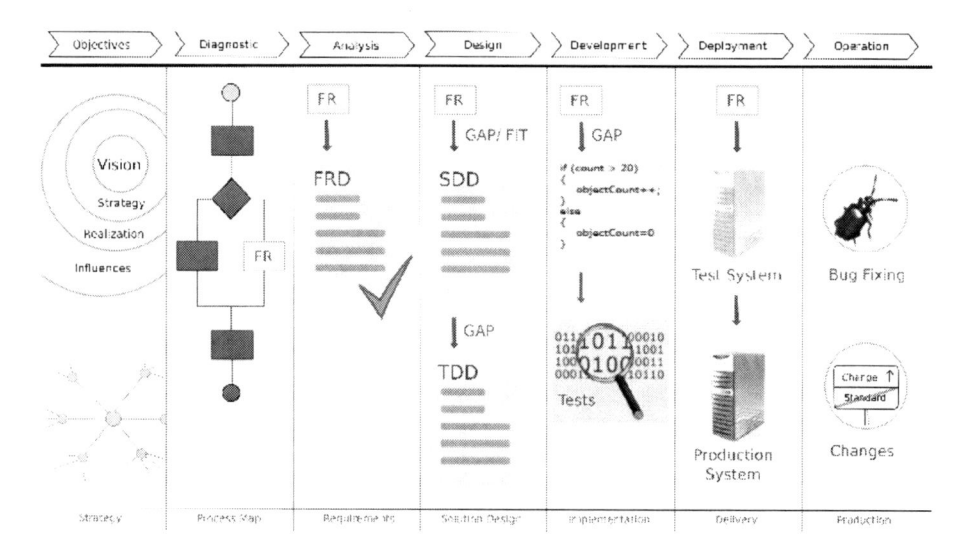

**Fig. 2.** Project4Sure methodology overview

In addition to the main methodology steps, Project4Sure provides common administrative features that are required in all stages of the project, such as contact management, a project calendar, a centralized to-do list and much more. This also includes modules that facilitate the creation of agendas for events and a common glossary that helps in defining common terms between customer, developers and consultants. Another very useful component is a central repository of risks associated with the project.

In order to integrate the platform with the environment of the project team and the customer, the Project4Sure platform provides management functionalities for document templates as well as stakeholder roles.

The first preparatory stage of the methodology is the *objectives* phase. Its purpose is to determine a consistent IT strategy together with the customer, as well as the scope of the project as seen from the management perspective. Consequently, the processes that are actually relevant for the project are identified - especially in consideration of future prospects.

Subsequently, the platform assists in the execution of the *diagnostic* phase, which is actually the first part of the analysis stage. As described previously, its main objective is the compilation of high level functional requirements and their dependencies. This leads to the concrete assembly of a hierarchical high-level process map and consequently to the definition of subprojects as well as a categorized functional requirement list.

Another significant part of this stage is the carrying out of a gap/fit analysis. Bundled tools, e.g. for functional requirements engineering, can increase the productivity of this step. Especially the import of processes modeled in Microsoft Visio into Project4Sure and the classification of their individual components as belonging to either the gap or the fit category is intuitive. Result artifacts of this stage are solution design documents (SDD) as well as technical design documents (TDD) in case of a gap.

The collaborative nature of the platform allows for an active integration of the customer and other stakeholders as well as the definition of approval workflows. Additionally, risks associated with the individual process steps can be documented and stored centrally.

With the current state roughly defined in the diagnostic step and the strategic goals defined in the objectives phase as described above, the execution of the *analysis* phase can be resumed on a more fine-grained level. Assisted by the Project4Sure platform, a more detailed functional requirements documentation is compiled. Platform features such as document versioning, the integrated release and approval management as well as the employment of customizable document templates facilitate these document-oriented tasks. The development of test case documents in cooperation with the customer is also connected to this phase. These documents are a precondition for substantial quality assurance.

As already mentioned, a data migration strategy has to be planned at the same time as well as the project execution itself, beginning with the definition of clear responsibilities and resources. Regarding the project planning, bundled tools allow for the generation of a rough-cut project plan "stub" from the defined functional requirements and their properties. This plan can be directly imported into Microsoft Project, while retaining references to the relevant documentation.

Corresponding to the Sure Step methodology, the *design* phase is subsequently executed. The Project4Sure system assists in this phase by providing workflows that facilitate change management. For example, changes to functional requirement documents have to be approved again. In addition, an overview on the states of the relevant documents is provided, making such change processes transparent for all stakeholders.

The consecutive *development* phase is supported by the platform's ability to automatically derive individual tasks from the functional requirement documents. Additionally included are software test management features that serve quality assurance purposes. The development phase also profits from the implemented risk management capabilities described earlier.

During the *deployment* phase, the system assists in further quality assurance tasks, including acceptance tests based on a staging environment that contains a test setup of the projected ERP system. In addition, training management and the preparation of the deployment of the production system are supported by the platform in this stage of the Sure Step methodology.

The staging environment with its test system also plays a big role in the *operations* phase. During this phase, the maintenance of the productive ERP system is warranted. The Project4Sure platform aids in this continuous process by providing a complete issue tracking system. This encompasses the management of submitted bugs and feature or change requests, connecting users of the system, support staff, decision makers and developers.

Conclusively, it can be said that Project4Sure accompanies the whole ERP project lifecycle from before its start all the way to its operational end state and beyond.

## 3.2 Potentials and Limits

Built upon the Sure Step methodology, Project4Sure offers all the advantages of a standardized procedure model while at the same time including its practical application. The project management platform allows the definition of project specific processes in addition to offering access to standards and templates defined for more general cases. Consequently, Sure Step templates are converted into clearly defined, workflow-driven processes. On this basis, Project4Sure can incorporate nearly all currently possible technologies into the requirements engineering process.

The advantages that are consequences of the software-based application of the Sure Step approach also encompass the possibility to track consistent version histories and to declare dependencies on all document levels. Additionally, reminder features support the responsible stakeholders in keeping the project on time. In combination with the web-based user interface that empowers even distributed teams to work together as if they were in the same place, the advantages add up to a significant increase in quality of projects realized using Project4Sure.

Project4Sure unfolds all of its potentials when also the browser-supporting and web-based components can be utilized. Consequently, its use is only optimal when connected to the internet. Offline work with Project4Sure is only possible in a very constrained fashion.

## 4 BPM 2.0

### 4.1 Overview

BPM 2.0 is a business process management concept that increases the flexibility of business processes (BP) by enabling business users (BU) to improve "their" business processes. The BPM 2.0 approach described in [3–6] aims at offering such a comprehensive BPM methodology by providing a procedure model encompassing all phases of the BPM life cycle. The term *BPM 2.0* refers to applying the Enterprise 2.0 concept to BPM. The suffix *2.0* indicates that integrating employees who execute business processes as part of their day-to-day tasks into the design of business processes is the core idea of BPM 2.0. In this contribution, BPM 2.0 is consequently defined as follows:

> *"BPM 2.0 is a business process management approach which encourages employees to improve "their" business processes. Web 2.0 technologies are utilized to enable contributions from employees with little BPM expertise."* [4]

This definition is extended by the definition given in [7] which requires that the developed process models are immediately executable by IT systems without requiring any programming.

Besides business processes, process innovations (PI) are the key artifact of BPM 2.0. PI are improvements to BP which are initiated and collaboratively developed by stakeholders like employees who are involved in executing the respective processes.

The BPM 2.0 approach comprises multiple components: (1) A role concept for implementing BPM 2.0 in the organization, (2) a procedure model detailing how these roles interact during the lifecycle of a process, (3) a software platform which allows BU to contribute to PI, (4) an extension to the procedure and role concepts that allows BU to contribute to the automation of their BP, and (5) a prototypical execution environment supporting component (4). [6] presents a case study examining the utility of BPM 2.0 in a real-world environment. In this case study, components (1) to (3) have been used. With mitigating the gap between business and IT during the implementation of ERP systems being the objective of this contribution, all components except component (5) will be introduced.

### 4.2 Procedure Model

Classic BPM lifecycle models like [8] or [9] distinguish between designing, implementing, executing, and analyzing BP. Innovation management lifecycle models like [10] exhibit a similar structure: Innovations are identified, selected, implemented, and finally evaluated. The main difference between management lifecycle models for innovations and business processes is that the former assume that a larger quantity of individuals is involved in creating innovations than in creating business process improvements. Therefore, it is necessary to implement review mechanisms for innovations.

However, both lifecycle models have to be adapted before being applied to BPM 2.0: Selecting PI requires a sufficient degree of maturity of these innovations in order to adequately assess their potentials and costs. Therefore, the BPM 2.0 lifecycle model must allow developing PI before *and* after the selection of process models. Fig. 3 depicts the BPM 2.0 lifecycle which combines the innovation [10] and BP management lifecycles [8] previously mentioned.

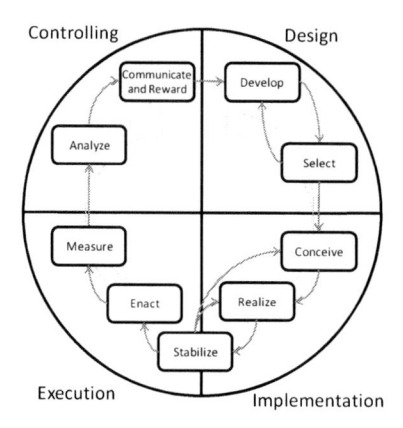

**Fig. 3.** BPM 2.0 management lifecycle

During the *design* phase, employees involved in the respective BP create and refine (develop) PI. By using a web based platform, options are discussed in discussion boards, documented in wikis, and formalized as graphical process models. By including potentially all stakeholders in this early stage, the risk of failing implementations is substantially reduced. Transferring design tasks to the employees allows fulfilling multiple requirements: Firstly, BP are improved continually, because it is in the best interest of the employees to change BP that impede their daily work. Secondly, they can swiftly and autonomously create answers to new challenges like changing market requirements [5]. Because multiple PI may be created in parallel, these innovations have to be selected: At first, stakeholders and employees evaluate proposed innovations during a collaborative assessment. In the next step, the process owner (PO) reviews promising innovations and – if accepted – triggers their implementation.

The *implementation* phase is about realizing PI both organizationally and technically. During this phase, PI are refined and change plans are conceived first. Then, these change plans are realized: Organizational structures are adapted, stakeholders trained, and IT systems are modified. The implementation progress is measured and – if necessary – the change plan is adapted to unforeseen challenges.

During the *execution* phase, the revised processes are brought to life by employees who conduct the processes. During the execution, the enactment component of the business process management system (BPMS) records key performance indicators (KPI) for further analysis.

During the *controlling* phase, the recorded KPI are analyzed in order to assess the performance of the processes. The results of this analysis are then published to all stakeholders in order to provide input for further PI. By comparing the KPI recorded before and after the implementation of a PI, the contribution of PI to the overall process performance can be estimated. Based on this estimation, rewards for the contributors to a PI are determined in order to encourage further contributions.

### 4.3 Automation

Applying BPM 2.0 to the automation of business processes is challenging, as technical models exhibit a higher degree of complexity due to the higher degree of formality and detail required. Therefore, [4] extends the BPM approach by specifying three metamodel levels that are tailored according to the requirements and capabilities of the involved users. In order to ensure that users need to deal only with the minimal complexity necessary, each metamodel is derived from the respective modeling goals.

1. *HC*: Business users *(BU)* create human-centric (HC) computation independent models (CIM) which focus on the business perspective of processes. In order to reduce the complexity of HC models, no technical details are included.
2. *HC+*: The HC models are refined by extended human-centric (HC+) models that enrich HC models with details that are necessary for automation like data flow or service calls. Like any platform independent model (PIM), HC+ models require a higher degree of formality. Thus, only business users with special training *(BU+)* are able to transform HC models into HC+ models. However, with the HC+ metamodel being a superset of the HC metamodel and a similar notation is used for both metamodels, the HC+ metamodel is simple enough for business users being able to understand ("read") HC+ models.
3. *IC*: The integration-centric (IC) models are used to define complex and technical interactions between processes, services, and existing IT systems. The modeling concepts are comparable to those at the HC+ level but require a much greater specification depth and experience in SW development. Therefore, only few users with specialized IT knowledge (IC experts; *ICE*) are able to use the modeling techniques and tools. Services and processes created at the IC level may be directly used at the HC+ level in a simplified form. Thereby a framework of reusable complex components is provided by the IC level for use within HC+ models.

Fig. 4 visualizes the interaction between these model levels and the corresponding roles as well as their relation to the modeling levels of the model-driven architecture (MDA) as laid out in [11]: (1) Business users design or refine a HC level model (e.g. as part of a PI). (2) Business users with special training enrich this model with technical details in order to make it executable. (3) With the HC+ model being simple enough for business users to passively understand them, business users can contribute their domain knowledge by using informal feedback functions like comments or wiki entries. (4) Business users with special training formalize these contributions by incorporating them into the HC+ model. (5) With HC+ models being executable, they can easily be transformed into Java source code by the code generator which is based on openArchitectureWare. This step allows HC+ process models to be automated by the already existing process execution engines (PXE) that often require Java classes of the process models for deployment. Contrary to the classical MDA approach laid out in [11], the BPM 2.0 approach requires no intermediary platform specific model (PSM) but generates the Java source code directly, as the Java-based process execution engine is the only target platform.

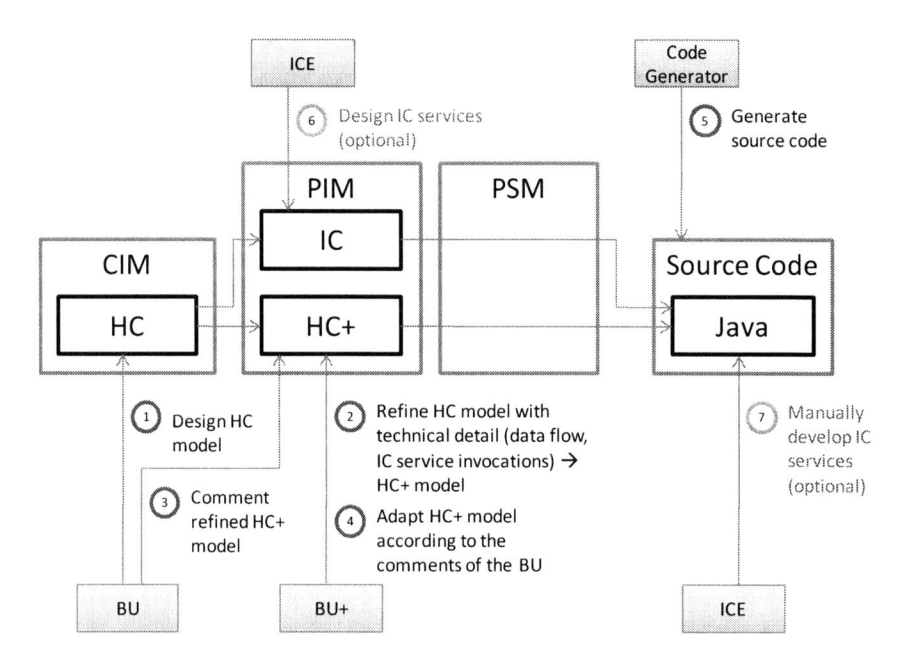

Fig. 4. Model transformation approach for BPM 2.0 [4]

By combining formal and informal functions of the modeling environment, the creation of the HC and HC+ models can be performed by users from the operational departments (BU, BU+).

However, in some cases, the expressive power of HC+ is not sufficient to efficiently model complex functionality. In these cases, a classical model-driven approach can be used: (6) An IC expert designs a service using the IC metamodel level. In the few cases, where designing IC services is not feasible as well, (7) IC experts can manually develop IC services with standard Java code.

The extended BPM 2.0 approach provides BU like business-oriented consultants with instruments as well as a methodology to directly contribute to the automation of process models. Thereby, operational departments can exercise more influence and control over the way their business processes are automated and swiftly adapt existing services or develop new ones. Fall-back mechanisms ensure that the approach can cope with complex scenarios as well.

As this approach is geared towards BPMS that automate tailored business processes, it can be applied to the customization aspects of ERP implementation projects as well as to the customization of already implemented ERP suites. It has the potential to ensure that all major stakeholders can contribute their knowledge as well as their specific requirements without requiring extensive technical knowledge.

### 4.4 Contributions

The BPM 2.0 approach allows ordinary business to develop a common understanding of the actual business processes of companies planning to undertake an ERP implementation project. With a clear understanding of the relevant business processes, deriving requirements for such a project is significantly simplified. Although BPM 2.0 allows developing business process models that exhibit substantial technical detail and that are automatable, the majority of the business users requires no technical know-how. All in all, BPM 2.0 promises to be a good complement for the Sure Step methodology.

## 5 Project4Sure Accelerated

The Project4Sure Accelerated (P4SX) approach extends the P4S approach by providing BU with more influence on the implementation of new Microsoft Dynamics implementations. While it relies on many aspects of BPM 2.0 like self-organization, the use of web-based platforms, this iteration of P4SX focuses on new implementations of ERP systems as opposed to BPM 2.0's focus on continuous process improvement.

P4SX exhibits a procedure model that is based on the Sure Step procedure model (cf. section 2). As depicted in Fig. 5, it essentially refines the phase *Analysis* and *Design* of the Sure Step procedure model.

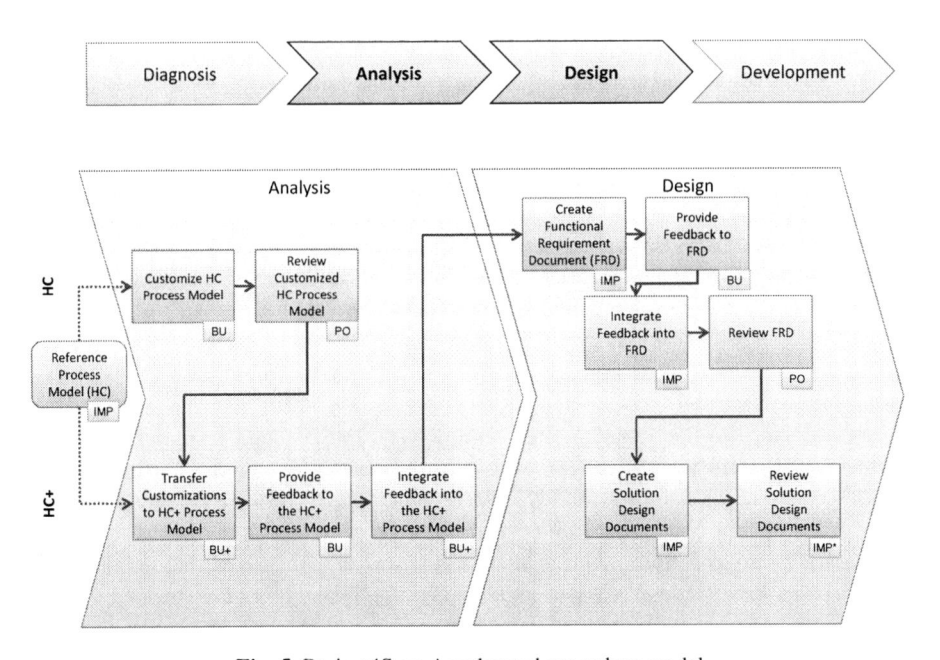

**Fig. 5.** Project4Sure Accelerated procedure model

In the *diagnosis* phase, the high-level automation requirements are matched to the high-level components of the Microsoft Dynamics NAV suite. Besides the overall implementation strategy, the components that need to be customized are identified.

Once the diagnostics phase has been completed, the necessary customizations to the ERP software are detailed during the *analysis* phase. For that purpose, BU identify the processes in the reference process model (RPM) that have to be customized and thereby pinpoint the changes required for the ERP software. The RPM comprises the processes of the Microsoft Dynamics NAV ERP suite and is provided by the consulting ERP implementation specialist (IMP). The changes to this RPM are incorporated by customizing its business-oriented (HC) process models. While empowering BU to participate in this analysis task ensures that differences between the real-world processes and the reference process model are reliably identified, using a reference process model as a starting point and template substantially reduces the overall effort required.

As many BU possess insufficient know-how in business process modeling, the quality of these customizations has to be ensured by two instruments: Firstly, a modeling specialist removes syntactic and semantic errors from the customized process models. Secondly, the process owner ensures that the customizations are correct and feasible from a business perspective during the review of the customized HC process model. Those instruments have been identified, refined, and validated during several case studies – including a case study conducted at a large European construction company [6].

Once the process models have been customized from the business perspective (HC level), business users with technical knowledge (BU+) transfer the customizations of the HC process models to the HC+ level. Similar to the BPM 2.0 approach, HC+ level models comprise technical detail like data flow and invoked services that are not considered on the business-oriented HC level. As the HC+ level meta model is a superset of the HC level meta model, BU can read and understand HC+ level meta models. This allows BU to provide feedback to the customizations the BU+ transferred to the HC+ level. With BU not possessing the methodical knowledge to edit these HC+ models directly, BU use informal and easy-to-use functions like wiki pages or post-it comments to enrich the HC+ model. In the next step, BU+ integrate these informal contributions into the formal process model.

Once the necessary customizations have been described on the HC level and refined with technical details on the HC+ level, the actual solutions concept is created during the *design* phase.

In compliance to the Project4Sure methodology, the consultant creates functional requirement documents (FRD) for each customization. In contrast to the process-oriented customizations of the analysis phase, FRD take a software component driven perspective on the required changes and may be attached to a process group, a process, or a single activity. As the FRD are basically wiki pages that contain little technical detail, BU can easily understand them and provide feedback, if a requirement is not well-aligned with the business needs. As it is likely that the input from BU will not always yield FRD that meet the expected quality criteria, the IMP has to integrate this feedback and ensure the correctness of the FRD. FRD are finalized once the PO has reviewed and accepted the respective FRD.

For each FRD, the IMP creates a solution design document (SDD) that describes in detail how the requirement is to be fulfilled by adapting the ERP system. In other words, the SDD is a description of how to implement the planned customizations. As it includes technical detail, the SDD is part of the HC+ level. In the succeeding *development* phase, software developers will take this document as a blueprint of how to customize the software by means of programming (on the IC level). Similar to the FRD, the SDD is a wiki document stored in the P4SX workspace.

## 6 Software Support

In order to ensure its operation in the day-to-day project work, the approach outlined in section 0 has to be supported by software systems. As shown by the success of projects utilizing Project4Sure, such platforms provide valuable benefits throughout the project lifecycle.

The Project4Sure methodology, in combination with the platform, empowers managers without any technical knowledge to monitor and control the progress of ERP implementation projects. The P4SX concept strives to transcend these possibilities: The customer takes a far more active role within the implementation project. A number of advantages result from this fact, notably a significantly reduced risk of project failure. In order to play such an active part however, the customer's experts need to have the required tools at hand.

For this very reason, the prototype of a P4SX platform was developed. It provides the foundation for future case studies that aim to validate the concept.

As both the BPM 2.0 and the Project4Sure platform are based on Microsoft SharePoint, their integration can be accomplished with little effort. The starting point for the effective software support of BPM 2.0 is the Project4Sure platform. The individual instruments for collaborative process modeling that the BPM 2.0 platform provides are embedded into its framework. The RPM containing the Microsoft Dynamics NAV processes is available in order to allow for easy adaption. Fig. 6 gives an impression of the reference process model.

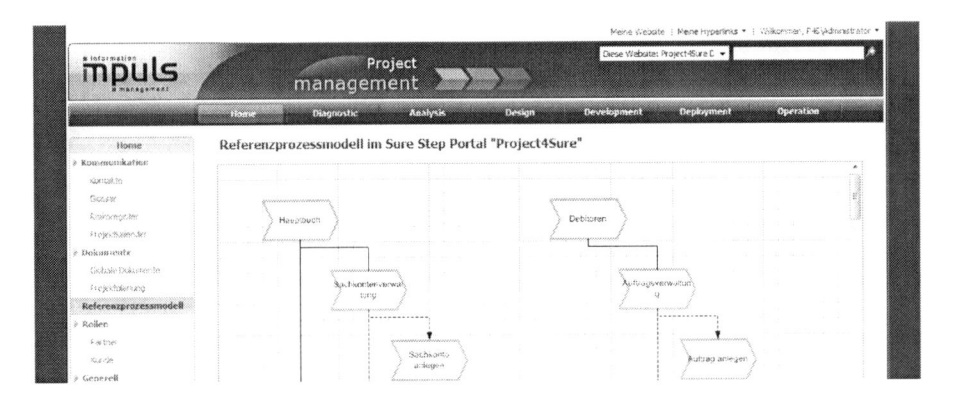

**Fig. 6.** Excerpt from the RPM of the P4S-X platform

In case customization becomes necessary, the concerned process model is first adapted on the HC level, followed by the HC+ layer. Additionally, hyperlinks contained in the process models refer to the corresponding FRD (cf. Fig. 7).

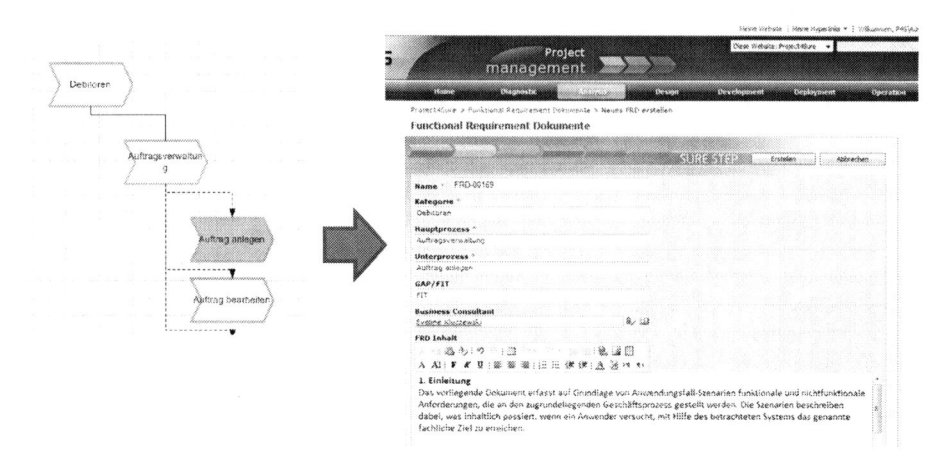

**Fig. 7.** Defining a FRD for a process within the RPM

Fig. 8 demonstrates how project planning and controlling are facilitated by the controlling cockpit of the Project4Sure platform.

**Fig. 8.** Controlling the implementation progress of FRDs with the P4S-X platform

In general, the platform thrives on the active participation of domain operatives and end users throughout the analysis and design phases of the project lifecycle. Naturally, errors can happen in the course of this: Information might be accidentally deleted or falsely structured, or incorrect contents could be contributed. The P4SX concept balances out such effects by involving the methodology specialist and regular reviews. In the long run, both concept and platform have to be able to handle user errors. By employing a versioning mechanism for all artifacts, it is ensured that no greater harm is done unintentionally.

## 7 Conclusion and Outlook

The core idea of BPM 2.0 is that the increased involvement of the business users results in a better specification of the business processes and functional requirements. Such a result has been successfully validated in a case study conducted in a large European plant construction company [6]. Using this new approach, there is a good chance of eliminating two of the biggest risks in software development: (1) the lack of user involvement and (2) incomplete requirements.

P4SX brings together the BPM 2.0 approach and the P4S project management platform based on Microsoft's Sure Step methodology. As described above, the HC and HC+ layer extend the P4S platform with two additional levels of abstraction resulting in a lower model complexity on the business user level. Therefore, it will be easier for the business users to specify and refine "their" business processes and software functionalities without the help of a specialist. The stronger coupling of the end users to the analysis and design phase will lead to a reduction of „late" change requests and therefore to lower project costs.

A prototype of the P4SX software platform already exists. In the next step, this prototype has to be validated within the context of several real world projects. As the total cost and failure risk of software projects are strongly correlated with change requests that occur during later project phases, as indicated by the chaos report [2], a good measure of the effectiveness of P4SX would be the ratio between FRDs changed after the design phase and the total number of FRDs. This ratio – ideally even as a distribution of change requests over the project phases – could be determined in projects that employ the P4SX platform and compared to historical data of similar projects executed without P4SX support.

## References

1. Emam, K.E., Koru, A.G.: A Replicated Survey of IT Software Project Failures. IEEE Softw. 25, 84–90 (2008)
2. Standish Group: Chaos Summary, The 10 Laws of Chaos (2009), http://www.standishgroup.com
3. Kurz, M.: BPM 2.0. Organisation, Selbstorganisation und Kollaboration im Geschäfts prozessmanagement Bamberg, Erlangen-Nürnberg, Regensburg (2009)
4. Billing, G., Kurz, M., Hettling, K., von Jouanne-Diedrich, H.: Applying BPM 2.0 in IT centric environments. Accepted paper. In: Rosemann, M. (ed.) Case Studies in Business Process Management. Springer, Heidelberg (2011)
5. Kurz, M.: BPM 2.0. Kollaborative Gestaltung von Geschäftsprozessen. In: Schumann, M., Kolbe, L.M., Breitner, M.H., Frerichs, A. (eds.) Multikonferenz Wirtschaftsinformatik 2010, pp. 729–740. Univ.-Verl. Göttingen, Göttingen (2010)
6. Kurz, M., Fleischmann, A.: BPM 2.0. Business Process Management meets Empowerment. In: S-BPM ONE 2010 (2011)
7. Fleischmann, A.: What is S-BPM? In: Buchwald, H., Fleischmann, A., Seese, D., Stary, C. (eds.) S-BPM ONE 2009. CCIS, vol. 85, pp. 85–106. Springer, Heidelberg (2010)
8. Weske, M.: Business Process Management. Concepts, Languages, Architectures. Springer, Heidelberg (2007)

9. Schmelzer, H.J., Sesselmann, W. (eds.): Geschäftsprozessmanagement in der Praxis. Kunden zufrieden stellen, Produktivität steigern, Wert erhöhen Hanser, München (2008)
10. Reichwald, R., Möslein, K., Huff, A.S., Kölling, M., Neyer, A.-K.: Service Innovation Leipzig (2008)
11. Miller, J., Mukerji, J.: MDA Guide Version 1.0.1, `http://www.omg.org/cgi-bin/doc?omg/03-06-01.pdf`
12. Shankar, C., Bellefroid, V.: Microsoft Dynamics Sure Step 2010. Packt Publishing, Birmingham (2011)

# Consolidating Business Processes as Exemplified in SAP ERP Systems

Andreas Hufgard[1] and Eduard Gerhardt[2]

[1] IBIS Prof. Thome AG, Mergentheimer Straße 76a,
97082 Wuerzburg, Germany
[2] University of Applied Sciences Coburg, Friedrich-Streib-Str. 2,
96450 Coburg, Germany

**Abstract.** A thorough semantic comparison of usage of business processes must be established as a preliminary stage to consolidating IT systems. In praxis, this step is frequently omitted from IT projects. This condition cannot be ascribed to lack of knowledge on the part of the project manager; rather, the reason lies in the high degree of complexity, intricacy and interdependency of business processes. Project managers are apprehensive of the time and effort involved in the early project phase and neglect it in favor of concrete action, and get bogged down in details for lack of a sound and logical overall approach. The result is system consolidation in the mere technical sense – business processes are neither standardized nor homogenized. In light of the significance consolidation bears on business (in the US in 2005 there were 7,736 mergers and acquisitions, totaling an average sum of 385 million USD [5]), it is costly to leave consolidation projects to chance. The following article introduces principles and procedures for consolidating business processes that aim to compensate for the deficit of scientifically documented findings.

**Keywords:** client consolidation, harmonization, standardization, merger, fusion, consolidation, restructuring, comparison, alignment, reorganization and business transformation of SAP systems.

## 1 Basics of Consolidation

The term consolidation stems from the Latin word "consolidare," which means to strengthen and make solid. When used in conjunction with an organization's business processes, consolidation usually refers to activities such as transforming and merging. It is worth noting that both words – transforming and merging – are an essential part of the term. Business process consolidation comprises the following steps:

Compare ➜ unify ➜ consolidate

To explain the method behind these consolidation steps the article is structured as follows. In the first chapter types and reasons for consolidation of IT systems are explained. Additionally the relevance of tool-aided analysis of data, which are stored in IT systems and which are necessary for the analysis of usage of business processes is discussed. The second chapter presents possible consolidation scenarios and their implications. The third chapter deals with the methodology of the comparison and consolidation of business processes. The last chapter summarizes the results.

## 1.1 Are Business Processes Synonymous with IT Systems?

Business processes are defined as temporal-logical sequences of activities geared toward changing input into output in accordance with transformation instructions. A distinction is made between determinate and indeterminate business processes, depending on whether the input, the output and the transformation instructions can be planned in advance. Determinate processes are characterized by an explicit ex ante determinability of input, output and transformation instructions with respect to type, quantity, time and place. This implies their complete controllability in terms of planning, execution and verification. Indeterminate processes differ in that at least one of the determinants mentioned above cannot be explicitly defined prior to its execution [1].

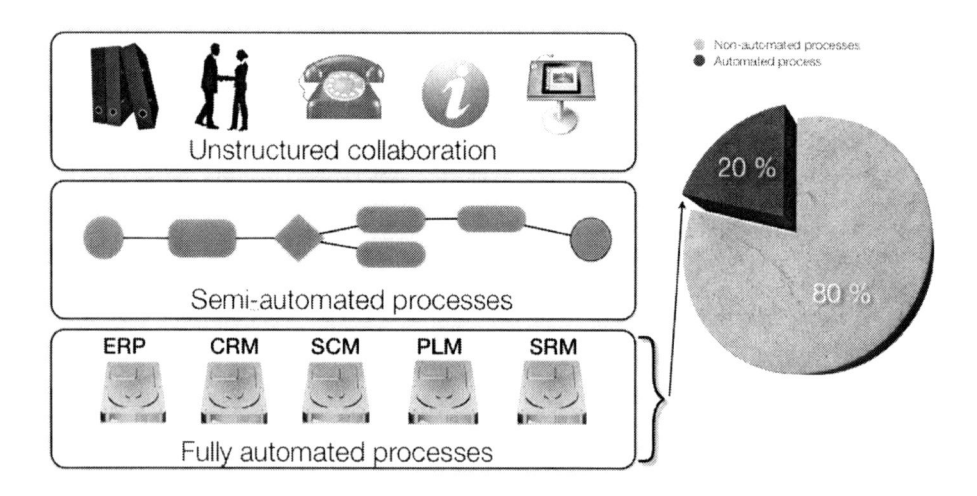

**Fig. 1.** Determinate and indeterminate processes [2]

### 1.1.1 Determinate and Indeterminate Processes

The above-mentioned characteristics of determinate business processes enable their execution to be completely automated via information technology – e.g. with business applications such as ERP and CRM (see Figure 1). According to one estimate, these processes make up approx. 20% of all business processes in organizations [3]. One of the fully automatable business processes is the payment of open items. The transaction is executed automatically in the SAP ERP system when payment of open items becomes due and the account balance permits payment.

The remaining 80% of the processes are indeterminate and either cannot be automated or only partially. IT plays "only" a supporting role in the execution of indeterminate business processes. Despite this limitation, the significance of information technology is substantial. Even supposedly non-IT-related processes in creative areas like development or design, cannot be performed completely without business applications, because, for example, employees must allocate their times to cost elements for cost-allocated billing.

In summary, it can be said that IT's degree of penetration in organizations is so high that nearly all business processes leave a data trail in business applications at some time. It is therefore ineffective to examine business processes as isolated from IT; they must be studied in conjunction with their supporting IT systems. And so it would logically follow that business process consolidation be based on the analysis of data trails left in applications by business processes. A neutral analysis of actual usage of business processes based on the data stored in applications provides the foundation for a clear and informative depiction of actual usage. This can then be used to identify differences in business process usage (in both systems) and to deduce their effect on consolidation of IT systems.

### 1.1.2 Differences in Process Usage

An isolated examination of the fully automatable process, "payment of open items", without the corresponding ERP system, will illustrate this assertion. Payment of open items in the SAP ERP system can either be effected at the earliest possible date with maximum cash back or at the latest possible date with minimum or no cash back. The result is the same – the open item is cleared. But the methods of execution differ. The way in which the business process is set up in the SAP ERP system depends on the organization's requirements. But if the organization's business processes are to be consolidated, it is essential to know whether the two companies vary in their use of the "payment of open items" process. If differences are identified in the early project phase, decision-makers can play an active role in determining how the new, common processes are to run in future; it enables employees and business partners to anticipate these differences and modify the SAP ERP system accordingly. If differences go unnoticed until the late project phase or indefinitely, this results in increased project times and expenses and delays; or problems are shifted to live operation when vendors and employees suddenly request support because open items are settled differently than before consolidation.

## 1.2 Types of Consolidation

Consolidating business processes has become increasingly important for organizations in the past few years. This is due to a need for internal and external systems integration.

### 1.2.1 Internal Consolidation

Internal consolidation becomes necessary when IT executives are forced by internal factors, such as cost pressures or restructuring requirements, to consolidate business processes and IT landscapes. According to a study by RAAD Research, approximately 15% of all SAP customers in Germany, Austria and Switzerland have several diversified and decentralized SAP systems [4]. This happens when SAP systems, such as SAP ERP or SAP CRM, are operated in subsidiaries, countries or user departments as autonomous and technically independent entities. These organizations have a powerful need to consolidate systems and harmonize business processes, since changes in process requirements necessitate multiple alignments in SAP systems, consuming considerable time and expense.

Even in the case of centralized SAP systems, approximately 40% of SAP customers recognize the need to improve operation of the application [4]. The reason for this could be that usage of an ERP system is heterogeneous in various organizational units, such as company codes (the smallest unit requiring a balance sheet in the SAP ERP system), plants or sales organizations. This means that in one ERP system, a company code automatically transacts payment of open items at the earliest possible date with the maximum cash discount, while in another, payment is transacted at the latest possible date without the discount. Customization of an SAP ERP system permits this degree of discrepancy in process usage within a single system. But this flexibility comes at a high cost, since both process variants must be maintained, supported and taught. This is why parallel usage of process variants within a single ERP system should only be allowed when required by country- or customer-specific conditions that promise an advantage and contribute to competitive differentiation.

### 1.2.2 External Consolidation

In addition to the scenarios previously illustrated, the trend toward consolidation is intensified through external system integration during mergers and acquisitions. The merging company's IT systems must be integrated into those of the existing or new company. The extremely low success rates of M&As attest to the complexity and risk of M&A-related activities. Numerous studies show that approximately 70% of all mergers and acquisitions resulted in a decrease of the company's value. The value of new corporations on the stock exchange was lower than the sum of each company's respective value prior to the merger or acquisition [5].

One reason for the extremely low success rate of M&As is the particularly difficult merging of IT systems, because combining separate companies' IT infrastructures requires substantial changes to be made in each company's processes. Regardless of whether consolidation is induced by internal or external pressures, the procedure remains the same. The business processes and IT systems impacted must be compared, differences identified and, based on these, concrete steps planned for implementation. The focus should not be on IT system but on the business processes it supports.

Another reason for the low success rate of consolidation projects is that there are almost no documented scientific results, methods and/or best practices from large consulting firms like Accenture for this type of project that are analagous to consolidation in business finance. In this area, for example, it is defined very precisely which balance sheet items may be consolidated with which balance sheet items in similar circumstances. There is a need for analogous guidelines and methods for the consolidation of business processes. Most publications that address consolidation illuminate only IT infrastructures. Business processes are excluded.

### 1.3 Consolidating SAP Systems

The term SAP consolidation is used when two or more clients or organizational units are combined in a single client or from several clients. The clients are always part of various SAP systems located on separate servers and sometimes even at different sites. In order to compare SAP systems effectively, the reference processes must be selected and evaluated by using productive data from each system. Current system usage visualized by reference processes marks the starting point for business process consolidation. This can either be evaluated manually, i.e. conducting a time-consuming analysis project, or via a tool-aided solution, for example by applying the method of Reverse Business Engineering (RBE).

The methods behind RBE were developed between 1998 and 2000 as part of a doctoral dissertation at Rainer Thome's Faculty for Business Administration and Information Technology in Wuerzburg. In collaboration with SAP, these methods were applied to SAP systems. The RBE check logic of productive SAP data facilitates the intelligent identification of processes currently "really used" and enables the structuring of an objective and verified as-is model. RBE "check steps" extract business process relevant data from SAP system, which enables the analysis of process models, based on an SAP system's productive data. Depicting the processes that are actually used establishes the starting point for a comparison of business processes run in different SAP systems. This article focuses on the examination of process usage in SAP systems based on the RBE-Methodology which is applied to derive the methodology for consolidation of business processes.

### 1.3.1 Technical Consolidation of SAP Systems

The consolidation process can be broken down into two steps. The first step comprises the technical side, which impacts or changes only the operation of the client on a centralized SAP system, in a specific data center. The goal of technical system consolidation is to shift a client from one system environment to another, and ensure it runs smoothly in its new setting. Full client consolidation merges two or more clients to create a single unit – the only remaining distinctions being their organizational elements (e.g. company codes, plants).

Table 1. Positive and negative effects of technical consolidation [6]

| Positive effects if consolidation is purely technical | Negative effects if consolidation is purely technical |
|---|---|
| • Expenses for site/location and office space are eliminated,<br>• Hardware infrastructure is scaled back,<br>• Communications and interfaces from one system to another no longer necessary,<br>• Cross-client tables must be compared and consolidated,<br>• Technical connection, system software, database software and services only needed once. | • Transformation costs for system comparison and adding missing functions and services in the target system,<br>• System complexity increases, while transparency decreases progressively,<br>• Tables increase in size,<br>• Risk of downtime becomes greater,<br>• Change impact testing and upgrade times increase,<br>• Problem identification and resolution requires more time. |

Synergetic effects achieved through technical consolidation are probably not as great as they first seem. From a technical viewpoint, cross-client tables and their contents, and all system-level processes are combined. This affects, say, number ranges and technical objects in the development environment. Together these make up around one third of the SAP data tables in the system. But the tables themselves have little to no effect on the business content in these tables. It is important to weigh the counter-productive effects against the productive ones. Technical consolidation adds to a system's complexity, increases the risk of downtimes and extends the duration of change cycles. So, always consider the situation, potential gains and possible risks very carefully before delving into a technical consolidation project. Table 1 shows some of the positive and negative effects of technical consolidation that eliminates decentralized systems and clients in favor of countries or business areas, and in which a centralized system is deployed worldwide:

### 1.3.2 Consolidating Business Elements in SAP Systems

The real benefits of consolidation become apparent only in the second step, which includes technical aspects, but incorporates business-related issues too. However, these types of projects are not easy to implement, since they are not relegated strictly to the IT department; they require collaboration across departments. As with all truly effective projects – particularly consolidation – business and IT must work hand in hand and company executives, organizational departments and the IT department must strive together toward a common goal. If consolidation of business-related aspects, such as standardization and harmonization of business processes, are neglected, consolidation will inevitably give birth to a highly complex "monster system". During the time of mainframes and SAP R/2, people talked of "dinosaurs" when describing systems that encumbered any organizational changes or rendered them impossible. To avoid creating an overly complex structure, it is essential to take pre-consolidation steps, such as standardizing user management and processes.

### 1.3.3 The Significance of Differences in Business-Related Usage

To reliably compare differences between systems, it is important to first compare real usage of SAP applications. Beware of merely juxtaposing all tables and program codes. This only generates large data quantities that reveal little about the system. For example, a comparison of all tables might reveal little more than the different language versions used in the system. But this data is meaningless if nobody uses them. This is why it is essential to compare aspects of the SAP infrastructure that are actively employed.

Inaccuracy resulting from manual analysis presents a considerable disadvantage. Frequently, entire areas of the system and crucial details are neglected – the serious consequence being that important functions might ultimately be missing from the target system. This leads to catastrophic consequences for the organization. System landscapes that have grown over time often lack transparency. And later, it is virtually impossible to identify precisely which processes and functions are used – and how and why. Most SAP users can only hazard a guess, or some might have a clear overview of a limited part of the process landscape. There are two reasons for this:

- Employee fluctuation within organizations
- The fact that SAP systems tend to become disorganized because of changes made in the system over time to adapt to real transformations within the organization.

And since this is the situation commonly confronted in most organizations, there is really no true alternative to a tool-based usage analysis that systematically reveals discrepancies in usage based on data stored in the systems. These business-related differences need to be either eliminated or harmonized before embarking on a consolidation project.

## 2 Recognizing Consolidation Scenarios

A consolidation scenario is defined as the way in which IT systems are merged. Depending on whether one is a leading system, there are two basic types of scenario (cf. Figure 2).

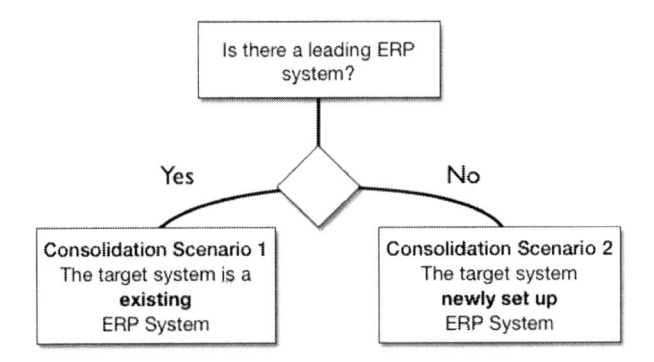

**Fig. 2.** Potential consolidation scenarios

### 2.1 The Target System is an Existing ERP System

Consolidation scenario 1 consists of an existing ERP system used as the target for all other ERP systems. If, for example, only two SAP ERP systems and the business processes modeled in them are affected by consolidation, two variations of this scenario are possible:

- SAP ERP system 1 ➜ SAP ERP system 2
- SAP ERP system 2 ➜ SAP ERP system 1

If additional ERP systems must be consolidated, the number of possible variations increases proportionally and the project costs and time involved become disproportionately high. One special characteristic of scenario 1 is the metric for comparison, or a target system. In this case, the business processes from the source system must be aligned with the requirements and technical restrictions of the target system. This eliminates the necessity for tedious discussions and coordination in the early project phases. The characteristics of scenario 1 are listed below.

## Positive aspects

- Rapid implementation of an operative system
  The reason for this advantage is that the source system is incorporated into a functioning ERP system. Consolidation takes place primarily at organizational level. Units from the source systems (company codes, plants, sales organizations, etc.) are integrated as new elements into an existing and functioning target system.
- Comparatively low implementation costs
  Normally the target system has a broader spectrum of functions. Conversely, this means exceptions to functions from the source system do not require much implementation time; most can be structured based on the existing scope of functions. Organizational units to be defined in the target system access existing functions and processes from this system.
- Low consolidation risk
  Consolidation projects are inherently high-risk. Consolidation risk is defined as the failure of established functions in the target system. It can be caused by functions in the source systems being forgotten or by the corruption of target system functions by transferring settings from the source system. This risk can be estimated in an existing, operating target system, since normally the functional scope and the processes in the target system are firm. Anomalies in functions and processes in the source systems should not be incorporated into the target system, unless as an exception. Their usage intensity (number of times accessed) and distribution (number of users) should be used as a benchmark.

## Important considerations

- High adaptation costs for master data migration
  A vital component of all consolidation projects is the adaptation of master data. In consolidation scenario 1, these master data structures have to be adapted to the target system requirements. Elaborate mapping algorithms must be defined and applied. If in the source system, for example, customers are managed in the "domestic vendor" account group, either an appropriate account group must be defined from the target system or a new one created.
- Retention of legacy data in the target system
  The longer SAP ERP systems are in use, the more they amass superfluous ballast – legacy data and unused company-specific developments or third party products. These modifications are normally developed when the system fails to provide adequate functions for certain company-specific processes. The average rate of company-specific modification for an SAP ERP system is approx. 18% [7], meaning that 18% of all functions used in SAP ERP systems are company-specific. The probability of these modifications being eliminated in an existing target system during a consolidation project is very low. Retaining company-specific developments generally incurs higher maintenance and training costs for the source system users.
- Increased complexity
  Due to the basic differences in executing certain business processes, such as process and discrete manufacturing, it is sometimes necessary to operate them in parallel in the target system to minimize risk. This may decrease the risk of

consolidation, but operating costs could increase, and the cost reductions anticipated through consolidating the systems will not be achieved – at least not immediately.
— Lack of harmonization
Harmonization of business processes in consolidation scenario 1 necessitates that business processes in the source system be adapted to comply with the requirements and technical restrictions of the target system. This is not true harmonization for the purpose of improving processes, since the target system's weak points and deficiencies are retained to avoid more than a modicum of technical changes to the system. For example, if the source system uses electronic banking to automate the upload of account transaction data to the ERP system, and the target system (for technical reasons) does not, this means the consolidated system will not be able to use this function. This is a huge step backwards for the source system. So, savings are postponed to the future, since harmonization is the actual driver of cost decrease.

## 2.2 The Target System is a Completely New ERP System

Consolidation scenario 2 consists of all ERP systems affected by consolidation being transferred to an ERP system that will be created from scratch. This is equivalent to fully reimplementing an SAP system and is usually considered when the systems to be migrated are highly company-specific.

### *Positive aspects*

— Harmonization from the outset
Homogenization of the system from the start is the greatest advantage in this scenario. It prevents similar processes from being operated in the same way, while merely being controlled differently. A system whose processes are standardized and homogenized when it goes live will experience an immediate reduction in operating costs.
— Elimination of unnecessary elements
When deploying a new SAP ERP system that includes requirements from all stakeholders (e.g. companies, organizational units and process owners), all company-specific modifications are checked to make certain they are future-proof, suitable, and meet the future company's requirements before they are transferred to the consolidated system.
— Replacement of company-specific modifications by standard functions
Company-specific developments can also be replaced by available standard functions from the latest SAP release.
— Easier master data migration thanks to suitable template
One advantage of this scenario should not to be underestimated: the ability to create master data structures that meet the requirements of all stakeholders but are free of any pre-assignments.

### *Important considerations*

— Long project times
As a rule, this scenario is characterized by long project duration because tedious organizational discussions about and coordination of future processes must take

place in the beginning phase. Since there are no de facto defaults, these need to be negotiated. This means, for example, an agreement must be reached on how payment of open items will be executed: at the earliest possible date with maximum cash back or at the latest possible date with minimum cash back. Experience shows that all stakeholders try to push through their familiar requirements in this phase. Negotiation of organizational issues by firms with differing corporate cultures greatly increases project times.
— High implementation costs and times
Implementing an SAP ERP system for the first time is generally associated with high costs and time investment, because the entire functional scope of the source systems must be implemented, tested and documented. This is often overlooked when decision-makers see that many processes and required technical settings can be transferred using transfer orders, without changes being made to the target system. But it is important to remember that a new system contains completely new, harmonized master data structures and organizational units. This may mean that decentralized procurement is replaced by centralized procurement. The technical settings of the procurement process remain the same, but distribution of tasks changes entirely, which means the organization and authorizations will need to be adapted accordingly.

### 2.3 Which Consolidation Scenario?

Which consolidation scenario is the right one for the project at hand is frequently decided on political grounds, i.e. without consideration for economic and technical issues. For example, during mergers and acquisitions, usually the acquiree's IT infrastructure is declared the target system. The business processes and the target organization's IT must be transferred to the new system landscape, although from a technical viewpoint, it might be better than the target system (for instance, it might have a more recent SAP ERP release, fewer company-specific modifications, etc.) To avoid this type of unsatisfactory solution, a consolidation scenario should be decided on under the consideration of the following aspects:

- Time: estimated project duration
- Expense: implementation, training, support costs
- Consolidation risk: failure of tried and tested functions in the target system
- How future proof: whether the target system can be upgraded to newer releases

A consolidation scenario can only be selected on the basis of comparison.

## 3 Compare Business Processes

The comparison of two SAP ERP systems should expose differences in usage to determine the best consolidation scenario (identification of source and target systems, etc.) Differences in usage are classified as identities and missing elements.

— **Identities:** These are functions, reports or processes used in both systems. The challenge lies in discerning whether functions, such as payment runs, are used in the same way in both systems. Contradictive and additive identities may occur.

In the case of contradictive identities, it's important to determine from the beginning which functions are affected in the target system and how, to prevent project delays. Normally one company has to adapt to the solution of another. The additive identities can be implemented in parallel in the target system. However, note that this solution incurs follow-up costs, as both solutions have to be operated and maintained in the target system.
- **Missing elements:** Missing elements are items like functions, reports or processes used in only one system. They can occur in both mandatory and reducible form. In the case of mandatory missing elements, it is essential that the affected functions be available in the target system to ensure the organization's future performance and sustainability. Reducible missing elements can be ignored in the first consolidation step in order to accelerate the initial phase.

The comparison matrix (cf. Table 2) indicates discrepencies in content. It is essential to pinpoint semantic differences for the same processes or identities at the next possible juncture; otherwise one risks comparing apples and oranges.

**Table 2.** Comparing content of two systems to be consolidated

| Business process | SAP ERP System 1 | SAP ERP System 2 | Comparison |
|---|---|---|---|
| Electronic bank statement | X | X | Identical key |
| Third-party transactions |  | X | Missing |
| Sample documents | X |  | Missing |
| Automatic payment runs | X | X | Identical key |

### 3.1 Semantic Identity Analysis

It is apparent in the matrix shown above (cf. Table 2) that the "electronic bank statement" process is used in both systems. At first glance, it appears to be an identity that should not cause any problems when the systems are consolidated. However, a semantic analysis shows that in system 1 the statements from the bank are imported to the SAP ERP system, interpreted and posted to the correct accounts with the aid of a third party product. In system 2, these tasks are performed using standard SAP ERP system functions. The semantic analysis was conducted by evaluating transactions used in conjunction with the business process and analyzing the entries in the relevant SAP tables. In view of the differing semantic of process usage, three issues will have an impact on the consolidation project.
- **Impact of system selection:** With respect to the business process "electronic bank statement," system 1 is not as future-proof as a target system because of its company-specific modifications. A high degree of individualization requires additional maintenance costs and impairs the system's ability to be updated, since proper functioning of this business process will have to be checked with each new release.

- **User impact:** Regardless of which system is defined as the target system, the impact on the users of the electronic bank statement is considerable. They have to be trained in how the electronic bank statement works in the new system. If system 2 is selected as the target system, users will have to be familiarized with the standard functions of the SAP ERP system with respect to this process. Furthermore, the number of users active in various processes is extremely important for the consolidation project. The number of users having to be trained in the new processes is a significant cost and time factor. The number of users can sometimes influence the selection of the target system in this regard.
- **Technical impact:** Discrepancies in usage of the "electronic bank statement" process make it necessary to adapt the target system and the channels of communication to the bank. When processing bank statement data such as transaction types, transferee, amount, etc. interpretation algorithms play a large role. They process the data and post amounts to accounts according to the rules specified in Customizing. Since in this example company-specific solutions are used, and an SAP standard solution on the other, it might be necessary to adapt the interpretation algorithms to the source system's business cases. For example, if in the source system incoming payments are assigned to open items with the aid of entries in the purpose field on the transfer form, and in the target system payments are assigned according to the name of the transferee, this will have to be changed in the target system.

Another identity from the comparison matrix (cf. Table 2) is the business process "automatic payment run". This process ensures that all open items are paid automatically and on time. The semantic analysis revealed that this process is used intensely in both systems and executed using standard SAP functions. It seems obvious to conclude that consolidation will not be a problem with respect to the automatic payment run. However, the analysis of the organizational elements contained in the process has revealed considerable divergences. The automatic payment run was organized centrally in system 1 and decentrally in system 2. This insight is based on user distribution, evaluated with the aid of the ABC analysis. IN system 1, the percentage of "A users", i.e. users who executed 80% of the payment runs more than 70% and in system 2, merely 30%. Users were assigned to the automatic payment run process based on transactions used to trigger the payment run.

- **Impact on organizational structure:** Differences in organizational structure make it necessary to reorganize a consolidated company. It is not possible to simply combine both departments; nor is it a good idea to retain both organizational forms (centralized and decentralized) with respect to the payment run process. Restructuring normally involves undeniable organizational resistance, since this includes redistributing areas of responsibility. For this reason, appropriate steps should be taken in the early project phase.
- **Impact on roles:** Reorganization or redistribution of tasks affects the SAP ERP system technically, because authorizations and roles that control user access have to be changed in line with the new task profiles. For example, if an employee is moved from banking to accounts payable, s/he will need

corresponding authorizations, and unnecessary ones must be deleted. If these activities are neglected, authorizations will become chaotic and difficult to keep track of. This will result in major discrepencies between actual system usage and potential usage based on authorizations granted.

## 3.2 Semantic Analysis of Missing Elements

Next, the impact of consolidation on the missing elements analysis will be examined. The comparison matrix (cf. Table 2) shows that sample documents are only used in system 1. This process involves the entry of specific posting transactions with reference to a sample document. The goal is to predefine selected account assignment elements to minimize entry time while increasing quality. From the perspective of system 1, there is a gap in the process if system 2 or a completely new system is defined as the target system. The following alternatives are possible in this case:

- Reduce: Eliminate the function in the target system
- Implement: Implement the missing function in the target system

The decision about whether to reduce or implement missing elements in the target system must be substantiated by semantic facts. Reduction is plausible when the affected processes, reports and functions meet the following criteria:

- Low usage intensity, e.g. small number of documents
- Isolated usage, e.g. limited to selected business cases/process instances
- Limited usage distribution, e.g. executed by few users

When opting to reduce, it's important to consider the impact on users. Affected users will need to be offered alternative solutions or workarounds for eliminated functions. When a decision is made to implement, the new functions in the target system must be checked with respect to the types of consolidation impact described. The example of the semantic analysis that revealed the use of sample documents shows that usage is limited to two process instances, posting of office requirements and telecommunications expenses. Elimination of this function, at least during the initial consolidation phase, was the best decision to minimize complexity.

The variations presented so far clearly indicate that a purely structural comparison of processes used in the systems to be consolidated is incomplete and fraught with risk. It is therefore essential to discover the semantic differences in process usage. To determine as many types of impact as possible, it is a good idea to examine the semantic differences in process usage based on the dimensions illustrated in Figure 3.

Impact on the external environment was not explained in depth above but has been included in Figure 3 for the sake of clarity. This occurs when the alignment of business processes influences the relationship or communication with stakeholders such as vendors, customers, banks, etc. Information can be gathered by analyzing the forms for these processes.

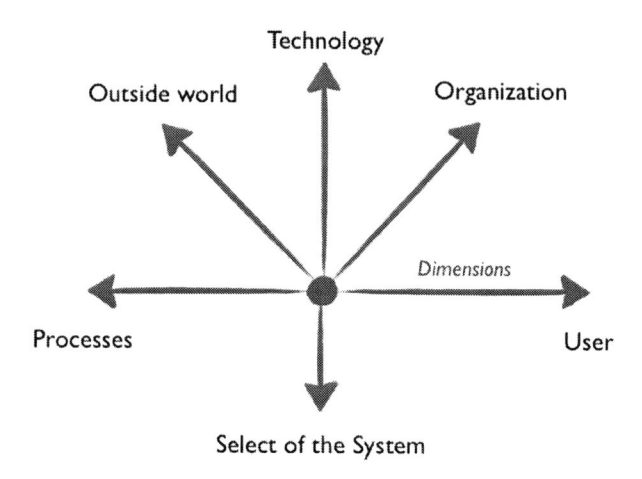

Fig. 3. Dimensions of impact of consolidation

## 4 Planning Consolidation Steps

The improved approach illustrated in steps 1 to 4 in Figure 4 can reduce costs and create a lean SAP system that meets all requirements. Step 5 acts as the link to the company's strategic transformation goals, but can also be used in conjunction with projects other than consolidation, such as re-design projects.

Fig. 4. Consolidation in five steps [6]

Step 1 consists of comparing the elements actually used, checking for identity and scanning for elements missing from the target system. Unused elements should also be identified and deleted.

## 4.1 Reduce and Simplify

Reduction in step 2 involves examining processes and users employed peripherally (i.e. either seldom or very frequently). An analytical approach to identifying low usage of processes, master data and transactions is to set a threshold value when comparing source and target systems. This paints a broader picture of usage and how its intensity varies, providing key facts for discussion with user departments. What should be the focus of migration? What is not so important?

Thanks to its comparison and analysis tools, the usage analysis achieves much more than simple technical migration of tables by the second step of consolidation:

- Only actively used elements are transferred from the source system.
- Knowledge about the elements really missing from the target system enables clear planning of enhancement time and costs.
- Concentration on frequently-used application areas ensures the new system's effectiveness.
- Elimination of seldom-used or obsolete objects reduces project costs.
- Target areas used only rudimentarily can be replaced by frequently-used processes, master data, etc. from the source systems, simplifying migration.

## 4.2 Standardize

The following rule is helpful to prepare for consolidation, to find a standard for a specific project, or to decide on an alternative: standardization cuts costs thanks to uniform rules and simplification. This should be the deciding factor when several alternatives are possible. A politically or legally dominant SAP client might set the standard for other consolidated clients. This can render specific transactions from the source client obsolete – in Financial Accounting, for instance – and these should not be transferred to the target system. Sometimes it can mean using a more advanced transaction from the source systems as the standard.

## 4.3 Harmonize

Harmonization entails discovering the most efficient and effective method for implementing a business model to align and reduce master data, functions or processes in similar areas. The harmonization analysis can also be used to compare difficult and complex business processes between two consolidation clients, to align them with one another. In contrast to standardization, the goal is not to harmonize the same settings across all clients, but to align similar master data, functions or processes with one another based on a single, focused business objective.

## 4.4 Transform

Business transformation entails gearing systems, processes and employees toward new goals. It determines the strategic and organizational guidelines and objectives for a consolidation project. Technical consolidation of SAP clients is not considered business transformation; it is merely one of the steps taken as part of an overarching strategic initiative.

All project managers and/or planners of consolidation projects should try to pass through all five steps. It is best to strip down, scale back and focus on business process issues before consolidating systems on a technical basis. The subsequent steps, standardization and harmonization, can be implemented independently of one another. Preparing systematically for business transformation is something that must be done repeatedly and extensively. Transformation must be goal-oriented and IT departments must be willing to work toward forward-thinking adaptation. This is not only useful when consolidating several different SAP systems, but also when incorporating new strategies, business models and processes into an SAP infrastructure. Business-IT transformations can free up space for innovations.

## 5 Summary

Consolidation projects cannot be launched without sufficient information on the starting point; lacking this, it is impossible to estimate the time, effort and challenges involved. Business process usage is pivotal for consolidation of IT systems and clearly shows that focus on technical aspects alone does not guarantee a project's success. Therefore, consider the following aspects at each consolidation stage:

1. **Compare**
   Conduct a semantic identity and missing elements analysis based on data in the IT systems to discover differences in process usage.
2. **Unify**
   The comparison analysis delivers a comprehensive consolidation road map, complete with identity keys, missing elements and their usage intensity and range. It also includes the potential impact of their reduction or transfer to the target system. This comparison can be used as the basis for selecting a consolidation scenario and the future organization of functions and processes in the target system.
3. **Consolidate**
   Technical steps such as master and transaction data migration and customization of the target system should be planned in the last phase.

Observe the recommendations made in this article, conducting a process usage analysis, including the required comparison techniques and consolidation projects will be based on facts.

## References

1. Gerhardt, J.: Dienstleistungsproduktion. Josef Eul, Köln, 105 (1987)
2. SAP, accenture: BPM-Technologie im systematischen Überblick: Ein Leitfaden zur Anwendung von Business Process Management, p. 19 (2009),
   http://www.evolvedtechnoligst.com

3. Hagemann, J., Rosenberg, A., Moller, C., Scavillo, M.: Business Process Management - the SAP Roadmap. SAP Press (2008)
4. RAAD Research, Kostenoptimierung bei SAP-Kunden: Betrieb frisst Innovation. In Computerwoche (March 3)
5. Laudon, K.C., Laudon, J.P., Schoder, D.: Wirtschaftsinformatik. Person Studium, 865, 973 (2010)
6. Hufgard, A.: ROI von SAP-Lösungen verbessern, p. 291, 299. Galileo Press, Bonn (2010)
7. IBIS Prof. Thome AG: RBE Plus Analysen. Unter, http://www.ibis-thome.de/305.html (access on March 23, 2011)

# Part III

# Technological Advancements

# Platform for Managing and Routing Cross-Organizational Business Processes on a Network Router

Nils Meyer, Markus Radmayr, Richard Heininger, Thomas Rothschädl, and Albert Fleischmann

Metasonic AG, Münchner Straße 29, Hettenshausen, 85276 Pfaffenhofen, Germany
{nils.meyer,markus.radmayr,richard.heininger,
thomas.rothschaedl,albert.fleischmann}@metasonic.de

**Abstract.** Today's business process- and workflow management is not limited to organizational borders but relates to network structures. Customers, partners and suppliers need to be supported on the basis of coordinated value added chains. The respective workflow engines however are in most cases sealed off by a corporate network and thus not reachable from outside without further ado. In this article we will revise our jCPEX! approach for connecting inter-organizational business process and present a solution where the jCPEX! platform resolves the mentioned impediment of private networks by being provided on a network router that connects the external net with the corporate network of an organization, making a separate DMZ superfluous for this purpose.

**Keywords:** jCPEX!, cross-organizational, interorganizational, business process management, network router.

## 1 Introduction

Due to globalization and increased market transparency, enterprises face raising competitive pressure. Fast technological developments causing shorter life cycles of products as well as more complex products require organizations to cooperate to meet these challenging requirements [1] [2]. "Different organizations contribute only those activities for which they provide the highest quality, productivity and innovation." [3]

Moreover, cooperation must not be static and long-lasting. In order to be able to quickly adapt to challenges like market change, prospects and risks, organizations must have the ability to replace their partners fast and at low costs. Partners are more and more selected just for a short to medium period of time [4].

As organizations use process-aware information systems to perform their workflows in an automated way, these requirements also need to be considered in the area of business process workflows that span beyond organizational boundaries [5].

In most cases, the workflow engine used for cross-organizational connection of business processes will be placed in the organizations internal corporate network to protect their private data from vulnerabilities and threats. For this reason an approach is needed to connect workflow engines of cooperating organizations, which are both not accessible directly through the internet.

In [6] we published requirements for interorganizational business process workflow and presented a solution for dynamically connecting business processes between organizations. In this paper we will briefly revise this approach and look into options to overcome the above mentioned restriction with workflow engines in the private net. Subsequently we will show an approach where our platform is placed on a network router to solve this issue.

Section 2 in short introduces the approach for dynamically connecting executable business processes through the jCPEX! platform. We go into the behavioural interface, the choreography that brings business partners together and serves as an interface the participants have to implement, and reveal what steps are necessary to bring the cross-organizational workflow finally to execution. In Section 3 we describe several alternatives to technically connect workflow engines separated in the respective corporate network, before presenting our way to resolve this with the jCPEX! platform installed on the enhancement mechanism of a network router in Section 4. The paper concludes with Section 5, a continuous example of connecting business process together by means of the jCPEX! platform, from the provision of the common choreography in the form of a behavioural interface, through the implementation and publishing of services compliant to the behavioural interface, till the execution of the whole process over the jCPEX! network router.

## 2 Cross-Organizational Workflow - The jCPEX!-Platform

In [6] we introduced the jCPEX! approach of connecting business processes beyond organizational boundaries in a dynamic way and compared different orchestration as well as choreography description languages to formerly determined requirements of interorganizational BPM. In the following, we give a brief overview of the basic concepts of the jCPEX! approach.

In jCPEX! we describe the communication between the involved partners as an implementation-independent choreography (classification see [7]) - the so called behavioural interface (BI). Implementation details are added by the jCPEX! platform, mainly in the form of rules for routing the message to the designated remote process.

The behavioural interface describes the observable behaviour (similar to private processes [8] or the view concept of [5]) of the participating processes and their communication via message exchange. It can be automatically extracted from a partner's private process or modelled separately from scratch.

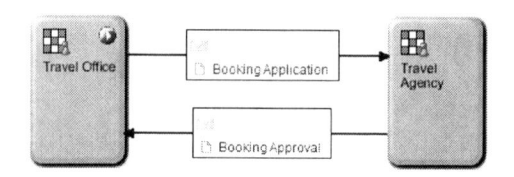

**Fig. 1.** Communications view of a behavioural interface

The behavioural interface can be seen as interface to the private processes of the participating partners. It facilitates replacement of a partner dynamically dependent on certain conditions – even at runtime. Fig. 1 shows a simple example of the communications view of a behavioural interface for a business travel booking process use case.

The workflow of the interface is described in more detail in the "internal behaviour" associated to each of the two subjects (Travel Office and Travel Agency) and is illustrated in Fig. 2. (the dotted lines are for better visualization only and show the message flow taken over from the communications view)

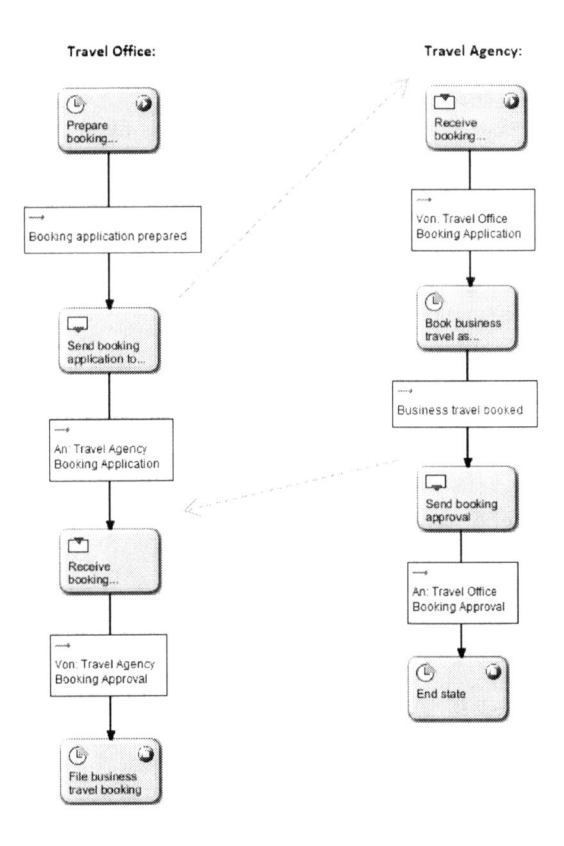

**Fig. 2.** Internal Behaviour of the business travel booking-BI

Several organizations can now provide an "implementation" of the behavioural interface by extending one side of the BI with their private and internal process. This processes will not be published and therefore not be visible to any of the partners. Only the fact that an organization offers a realization of a certain behavioural interface will be announced on the jCPEX! platform (for more detail of the whole concept please refer to sections 4 and 5).

Before executing a cross-organizational process, the organization starting the process has to specify rules that determine which remote process shall be chosen in certain conditions. These rules can interpret e.g. the selected receivers or attached data forms (called business objects in the case of S-BPM). If, for example, an employee wants to go on business travel to Japan (field "destination" in the business travel application form), another travel agency is chosen as if she travels inside Europe.

Also the triggered (receiving) organization has to specify rules for its supported behavioural interfaces to establish a connection on the jCPEX! platform between the specific BIs and the concrete internal processes. With this concept, service providers are capable of providing different internal processes (implementations) for one cross-organizational case, all conforming to the same behavioural interface. This is beneficial e.g. for providing regular customers with special services or to distinguish customers on regional criteria.

In most of the cases, the workflow engine running the (private) processes will be situated in the corporate network and thus not be accessible from the internet without explicit defined exceptions. For interorganizational cooperation through business processes it is however necessary that the workflow engine can receive messages from the partner's processes.

The next section will describe the challenges with services sealed off by a corporate network and present common solutions for connecting such services that are not reachable from outside without further ado as well as their respective advantages and drawbacks.

## 3 The Difficulty with Workflow Engines in the Corporate Network

Organizations executing business processes will normally locate their workflow engines in the private corporate network to protect them from unsafe internet traffic. As a consequence, mechanism are required to establish a connection for dispatching messages between workflow engines of organizations taking part in interorganizational process workflows.

In the following we present five possible solutions for connecting secured workflow engines that are not directly accessible.

### 3.1 EDIFACT over Internet

One of the most used standards for B2B communication is United Nations Electronic Data Interchange for Administration, Commerce and Transport (UN/EDIFACT or, more commonly EDIFACT).

EDIFACT is the international Electronic Data Interchange (EDI) which was developed by the United Nations Economic Commission for Europe in the year 1990. The aim of this standard was to standardize paperless trading by the creation of tools that would make electronic interchange of data in international trade a secure, effective and cheap alternative [15].

Although EDIFACT is a well situated standard and, especially in Europe widely used there is no standard or best practice for the cross-organisational use of EDIFACT. This has the advantage that, theoretically, companies can choose its favourite way to exchange business documents. However, due to dependencies to other companies an organisation could be forced to exchange its business documents in different ways.

One commonly way for interchanging electronic business documents is value-added networks (VAN). These networks have been specifically designed and operated for EDIFACT. Each trading partner has a mailbox within a VAN and if an EDIFACT message sent to a trading partner is put into its mailbox. The trading partner can receive messages from there [16]. Although all VANs are connected with each other so that any trading partner on any VAN can reach any other trading partner on any other VAN, the obvious problem is that a trading partner has to have access to a VAN.

Another common way is the use of FTP or e-mail (Fig. 3) for the exchange of EDIFACT documents which could also be done by a workflow engine.

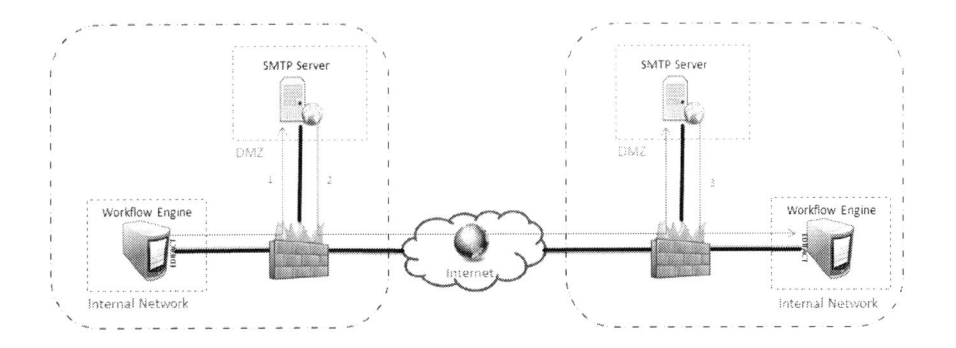

**Fig. 3.** EDIFACT over e-mail

### 3.2 Point to Point Integration

Another solution for the integration of workflow engines is to connect them pairwise over the internet (Fig. 4). Each workflow engine is configured with the information how it can reach the other workflow engine. For cross-organisational processes it can reach the other workflow engine which also needs to be configured to communicate with the other engine.

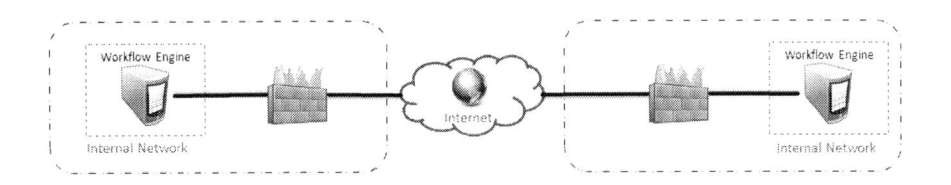

**Fig. 4.** Point-to-Point connection of workflow engines

As workflow engines are usually hosted in the internal network of a company, the firewall needs some exceptions to assure the data transfer between the business partners.

While the point-to-point integration provides basic integration functionality, it has limitations that are relevant in more complex integration scenarios. Apart from security problems in opening ports in the firewall and forward them to the workflow engine, this solution has also a rather static character. Each new business partner has to be manually integrated in the workflow engine which should work on a higher technical abstraction layer.

### 3.3 Publish/Subscribe Technology

Message queues can be noted as a further solution. They represent the publish/subscribe-technology, which is characterized by one (or more) producers and consumers of data. The producer might publish data to a given endpoint, whereas consumers are subscribed to this endpoint and get data at some point [16].

Message queues provide an asynchronous way to connect workflow engines, meaning that the sender and receiver of the message do not need to be directly connected. The sending process places the message onto the queue where it is stored until the receiving process picks it up (illustrated in Fig. 5). These message queuing systems usually provide enhanced resilience functionality to ensure that messages do not get "lost" in the event of a system failure [18]. The message queuing system will typically be installed in the DMZ of the organization to be accessible through the internet through defined and opened ports. Depending on the used transport protocol, this can of course also be the standard web port 80.

Nevertheless, extra hardware like a web server is necessary for this approach, and there are several issues regarding consuming intervals, buffer overflows and loss of process control. Apart from that, queuing technologies do not support business logic by default and enhancements may be difficult to implement.

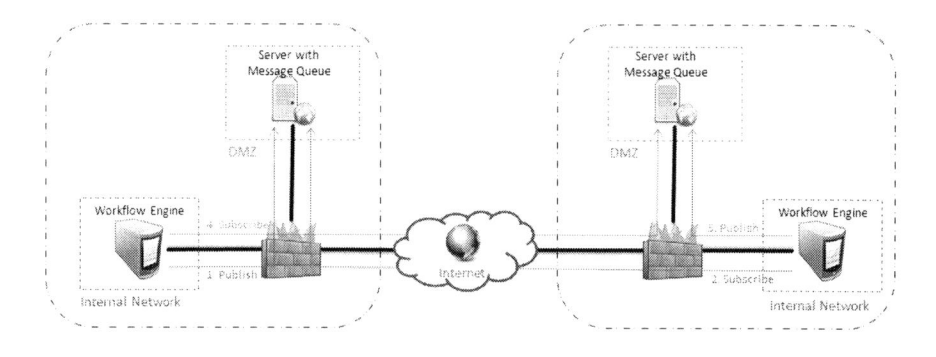

**Fig. 5.** Publish/Subscribe architecture for connecting workflow engines

One scientifically well documented approach for a publish/subscribe System is PADRES which is described in [21]. In combination with the NIÑOS runtime, a distributed business process execution architecture, it is possible to execute Business.

Process Execution Language (BPEL) programs in a decentralized, orchestrated PADRES environment and according to [22] NIÑOS would also be applicable for realization of cross-enterprise business process management, where no one single entity runs and controls the entire business process, but rather the process emerges as a choreographed concert of activities and subprocesses run by each organization.

NIÑOS uses agents which assures the communication between the Web Service Protocols and the BPEL engine. [22].

### 3.4 Enterprise Service Bus

One of the latest solutions for integrating cross-organizational workflows could be an Enterprise Service Bus. "An Enterprise Service Bus is a standard-based integration platform that combines messaging, web services, data transformation and intelligent routing in a highly distributed, event-driven Service Oriented Architecture" [17] In other words an ESB provides a distributed, message-oriented architecture which supports traditional Enterprise Architecture Integration features such as message routing and transformation within the context of integration based upon "business services" and XML messages. It should be the technology that adds 'intelligence' to the integration infrastructure which also enables interactions between multiple systems and organizations.

With an ESB solution it is possible to connect workflow engines in a cross-organizational context over web services including dynamic message dependent routing to remote workflow engines. Similar to a message queue approach, a (web) server in the demilitarized zone (DMZ) is required for the ESB, which then routes the communication to the workflow engine in the organization's internal network.

### 3.5 Web Services

According to the W3C working group note about "Web Services Architecture" [14], a web service is a software system created with the intention of enabling the interoperable machine-to-machine communication over a network. The interface description has to be in a machine-processable format, such as WSDL, and other information systems may connect to the web service via SOAP messages, also defined within the interface. SOAP messages are usually transferred via HTTP as serialized XML and in connection with other relevant network standards [14].

As we have mentioned, the lack of a missing established industry standard regarding the connection of business process management suites, led to the development of proprietary interfaces. Those might normally be designed to interconnect based on HTTP with messages in any XML format. Several advantages such as low difficulty and fast development result from this design decision. SOAP, XML, HTTP and numerous other web standards created a solid platform and infrastructure for this kind of information systems.

Consequently, web services facilitate the interoperability between organizations. As necessary network protocols are usually permitted by the network administrators, no additional security problems are invoked with the implementation of such a process gateway in a demilitarized zone. The only limitation may result from the modeling standard and the workflow integration of web services. Workflow engines may easily work together on an interorganizational basis, if these constraints can be resolved. As Web Services are only the technology of calling a remote service or method, no enhanced functionality is related to this approach automatically. This is up to the workflow engines or some middleware that has supplementary to be added, which again results in the need of an additional server.

We have presented EDIFACT, point to point integration, publish/subscribe technology, enterprise service bus and Web Service as technologies to connect workflow engines of different organizations. Of course they can usefully be combined for more significant solutions. In the next section we will introduce our approach and show, which of these technologies we applied for the jCPEX! platform.

## 4 jCPEX! on a Network Router

As shown in the previous section, several approaches are available for inter-organizational connection of process management engines respectively workflow management suites. This section covers the introduction and description of our approach, focusing on hands-on examination. First, an overview of the jCPEX platform is given, followed by an introduction to our interface called "Behavioural Interface", and finally we end with a critical survey of advantages and possible misleads of our approach.

### 4.1 Overview jCPEX! Platform

In the previous section we discussed available possibilities for technically connecting workflow engines beyond organizational boundaries..

Our approach obviously does have several analogies with the concept of an ESB presented in 0: The jCPEX! platform serves as a hub for the integration of distributed workflow engines and as an interpreter taking care of a frictionless communication between the process engines for interorganizational workflow. As a result, the workflow engines do not need to have a direct connection by what it does not matter if they are sealed off in the internal corporate network.

Furthermore, Web Services (section 3.5) are used to transport the messages from the sending process to the jCPEX! platform on the process router as well as to further forwarding it from the jCPEX! platform to the receiving process instance. Web Services offer the advantage that XML is supported as message format as well as the standard hypertext transport protocol can be used for transportation, which should minimize troubles with interposed firewalls.

The following technologies are combined on the jCPEX! platform:

- Web Services (technical)
- SMILA (semantic search)
- USDL (metadata description language)

jCPEX! integrates these technologies to create a platform, providing the possibility of a highly agile connection between business partners. Fig. 6 gives an outline of the architecture.

We assume a large number of business process management suites installations. Therefore, it would be very easy to connect these installations with a standardized protocol, a flexible platform and a capable interface.

Fig. 6 delineates the basic architecture of our approach. The company's business process management engine is installed in the private corporate network and runs the orchestrated workflows. For interorganizational business processes, the messages are forwarded to the jCPEX! platform located on the enhancement mechanism of a network router, Cisco's Service Ready Engine Virtualization (SRE-V), which will be described later in this section. Cisco's SRE-V hosts the web service, SMILA and the USDL repository, providing all necessary process routing functionality.

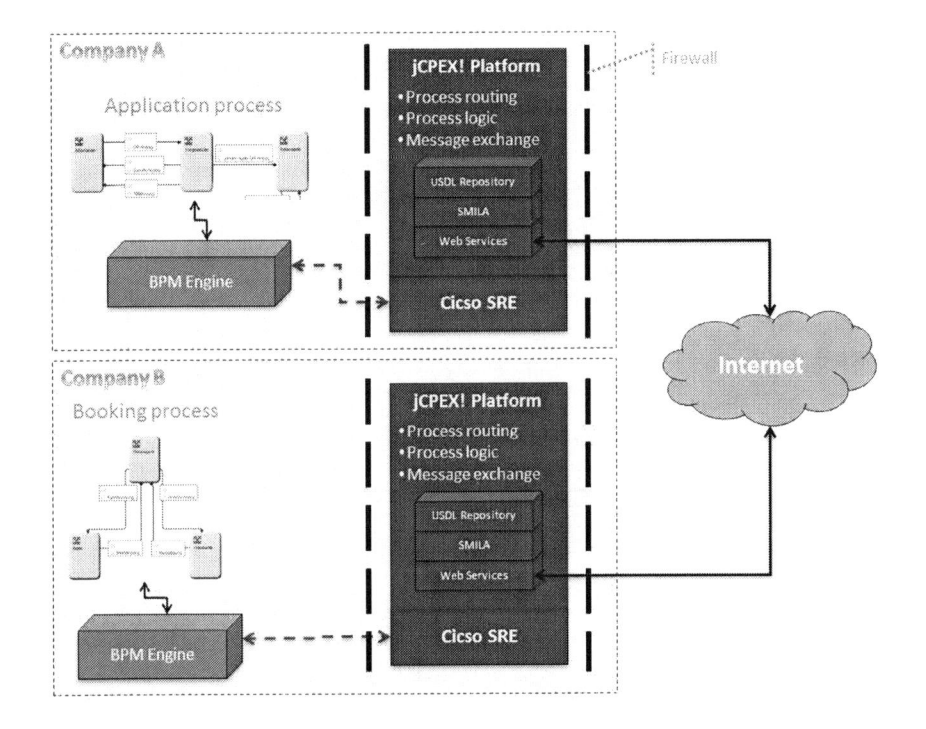

**Fig. 6.** jCPEX! Platform

**Cisco Service Ready Engine Virtualization.** The usage of available infrastructure resources might be one of the most important aspects and goals of jCPEX!. Consequently, we decided to implement the prototype of our platform on Cisco's Service Ready Engine, which is a high-performance router blade for Cisco ISR G2. This Service Ready Engine supports different applications, whereas we chose the virtualization platform SRE-Virtualization [11]. This platform provides VMware vSphere Hypervisor, a full featured virtualization engine, with numerous benefits [10] [11]:

- Remote management with network and server separation
- Centralized management and troubleshooting
- Compact, all-in-one networking and computing system, no additional server required
- Reduced total cost of ownership (TCO) of branch-office infrastructure

In case of our prototype, we decided to install Ubuntu Server Edition 10.10 as operating system within this virtual environment. Additionally, we configured a database management system and a java servlet container.

**Web Service.** As mentioned above, Web Services are used for communication between the workflow engines and the jCPEX! platform as well as between the distributed jCPEX! platforms of the participating organizations. Therefore, web services build the technical layer for communication.

**SMILA.** This extensible framework is developed for building search solutions to access unstructured information. The jCPEX! search realized with SMILA is used by service providers for searching for process interfaces (BIs) that can be implemented and offered as a service. Customer use the search, accessible on the own jCPEX! platform, to find implementations of behavioural interfaces (services) one can use in its business process. Both, behavioural interfaces and their implementations are described in USDL and stored in a repository wherefrom the SMILA search retrieves its data [13].

**USDL Repository.** The Unified Service Description Language (USDL) is a platform-independent language for describing services. This language consists of three domains: business, operational and technical. These domains ensure the complete electronic representation of business services including all possible and needed facets. For instance, all legal and trading notes are included. As already mentioned, in jCPEX! the metadata of process interfaces (e.g. description of the service, capabilities, ...) and implementations (description of the service provider, service level agreements, legal, ...) as well as the choreography description (currently in PASS, a process description language based on pi-calculus) are stored in USDL [12].

The storage of these USDL documents is provided by a repository especially developed for this purpose. The so called USDL Repository provides storage, SMILA based search functions, browsing, management and numerous additional features concerning USDL documents.

### 4.2 Behavioural Interface

We have described so far the technical implementation of our jCPEX! platform. Conceptually, the Behavioural Interface is one of the key concepts of the approach. It contains the interaction behaviour between involved actors and therefore represents the choreography for all concerned parties. Moreover, the behavioural interface contains additional information to comparable interfaces such as WS-CDL [6]. This enhances our approach in comparison to existing solutions.

Another advantage of the behavioural interface is that it automatically can be derived from the internal private process if the subject-oriented modelling language (a discussion of S-BPM can be found in [19]) is use. Below, we will show this procedure in short. Initial point is the process in Fig. 7, a business travel booking service provided by a travel agency. The process is shown in his communications view that means, all involved subjects are presented with the message flow between them. Subject Travel Agent, which communicates with the external subject Travel Office representing the customer, can be seen as the interface to this process. To get the observable behaviour of this process viewed from the customer's position, we have to replace all communication relations to internal subjects, which are insignificant for the choreography with the customer, with internal function. In a second step, redundant internal functions originated from the first step can be aggregated. The result is a choreography called behavioural interface in our approach, which can be used to create and verify opposing processes and additional implementations.

The next section illustrates our approach in detail. This includes the description of the whole business process management lifecycle.

## 5 Detailed Illustration of the jCPEX! Approach

In this section we go through the individual steps necessary for modelling and executing a cross-organizational business-process with the jCPEX! platform to further clarify the jCPEX! concept and the benefits of using the introduced network router approach. For modelling we use the S-BPM modelling language as we implemented the necessary web services for the S-BPM based Metasonic Suite only so far.

**Providing a service.** We continue the example from section 2 where we showed an exemplary behavioural interface for a business travel booking service. This behavioural interface could have been modelled from scratch e.g. by an independent institution like an umbrella organization for travel agencies, or be automatically extracted from the entire modelled process of a certain travel agency (Fig. 7.).

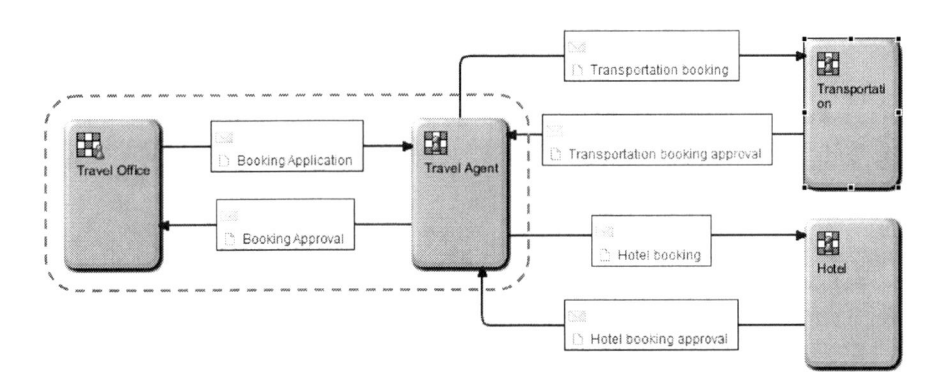

**Fig. 7.** Process model of business travel booking service

The green doted rectangle points to the fragment of the process model that conforms to the behavioural interface, at least in the communications view. This part was then extended with internal process details, which have been simplified for this showcase. In fact, the process "behind" the subject communicating with the service consumer (Travel Agent) would be of course much more complex in a real scenario.

In case the behavioural interface was extracted by the organization providing the service, the behavioural interface will be published on the jCPEX! process router associated with this travel agency's workflow engine. On the process router it is also stored that the referenced workflow engine provides a concrete realization of the service offered by the interface. The business and operational aspects of the provided service is described with USDL (see section 4.1). To link the implemented public behavioural interface with the concrete business process, a rule is defined that instructs the jCPEX! process router which process to initiate if a message related to a certain behavioural interface is arriving.

**Using a service.** Organizations requiring a particular service can use the search capability provided by their internal jCPEX! platform to detect a suitable offer. Services can be searched by business- or operational properties defined in the USDL for each process. In the future it should also be possible to automatically find services that fit my process. Process pattern matching [9] and the distributed automatic service composition approach [20] will be examined for that purpose. The appropriate behavioural interface can then be downloaded into the modelling tool and be extended with the required process elements. As there can be more than one provider offering an implementation for a certain behavioural interface, a rule has to be created on the side of the triggering process to determine the favoured provider to be used on execution. It is possible to define multiple rules to invoke different service providers in distinct cases. As already mentioned, these cases can e.g. be distinguished by certain data delivered with the message. In our example, the destination of the business travel would be a candidate for distinguishing certain travel agencies.

**Additional implementations of a behavioural interface.** Just like consumers, also further service providers – in our case travel agencies - are able to search and implement published behavioural interfaces to provide an implementation of the service on their part. After realizing the internal process, the corresponding behavioural interface will be duplicated on their local jCPEX! process router and the description of the provided service is published in the form of USDL at the same place. Equivalent to the first service provider mentioned above, a rule is mandatory to be able to forward incoming messages for a certain behavioural interface to the concrete process deployed on the internal workflow engine.

**Execution.** When it comes to execution of the interorganizational business process, the workflow engine detects that the receiver of a certain message is located outside the local engine and forwards the message to the Web Service interface of the jCPEX! process router. On this platform, the rules associated to the used behavioural interface (with uid-4df67bf4-ba8c) are analysed to determine the appropriate receiver. In the travel booking example shown in Fig. 8 the travel destination is Japan, and the according rule determines Travel Agency 1 as the intended receiver of the message. The jCPEX! platform routes the message forward to the jCPEX! process router of Travel Agency 1. The receiving jCPEX! platform is responsible for determining the according process on the internal workflow engine, and handles this by interpreting the rules available for the behavioural interface underlying the received message. In our case, no conditions are defined and all incoming messages for this behavioural interface are routed to the process with the internal id *process1283413933*. This, again, is realized by a Web Service call to the workflow engine. The router is configured in a way that it has access to the appropriate service of the workflow engine in the private corporate network.

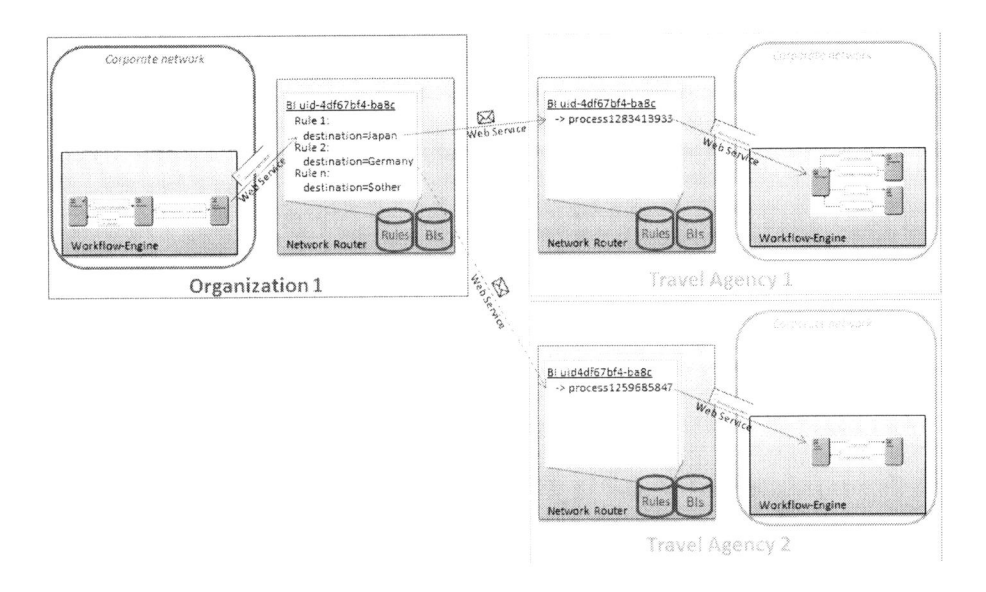

**Fig. 8.** Execution of a cross-organizational business process with jCPEX! on a network router

For the message back to the customer organization (booking approval) it is neither required to have rules on the travel agency's side nor on the side of the originating organization since the message has only to be routed to the original sender and triggering process, whose identifications are stored in the transmitted message

In our prototype we only realized the necessary Web Service interface for the S-BPM based Metasonic Suite, but the jCPEX! approach is in fact applicable for all workflow engines providing an implementation of the specified interface.

## 6 Critical Survey

As we have shown, our approach and the implementation of our prototype addresses missing solutions in the field of business process management. However, we would like to bring up core benefits and possible misleads within this subsection. Both aspects will consequently result in further research and future work.

Subject-oriented business process management (S-BPM) has significant advantages in modelling the interaction behaviour of actors. Thus, modelling the explicit communication of participants is inevitable linked with S-BPM. Process modellers do not need to change their modelling behaviour and do not need to acquire new modelling skills.

Furthermore, integrating the jCPEX! platform enables organizations to route their processes on a rule-based manner. This allows the connection of several workflow engines, whereas our platform takes over message routing and connects the process to the adequate receiver. This task includes the possible integration of business logic, such as verifying tasks and quality assurance.

On the other hand, we should note the missing and still developing standardization of the Behavioural Interface. This may result in yet another inter-organizational business process management description language. This subject definitely needs ongoing research. At the moment, the behavioural interface is specified with the subject-oriented modelling description language PASS. While focusing on our novel interface, it should also be examined, if older specifications such as WS-CDL or Let's Dance may meet our requirements to describe the behavioural interface. However, we already discussed missing features of existing solutions earlier [6].

## 7 Conclusion and Future Work

In this paper we presented an approach to overcome the issue of connecting workflow engines located in the private corporate networks of different organizations participating in interorganizational business processes workflow.

Starting with briefly revising our jCPEX! approach for cross-organizational workflow management we demonstrated the benefits of using the jCPEX! platform installed on the extension mechanism of a network router. Usually, workflow engines of organizations executing business processes are protected from various external threats by hiding them in the internal corporate network where only authorized internet-traffic is passed through. There are several options to allow workflow engines to be reached from outside, each of them causing more or less administrative and set up effort. By using the jCPEX! platform for managing the communication between the involved participants on a network router in the DMZ, this effort can be reduced to a minimum without cutting back immunity standards. Subsequently we presented the entire approach where two organizations handle their interorganizational business process via the jCPEX! platform on their respective network router.

Next steps will introduce a "process firewall", a mechanism that allows partners to reject messages from certain sender ("allow all" with exceptions) or to just accept messages from authorized sender ("deny all" with exceptions). A use case for this requirement could be e.g. to accept letters of credit from my local bank only.

Another issue we will tackle in the future is to make use of the router API to facilitate further use cases. By using the router API we want to make the platform aware of the network state. It is then possible to cache a message if the WAN connection is down and resend it as soon as the connection is established again.

For the jCPEX! approach we are working on the integration of algorithms to verify the soundness and correctness of the processes implementing a behavioural interface (does the implementation conform to the interface) development at the University of Darmstadt [9]. This algorithm is also applicable to be used for searching for implementations that do not match exactly a particular behavioural interface but could be used after minor adjustments.

## References

1. Grefen, P., Eshuis, R., Mehandjiev, N., Kouvas, G., Weichhart, G.: Internet-Based Support for Process-Oriented Instant Virtual Enterprises. IEEE Internet Computing, 30–38 (November/December 2009)
2. Pieper, R., Kouwenhoven, V., Hamminga, S.: Behond the Hype - e-Business Strategy in Leading European Companies. Van Haren Publishing (2001)

3. Decker, G., Weske, M.: Interaction-centric modeling of process choreographies. Information Systems (2010)
4. Timmers, P.: Electronic Commerce - Strategies and Models for Business-to-Business Trading. John Wiley & Sons, Chichester (1999)
5. Chebbi, I., Dustdar, S., Tata, S.: The view-based approach to dynamic inter-organizational workflow cooperation. Data & Knowledge Engineering 56(2), 139–173 (2006)
6. Meyer, N., Feiner, T., Radmayr, M., Blei, D., Fleischmann, A.: Dynamic Catenation and Execution of Cross Organisational Business Processes - The jCPEX! approach. In: S-BPM ONE 2010 - The Subject-oriented BPM Conference (2011)
7. Decker, G., Kopp, O., Barros, A.: An Introduction to Service Choreographies. Information Technology 50(2), 122–127 (2008)
8. Ziemann, J., Matheis, T., Freiheit, J.: Modelling of Cross-Organizational Business Processes - Current Methods and Standards. Enterprise Modelling and Information Systems Architectures 2, 23–31 (2007)
9. Aitenbichler, E., Borgert, S., Mühlhäuser, M.: Distributed Execution of S-BPM Business Processes. In: S-BPM ONE 2010 - The Subject-oriented BPM Conference (2011)
10. Cisco Services-Ready Engine Modules At-a-Glance, http://www.cisco.com/en/US/prod/collateral/modules/ps10598/at_a_glance_c45_556153.pdf (downloaded April 7, 2011)
11. Services Ready Engine Virtualization Self Training Guide, http://www.cisco.com/en/US/prod/collateral/ps10265/ps11273/installation_guide_c07-640002.html (visited on April 7, 2011)
12. Internet of Services: about USDL, http://www.internet-of-services.com/index.php?id=288&L=0 (visited on April 7, 2011)
13. SMILA - Unified Information Access Architecture, http://www.eclipse.org/smila/ (visited on April 7, 2011)
14. Web Services Architecture, http://www.w3.org/TR/ws-arch/ (visited on April 7, 2011)
15. United Nations Economic Commisssion for Europe, Un/Edifact Draft Directory. Un/Edifact Draft Directory Part 1 Introduction
16. Bussler, C.: B2B integration: concepts and architecture. Springer, Berlin (2003)
17. Chappell, D.E.: Enterprise Service Bus - Theory in Practice. O'Reilly, Sebastopol (2004)
18. Message queue (Wikipedia), http://en.wikipedia.org/wiki/Message_queue (visited on April 4, 2011)
19. Fleischmann, A.: What is S-BPM? In: Buchwald, H., Fleischmann, A., Seese, D., Stary, C. (eds.) S-BPM ONE 2009. CCIS, vol. 85, pp. 85–106. Springer, Heidelberg (2010)
20. Hu, S., Muthusamy, V., Li, G., Jacobsen, H.-A.: Distributed Automatic Service Composition in Large-Scale Systems. In: Distributed Event-Based Systems Conference (DEBS), pp. 233–244 (2008)
21. Jacobsen H.-A., Cheung A., Li G., Maniymaran B., Muthusamy V., Kazemzadeh R.S.: The PADRES Publish/Subscribe System, Middleware Systems Research Group. University of Toronto, Canada, http://msrg.org/papers/PADRESBookChapte (visited on May 30, 2011)
22. Li, G., Muthsusamy, V., Jacobsen, H.-A.: A distributed service-oriented architecture for business process execution. ACM Transactions on the Web 4, 1–33 (2010)

# ePASS-IoS 1.1: Enabling Inter-enterprise Business Process Modeling by S-BPM and the Internet of Services Concept

Stephan Borgert[1], Joachim Steinmetz[2], and Max Mühlhäuser[1]

[1] Technische Universität Darmstadt
{stephan,max}@tk.informatik.tu-darmstadt.de
Hochschulstrasse 10, 64289 Darmstadt, Germany
[2] Technische Universität Braunschweig
joachim.steinmetz@tu-braunschweig.de
Mühlenpfordtstr. 23, 38106 Braunschweig, Germany

**Abstract.** The future "Internet of Services" (IoS) will provide an open environment allowing market participants to offer and consume services over Internet marketplaces. It gives businesses the opportunity to outsource parts of their business processes. This leads to networks of cooperating businesses with a distributed execution of processes and provides a good support for inter-enterprise modeling. Many methods have been proposed to describe such processes, however most only focus on certain aspects and fall short of others. We present ePASS-IoS, a unified approach to describe processes and service choreographies with well-defined execution and verification semantics. With the formulation of the well-known workflow and interaction patterns in ePASS-IoS, we show that its expressiveness is adequate. To clearly define the semantics of the language, we formalize it using a process algebra.

**Keywords:** Business Process Modeling, Subject Oriented Modeling, ePASS, Formal Semantics, $\pi$-Calculus.

## 1 Introduction

Globalization is continuously growing and with it, the challenges for today's enterprises. New goods appear more and more frequently, while existing goods disappear within shorter time slices. Hence the number of potential business partners is increasing. Therefore, suitable solutions for inter-enterprise business process management are becoming more important. The topic of inter-enterprise business process modeling is attracting a growing interest and a couple of works have investigated challenges and requirements for such business processes [4,16,18,35,19,20].

On the other side, we can observe two other major market trends. First, the success of so-called "apps", which are end-user applications that can be easily purchased on Internet marketplaces and installed on the user's computer. Second, the SOA architectural style is increasingly used inside enterprises to reuse functionality in the application tier. The vision of the Internet of Services (IoS) lies in the connection of these two trends: software services should become tradable goods and enable the reuse of software components across businesses. In the IoS, multiple businesses cooperate and use interacting software services to implement business functionality due to the Process as a Service (PaaS) concept [10]. There are different ways how such software services are provided from a technical perspective, but we can mainly distinguish between two categories. First, there are services provided by process execution engines, such as a BPEL [26] engine. Second, there are services directly implemented in a programming language, such as Java. Regardless of this technical implementation, the behavior of such services can be described in the form of a process model, maybe on a somewhat abstract level.

In order to enable faster and easier inter-enterprise cooperation, we introduce an approach which uses the S-BPM paradigm in combination with the IoS [1]. We have chosen the "Parallel Activity Specification Scheme" (PASS[11,13]) as foundation for our extensions because we consider it the most suitable approach for these purposes. We denote the language elements which are introduced in[12] as ePASS. More reasons and advantages of ePASS in comparison with other languages are given in the explanation of the requirements and in the introduction of S-BPM in section 3.1.

Firstly, we describe the challenges and derive requirements from them. We identify two requirements that can not be fulfilled with current PASS solutions. First of all the modeling language must support the description of choreographies. The proof of this has been due up to now and will be given in section 3. The second requirement is the need for a formal verification semantics. For this we will use the $\pi$-calculus [25] in section 4 to formalize ePASS-IoS. We expect the reader to be familiar with the formal syntax and semantics [31] of the $\pi$-calculus. In section 5 we will discuss how ePASS-IoS fulfills the remaining requirements. The research context of this paper is focused on aspects enabling the automatization of testing interaction soundness in particular, and enabling soundness testing in general. Other important aspects like matching of non-functional properties or the automatical negotiation of contracts are out of the scope of this work. The following two contributions are elaborated in this paper:

1. It is shown that ePASS-IoS fulfills existing choreography requirements. An existing comparison of languages has been extended.
2. A $\pi$-calculus based formal semantics for ePASS-IoS 1.1 is given.

## 2 Challenges for S-BPM: Inter-enterprise Business and Internet of Services

### 2.1 Inter-Enterprise Business Process Modeling

In this section, we will firstly describe challenges for inter-enterprise process modeling. Secondly, we derive requirements which from these challenges and finally we explain how the challenges are met by fulfilling the requirements.

A recent work which describes important challenges for inter-enterprise process modeling is [4] which we adopt.

**C1) No central governance of the global process:** This state is usually desired from each partner and is the most appropriate.
**C2) Autonomy of business partners:** Each partner will model, execute, monitor, etc. its own part of the business process and needs the capability to hide internal aspects of its own process part.
**C3) *Directly* executable *organisational* process models:** Mathias Weske states five different levels of business processes [34]. The last three ones are the levels of the *Organisational, Operational* and *Implemented* business processes. The processes of the organizational level serve for providing and consuming purposes and therefore the processes on this level must be executable. Furthermore, these process models must be *directly* executable or should be fully automatically generatable into directly executable process models. Otherwise, the risk for a nonconformance between the process model and the actual process can be very high. This would lead to incompatibility of the distributed process parts. Usually, organizational process models and their inputs and outputs are described in text files, what makes it even harder to get them directly executable.
**C4) Support of organizational units and roles:** Processes within an enterprise are based on an existing organigram and different business roles of persons. This intra-enterprise structure has to be preserved to realize a well-formed mapping to the inter-enterprise structure.
**C5) Support of formal activity and data semantics:** In order to enable interoperability, the description language for the interface must have an unambiguous semantics. This holds also for the activities that must not or should not be hidden.

We derived the following three basic requirements from the challenges under consideration of the IoS use case and state one more important requirement.

### 2.2 Requirements

**R1) Choreography description:** The modeling language must support the description of choreographies. Choreographies allow to describe which services are interacting and constraints on their message exchange patterns. In addition, it must be clear from the process model *who* has to do what. This aspect is often insufficiently expressed in mainstream languages, such as BPMN [27], but it is important to know who is responsible for each activity once the process is executed in a distributed environment. Hence, we will introduce the concept of *subjects* below. Challenges C1), C2) and C5) are addressed by this requirement.
**R2) Formal semantics for model execution, verification and data specification.** The formal specification of process modeling languages is done mainly for two reasons. First, the process model gains clear *execution semantics*, allowing it to be directly executed in an execution engine. Second, the model gains *verification semantics*. If the model can be transformed to a Petri Net [28] or a process calculus, etc., then automated verification techniques can be applied to it. Most importantly, in the IoS scenario we want to ensure *interaction soundness* between the services. Verification is desirable in general, because it allows to detect service incompatibilities before their execution, i.e., at composition time.

The current PASS language is equipped with a formal execution semantics and a workflow engine for direct execution exists [24]. Due to this fact we consider PASS and ePASS-IoS as very exact modeling languages which is highly important property of BP modeling languages as well. A formal verification semantic is introduced for ePASS-IoS in this paper. Formalizing of data can be done by a couple of methods. Our approach is explained in section 4 and will tackle the challenges 3) and 5) given above. The formal syntax and the unambiguous semantic provide formal activity like verification methods. The formal verification will enable correct business processes through all 3 level "Organisational, Operational and Implemented", which leads into directly executable and consistent models.

**R3) Hierarchability:** Hierarchability denotes the ability to move up and down in terms of the abstraction level in the process model. This offers three important benefits. Firstly, it enables to model each of the three necessary business process abstraction levels by the same model. These levels are stated in C2) and are the levels of *Organizational, Operational* and *Implemented* business processes. ePASS and ePASS-IoS remove the gap between operational- and implemantion-level by the natural language inspired modeling concept and the capability of refinement. More details are given in section 3.1. The PASS language already delivers hierarchability by the concept of composition of subject. Just as a composition of services is a service as well, a composition of subjects is also a subject. For example, a subject oriented business process is modeled for a team in a company. The result of the process will propagate to another team of the same devision. Now, one subject can be decelerated as an external subject and can be used by other processes as an usual subject. By recursively applying this concept, any arbitrary level of abstraction is reachable with the same modeling concept. This is a large advantage on top of other languages like BPMN[27] or EPC[32]. The intension of these language is to describe the whole process within one model. BPMN consist of many elements and concepts and could be used to emulate the same kind of hierarchisation but it is not supported inherently. BPEL provides the same concept because it orchestrates services to composed services. One drawback of BPEL is that the language is not suitable for business man because of its character of an graphical, imperative programming language. Another drawback is the strong limitation to only 8 very simple interaction patterns which are prescribed by the WSDL 2.0[6]. To overcome this limit, BPEL can be equipped with an formal semantics as well as it is done for example in [22,23,21,33]. Secondly, it enables to avoid one-shot transformations. Instead of transforming from an abstract process notation to an executable notation, such as transforming from BPMN subsets to BPEL [26], all technical refinements should be directly possible within the same model. This enables us to directly execute the model and hence to keep the modeled process consistent with the executed process at all times. This requirement comes up and is driven by the challenge C3) and is a major benefit for BPM. Thirdly, businesses consider their processes often as trade secrets and are not willing to fully disclose them. The concept of hierarchability allows us to describe processes on a higher abstraction level, which is still sufficient for verifying service interactions, but they are no longer executable. Together with a well-defined semantic of the language, it is also possible to programmatically derive this *external behavior* of a service from the detailed process model. Challenges C2), C3) and C4) are addressed by this requirement.

Beside the requirements we derived from the challenges, we state one important requirement which should meet by every BP modeling language.

**R4) Expressiveness despite usability by business users:** S-BPM is supposed to be particularly usably by business users. More details are given in section 3.1 and [12]. In [14] is shown how the workflow patterns[9] can be expressed. Finally, we describe in this paper how ePASS-IoS meets the requirements of choreography description languages.

## 3  ePASS-IoS as Choreography Description Language

### 3.1  Introduction to S-BPM

To define new business processes, or to describe or adapt existing ones, many roles are often involved in enterprises. Examples for such roles are business analysts, method strategists, process engineers and others. This leads to misunderstandings during the communication between participants of different roles. The reasons for this are well known: Every participant has their own knowledge of different domains. Also, they have their own views on the process and its tasks, and/or different domain specific terms or modeling languages are used. To tackle this problem the Subject Oriented Business Process Management (S-BPM) approach uses a certain concept that is derived from natural languages. Every natural language consists of the structure elements subject, predicate and object. Furthermore, every ordinary human being speaks at least one natural language, and is therefore familiar with this concept. S-BPM processes consist of the same elements and thus we consider it as most appropriate for business

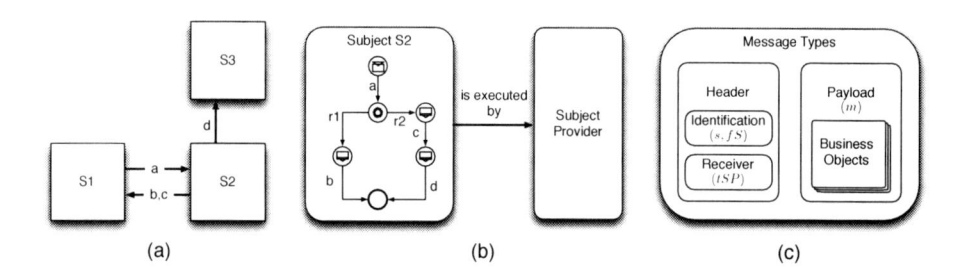

**Fig. 1.** The business process in (**a**) consists of three subjects $S1, S2, S3$ which exchange the messages $a, b, c, d$ among each other. During runtime, subjects are provided by subject providers which execute the internal behavior of the subjects (**b**). The structure of the messages is illustrated in (**c**).

users. The *Subjects* are conceptual placeholders for subject providers which are the actual actors at runtime. The *Predicates* are activities which can be performed by a subject provider. The basic activities are *Send*, *Receive* and *Action*. The *Objects* are the messages that are exchanged among subjects. Figure (1a) depicts a simple subject oriented business process model with the subjects **S1, S2** and **S3**. The subjects S1 and S2 exchange messages of the message type **a** and **b,c** while S2 and S3 exchange messages of the type **d**. In natural language we would say: S1 (subject) sends (predicate) the message **a** (object) to S2 (indirect object).

**Subjects** (Figure 1(a),1(b)) have a certain process specification which defines the internal behavior of the subject providers. All language elements of ePASS-IoS are explained in more detail in subsection 3.3. The simplified internal behavior of the subject S2 consist of the three basic activities: *Receive, Action, Send* and the *End* element. The internal behavior has the following meaning: Firstly, a message $a$ is received. Then a function is invoked which can deliver the two different return values $r1$ and $r2$. If the return value equals $r1$, then message $b$ will be send and the process will *End*. If the return value equals $r2$, then firstly the messages $c$ and $d$ are sent in a sequence and finally the execution of the internal behavior will *End*.

**Subject provider** (Figure 1(b)) are instances of subjects and execute the behavior of the subject at runtime. While a subject is only a conceptual unit, the subject provider is a living or processing unit, which interacts with other actors at runtime. Therefore, we use the term subject provider for everything that 1) has a well defined process behavior and 2) executes this behavior during the runtime of the process. One example for subject providers are humans, since they receive e-mails, files, voice commands, etc. in a business process, then they do something with these entities and finally they pass on their results. Manufacture robots also get devices or components for processing, and their behavior can be modeled with the same constructs. A subject provider can also be a software system like a stakeholder relationship management system (SRM) or an entity relationship management (ERM) system. A more practical example is a subject called *baker*. It defines the kind of subject which will be used in the process. Subject providers could be the baker Winston Smith living in city $A$ or the baker Paul Roberts living in city $B$. The process model itself should be independent from its context of execution. If the process is executed in $A$, than the subject provider Winston Smith will be used during runtime, because he lives there. Otherwise, if the process is executed in $B$, than the subject provider Winston Smith will used during runtime.

**Message types** (Figure 1(c)) consist of a **header** part and the **payload** part $m$. The header contains information for addressing and matching the messages. The message broker reads the receiver set $tSP$ of subject providers and delivers the payload and the identification information to them. The subject providers need the identification information to control their internal behavior. In this work, the set of subject providers is not supported yet. Therefore, we limit the set to one element. As we will explain in more detail below, the control flow of the internal behavior depends on the identification information. The payload is assembled by one or more **business objects**. Business objects are well defined forms or representatives for real world objects like products that have to be delivered, a physical package or everything else exchanged by enterprises. As example we choose a message content called book post. It consists of the business objects *book*, *delivery note* and a *cardboard box*. A message is an instance of message type and will be sent to the customer.

### 3.2 Architecture and Methods

ePASS-IoS consists of a graphical syntax, a formal execution semantics and a formal verification semantics. We focus on the syntax and the formal verification semantics in this paper. To enable formal verification the formal verification semantic is used to translate the process model into a formal model. While the process model is independent from the system architecture, the formal model is derived from the process model under consideration of architecture components. Figure (2) depicts the architecture of the ePASS-IoS system. The service marketplace enables the trading of businesses processes by the Process as a Service concept. Each enterprise can be a process provider or a process consumer. Process provider will register subjects of their processes which serves as connection point. Process consumer will find these subjects and can establish a connection to them during the process execution. To realize both tasks the communication channel (2a) between an enterprise and the service marketplace is used. Certainly, the service marketplace has one channel for each Enterprise as indicated in Figure 2.

A process instantiation (2A) can be triggered by two different events. Firstly, a request is sent by a **Client** application of the own enterprise (2b). Such an application can be everything that is used by a subject provider, e.g. a local or mobile

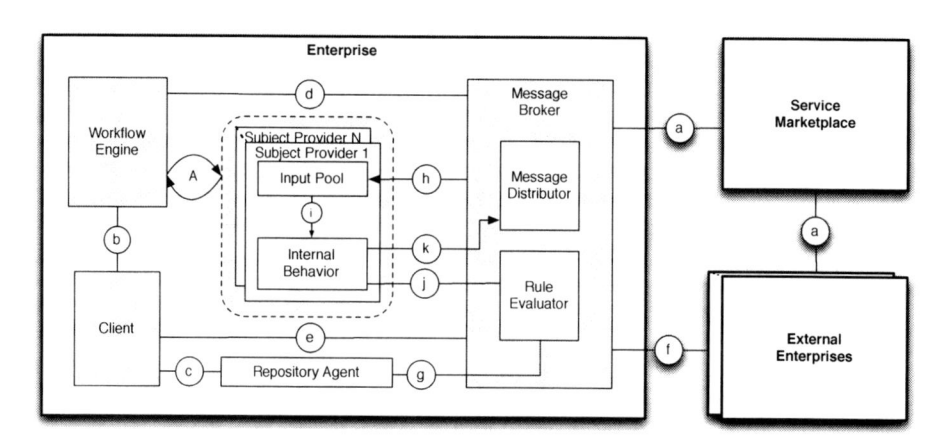

**Fig. 2.** Marketplaces serve as broker for processes. The messages are brokered by message brokers of each enterprise to the corresponding message providers.

application, a web browser application or an enterprise application like a stakeholder relationship management system (SRM). The client can get information about the process (2c) from the **Repository Agent** which is an front-end of the repository and stores all descriptions which are necessary for the BPM. All necessary information are sent to the workflow engine (2b) to instantiate the process. It constructs a new subject provider agent, notifies the message broker via channel (2d) and the client via channel (2b). Every further communication between the client and its subject provider agent is done via channel (2e).

Secondly, a request is sent by an external subject form an external enterprise (2f) and is received by the message broker. In this case the message broker evaluates the concerning rules using the Repository Agent (2g), sends an instantiation trigger to the workflow engine (2d), receives address information of the subject provider agent and delivers the message into the **Input pool** of the subject provider (2h). The input pool is a channel based message buffer and enables asynchronous communication between subject providers. Furthermore it increases interaction soundness by reducing the probability of communication deadlocks. The concept is simple: The input pool just stores messages. When the **Internal Behavior** agent of the subject provider requires a message, it is propagated to it via channel (2i). Deadlocks will only occur when both communication partner are in a receive state or one execution partner is already finished. A wrong send order of messages does not lead to a deadlock. An example is a subject provider $SP1$ which internal behavior expects first a message $m_1$ and then a message $m_2$. If the input pool of $SP1$ gets first the message $m_2$, the internal behavior agent just waits until the message $m_1$ arrives at the input pool. Then it will firstly receive $m_1$ via channel (2i) and then message $m_2$. The internal behavior agent can directly communicate to the **Rule Evaluator** agent to get sets of candidate subject providers (2j). This could be necessary for inter-enterprise communication. The set of subject providers of the own enterprise is usually known and does not change frequently. Hence, for intra-enterprise communication the selection can often be performed automatically. Further more the internal behavior agent performs all actions which can be defined by the language set shown in Figure 3. Are the receiver subject providers selected, the candidate set is sent to the message broker (2k) which will process it via the **Message Distributor**.

### 3.3 Language Elements of ePASS-IoS

The 15 language elements of the ePASS-IoS language are depicted in Figure (3). The elements 1...6, 8, 9, 14 and 15 are standard elements of ePASS and have already been explained in [12]. We introduce the syntax of the elements in this section while more details and the formal semantics of the elements are given below. The **Subject**s (1) and the **Channel**s between them (2) are used on the organizational and on the operational business process level and is denoted as layer $L_1$. Subjects are connected by unidirectional channels, which enable the communication between them. At runtime message can be sent and received by subject providers. The messages can have different message types.

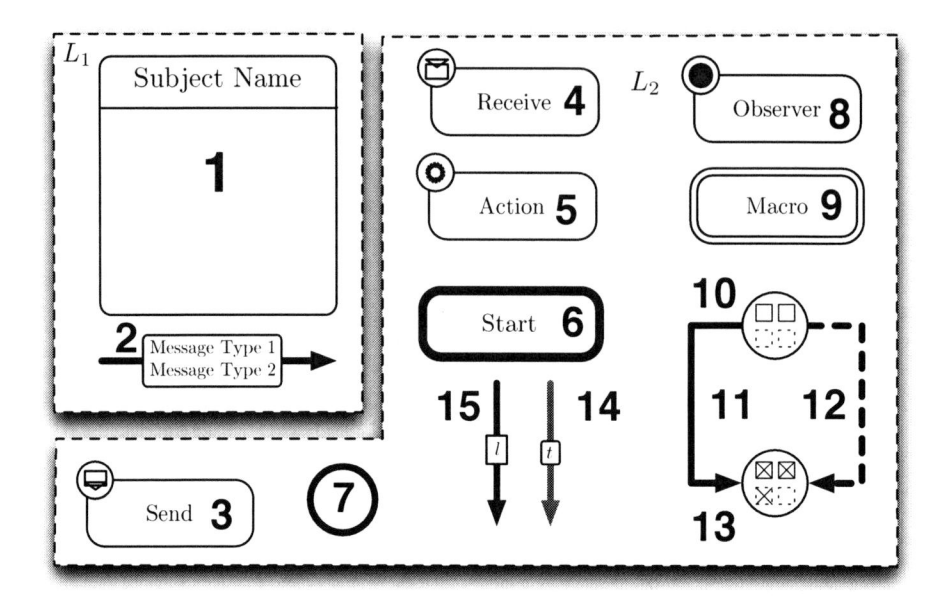

**Fig. 3.** Language Set of ePASS-IoS 1.1

The elements on the layer $L_2$ are used for modeling the internal behavior on the operational business process level at the border to the implementation level. The actions of the internal behavior can be refined with Java code which can be interpreted by the workflow engine. Therefore it is simple to connect the internal behavior of the subject provider to the IT of the implementation level. **Send** (3), **Receive** (4) and **Action** (5) are the basic activities. The internal behavior of subjects has exactly one **Start** activity (6) and can have an arbitrary number of **End** activities (7). Start activities are denoted by a bold border. Every activity can be a start activity. The **Observer** (8) manages interrupts and exceptions. When such an event happens, it leads the control flow to an alternative behavior. The **Macro** (9) just gives the ability to define a subgraph of internal behavior for the purpose of reusability. Control flow edges are used together with all the other elements of the $L_2$ layer. Label $l$ of the edge (15) has different meanings which will be explained in more detail below. Edges of type (16) are **Timeout** edges. The label $t$ denotes an absolute time. If this time is met the control flow will go along these edges. Nodes declared with (6) can have an arbitrary number of out-edges and the End node (7) can have an arbitrary number of in-edges. All other nodes can have an arbitrary number of in- and out edges. The semantics of this pattern is an exclusive choice split and join. In order to fulfill a task, certain activities often have to perform and others could be performed in addition. This is the reason for the activities (10) and (13) which are called **Modal split** and **Modal join**. They form a combination of an AND- split and join pair and an OR split and join pair. If OR traces (12) will be executed, then they will be executed in parallel to the AND traces (11). Fully automatic subject providers can perform the AND traces in parallel while human subject providers can perform them in a sequence or switch among them during the execution. These two operators are inspired from [14] where the *Checklist* operator is defined. This operator is a gateway because there is only one symbol for split an join and that is the difference to our modal split and join pair. A formal semantic was not given for the Checklist operator.

## 3.4 Requirements for Choreography Description Languages

The following requirements of Table 1 are obtained from [17,8] and are used to evaluate ePASS-IoS.

**Graphical notation (+)** The notation is given by the ePASS-IoS workflow language notation which is very similar to the original PASS notation.

**R1. Multi-lateralinteractions (+)** The number of subjects is not limited and every subject can be provided by any number of subject provider at the same time. That holds already for the graphical layer. The formal verification model of ePASS-IoS supports only one subject provider.

**R2. Service topology (+)** The subject interaction or process layer $L_1$ provides the essential structural view of the choreography.

**R3. Service sets (+)** Every subject is a placeholder for an arbitrary number of subject providers.

**R4. Selection of services and reference passing (+)** The subject providers are normally selected during runtime. The message broker manages the message delivery and one part of the message is the backchannel of the sender.

**R5. Message formats (+)** The messages are defined by XSD specifications.

**R6. Interchangeability of technical configurations (+)** As mentioned above, the process model, the embedding information of the enterprise and the embedding information of the IT of the enterprises are separated. The technical configurations are stored in the IT embedding part.

**R7. Time constraints (+)** Timeout edges can be defined on the workflow level and the edges are mapped to the formal model as well.

**R8. Exceptionhandling (+)** Exceptions and interrupts can be handled by the observer.

**R9. Correlation (+/-)** The ePASS-IoS models are models of a process instance. Different process instances can be handled by the workflow engine. There is no language element of ePASS-IoS that enables to handle different conversations to the same interaction partners. However, the correlations can be handled on the implementation layer $L_3$. That means, that Java code can be written for the involved activities.

**R10. Integration with service orchestration languages (+)** The choreographies modeled by ePASS-IoS are directly executable. Therefore the orchestration support is inherent.

**Table 1.** Choreography requirements (CR) feature matrix for BPM languages

| Requirements | BPEL | BPEL$^{light}$ | BPEL$^{gold}$ | WSFL | WS-CDL | Let's Dance | BPMN | iBPMN | BPSS | SCA | ePASS-IoS |
|---|---|---|---|---|---|---|---|---|---|---|---|
| Graphical notation | + | + | - | + | - | + | + | + | - | - | + |
| CR1. Multi-lateral interactions | + | + | + | + | + | + | + | + | - | n/a | + |
| CR2. Service topology | - | - | + | + | +/- | - | +/- | + | - | + | + |
| CR3. Service sets | +/- | +/- | + | - | - | + | - | - | - | + | + |
| CR4. Selection of services and referencepassing | +/- | +/- | + | +/- | +/- | +/- | - | - | - | n/a | + |
| CR5. Message formats | + | + | + | + | + | - | + | + | + | + | + |
| CR6. Interchangeability of technical configurations | - | + | + | + | - | - | - | - | - | - | + |
| CR7. Time constraints | + | + | + | - | + | +/- | + | + | + | n/a | + |
| CR8. Exception handling | + | + | + | + | + | - | + | + | + | n/a | + |
| CR9. Correlation | + | + | + | - | + | - | - | - | - | n/a | +/- |
| CR10. Integ. with service orchestration languages | + | + | + | +/- | - | +/- | +/- | - | +/- | n/a | + |

## 4 Formal Foundation of ePASS-IoS 1.1

After a syntactical introduction of ePASS-IoS 1.1 and its graphical elements in chapter 3.3 we lead on with the semantics ofePASS-IoS.

The π-calculus [25] provides formal concepts which were invented to describe concurrent dynamic processes. We will demonstrate that this process algebra fits to the concepts of subject oriented business process modeling with the necessary formal precision. The syntax and structural operational semantics (SOS) [29] of π-calculus is defined by Sangiorgi and Walker in [31]. The formal syntax is given in Table 2 and defines all possible operators and channel definitions. The labeled transition semantics of π-calculus is introduced in Table 3.

Although many different extensions of π-calculus [5,15] were enhanced the concepts with special features we are using the basic version of π-calculus for obtaining universality.

In the following section we demonstrate the complete mapping of ePASS-IoS 1.1 concepts (Figure 3) to π-calculus. We start with basic elements and force first examples with basic communication including send and receive activities.

**Table 2.** Syntax of $\pi$ Calculus

| Processes $P$ ::= | $\mathbf{0}$ | Inactive Process |
|---|---|---|
| $\mid$ | $\pi.P$ | Prefix |
| $\mid$ | $P + Q$ | Sum |
| $\mid$ | $P\mid Q$ | Parallel |
| $\mid$ | $\nu \tilde{z} P$ | Restriction |
| $\mid$ | $K\lfloor \tilde{a} \rfloor$ | Identifier |
| Prefixes $\pi$ ::= | $\bar{x}\langle \tilde{y} \rangle$ | Send |
| $\mid$ | $x(\tilde{z})$ | Receive |
| $\mid$ | $\tau$ | Hidden Action |
| $\mid$ | $[x = y]\pi$ | Match |

**Table 3.** Labled transition semantic of $\pi$-calculus [31]

$$\text{OUT } \frac{}{\bar{x}y.P \xrightarrow{\bar{x}y} P}$$

$$\text{INP } \frac{}{x(z).P \xrightarrow{xy} P\{x/z\}}$$

$$\text{TAU } \frac{}{\tau.P \xrightarrow{\tau} P}$$

$$\text{MAT } \frac{\pi.P \xrightarrow{\alpha} P'}{[x=x]\pi.P \xrightarrow{\alpha} P'}$$

$$\text{SUM-L } \frac{P \xrightarrow{\alpha} P'}{P + Q \xrightarrow{\alpha} P'}$$

$$\text{CONST } \frac{}{K\lfloor \tilde{a} \rfloor \xrightarrow{\tau} P\{\tilde{x}/\tilde{y}\}} \quad K := (\tilde{x}).P$$

$$\text{PAR-L } \frac{P \xrightarrow{\alpha} P'}{P\mid Q \xrightarrow{\alpha} P'\mid Q} \; bn(\alpha) \cap fn(Q) = \varnothing$$

$$\text{COMM-L } \frac{P \xrightarrow{\bar{x}y} P' \; Q \xrightarrow{xy} Q'}{P\mid Q \xrightarrow{\tau} P'\mid Q'}$$

$$\text{CLOSE-L } \frac{P \xrightarrow{\bar{x}(z)} P' \; Q \xrightarrow{xz} Q'}{P\mid Q \xrightarrow{\tau} \nu z(P'\mid Q')} \; z \notin fn(Q)$$

$$\text{RES } \frac{P \xrightarrow{\alpha} P'}{\nu z P \xrightarrow{\alpha} \nu z P'} \; z \notin n(\alpha)$$

$$\text{OPEN } \frac{P \xrightarrow{\bar{x}z} P'}{\nu z P \xrightarrow{\bar{x}z} P'} \; z \neq x$$

### 4.1 Termination

Termination of a subjects internal behaviour is denoted by the *End* activity of ePASS-IoS 1.1. The *End* activity is mapped to the NIL-operator of $\pi$-calculus. Milner used this feature from $\lambda$-Calculus [7,2] in which it is describing an empty list to describe the "empty process" with the symbol "**0**". An empty process is a process which is inactive and has no active function. Mostly the NIL operator is used to terminate a sequential list of agent activities and thus the agent. To describe such termination the syntax of the original PASS [11] provides functional states with final flags. The symbol of a circle is reused in ePASS-IoS 1.1. On the left-hand side of Figure 4 the language element of ePASS-IoS is depicted. On the right-hand side the process agent *End* is defined in $\pi$-calculus with the symbol **0** as an empty process.

$$End := \mathbf{0}$$

**Fig. 4.** End activity

### 4.2 Action Activity

This action is either performed manually or automatically. In the manual case, the users get a message what they have to do and state the result manually afterwards. As an example, we can imagine a check of a proposal. After the check they can state about a rejected or accepted proposal. Actions can also be performed automatically. For this purpose software code in Java can be written and attached to the actions. This concept is already defined in PASS and is called refinement of the activities.

An action is in every case a mapping from an input value to exactly one output value. Figure 5 shows the node symbol of the activity in ePASS-IoS. It can be labeled with a name and annotated by additional properties. The example in Figure 5 shows this annotation with in the square brackets. The function name $act$ is used as internal channel between the declaration agent $A_D$ and the functional agent $A_F$. The agent $A_F$ receives a input value tuple $\tilde{x}$ and a timeout value $t$ from this interface. If the internal action $\tau_F$ is executing within the scheduled time the response $r$ is responded to the declaration agent $A_D$. Otherwise the timeout response $r_t$ is received and a different activity $\langle \cdot \rangle$ will be executed as next. The timeout behavior is considered as non deterministic $(+)$ because the results of the action is not known during pre runtime. A further support of time as just a $\tau$-branch is not necessary since only the cases timeout happens and timeout does not happen have to be considered. The symbol $\langle \cdot \rangle$ is a placeholder for representing the next activity. For example the $\langle \cdot \rangle$ can be the end activity $\mathbf{0}$ and the subjects behavior will terminate. Before the verification task all placeholder values $\langle \cdot \rangle$ are specified with concrete terms.

$$A_D := \overline{act}\langle \tilde{x}, t \rangle . (\sum_{i=0}^{n} r_i . \langle i \rangle + r_t . \langle m \rangle)$$

$$A_F := act(\tilde{x}, t) . \tau_F . (\sum_{i=0}^{n} \overline{r_i} . A_F + \overline{r_t} . A_F)$$

$$A := \nu(act, r, r_t)(A_D | A_F)$$

$$Action := \sum_{i=1}^{m} \tau . \langle i \rangle$$

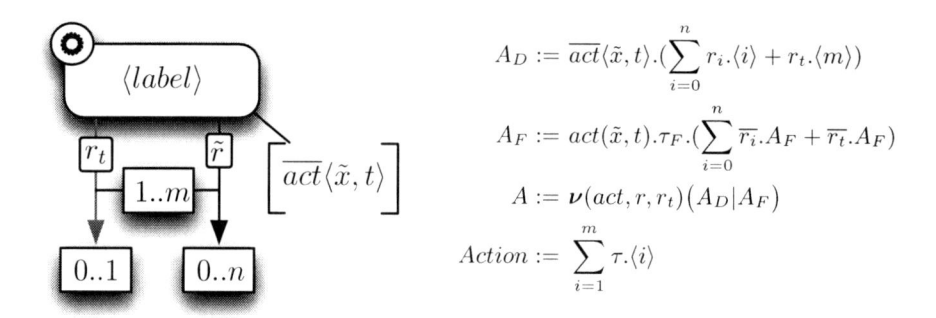

**Fig. 5.** The agent $A$ is an extensive model for the action activity. It is composed of the declaration agent $A_D$ and the function agent $A_F$. $A$ can be simplified to the agent *Action* by applying the rules of the SOS semantics.

At this point we demonstrate the simplification of the $\pi$ expression of the action activity as shown in Figure 5. We will use step by step the rule semantics of Table 3. First, we apply the rule CLOSE-L. The request channels $\overline{act}\langle\tilde{x},t\rangle$ and $act(\tilde{x},t)$ synchronize. Then the invisible action $\tau_F$ is executed. The request channels $r$ join by appling rule CLOSE-L and other functional agents are allowed to be executed. The semantic rules simplify the $\pi$ expression into a sequence of two $\tau$ followed by $m$ $\tau$-branches. We remove the leading two $\tau$ for simplification because they do not have an affect on the control flow and the states space of the whole system is reduced by this.

$$A_D := \overline{act}\langle\tilde{x},t\rangle.\Big(\sum_{i=0}^{n} r_i.\langle i\rangle + r_t.\langle m\rangle\Big)$$

$$A_F := act(\tilde{x},t).\tau_F.\Big(\sum_{i=0}^{n} \overline{r_i}.A_F + \overline{r_t}.A_F\Big)$$

$$A := \nu(act,r,r_t)(A_D|A_F)$$

$$\stackrel{\text{CLOSE-L}}{\Longrightarrow} = \nu(\ldots)\Big(\big(\sum_{i=0}^{n} r_i.\langle i\rangle + r_t.\langle m\rangle\big)|\tau_F.\big(\sum_{i=0}^{n} \overline{r_i}.A_F + \overline{r_t}.A_F\big)\Big)$$

$$\stackrel{\tau_F}{\Longrightarrow} = \nu(\ldots)\Big(\big(\sum_{i=0}^{n} r_i.\langle i\rangle + r_t.\langle m\rangle\big)|\big(\sum_{i=0}^{n} \overline{r_i}.A_F + \overline{r_t}.A_F\big)\Big)$$

$$\stackrel{\text{CLOSE-L}}{\Longrightarrow} = \nu(\ldots)\Big(\sum_{i=0}^{n}(\tau.\langle i\rangle|A_F) + \tau\langle m\rangle|A_F\Big)$$

$$= \nu(\ldots) \sum_{i=1}^{m}(\tau.\langle i\rangle|A_F)$$

$$\equiv \nu(\ldots) \sum_{i=1}^{m}(\tau.\langle i\rangle|\mathbf{0})$$

$$\equiv \nu(\ldots) \sum_{i=1}^{m}\tau.\langle i\rangle$$

$$\Longrightarrow A := \tau_{act}.\tau_F.\Big(\sum_{i=1}^{m}\tau.\langle i\rangle\Big)$$

$$Action := \sum_{i=1}^{m}\tau.\langle i\rangle$$

### 4.3 Send Activity

The send activity is build up from 4 action activities (see Figure 6). In chapter 3.2 the message broker was defined as one element within the ePASS-IoS architecture. This broker can evaluate a set of message receivers based on internal rules. Therefore the first action of a send activity is to define an evaluation request. The request is sent to the rule evaluator of the message broker which responses a list of candidates for subject providers. Next, one or more subject providers are chosen. If no candidate was found the request definition can be revised. Otherwise, the set of selected subject provider is propagate to the message distributor of the message broker. As already mentioned, we support only one subject provider in this paper. The first parameter of the send activity is the *backchannel s*. This channel is an identifier of the sender and can be used by the receiver to response messages. The parameter $fS$ is an abbreviation for *from subject* and is used by the receiver to control the control flow of its internal behavior. The set $tSP$ is the set of subject providers which are to receive a message and finally, $m$ is the actual message. The parameter $s$ and $fS$ are inserted by the transformation algorithm.

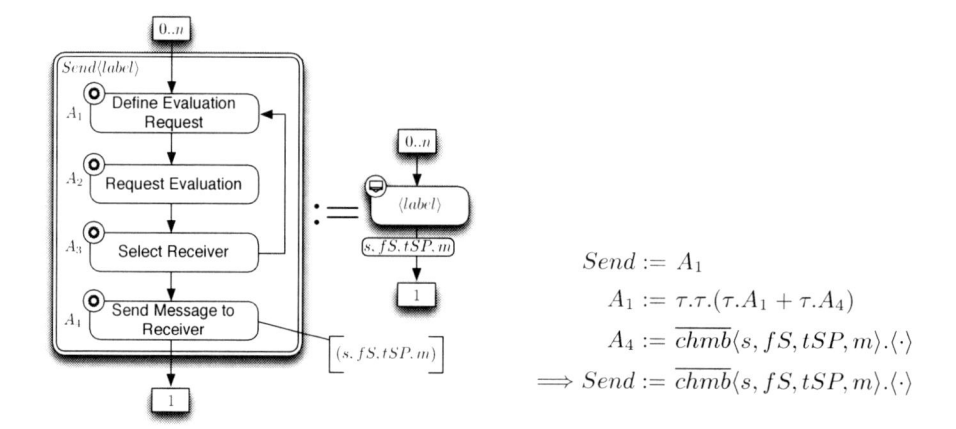

$$Send := A_1$$
$$A_1 := \tau.\tau.(\tau.A_1 + \tau.A_4)$$
$$A_4 := \overline{chmb}\langle s, fS, tSP, m\rangle.\langle \cdot \rangle$$
$$\Rightarrow Send := \overline{chmb}\langle s, fS, tSP, m\rangle.\langle \cdot \rangle$$

**Fig. 6.** *Send* activity

As showed in the mapping of Figure 6 the send activity can be simplified as well.

### 4.4 Input Pool

Here the mapping of the concept "input pool" is described. This concept was already introduced by PASS. Since it has an effect to the communication behavior of the subject provider, we have to take it into consideration for the formal verification semantics. For implementing the asynchronous communication between subjects with the synchronous π-calculus the input pool is needed to buffer messages in an inventive manner. Instead of using one buffer (FIFO, LIFO or bag) for one channel as described in [3] the concept of an input pool provides a finite set of unlimited buffers for each subject. Thereby buffers are identified by its sender and by the message type. In Figure 7 the example of two senders and three message types is depicted. All incoming messages of a subject are received by the unambiguous input channel of its input pool. In the example of Figure 7 the **channel ch** is received the name of the **sender s** and the **message m**.

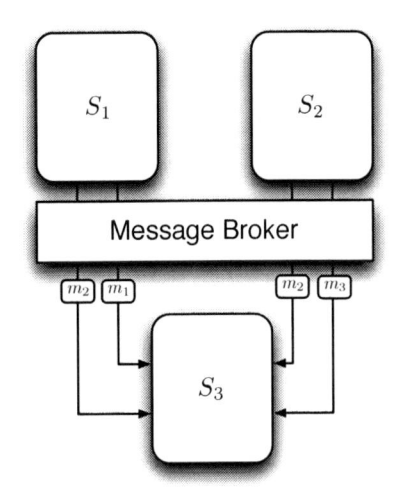

$$IP^0 := ch(s,m).\overline{s}\langle m \rangle.IP^0$$

$$IP^1_{s1} := s1(m).([m = m_1]\overline{s1m1}.IP^1_{s1} + \\ [m = m_2]\overline{s1m2}.IP^1_{s1})$$

$$IP^1_{s2} := s2(m).([m = m_2]\overline{s2m2}.IP^1_{s2} + \\ [m = m_3]\overline{s2m3}.IP^1_{s2})$$

$$B_{s1m1} := s1m1.(\overline{s1m1i}.0|B_{s1m1})$$
$$B_{s1m2} := s1m2.(\overline{s1m2i}.0|B_{s1m2})$$
$$B_{s2m2} := s2m2.(\overline{s2m2i}.0|B_{s2m2})$$
$$B_{s2m3} := s2m3.(\overline{s2m3i}.0|B_{s2m3})$$

$$IP_{S_3} := \nu(s1,s2,s1m1,s1m2,s2m2,s2m3)(IP^0|IP^1_{s1}|IP^1_{s2}|B_{s1m1}|B_{s1m2}|B_{s2m2}|B_{s2m3})$$
$$S_3 := \nu(s1m1i,s1m2i,s2m2i,s2m3i)(IP_{S_3}|IB_{S_3})$$

**Fig. 7.** Input pool

After differentiating between the sender it has to be select the right message type by using the match prefix of $\pi$-calculus. By means of this approaches the corresponding buffer can be selected. For example the message $m_2$ was send by the sender $s1$ the buffer $B_{s1m2}$ is selected. This buffer receives the message via the channel $s1m2$ and tries to forward the received message to the receiver activity through its internal channel $\overline{s1m2i}$. To avoid a blocking process, the buffer agent is replicating itself ($|B_{s1m2}$). The input pool can provide a finite set of unlimited buffers by this approach. The total formalizing of the subject $S_3$ is the composition of its internal behavior $IB_{S_3}$ and the input pool $IP_{S_3}$.

### 4.5 Receive Activity

If the input pool of a subject contains messages for the subject, the receive activity can be activated. In the example of Figure 8 m different messages can be received alternatively. A receive activity can be connected to the input pool with internal channels $s_jm_ki$. The postfix $i$ denotes internal. $A := \sum_j \langle Sender \rangle \langle Message \rangle i.A_j$ Once the corresponding buffer of the input pool contains a message it will processed by the internal behavior of the subject.

In Figure 8 the two agents *Receive* and *Receive$_t$* are defined. The second one supports timeouts. The content of the message does not matter for verification purposes.

$$Receive := \sum_{j=1}^{n} s_k m_l i.\langle j \rangle$$

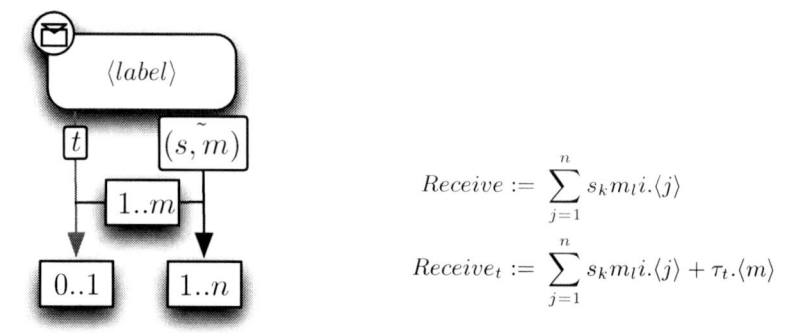

$$Receive_t := \sum_{j=1}^{n} s_k m_l i.\langle j \rangle + \tau_t.\langle m \rangle$$

**Fig. 8.** Receive Activity

### 4.6 Modal Split and Modal Join

As already mentioned in section 3 these two operators are inspired from [14] where the *Checklist* operator is defined. The *Modal split* is splitting the control flow and the *modal join* is joining the branches. The adjective *modal* is derived from modal logic. Modal logic is an extension of the predicate logic with 2 operators. The ◊ represents the possibility of a proposition and the □ symbolizes the necessity of a proposition. The both concepts are used in ePASS to represent control flow branching. In the graphical representation of ePASS-IoS necessary control flow branches are drawn through and the possible control flow branches are dashed. In the example of Figure 9 the activities $M_1$ and $M_2$ are necessary while the activities $M_3$ and $M_4$ are optional. All activities can be executed concurrently. The $M_i$ are abbreviations for an arbitrary fragment of internal behavior definitions of subjects. They are called macros and will be explained in more detail in section 4.8. Within the $\pi$ expression of the example the guard-channel $g$ is used to ensure the necessary execution of the activities $M_1$ and $M_2$. Additionally the guard is used in combination of the non-deterministic choice

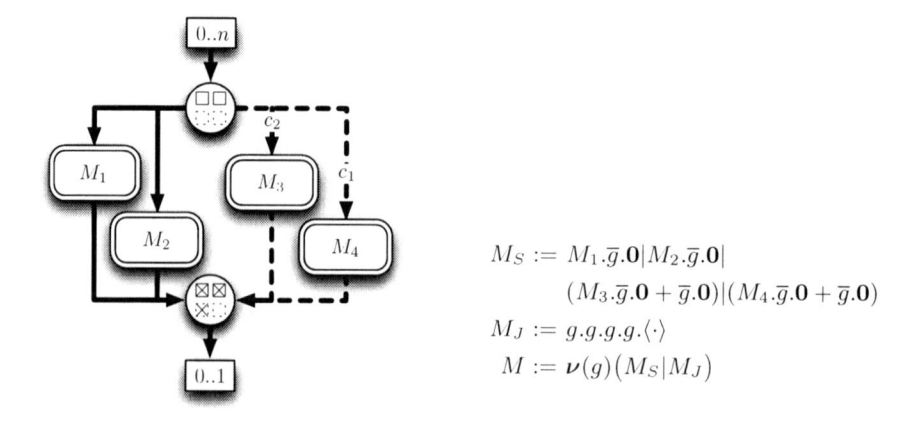

$$M_S := M_1.\overline{g}.0|M_2.\overline{g}.0|$$
$$(M_3.\overline{g}.0 + \overline{g}.0)|(M_4.\overline{g}.0 + \overline{g}.0)$$
$$M_J := g.g.g.g.\langle \cdot \rangle$$
$$M := \nu(g)(M_S|M_J)$$

**Fig. 9.** Modal split and modal join activities

operator to indicate the termination or the skipping of the possible activities $M_3$ and $M_4$. The agent of the modal join activity is waiting on this 4 guards before it releases the control flow.

## 4.7 Observer

The ePASS-IoS observer provides the capability to model a backup solution additional to the usual regular behavior. We will introduce interrupts and exceptions, show the corresponding ePASS-IoS processes and map this behavior to $\pi$-calculus.

**Happy Path:** First of all we show a short example of a regular behavior, which can be interrupted by an event or abandoned by exceptions. We call such a regular behavior is called happy path. Figure 10 shows an example of a happy path, which will be used further to explain the concepts of the observer. The path starts with the receive activity $A_1$ and continue with 2 sequential ordered action activities $A_2$ and $A_3$. The end activity $A_4$ is terminating the happy path $A_1$ to $A_3$.

$$HP := s_j m_k i.\tau_{A_2}.\tau_{a_3}.0$$

**Fig. 10.** Happy path

**Implementing interrupts by using the observer:** The happy path of Figure 10 can be interrupted by an event. To describe such behavior the ePASS-IoS observer provides concepts to implement such interrupts. In $\pi$-calculus the parallel operator is used to provide additional behavior next to the happy path HP. Firstly, the happy path HP was extended by an alternative path. The old path and the new path are extended with the guards $g_1$ and $g_2$. This is illustrated in Figure 11. The observer sends any amount of $\overline{g_1}$ until the receive activity $A_6$ receives the interrupt message $im$ from the subject $s_1$. Then the observer switches to sending $\overline{g_2}$. Therefore the control flow passes the action $A_3$ and is steered over the action $A_5$. The branching interrupt ends in the same terminating activity $A_4$.

**Observers enable exception handling:** Another important concept is the exception handling within business processes. In the example of Figure 12 the observer $O(A_3)$ can catch the 2 exceptions $exm_1$ and $exm_2$ which can be thrown by the agent $A_3$. These exceptions are just other possible results of $A_3$. Therefore the transformation algorithm has to connect the results with the concerning agents $A_5$ and $A_6$.

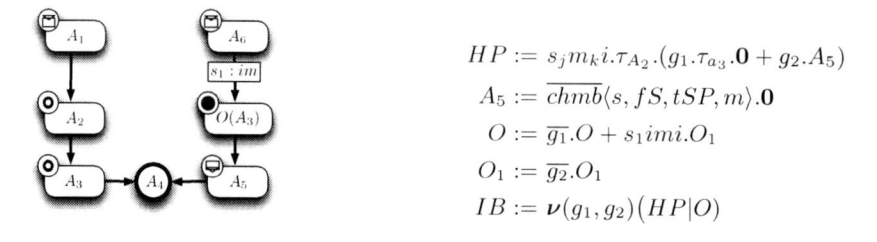

**Fig. 11.** Interrupts

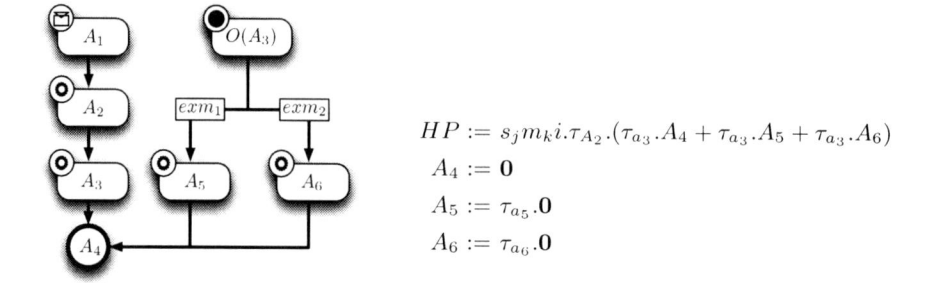

$$HP := s_j m_k i.\tau_{A_2}.(g_1.\tau_{a_3}.\mathbf{0} + g_2.A_5)$$
$$A_5 := \overline{chmb}\langle s, fS, tSP, m\rangle.\mathbf{0}$$
$$O := \overline{g_1}.O + s_1 imi.O_1$$
$$O_1 := \overline{g_2}.O_1$$
$$IB := \boldsymbol{\nu}(g_1, g_2)(HP|O)$$

**Fig. 12.** Exception handling

$$HP := s_j m_k i.\tau_{A_2}.(\tau_{a_3}.A_4 + \tau_{a_3}.A_5 + \tau_{a_3}.A_6)$$
$$A_4 := \mathbf{0}$$
$$A_5 := \tau_{a_5}.\mathbf{0}$$
$$A_6 := \tau_{a_6}.\mathbf{0}$$

### 4.8 Macro

If some internal behavior have to be used more than once, the concept of a macro can be used. Figure 13 shows an easy example. The branching behavior from the activity $A_2$ to the activities $A_3$ and $A_4$ can be encapsulated into the macro $M$. This macro can be used by the model developer in an efficient manner.

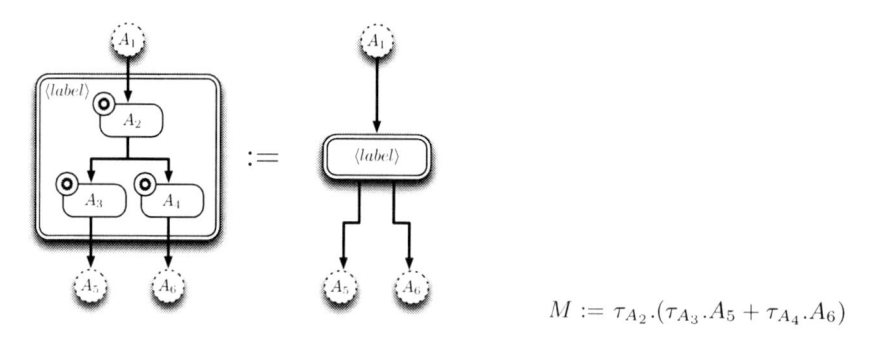

$$M := \tau_{A_2}.(\tau_{A_3}.A_5 + \tau_{A_4}.A_6)$$

**Fig. 13.** A macro is just a sub-composition of a subject

By using the concrete mapping between each ePASS-IoS element and the π-calculus, as shown above, it is possible to transform an arbitrary business process model from ePASS-IoS to a π-calculus term. Exploiting the SOS rules leads to a labeled transition system of the whole business process model. This system can be analysed by using model checking methods.

## 5 Conclusion

We have introduced ePASS-IoS 1.1 as a new variant of S-BPM notations. It is an extension of ePASS and focuses on supporting the internet of service paradigms.

We have shown that ePASS-IoS is able to fulfill almost all requirements of a choreography description language. The support of correlations should be better. Up to now, correlations can only be supported if the maximal number of subjects is known during design time. In this case, the necessary number of subjects can be modeled. The extension of the graphical syntax and the concerning semantics is a future task.

A $\pi$-calculus based formal verification semantics is defined in this paper. It provides the ability to check the process models on soundness and interaction soundness. For more information about possible verification processes we recommend the work of Frank Puhlmann [30].

**Acknowledgments.** This work was supported by the Theseus Programme, funded by the German Federal Ministry of Economy and Technology under the promotional reference '01MQ07012'. We thank Albert Fleischmann for fruitful discussions and valuable comments.

## References

1. Aitenbichler, E., Borgert, S.: Application of subject-oriented modeling in automatic service composition. In: Buchwald, H., Fleischmann, A., Seese, D., Stary, C. (eds.) S-BPM ONE 2009. CCIS, vol. 85, pp. 71–82. Springer, Heidelberg (2010)
2. Barendregt, H.: The lambda calculus: its syntax and semantics. Elsevier, Amsterdam (1981)
3. Beauxis, R., Palamidessi, C., Valencia, F.: On the asynchronous nature of the asynchronous $\pi$-calculus. In: Degano, P., De Nicola, R., Bevilacqua, V. (eds.) Concurrency, Graphs and Models. LNCS, vol. 5065, pp. 473–492. Springer, Heidelberg (2008), http://dblp.uni-trier.de/db/conf/birthday/montanari2008.htmlBeauxisPV08
4. Bouchbout, K., Akoka, J., Alimazighi, Z.: Proposition of a generic metamodel for interorganizational business processes. In: Proceedings of the 6th International Workshop on Enterprise & Organizational Modeling and Simulation, EOMAS 2010, CEUR-WS.org, Aachen, Germany, pp. 42–56 (2010), http://portal.acm.org/citation.cfm?id=1866939.1866943
5. Boudol, G.: Asynchrony and the Pi-calculus. Research Report RR-1702, INRIA (1992), http://hal.inria.fr/inria-00076939/PDF/RR-1702.pdf
6. Chinnici, R., Moreau, J.J., Ryman, A., Weerawarana, S.: Web services description language (wsdl) version 2.0 part 1: Core language. World Wide Web Consortium, Recommendation REC-wsdl20-20070626 (June 2007), http://www.w3.org/TR/wsdl20/ (last accessed on May 22, 2011)
7. Church, A.: The Calculi of Lambda Conversion. Princeton University Press, Princeton (1941), http://portal.acm.org/citation.cfm?id=1096495
8. Decker, G., Kopp, O., Leymann, F., Weske, M.: Interacting services: From specification to execution. Data Knowl. Eng. 68, 946–972 (2009), http://portal.acm.org/citation.cfm/?id=1598082.1598333

9. van Der Aalst, W., Ter Hofstede, A., Kiepuszewski, B., Barros, A.: Workflow patterns. Distributed and parallel databases 14(1), 5–51 (2003)
10. Fingar, P.: Dot Cloud: The 21st Century Business Platform Built on Cloud Computing, 1st edn. Meghan-Kiffer Press, Tampa (2009)
11. Fleischmann, A.: PASS - A Technique for Specifying Communication Protocols. In: Proceedings of the IFIP WG6.1 Seventh International Conference on Protocol Specification, Testing and Verification VII, pp. 61–76. North-Holland Publishing Co., Amsterdam (1987), http://portal.acm.org/citation.cfm/?id=645831.670083
12. Fleischmann, A.: What is S-BPM? In: Buchwald, H., Fleischmann, A., Seese, D., Stary, C. (eds.) S-BPM ONE 2009. CCIS, vol. 85, pp. 85–106. Springer, Heidelberg (2010), http://dx.doi.org/10.1007/978-3-642-15915-2_7
13. Fleischmann, A., Lippe, S., Meyer, N., Stary, C.: Coherent task modeling and execution based on subject-oriented representations. In: England, D., Palanque, P., Vanderdonckt, J., Wild, P.J. (eds.) TAMODIA 2009. LNCS, vol. 5963, pp. 78–91. Springer, Heidelberg (2010)
14. Graef, N., Nils, T.: Evaluation, Mapping und quantitative Reduktion von Workflow Patterns (Control-Flow), Bachelor thesis, University Karlsruhe, Institute of Applied Informatics and Formal Description Methods (AIFB) (2009)
15. Herescu, O.M., Palamidessi, C.: Probabilistic asynchronous π-calculus. In: Tiuryn, J. (ed.) FOSSACS 2000. LNCS, vol. 1784, pp. 146–160. Springer, Heidelberg (2000)
16. Huemer, C., Liegl, P., Schuster, R., Werthner, H., Zapletal, M.: Inter-organizational systems: From business values over business processes to deployment. In: 2nd IEEE International Conference on Digital Ecosystems and Technologies, DEST 2008, pp. 294–299 (February 2008)
17. Kopp, O., Engler, L., van Lessen, T., Leymann, F., Nitzsche, J.: Interaction Choreography Models in BPEL: Choreographies on the Enterprise Service Bus. In: Fleischmann, A., Schmidt, W., Seese, D., Singer, R. (eds.) S-BPM ONE 2010 - the Subjectoriented BPM Conference. CCIS, Springer, Heidelberg (2011), http://www2.informatik.uni-stuttgart.de/cgi-bin/NCSTRL/NCSTRL_view.pl?id=INPROC-2011-04\&engl=1
18. Legner, C., Vogel, T., Löhe, J., Mayerl, C.: Transforming inter-organizational business processes into service-oriented architectures method and application in the automotive industry. In: KiVS 2007 - Kommunikation in Verteilten Systemen, p. 12 (2007)
19. Legner, C., Wende, K.: The Challenges of Inter-organizational Business Process Design - a Research Agenda. In: Proceedings of European Conference on Information Systems, ECIS 2007, pp. 1643–1654 (2007), http://www.alexandria.unisg.ch/EXPORT/DL/36606.pdf\hfill
20. List, B., Korherr, B.: An evaluation of conceptual business process modelling languages. In: Proceedings of the 2006 ACM Smposium on Applied Computing, SAC 2006, pp. 1532–1539. ACM, New York (2006), http://doi.acm.org/10.1145/1141277.1141633
21. Liu, Y., Müller, S., Xu, K.: A static compliance-checking framework for business process models. IBM Systems Journal 46(2), 335–362 (2007), http://dblp.uni-trier.de/db/journals/ibmsj/ibmsj46.html#LiuMX07
22. Lohmann, N.: A feature-complete petri net semantics for WS-BPEL 2.0. In: Dumas, M., Heckel, R. (eds.) WS-FM 2007. LNCS, vol. 4937, pp. 77–91. Springer, Heidelberg (2008), http://dblp.uni-trier.de/db/conf/wsfm/wsfm2007.html#Lohmann07

23. Lucchi, R., Mazzara, M.: A pi-calculus based semantics for WS-BPEL. J. Log. Algebr. Program. 70(1), 96–118 (2007), http://dblp.uni-trier.de/db/journals/jlp/jlp70.html#LucchiM07
24. Metasonic: Metasonic Suite (2011), http://www.metasonic.de/ (last accessed on March 20, 2011)
25. Milner, R.: Communicating and mobile systems: the π-calculus. Cambridge University Press, Cambridge (1999)
26. OASIS: Web Services Business Process Execution Language Version 2.0 (2007), http://docs.oasis-open.org/wsbpel/2.0/wsbpel-v2.0.pdf (last accessed on March 20, 2011)
27. OMG: Business Process Modeling Notation. 2.0 edn. (2011), http://docs.oasis-open.org/wsbpel/2.0/wsbpel-v2.0.pdf (last accessed on March 18, 2011)
28. Peterson, J.: Petri Net Theory and the Modeling of Systems. Prentice-Hall, Inc., Englewood Cliffs (1981)
29. Plotkin, G.D.: A structural approach to operational semantics. Tech. Rep. DAIMI FN-19, University of Aarhus (1981)
30. Puhlmann, F., Weske, M.: Interaction soundness for service orchestrations. In: Dan, A., Lamersdorf, W. (eds.) ICSOC 2006. LNCS, vol. 4294, pp. 302–313. Springer, Heidelberg (2006)
31. Sangiorgi, D., Walker, D.: The π-calculus: a Theory of Mobile Processes. Cambridge University Press, Cambridge (2003)
32. Scheer, A.: ARIS-business process modeling. Springer, Heidelberg (2000)
33. Weidlich, M., Decker, G., Weske, M.: Efficient Analysis of BPEL 2.0 Processes Using π-Calculus. In: Li, J., Guo, M., Jin, Q., Zhang, Y., Zhang, L.J., Jin, H., Mambo, M., Tanaka, J., Hayashi, H. (eds.) APSCC, pp. 266–274. IEEE, Los Alamitos (2007), http://dblp.uni-trier.de/db/conf/apscc/apscc2007.html#WeidlichDW07
34. Weske, M.: Business Process Management: Concepts, Languages, Architectures. Springer, Heidelberg (2007)
35. Ziemann, J., Matheis, T., Freiheit, J.: Modelling of Cross-Organizational Business Processes. In: EMISA, pp. 87–100 (2007)

# Part IV

# Experience Reports

# CGAA/EES at NEC Corporation, Powered by S-BPM: The Subject-Oriented BPM Development Technique Using Top-Down Approach

Shinji Nakamura, Toshihiro Tan, Takeshi Hirayama, Hiroyuki Kawai,
Shota Komiyama, Sadao Hosaka, Minoru Nakamura, and Katsuhiro Yuki

NEC Corporation, Minato-Ku, Tokyo, Japan
s-nakamura@dn.jp.nec.com, t-tan@aj.jp.nec.com,
t-hirayama@ab.jp.nec.com, h-kawai@bu.jp.nec.com,
s-komiyama@cp.jp.nec.com, s-hosaka@fq.cnt.jp.nec.com,
m-nakamura@zf.jp.nec.com, k-yuuki@zi.jp.nec.com

**Abstract.** It is not that difficult to visualize business processes as a model and execute them using today's BPMS products. However, it is difficult for a worker at a work site to simply and clearly model processes to be executed, and then express with certainty the business scenario within the entire company's activities to which those processes are related. In addition, a shorter cycle for continuous BPM improvement activity is strongly desired, where the model is improved from results gathered as processes based on that model are executed. The "CGAA/EES development methodology" developed by NEC provides an overall optimization solution that overcomes these issues by bringing a top-down approach to subject-oriented BPM.

**Keywords:** subject-oriented BPM, top-down approach method, subject structuring, subject-oriented SOA.

## 1 Introduction: BPM as Developed by NEC

We explain the CGAA/EES (Enterprise Eco Service) approach by first introducing BPM as conducted at NEC corporation with the model hierarchy and the BPM cycle. Section 2 is about the history of NEC BPM solutions and the issues that led to implement CGAA/EES. Chapter 3 deals with the S-BPM approach as a basis of the CGAA/EES features which are presented in section 4. The CGAA/EES development methodology is outlined in more detail in chapter 5, while we conclude with the benefits in section 6.

### 1.1 A Model Hierarchy that Expresses and Optimizes Corporate Activity

Corporate activities at NEC corporation are expressed using the following three hierarchies (see fig. 1):

- Business model
- Business scenario
- Executable processes

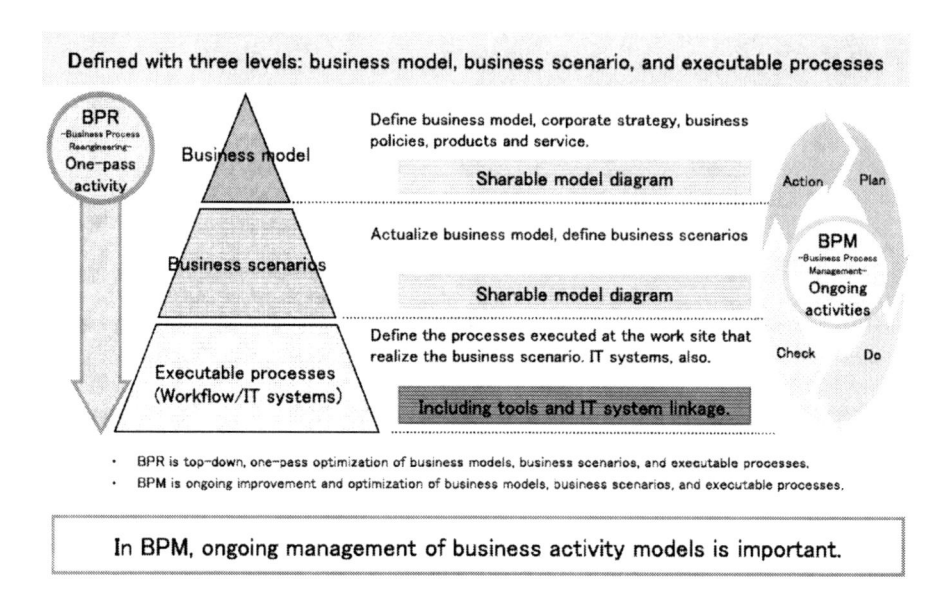

Fig. 1. A model hierarchy that expresses and optimizes corporate activity

The business model layer defines the business model and business strategy, along with the products and services that are provided. The business scenario layer defines the business scenarios that carry out the business model. Models on the business model layer and business scenario layer models are diagrams that express company activities and which should be shared within the company. The executable process layer defines the processes that are executed during execution of business scenarios at the actual work site. The executable processes represent the concrete procedures that allow workers to accomplish actual tasks at the work site. They are expressed as work flows that include procedures using tools and IT systems.

BPM (Business Process Management) and BPR (Business Process Reengineering) [1] look similar, but BPR is a method that makes one-time-only top-down improvements going from the business model layer to the business scenario layer and to the executable process layer. On the other hand, BPM is an optimizing method that makes continuous improvements to the business model layer, business scenario layer, and executable process layer. Because it implements this sort of continuous improvement cycle, BPM requires a mechanism that allows continuous maintenance and management of these three layers.

## 1.2 BPM Cycle

The BPM improvement cycle differs, depending on whether it is being implemented for the business model layer, business scenario layer, or executable process layer (see fig. 2).

The "top-down BPM cycle" targets all corporate business activities. This is BPM that is applied top-down from the business model layer, including business strategy updates to business scenarios and executable processes. Taking from three months to one year or more, the length of time and expense are a heavy burden on the company that implements it.

In the "business scenario improvement BPM cycle" the business strategy is already determined. This BPM activity actualizes the business strategy in the business scenario and executable process layers. Its length is approximately two weeks to three months. One cycle of activity is not supposed to take a long time.

The "work site improvement BPM cycle" executes the business scenario. Therefore, it is BPM as implemented from the perspective of actual workers at the work site. In this cycle, small-scale improvements are implemented again and again as they are noticed during daily work, being quickly reflected in tasks at the work site. The length of this improvement cycle is extremely short, ranging from approximately one day to at most two weeks. With this sort of short-length BPM cycle, the diagrammed model should be immediately reflected in tasks at the work site.

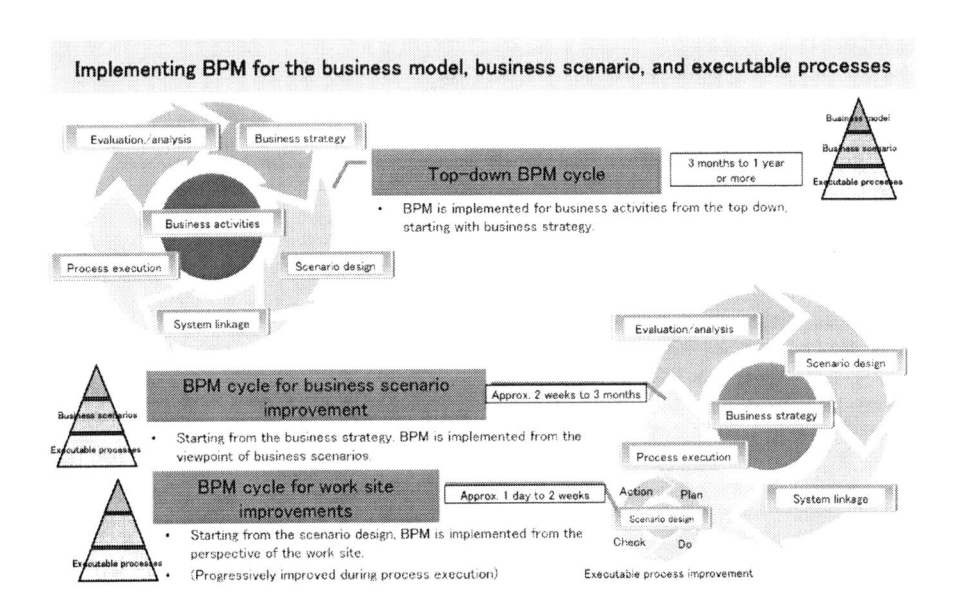

**Fig. 2.** BPM Cycle

It is important to clarify the business model before implementation of the "business scenario improvement BPM cycle", and it is also important to clarify each business scenario before implementation of the "work site improvement BPM cycle". It is important that the goals of the improvements to be implemented from these cycles are also clearly expressed. Especially, BPM in the executable process layer carries the risk that only partial optimization will result. To achieve overall optimization, it is important to make progress by repeatedly implementing small improvements instead of implementing large changes at one time, while always being aware of the current position within the company's overall activities.

## 2 History of NEC BPM Solutions

### 2.1 CGAA: Class of General Available Application

CGAA was originally a development environment for SOA/MDA-oriented application software. It consists of a framework, class library, and development methodology. Later, BPM software was introduced and a methodology was developed to cover everything from upstream business process definitions to system requirement definitions. Currently, it has become independent from software application development, and is now provided as a separate BPM solution.

There are two NEC BPM solutions: CGAA/ARIS and CGAA/EES.

### 2.2 CGAA/ARIS

CGGA/ARIS is a BPM solution that includes development methodologies and tools using the ARIS platform [2] from the Software AG company. It is a BPM solution for visualizing (AsIs analysis) and improving (ToBe creation) business model layers and business scenario layers. CGAA/ARIS expresses business granularity in four functional layers, defining them in a top-down fashion (see fig. 3):

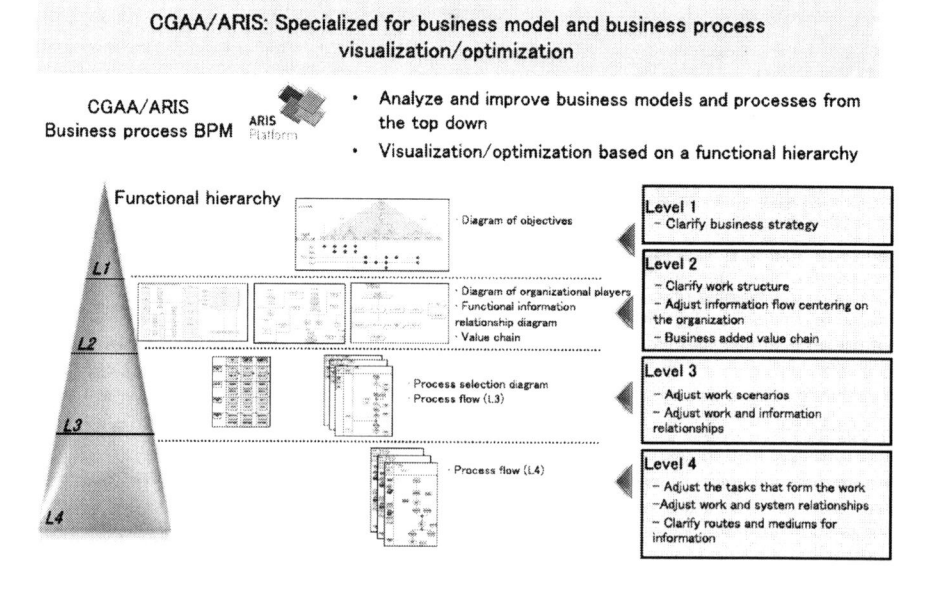

**Fig. 3.** CGAA/ARIS BPM Solution

Level 1: Business strategy definition
Level 2: Business model definition
Level 3: Process model definition
Level 4: Task definition

Because "functions to implement business strategy" are defined and organized at each level, organization from a functional perspective (process orientation) is the focus in optimizing the entire company's activities.

## 2.3 Issues

Experience from many deployments of CGAA/ARIS has made a number of problems apparent. First of all, when analysis centers on functions, it is difficult to model processes that are linked to many departments or people. An expert consultant is needed. Because the person responsible for the actual work cannot define the model by himself or herself, defining processes that correctly represent the actual situation becomes both expensive and time-consuming. Ready-made templates are also available to address this problem, however, no matter which is used, it is difficult to accurately represent the actual conditions at the company.

Another problem is the excessive length of the BPM cycle. Even after processes have been defined, their effectiveness and defects cannot be quickly understood, due to the time required to install them in the system and activate them. By the time the results of executing these processes have been observed and new improvement points have been discovered, the business conditions upon which the processes are based may have already changed. In an age like today, where the business environment is rapidly changing, BPM activity will have a negative effect if it does not follow those changes. It will waste not only the effectiveness of improvements, but also money.

To overcome such problems, CGAA/EES was developed as methodology that models business using a subject-oriented, not function definition approach. It is a comprehensive BPM improvement activity that uses a top-down approach starting with business strategies.

## 3 Features of Subject-Oriented BPM

### 3.1 What Does "Subject-Oriented" Mean?

The subject-oriented approach is a technique where affairs are understood from the perspective of the person or object that is the subject [3] [4] [5].

Generally, language is made up of three main parts: subject, predicate, and object (see fig. 4). The same applies when diagramming business processes. In process orientation, the predicate is described from the perspective of procedures. With object orientation, the object is described from the perspective of items or services. In contrast to these, subject orientation describes the subject from the perspective of the parties involved. This technique of diagramming business processes centering on those involved parties is called a subject-oriented approach [3].

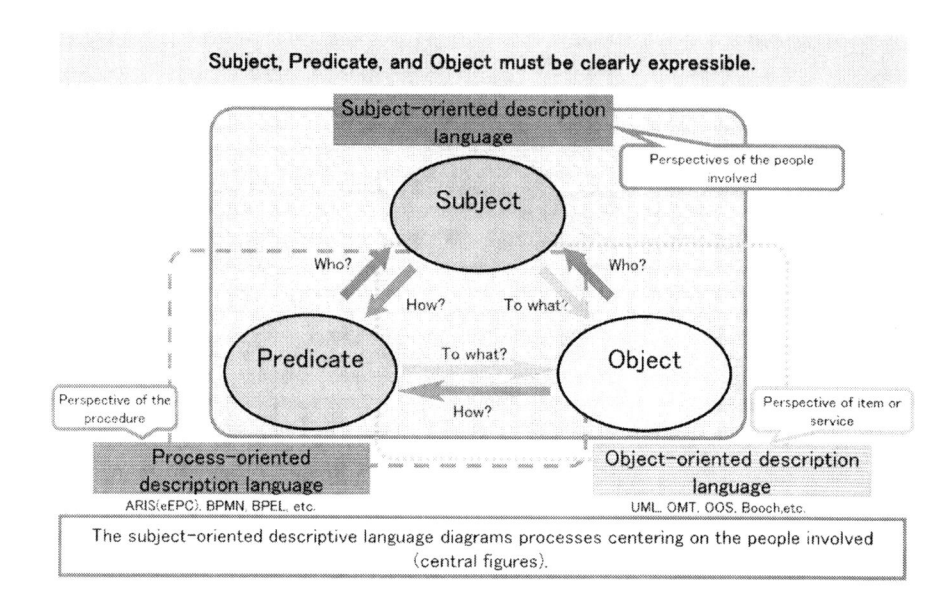

**Fig. 4.** Requirements for a Modeling Language that Diagrams Business Processes

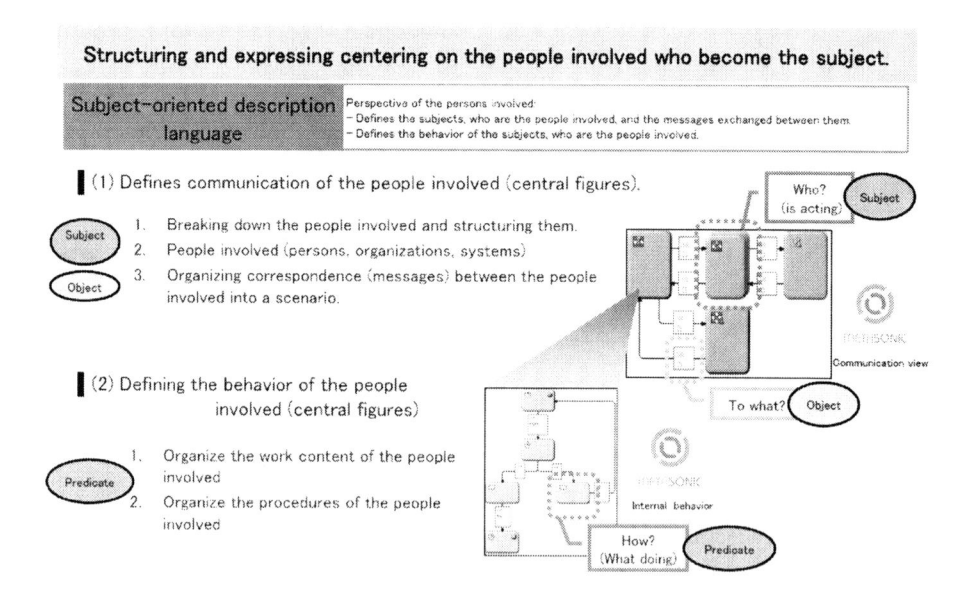

**Fig. 5.** Subject-oriented description language model

## 3.2 Subject-Oriented Description Language Model

When using the subject-oriented approach we applied Metasonic Suite for diagramming models. It diagrams a "Communication View" (subject interaction diagram), which defines the communications between involved parties, and "Internal Behavior" (subject behavior diagram), which defines the behavior of the involved parties [3] (see fig. 5).

### 3.3 Defining Communication between the Involved Parties

For each aspect of the business, related involved parties are identified and placed in the communication view. These involved parties are the subjects. Exchanges between the subjects are defined as messages, and used to model actual communications.

For comparison, let us consider process-oriented functional definition. As mentioned before, in functional definition, we must depend on the expertise of a consultant to define the granularity of each function. Even though a criterion of "a function to achieve an objective," the results of functional definition will not be consistent.

On the other hand, granularity is not an issue when diagramming with the subject-oriented approach because the boundaries between subjects are very distinct. The areas where communication occurs form the boundaries. This is the concept best understood by the workers actually working at the work site, which means a highly-skilled consultant is not required. This is the element that most contributes towards making business modeling easy, an important point in allowing reality to be modeled as it really exists.

### 3.4 Defining the Behavior of the Involved Parties

When the subjects and their communications have been clarified, the behavior of the subjects can be defined from the perspective of the subjects themselves. When diagramming, it is best to consider only the work of the subject in question. Because the communication between subjects is already defined in the communications view, only the exchange of messages needs to be considered for subjects other than the one being diagrammed.

For comparison, let us consider the definition of behavior in process-oriented functional definition. In process orientation, swim-lanes are frequently used. However, when defining behavior using swim-lanes, the behavior cannot be diagrammed unless the content of the work performed by the roles in each lane is understood. In the actual workplace, a person has little understanding of the content of work performed by the people with whom the person he or she is communicating. This is the root cause of the excessive time required for investigation and interviews when diagramming this through swim-lanes.

Because behavior is defined from the perspective of the subject when using subject orientation, modeling can be performed with the subject considering only his or her own work. This is also an important element in making business easy to model.

By modeling in this way, focusing only on the work of each subject individually, the actual work processes can be correctly modeled when the communication perspective is added. This is the biggest advantage of the subject-oriented approach. It means there is no need for consultants with high-level expertise. It is a situation where the workers performing the actual work are the subjects and can implement BPM.

## 4 Features of CGAA/EES

### 4.1 Subject-Oriented BPM Targeted by NEC

The advantage of subject-oriented BPM is that processes can be easily and clearly understood from the viewpoint of the involved parties at the work site. This is a very powerful solution for BPM activity on the executable process layer. However, there is always a concern that if BPM improvement activity is continued only from the worker's viewpoint, it will only result in partial optimization.

NEC has spent many years considering overall optimization using top-down BPM. Applying this knowhow, NEC has developed a technology for performing top-down subject-oriented modeling from the business model and business scenario layers, down to the executable process layer. Through this, the relationships between the business strategy and executable processes are clarified, making possible BPM improvement that considers overall optimization.

The features of the CGAA/EES development methodology are described below.

### 4.2 Features of the CGAA/EES Development Methodology

As a subject-oriented BPM analysis technique, the CGAA/EES development methodology implements overall optimization from a communications perspective and business scenario perspective (see fig. 6). Through analysis from a subject (role) perspective, not a conventional functional perspective, it provides a simple analysis

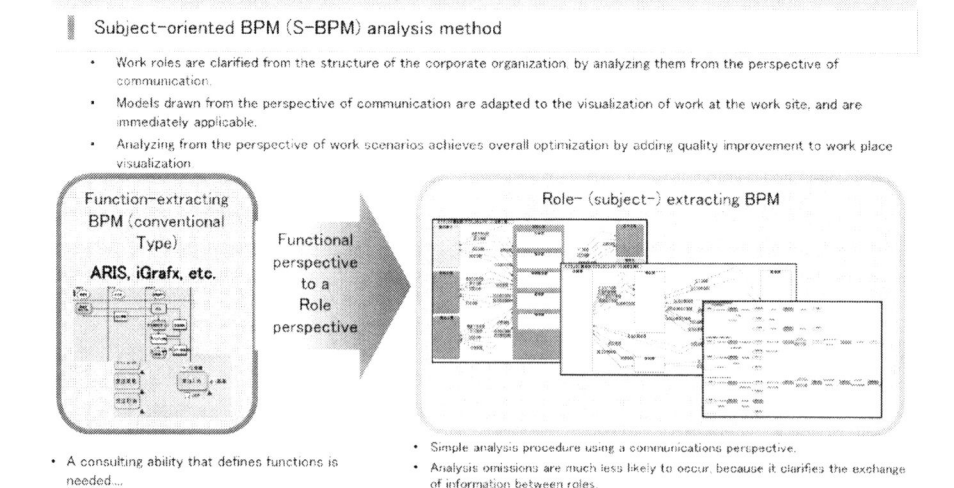

**Fig. 6.** Features of the CGAA/EES Development Methodology

procedure that does not require a consultant with high-level expertise, and where different results from different analysts are not likely to occur. Another feature is that it diagrams a simple model that is grounded in reality, which makes analytic omissions less likely.

### 4.3 Subject Structuring

First of all, "subject" indicates the subject that executes the executable process. However, when considering overall optimization, it is not always effective to deal with "subjects" at the level of the central person who performs work at the work site. Therefore subject structuring is performed by bringing in the concept of an abstract subject that represents a unit larger than a conventional subject (defined as a "subject community" by Metasonic AG). Using this concept, the work of large organizations and business divisions can be modeled.

At the same time, the information that forms the input and output (messages) of subjects and subject communities can be clarified (see fig. 7). This is the same as defining the interfaces of subjects and subject communities. At this point, subjects and subject communities can be handled as "black boxes," and it is not necessary to be aware of the concrete means by which inputs become outputs.

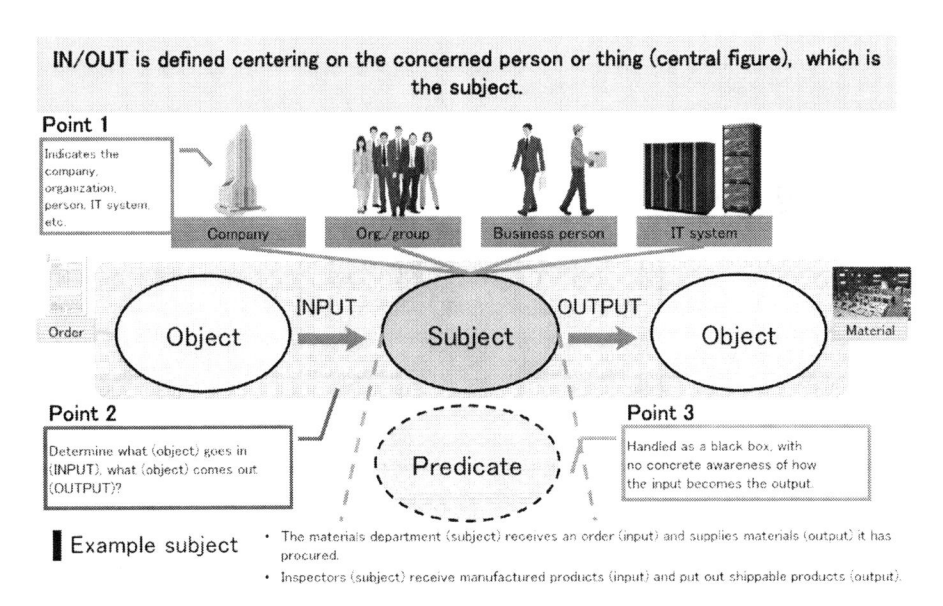

**Fig. 7.** Subject-based Thinking

In addition, subject communities are not only simplified groups of subjects. Groups can also be made between subject communities. In this way, subject structuring can be accomplished using a multi-layer hierarchical representation. For example, subject structuring is possible from the highest level of very large organizations, such as entire companies (see fig. 8).

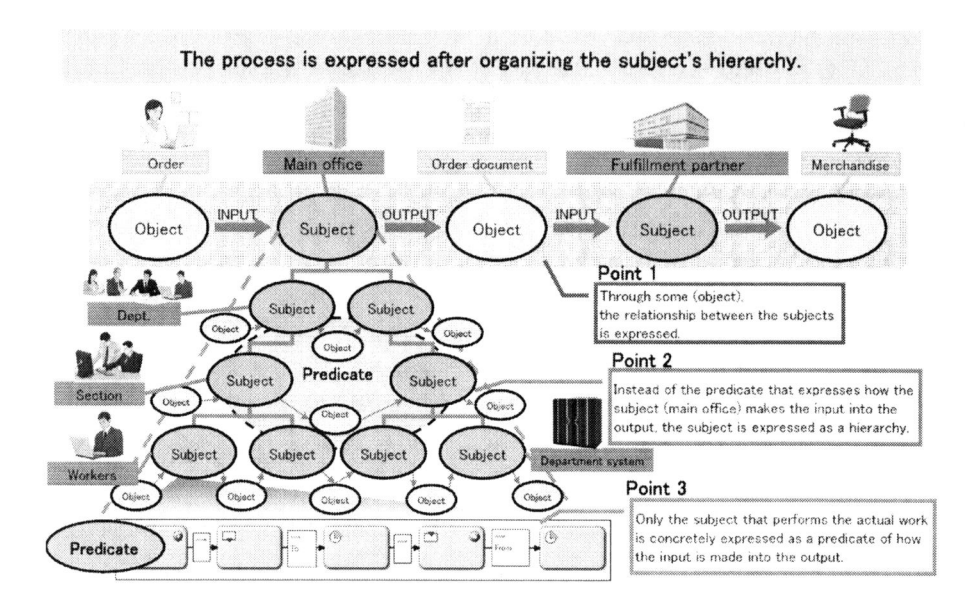

Fig. 8. Establishing Relationships and Hierarchies for Subjects

### 4.4 Business Scenario Visualization

When expressing "overall corporate activity", awareness of business scenarios is essential. However, when diagramming executable processes, especially at the start of deployment, it often happens that just one part of the business scenario is being diagrammed, and there is a strong risk of falling into conditions of local optimization and complacency. Even when diagramming executable processes belonging to only one part of the business scenario, it is essential to remain aware of the business scenario as a whole.

In the process-oriented approach, this business scenario is expressed as a chain of functions. On the other hand, with CGAA/EES subject-oriented modeling, the business scenario is expressed using a chain of subjects or subject communities. As mentioned earlier, high-level consultants are not required because the scenario is expressed using subjects or subject communities, and this expression can be very close to reality.

### 4.5 Top-Down Technique

When diagramming executable processes, there are always the nagging problems of process sizes and subject sizes (subject communities). They should be designed in a way that keeps the sizes of processes and subjects/subject communities from becoming a discouraging factor, not only during visualization, but also during ongoing BPM implementation. However, more often than not, sizes of processes and subject/subject communities become troublesome, due to unrealistic design, design based on feelings instead of facts, and consolidation work that occurs during later improvements and requires alterations to the model.

CGAA/EES addresses these problems by establishing the size of executable processes and the subjects that actually execute them, using the top-down technique for subject structuring and business scenario visualization (see fig. 9). When seen as a whole, process and subject design are a sticking point for continuous BPM activity and defining services in subject-oriented BPM.

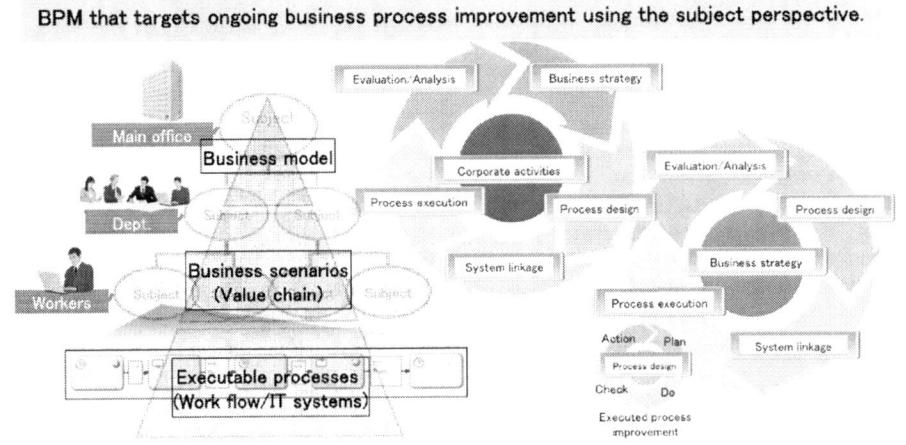

**Fig. 9.** Subject-oriented BPM Using the Top-Down Technique

## 5 CGAA/EES Development Methodology

### 5.1 Subject-Expansion Model

With the CGAA/EES development methodology, business activity, business scenarios, and executable processes are modeled using a subject-expansion model. Executable processes are arrived at through analysis of the business model and subject structure from the subject perspective (see fig. 10).

(1) The basis of the subject structure is clarified by organizing the company's business model. (2) The subjects of the executable processes are arrived at from the overall corporate activity by making (breaking down) the subject structure into a hierarchy. (3) The executable processes are diagrammed, clarifying their relationships to the business scenario.

The subject structure is expressed in six layers: the entire company (SL0), main office and company sites (SL1), business units (SL2), department granularity (SL3), section granularity (SL4), and subsection granularity (SL5). The subjects structured here are not those that can execute processes, but are subject communities of abstracted subjects (SL: Subject Layer).

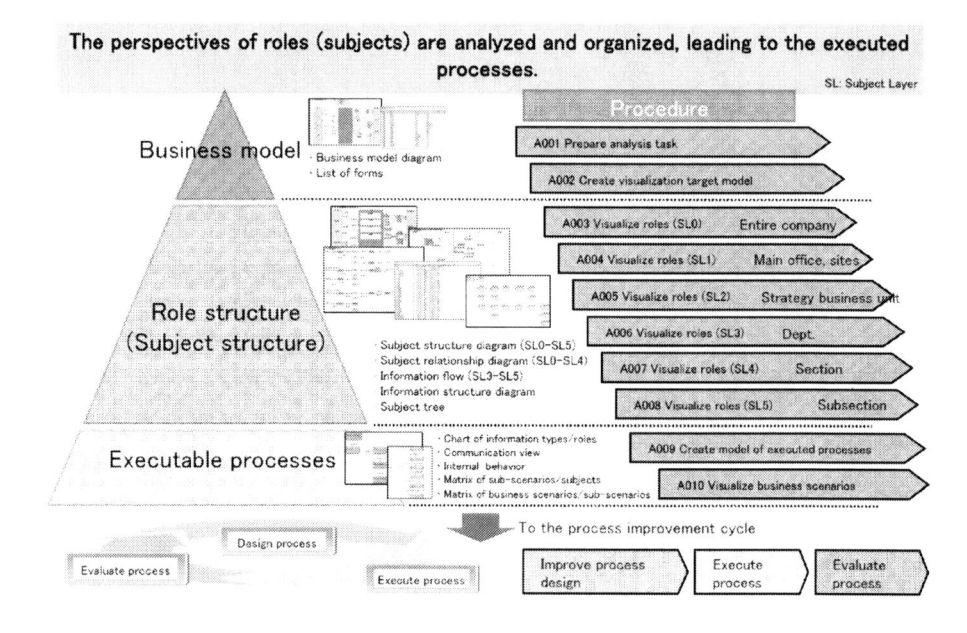

**Fig. 10.** Subject-Expansion Model

### 5.2 Business Model Layer: Procedures A001 to A002

Subjects that represent the entire company and subjects that represent its stakeholders are expressed through their handling of forms. In CGAA/EES, forms are used as one element in capturing reality. The stakeholders who handle forms are organized by organizing the forms into a "form list." Activities of the entire company can then be expressed by drawing a "business model diagram" (see fig. 11).

(1) Actual existing forms are examined, and the stakeholders who handle those forms are sorted by organization name (company name or organization name within the company). (2) The forms are also organized according to their properties (medium/EDI, existence of changes, etc.) in the form list. (3) Centering on the subject being analyzed, subjects with which there is a sales relationship (left-hand column) and subjects with which there is a buying relationship (right-hand column) are distinguished, and diagrammed on the business model diagram. (4) Forms that are identified in the form list are diagrammed on the business model diagram as forms exchanged between subjects.

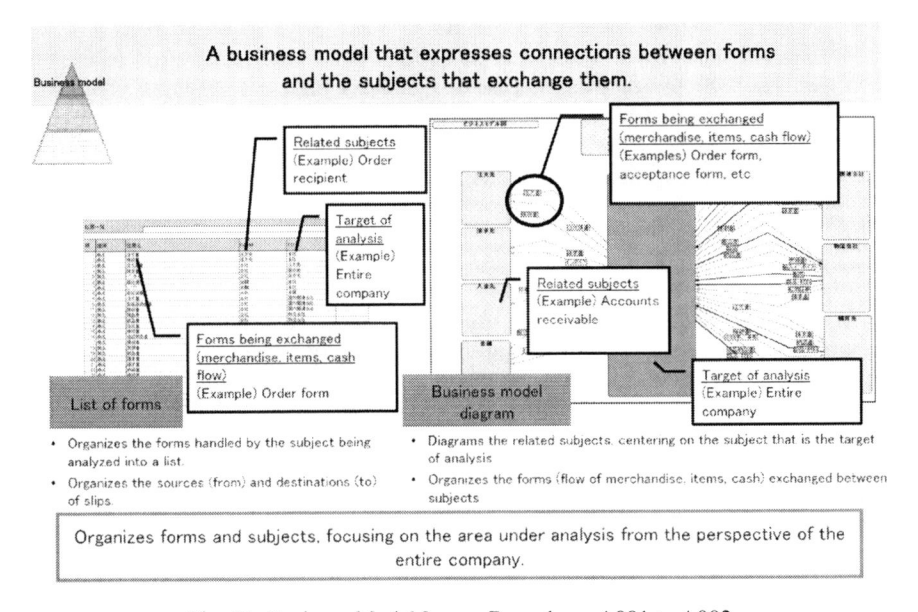

Fig. 11. Business Model Layer: Procedures A001 to A002

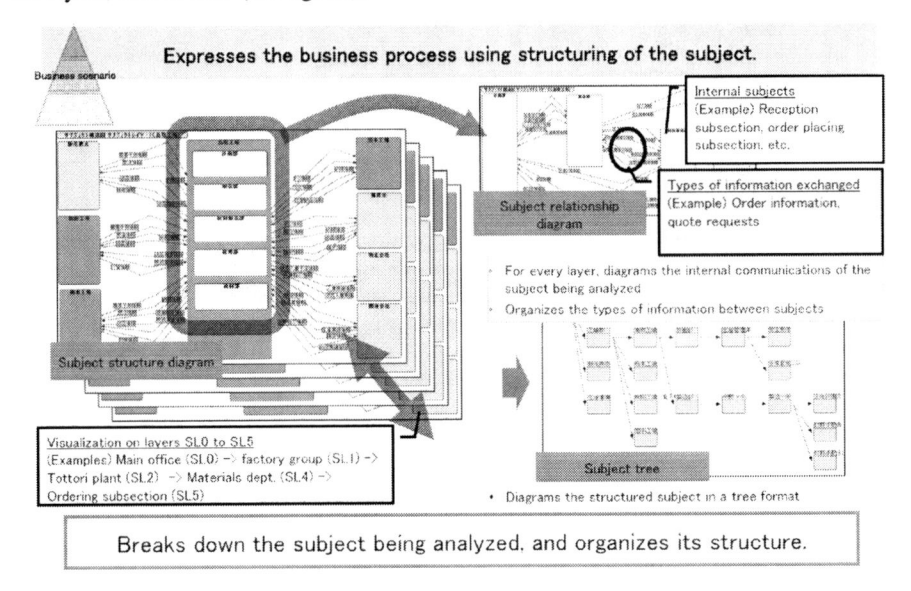

## 5.3 Subject Structuring: Procedures A003 to A008

The subject structure is expressed as the relationships that are external to the subject being analyzed (subject structure diagram) and internal relationships of the subject being analyzed (subject relationship diagram). In addition, the subject structure is expressed in six layers, SL0 to SL5 (see fig. 12).

Fig. 12. Subject Structuring: Procedures A003 to A008

(1) Centering on the subject being analyzed, subjects with which there is a sales relationship (left-hand column) and subjects with which there is a buying relationship (right-hand column) are diagrammed on the "subject structure diagram." Exchanges between subjects are organized and described according to the information type. (2) The subject being analyzed is broken down into relationships between subjects on a single layer and diagrammed as the "subject relationship diagram." (3) Subjects that have been structured by being broken down are diagrammed as a "subject tree diagram."

The SL0 "subject structure diagram" is drawn with the same granularity as the "business model diagram" and takes the highest subject structure position.

In the subject breakdown, CGAA/EES uses "organization" as one more element for thinking about reality. However, the broken-down subject is not necessarily limited to matching organizational granularity. Subjects are also categorized from the perspective of roles. This takes into consideration the multiple roles within the existing organization, extracting and clarifying them. Finally, on the SL5 layer, this connects to the size of the process and executable subject.

Also, in the business model diagram, exchanges between subjects are handled as forms, but in the subject structure, they are instead handled by information types (information). By doing this, even if the same forms are exchanged, it is possible to express different meanings. This is important in expressing business processes.

### 5.4 Scenario Visualization: Procedures A006 to A008

This clarifies the business scenario within subject structuring. The relationships between subjects and between information types diagrammed in the subject structuring diagram are expressed as flow, focusing on their sequence (see fig. 13).

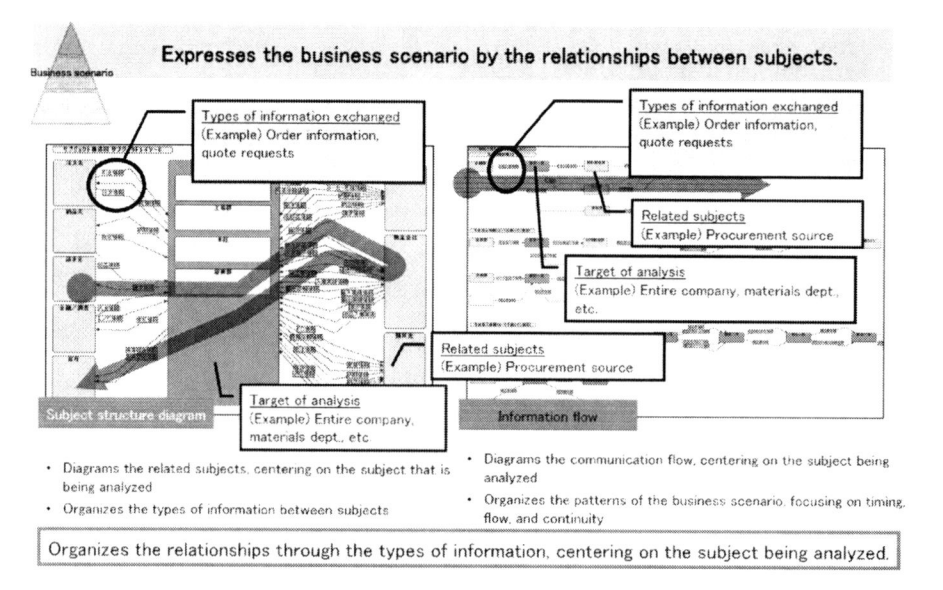

**Fig. 13.** Scenario Visualization: Procedure A006 to A008

(1) The relationships between subjects and information types are focused on and diagrammed as "information flow." (2) The number of information flows is decided from the perspective of the information types that trigger them. (3) Information flow is organized from the SL3 layer that composes the business scenario. SL4 and SL5 also organize business scenarios in the same way.

Scenarios that are expressed as chains of functions in the process-oriented approach are organized in the subject-oriented approach in this way from the perspective of subjects and the flow of information types that go between them. This is the big difference when expressing them from the perspective of subjects instead of functions.

## 5.5 Executable Process Model Creation: Procedure A009

Using the SL5 subjects clarified through subject structuring, we can arrive at the scope to be defined with processes and the subjects who can execute them (see fig. 14).

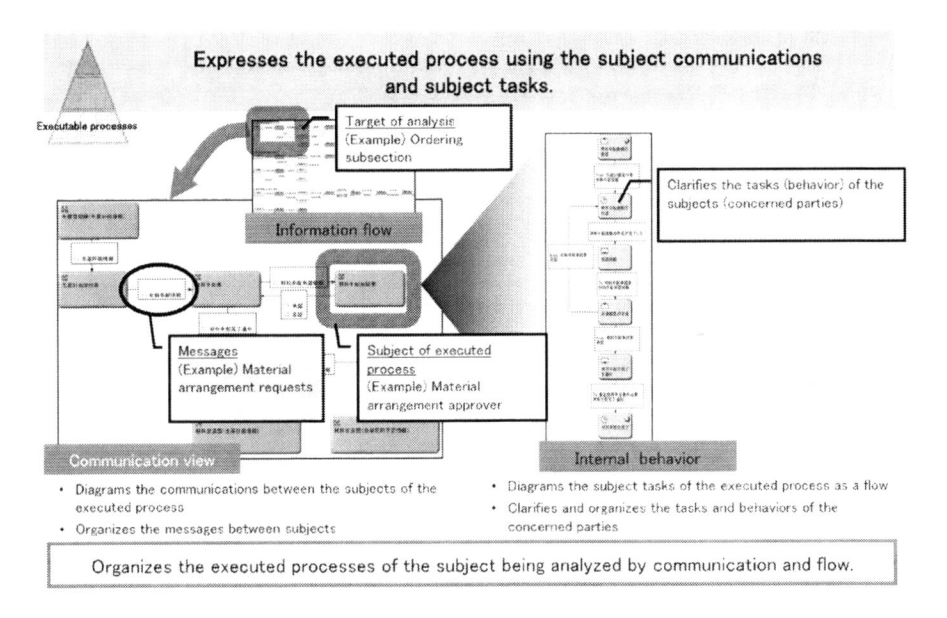

**Fig. 14.** Executable Process Model Creation: Procedure A009

(1) The communication view is created with the SL5 subjects that have been clarified through subjects structuring and the size of processes. (2) Subjects that exist within SL5 subjects are identified and defined in the communication view as subjects who can execute processes. (3) The work of the identified subjects who can execute is defined as internal behavior.

## 5.6 Business Scenario Makeup: Procedure A010

The created communication views are connected, until they reach the units that make up the business scenarios (see fig. 15). (1) The SL5 subjects in the communication view are connected, making up the SL4 scenarios. (2) The SL4 business scenarios are further connected to make up the SL3 scenarios.

By clarifying the relationships between the communication views and the business scenarios, the positions of the subjects who can execute are clarified in the business scenario, organizing the fundamental information for overall optimization.

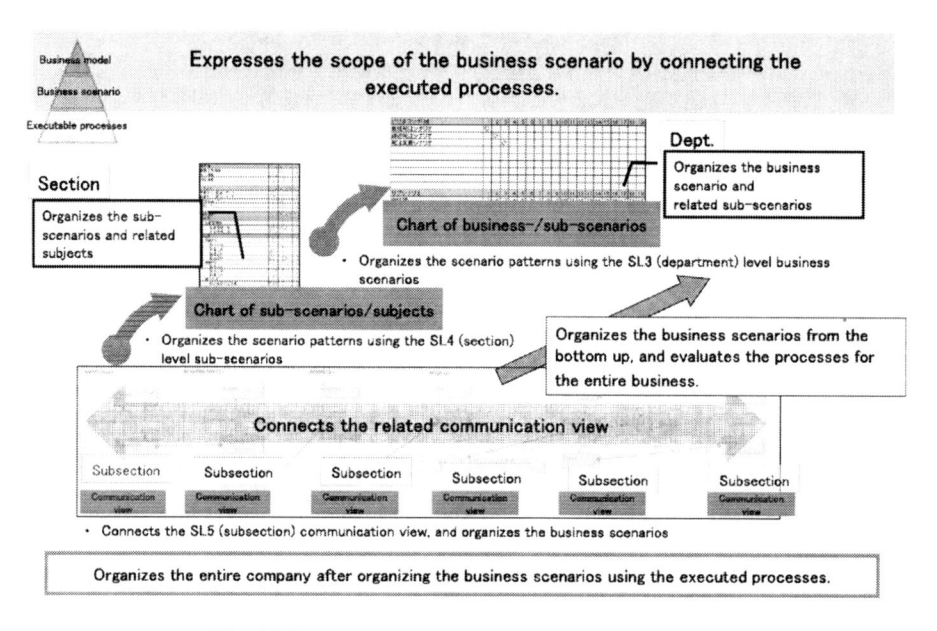

Fig. 15. Business Scenario Makeup: Procedure A010

## 6 Conclusion

CGAA/EES is a development methodology based on subject-oriented BPM that achieves BPM cycle implementation and overall optimization (see fig. 16). It

- Achieves BPM for small group activities
  Implements the BPM cycle at the minimum unit size of small group activities at the SL5 subsection level.
- Achieves a BPM foundation with immediate improvement action.
- Achieves BPM deployment in phases
  An approach that allows gradual expansion of the scope of BPM, starting from the introduction of hierarchical executable processes.
- Achieves company-wide optimization

  Achieves overall optimization while also achieving BPM for small-group activity by visualizing overall corporate activity as well as business scenarios.
- Achieves easy visualization and improvement

Besides achieving overall optimization, visualization and improvement are easily accomplished using subject-oriented visualization without the need for consultants with high-level expertise.
- Achieves synchronization of the model and the work site
Controls the gap between the model and tasks at the work site by diagramming executable processes.

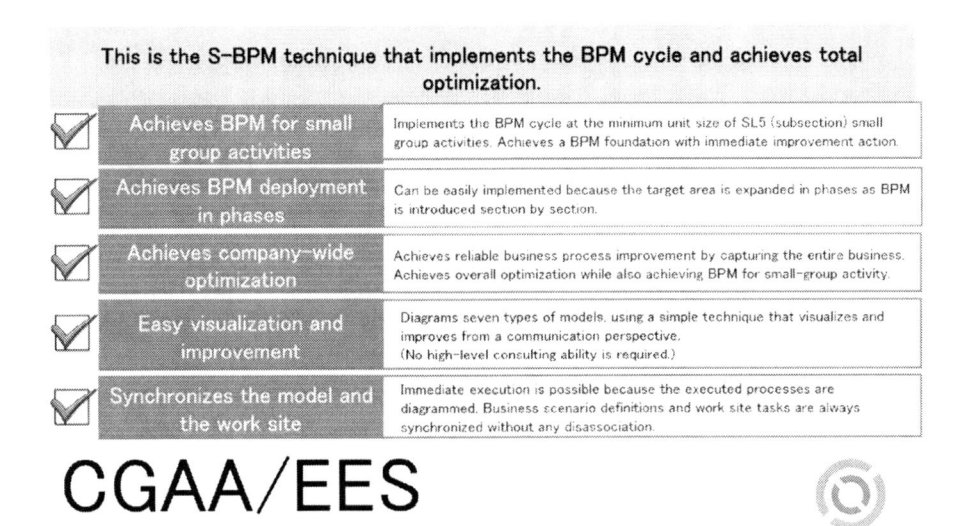

Fig. 16. Conclusion

## References

1. Hammer M., Champy J., Business Reengineering. 6. Auflage, Frankfurt am Main 1996
2. Scheer, A.-W.: ARIS – Modellierungsmethoden, Metamodelle. Anwendungen, Berlin (1998)
3. Fleischmann, A., Schmidt, W., Stary, C., Obermeier, S., Börger, E.: Subjektorientiertes Prozessmanagement, München (2011)
4. Fleischmann, A.: What is S-BPM? In: Buchwald, H., Fleischmann, A., Seese, D., Stary, C. (eds.) S-BPM ONE 2009. CCIS, vol. 85, pp. 85–106. Springer, Heidelberg (2010)
5. Schmidt, W., Fleischmann, A., Gilbert, O.: Subjektorientiertes Geschäftsprozessmanagement. HMD – Praxis der Wirtschaftsinformatik. Heft 266, 52–62 (2009)

# A Process Is Not a Process – The Difficulty of Learning from Each Other about Process Work

Martin Turinsky

AUDI AG, 85045 Ingolstadt, Germany

**Abstract.** To enable different technical departments to learn from each other in their process work or ideally to complement each other, a better understanding of each other's intentions in process work has to be developed. For the primary disciplines of process documentation, process optimisation and process control, essential context situations are illustrated and the necessary levels of detail as well as the bridge to IT design are discussed.

**Keywords:** Process documentation, Process optimisation, Process control, Depth of detail, Structure configuration, IT design.

## 1 Motivation

Consistent terminology, modeling notation, and levels of detail are conditions for allowing different departments in a large organization like Audi to develop a common understanding of processes, but also to learn from each other about their process work, e.g. by discussing different approaches. In this paper we thus reflect on terminology and notation in section 2, before we discuss these aspects together with the appropriate level of detail for process documentation, process optimisation and process control in the chapters 3 to 5. In chapter 6 we conclude with some special objectives of process analysis and documentation, related to quality management and IT. Chapter 6 addresses some special objectives of process analysis and documentation, related to quality management and IT. In chapter 7 we conclude with some thoughts on future developments in BPM.

## 2 Terminology and Process Notation

Today, the term "process" is used almost at will. You will hardly ever hear five minutes of business small talk without the word "process" being uttered.

Besides the slack use of the term as a synonym for task, activity or function, it is thoroughly applied in the sense of a "defined procedure". Nevertheless, there remains great scope for interpretation and application of the term. The consequence is that we talk at cross-purposes, and this leads to unnecessary misunderstandings.

The different ideas about how the term "process" should be used are models formed from different contexts and experiences. However, a model is nothing but a simplified and limited reflection of reality that serves a certain explanatory purpose. So the question is not whether somebody uses the term "process" incorrectly, but rather what he uses the term for.

We can distinguish between three evolutionary steps in process management, each of which makes a substantial contribution to clarification of the concept (see fig. 1).

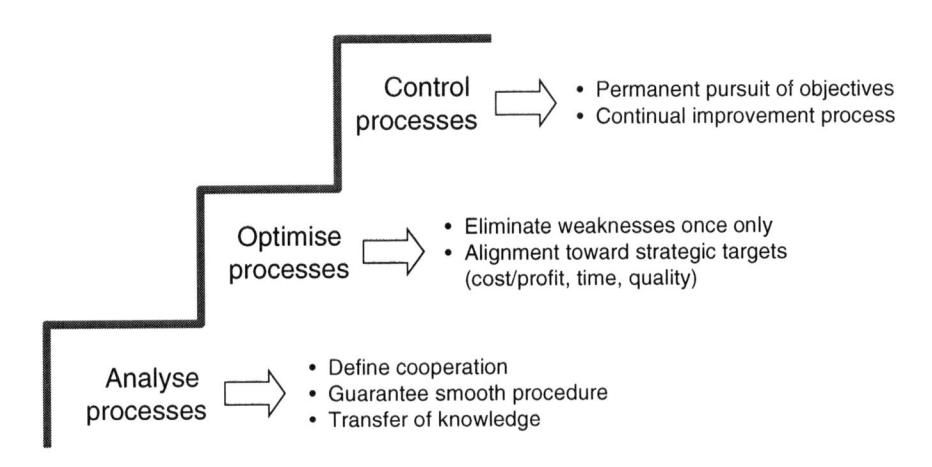

Control processes ⇨
- Permanent pursuit of objectives
- Continual improvement process

Optimise processes ⇨
- Eliminate weaknesses once only
- Alignment toward strategic targets (cost/profit, time, quality)

Analyse processes ⇨
- Define cooperation
- Guarantee smooth procedure
- Transfer of knowledge

**Fig. 1.** Evolutionary steps in process management

While this is an initial approach to explaining the complexity of the world of processes, it only covers the differences in the objectives pursued to a limited extent. Expanding these views will ultimately lead to the consideration of a number of special objectives in the process model, especially those in IT design.

Only if the same language (notation) is used to describe processes, it will be possible to communicate about them meaningfully. A language is defined as a combination of vocabulary and grammar. Applied to process work, this means that the essential terms are defined and are more-or-less uniformly applied. It is advisable to define terms as closely as possible to their meanings in everyday language. Subtle artificial terms are doomed to failure.

Grammar is easier to teach if the effects of the modeling conventions are to be found in a central process modeling tool which requires, for example, special training for it to be used. The temptation to use all the different capabilities that such a tool offers has to be resisted, or else its propagation will be limited to a few method specialists. An essential precondition to achieve the level of propagation needed is rather the drastic reduction to a few descriptive features and linking elements.

Even with the very term "process", a common denominator has to be found between the various stakeholders involved. The definition of the term "process" in the meaning of added value is hardly vulnerable and yet highly specific. In other words: a process is the conversion of a defined input to a defined output via a sequence of activities (process steps).

## 3 Purpose: Transparency

### 3.1 Transparency for Added Value

#### 3.1.1 Top-Down Principle
To illustrate the business activities, focus is placed on the added value of the company strictly in accordance with the definition of the term "process" assumed above. Consideration is given precisely in accordance with the top-down principle. Processes on the uppermost level of detail are highly generic ("artificial"). In industrial corporations, process level one usually comprises the processes of product development, customer acquisition, order fulfilling and to a greater or lesser extent management and support processes for human resources, finance, IT, etc. Here, the process designations definitely testify to a certain inventiveness.

Considered in isolation, this granularity makes the business being described impossible to recognise. It does not matter whether the product is dishwashers, aeroplanes or diapers: the processes are the same. Above all, in multi-product companies it is almost inevitable that these generic processes, uniformly defined by a central office for all company divisions, have acceptance problems. A level zero, representing the "business section", can prevent this.

Within a business section, the process level described is extremely meaningful. A focus is placed on the essential company achievements. In the product development process products, for which the customer should pay the price asked, are developed to market and production maturity. This is the very basis for the existence of a company. The customer's enthusiasm for the brand and product are stimulated in the sales process, inciting him to make a purchase or place an order. The customer order process completes the order. The specified product is manufactured and delivered. After the sale has been made ("After Sales") the product is serviced and any defects that may have occurred are eliminated to maintain the usefulness of the product, creating an essential basis for brand loyalty. In order to do this, staff has to be employed, suitable IT systems have to be operational and scarce resources have to be utilized effectively and efficiently.

#### 3.1.2 Display Format
Processes, describing the essential activities of a company at the very highest level are usually illustrated in the form of a simple value added chain [1] (see fig. 2).

Even here, it is extremely advisable to specify each input and output. That makes it clear what service is to be rendered and what added value is to be achieved here; where the process starts and where it ends. An illustration in the form of value added chains is also usually sufficient for the next level of detail, assuming the number of sub-process steps remains manageable.

Essentially, the first two process levels are shaped by the commercial purpose of the company. Not even the company strategy has significant influence on the processes on this level, unless they involve the development of new fields of business. Examples of these in the automotive industry are new processes for mobility services or vehicle-related IT solutions. However, the company strategy does have a great effect in the target figures for process achievement (see sec. 5.1).

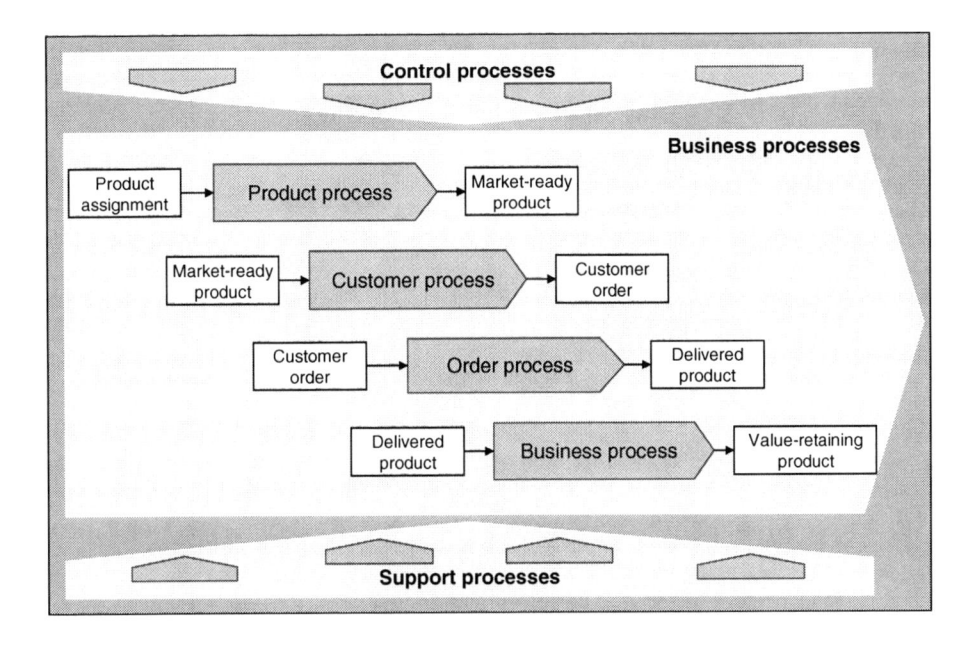

Fig. 2. Typical process house of a company in the commodities industry

## 3.2 Transparency as Basis in Cooperation between Involved Parties

A process model will produce a considerable increase in value whenever the participants responsible for executing a process step are named. That may sound banal, but it does have a significant influence on the description of a procedure. The upshot of the decision to specify the participant responsible for execution is that the process step is always cut when there is a change of responsibility. In other words a process step ends at the latest when an output is passed on to the next entity. For the parties involved in the process, these handover points therefore constitute the critical interfaces in the process and as a consequence, processes often reflect the customer/supplier relationships within the company. The resulting cooperation model is especially valuable for the understanding of the company activities when the model does not end at the functional boundaries between divisions, but rather highlights the interplay between the different parties involved.

Two companies performing the same business activities will perform the process differently simply through their different organizational structures and their different distributions of tasks. This has far-reaching consequences. A standardisation of processes across the subsidiaries of a group will be difficult to realise without harmonising the organizational structure.

### 3.2.1 The Status of Process Orientation in German Companies

A recent study in which 83 major German industrial corporations were surveyed (19 of them listed in the DAX30 and 21 in the MDAX share indexes) showed that the procedural organisation in German companies remains predominantly function-orientated [2] (see fig. 3).

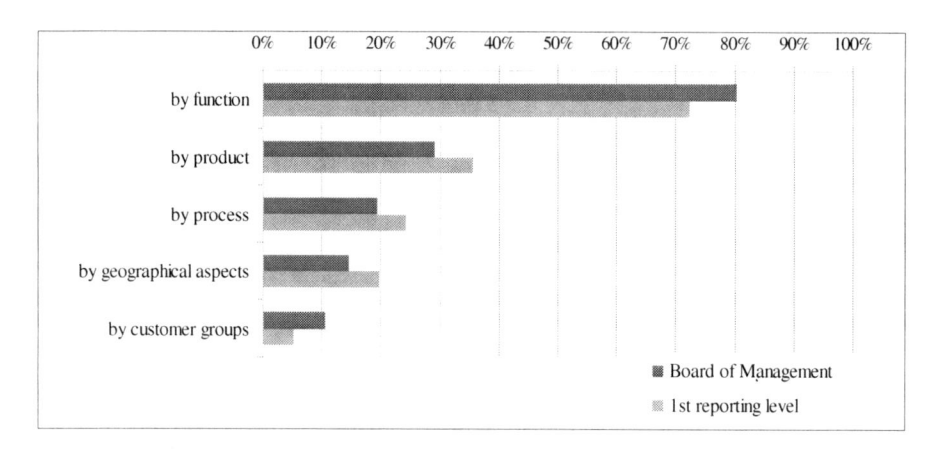

**Fig. 3.** Structuring principles of German industrial companies

Three principle results are derived from the further findings of the study [3]:

1. With respect to the measurability and controllability of corporate processes, there remains substantial need for action to meet the future challenges with regard to the speed of decision-making and the service provision.
2. In the majority of cases, responsibility for processes has not been consistently assigned. While designated process coordinators exist in many companies, these do not enjoy the levels of authority needed.
3. The companies are attaching increasing strategic importance to process orientation, and yet in practice, the level of implementation remains unsatisfactory.

The structural organisation at Audi is also predominantly function-orientated. On the first reporting level below the Board of Management are the Development, Procurement, Production, Sales & Marketing, Human Resources and Finance divisions – a classical structure.

The functional line organisation also characterises the behavioural orientation of the workforce and the vertical career paths. The concentration of similar functions and thus of the associated employees from related technical disciplines creates a local commitment and the critical mass for the development of technical experts. For the individual departments and function divisions, this certainly generates the effect of a learning organisation. Over the last decades at Audi, this has led to a highly functional professionalism which can be seen in technically sophisticated products and outstanding quality with the quest for perfection even in the non-technical disciplines (e.g. marketing).

### 3.2.2 Display Format

Processes that regulate the cooperation between the entities involved must place its focus heavily on the assignment of activities to the units performing the activity in order to derive any need for adjustment in the organizational structure. A proven format is the "swimming lane diagram" (here in the horizontal version) [4] (see fig. 4).

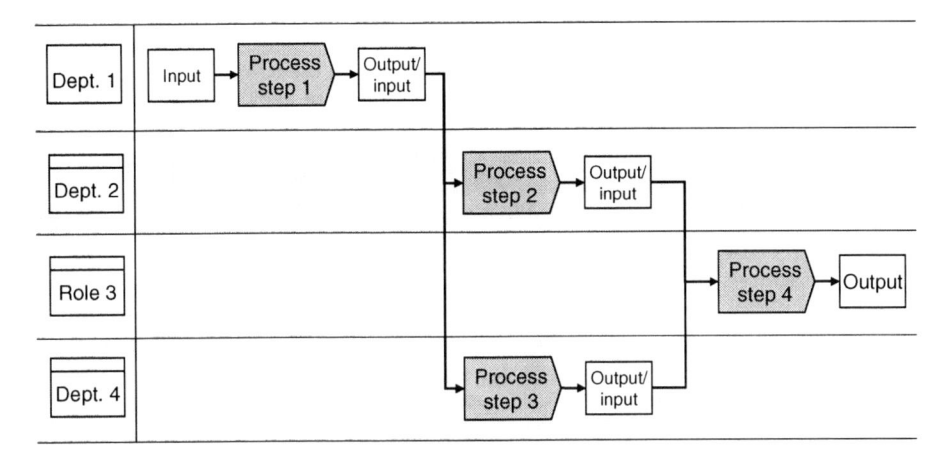

Fig. 4. "Swimming lane diagram"

The process description follows the pattern of process definition: Input – Process step – Output. Sorting the process steps and the output according to the responsible entity creates the swimming lanes. The participant responsible for executing a process step and for delivering the output is specified in the left-hand column. Primarily, these are the existing organisational units or councils. In certain cases, more abstract roles are required (supplier, customer, controlling, head of department). With a ratio of about 1:10 of higher-order to lower-order process levels, this format is highly suitable for illustrating the middle levels. Because the graphic illustration in the form of swimming lanes is not particularly economical with space, large process-wallpapers are often created. To survey the actual situation with the aim of optimising processes and structures, this format can be extremely useful as it is possible to put your finger directly on the pain points. For a management presentation, such illustrations usually only demonstrate intensive work on the issue. A more compressed representation is generally necessary for decision making.

## 3.3 Strengths and Weaknesses of a Hierarchical Process Model

Most people who work with process modeling have an imagination of a hierarchical tree structure when they think about a company process model. Such a model does indeed create a good understanding of the interrelationships within a company, up to a certain depth of detail. The hierarchical process model offers a rational way of navigating through the landscape of processes and their levels of detail. It thus forms a good basis for the publication of the process knowledge of a company in the employee portal.

Ideally, this imagination will contain process steps of roughly the same size on all process levels. But onto what should this granularity be fixed? Onto the period of time, the scope of tasks, their complexity or the evaluated value added difference between input and output? It is not unusual to get different process descriptions when different process modelers deal with the same process. The same thing applies for the attributes to be analysed. The objective of process modeling thus defines which questions have to be asked, which data have to be collected and which information has to be generated.

Even more serious is the drawback that the tree structure makes networks between the process sections invisible, although these are necessary to explain the various interrelationships. On a high process aggregation level, certain networks have to be ignored in detail. This is accepted to achieve a condensed representation. We are appeased, because we expect these networks to reappear as we descend through the process detail levels.

Metaphorically speaking, we go downstairs to floors where we find separate rooms with just a few joining doors. A database-based process modeling tool makes these links possible in principle, but in practice extensive networking will often fail on the fact that the dependencies generated can no longer be managed.

The hierarchical process model is based on the idea of a logical sequential flow. This doubtlessly creates order, but it also prevents the correct perspective for many necessary explanations (see chapter 4).

## 3.4 Limits of Company-Wide Process Documentation

While the subdivision of processes onto ever finer process steps give a deeper insight, the complexity increases exponentially with each level, and it does so not only because of the factor of the average number of sub-process steps (e.g. 1:10), but also because the dynamics of change increase with each level of detail and the need for relevance to the current situation becomes ever more difficult to guarantee. Every extension by just one level of detail therefore has to deliver a benefit in the form of additional information. Input, process step, output and determination of the process step owner are not enough.

Within a field of business, it is usually sufficient to present the first two process levels in the form of a value added chain. For an experienced member of staff, such process levels are trivial. Nevertheless, they do create a rough framework for orientation that puts the focus on the result to be jointly achieved (in the form of a product or a service), especially in functionally structured organisations. This corporate process model (process house) can form the basis for the installation of process owners, which could reconcile the conflict between partly contradictory divisional interests, assuming they are given the necessary authority.

In companies that are not structured according to processes, the persons responsible for execution must be explicitly specified at the latest in the following level of detail as specific company procedures then have to be defined. In such organizations, processes flow cross-functionally with partly substantial challenges at the corresponding interfaces. Sub-services are optimised and perfected, but frictional losses occur right along the value added chain when these sub-services are linked, and this has a negative effect with regard to time deadlines and costs. But even the documentation of processes in the graphical form of the swimming lane diagram (according to responsibilities) is only worthwhile to a certain depth of detail. Transparency and relevance to the current situation also have their price here (see fig. 5). The definition of the optimum depends on different factors such as frequency of throughputs, number of participants involved, fault risk or staff qualification. In many cases, a procedural description in concise headwords is sufficient. Usually, a graphic illustration is no longer required to control a previously optimised regular procedure.

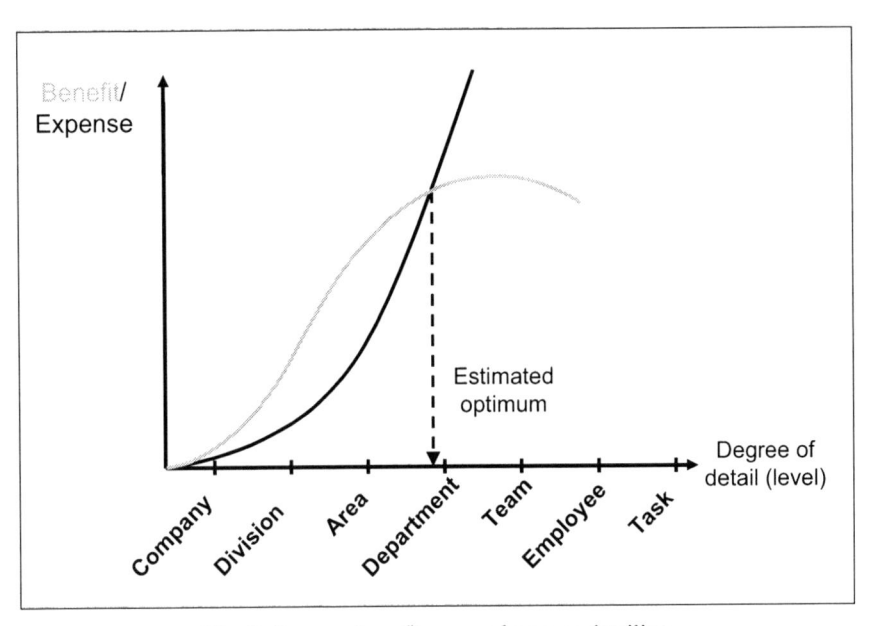

**Fig. 5.** Expense/benefit curve of process detailing

The economical principle that marginal costs are not to exceed the marginal benefit should also be applied when choosing a depth of detail for a permanently updated company process model[1]. Even if it is not possible to reliably determine the curve, we are most certainly permitted to trust in our experience here.

The optimum can be shifted to greater depth of detail with more information content. The information and data that are linked by inputs/outputs are a valuable basis for coherent IT master data management. Here we can find potential that remains largely untapped.

On the workplace level, documentation can be useful for new members of staff and for describing deputization arrangements. Documentation for operating IT systems or checklists for detail procedures that are critical for safety (aeroplane takeoff) are examples of rational process descriptions on the detail level.

The risk of "exaggeration", i.e. the risks of describing a process in too much detail, is much higher than usually expected. This does not mean just the wasteful use of resources for unnecessary documentation, but rather the loss of credibility for the potential of process management.

## 4 Purpose: Optimisation

### 4.1 From "As is" to "to Be"

There are many different factors that can trigger a process optimisation project: growing numbers of throughputs with limited resources, reductions in staffing or

---

[1] The degree of detail is represented here by the size of the organisational unit. This is only a weak indicator, but at least better than an arbitrary number for the detail level.

budget, lasting deviations from specified targets, increasing amounts of reworking and much more besides. Sometimes, it is initially just a diffuse lack of satisfaction on the part of the process owner or participant, or a weakness in the process is discovered by chance during mandatory process documentation as part of the quality management system.

As diverse as the reasons are, the potential discovered can be just as varied. If deficiencies are found in the sequence of the procedure, if test steps or approvals are to be eliminated or if tasks are to be distributed differently, then the optimisation measures will feed through to the documented target process model. Often however, potential is discovered and processed as part of optimisation measures that is not at all apparent in a process representation, as described above with the example of the swimming lane model: The process is optimised, yet the change cannot be seen in the process model. Process improvement measures can affect staff qualification, improved communications, the adaptation of the IT solutions employed and much more besides.

The process model is then used within the optimisation project "simply" to systematically record the strengths and weaknesses of the current situation. However, the service provided by this cannot be overstated.

If the persons involved in the process meet up for a workshop together and discuss the actual process, the result will not only be a description of the actual process, but there will also be an immediate discussion of the difficulties that occur in the process cycles. The weak points can then be located directly in the process. Very often, potential solutions are presented here and a vision of a future target process is imperceptibly formed.

A more radical approach is often demanded in which work should immediately start on the creation of a target process. Such an approach can sometimes exploit the creative potential of the persons involved more effectively. But this approach must not be sold with the argument that we do not need to squander our time with the current actual process. At the end of process optimisation or of a process redesign, there is the far more difficult task of changing over from the current process to the target process in the real world, not just on the model level. This path can only be successfully taken if we have a good idea not only of where we want to go, but also of where we are coming from. Even if we dare to enforce the change with hierarchical authority, the doubters and the apparent losers of the change will intone the song of "everything was better the way it used to be", all along the long path to establishing the target situation. Then we have to remember the drawbacks of the past clearly and sustainable or else we will always face the risk of relapsing.

In my experience, space for creative solutions is not distorted by the classic approach with the first step of analysing the actual process. Rather, it creates the security that proposals for change that really can be implemented have been developed in the awareness of real requirements.

## 4.2 Choice of Detail Level

Like the complexity of the possible indications of a need for improvement, the complexity of the triggers for an optimisation project leads to problem-related process views. These must only be orientated toward a hierarchical top-down process model if it really can help to solve the problem.

That does not mean that the hierarchical process model is unable to make a valuable contribution to process optimisation. Usually, a rough localisation of the project scope is possible, allowing the entities involved to be identified.

However, as soon as we start the analysis, we must remain focused on the optimisation objective. Depending on the focus, process mapping can link different detail levels, skip sections, create new relationships that have been lost in the tree structure of the hierarchical model (see section 3.3). As a rule, process consideration follows a T-model in optimisation projects. When identifying fields of activity, we try to maintain a high level of aggregation. When a field of activity has been identified for optimisation, there will follow a deep drilling in which the detail processes are scrutinised.

It is also desirable for the findings to be input into the updating of the hierarchical process model at the end of the project. But this usually fails in the fact that the persons involved in a project turn their attention to new tasks once the project ends. Process work after a project has ended, is a bit like cleaning up the kitchen after the dinner has been cooked and eaten. Everybody tries to get out of it. Only rarely there is a transfer to the hierarchical process model, so the knowledge acquired remains largely in the project group.

## 5 Purpose: Controlling Efficiency

### 5.1 Process Monitoring

Processes gain attention if performance indicators can be found for them, if targets can be assigned, if the achievement of targets can be monitored and if corrective measures can be initiated in case of deviation. Whoever claims to operate process management has no choice but to use indicators, because management means the target-orientated control of activities. But we can only control what we know and what we regularly measure. That forces us to describe our processes and to define our performance indicators.

Indicators for measuring the overall company performance can be easily assigned to the first level. On the highest aggregation level, they can be found, in part, in the annual report: sales, revenue, results. As indicators for the overall efficiency of a company, this is not enough, but it is nevertheless recommended to remain economical with the choice of performance indicators.

Indicators must be transparent and the underlying targets must be achievable and binding. On the first aggregation level, these targets are a manifestation of the company strategy. The detailed indicators must have a logical relationship to the higher-order indicators, and must be just as easy to explain. Indicators can only be effective as control parameters if they are known and accepted. This hypothesis alone represents a natural limitation with respect to the quantity.

As a rule, indicators form the target dimension of the company with respect to growth (sales volume), results (costs, revenue), quality and customer perception (satisfaction/enthusiasm) (see fig. 6). For the process arrangement you usually apply a specification with respect to quality, throughput (volume), use of resources (cost) and time. These target dimensions are in competition with each other.

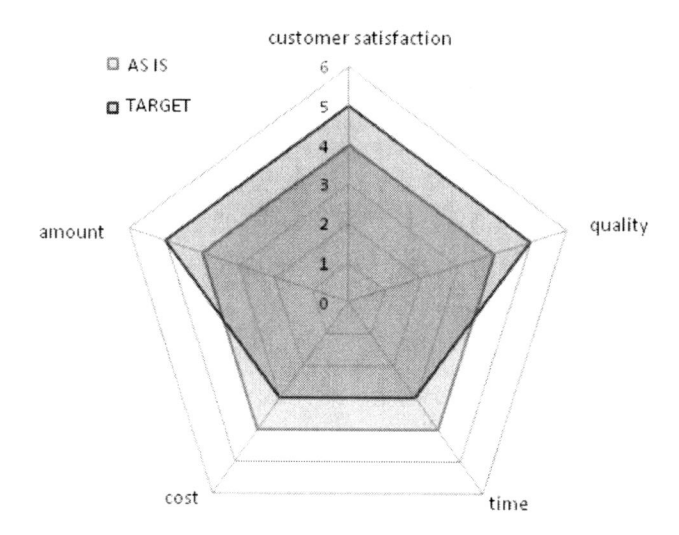

**Fig. 6.** Target dimensions for process control and optimisation

The dimension of time is especially important, both in the sense of duration and throughput time, and in the sense of adherence to schedules. Shorter process times will cause shorter commitment of resources, which not only reduce process costs, they also help to get new products onto the market more quickly and thus to achieve higher prices.

For operational process control, their availability and acceptance also have to be taken into account when choosing indicators. Again in this respect, the throughput time and adherence to schedules are the central process indicators, alongside quality and volume. Throughput time and adherence to schedules, direct throughput rate and reworking can be simply and promptly analysed, even on the lower process levels. Process costs and customer satisfaction are much more complex to record.

The implementation of target specifications can only succeed if they are also used to measure the responsible managers. Accordingly, the process objectives must be anchored in the management target agreement system. This will provide the necessary degree of obligation. However, in a functional organisation, responsibility for achieving process objectives is usually only the same as line responsibility for a few controlling and supporting functions. In other words, the achievement of objectives for cross-departmental processes is influenced not only by one manager, but is the result of the interrelationships of several organisational units. Again here, structural weaknesses can be countered by the involvement of process councils or process owners.

## 5.2 Depth of Detail

Essentially, each process requires a regular monitoring: Is that process result still needed? Is it being performed efficiently enough? Every manager responsible for results must permanently answer these questions. As long as it is easy to monitor the value added and as long as failings are readily visible, there is no need for a complex, indicator-based monitoring system to be installed. All measures in the company are subject to the economical principle that marginal costs are not to exceed marginal benefits. Many balanced scorecards would be drastically thinned out if this standard were to be applied. If however, organisational units from different functional divisions are involved, a control using performance indicators is necessary. The boundary of detail is therefore in the processes that govern the cooperation between organisational units. Enduring indicator monitoring thus ideally complements the hierarchical process model and increases its value contribution.

If we can supply up-to-date performance indicators for the company process model which are part of the management targets agreement, we will have finally helped process management to achieve its breakthrough.

## 6 Special Objectives of Process Analysis and Documentation

In the chapters 3 to 5 we looked at three important steps in the BPM cycle: analysis and documentation (modeling), optimization and process control. These activities not only serve increasing the transparency and optimization of what is happening in the enterprise. They are also closely related to quality management and the shape of the IT support of processes, on the strategic level as well as on the executions (operational) level. These aspects are the subject of our conclusion in the following sections.

### 6.1 Quality Management Standards (EN ISO 9001)

How mandatory should and can process documentation be? This question has to be answered at the latest when the processes are documented as part of a quality management program, where they are regularly approved in accordance to a certification standard. The demand for obligation is automatically coupled to the question of responsibility. This responsibility is reliably defined wherever line responsibility and process responsibility coincide. In functional structure organizations it is also assured on the lower process levels. On the higher-order level, councils or process owners are required to accept responsibility for the process results or at least for its coordination.

If the process analysis is performed top-down as part of a quality management system, the hierarchical process model can be used as an organisational framework. But part of the obligation for documentation is also displayed in isolated processes, as the need for regulation is problem-based and not always foreseeable, similar to the need for process optimisation.

Agreement can be achieved even less if documentation has already been created independently of the hierarchical process model. Much of the process documentation in German companies was created on the basis of an element-orientated standard (ISO 9000:1994). When changing over to a process-orientated standard (ISO 9000:2000), much was done in an attempt to retain the documentation work already performed. There is understandably a low level of willingness to dissect these now isolated processes and to reorder them. However, if you neglect to link the documented process knowledge to the hierarchical process model the transfer of knowledge is blocked. A compromise could be to assign the isolated processes on a higher aggregation level so that they can at least be put into the right process context.

## 6.2 Processes for Deriving the Requirements of IT Support

The principal task of IT solutions is to support the company processes. Work should be made easier. Information should be fed to the right places. In other words, the process requirements must be identified before any IT adaptation relevant to processes is made, and processes must again be optimised before any major IT implementation is introduced. Almost every company process is now IT supported. The implementation of process changes is therefore complex and expensive, because the adjustments also have to be made on the IT applications employed. In so far, it is not understandable that expensive IT solutions are implemented without conducting inexpensive process examinations beforehand.

Essentially the remarks made in section 4 apply to this early phase of preparing an IT implementation. The potential here would be even greater if the ascertainment of the flow of information is compulsory. A process description for the IT context inevitably has to pursue the path taken by data more closely. If this is only done from the perspective of an isolated, detached IT application, it will be similarly unsatisfactory as the isolated process description of a functional division. Instead of successively creating a company-wide information architecture, we are usually content with the data model of this one application, mostly represented as an entity relationship diagram.

## 6.3 Processes for a Strategic IT Construction Plan

Here, the IT division employs the hierarchical process model as a basis for assigning IT systems to processes. The result is a IT construction plan of applications. Based on this actual assignment, strategic plans for a target architecture can be developed and the implementation steps can be highlighted in corresponding IT projects.

This interlinking between process and IT also helps the IT division to make the value contribution of IT within the company clearer. A rational extension could be the strategic construction plan of information.

## 6.4 Process Descriptions in Reality and Close to Reality

In the sections before we talked about representing reality in models in order to reduce complexity and to have a common language to communicate about what is happening in reality. As mentioned before, nowadays most company processes are supported by IT. This means – by the end of the day – a process model needs to be brought back to reality by implementing it as an executable workflow.

Executable process descriptions can be found for the direct implementation of workflows or in the program code, generated by CASE tools (Computer Aided Software Engineering). To date, CASE approaches still enjoy a niche existence, even if they have been successfully tested in the laboratory and implemented in small-scale applications.

Also the workflow approaches still have not reached the predicted breakthrough even with BPML, BPEL, SOA, BPO or as here S-BPM: The euphoria that I have also shared at times has often turned into disillusionment, sometimes quickly, sometimes gradually. With all of these different approaches, we are trying to overcome the boundary between the model level and reality. However, we are inevitably moving on a detail level that is extremely vulnerable to change.

A certain degree of scepticism remains even with S-BPM. The potential of the approach is visible and even successfully implemented in Audi, but so far only at the edge of the process map in administrative activities. Only if the approach enters the core business and cooperates with the established IT solutions, the added value will be proven.

## 7  A Next Step for Processes Management

The subject oriented approach could also help to decrease the costs and increase the quality of permanent process documentation. Process recording, evaluation and publishing could be delegated from the process modeling experts to the process participants if we could use a WIKI approach. Process optimisation could be integrated in a social collaboration platform like it is done already for creating and assessing ideas for innovations. This combination of a process modeling tool with a social collaboration platform could promote process management into a new level.

## References

1. Porter, M.E.: Competitive Advantage – Creating and sustaining superior performance. Frankfurt/Main (2010)
2. Liebert, T.: Process-orientation in corporate organisation – An empirical study of process-orientation in major German companies and its effect on organisational efficiency (forthcoming 2011)
3. Picot, A., Liebert, T.: Stand von Prozesscontrolling und –management in deutschen Großunternehmen – Ergebnisse einer empirischen Untersuchung bei Industrieunternehmen. In: Zeitschrift für Controlling und Management, 55. Jg., Sonderheft Prozesscontrolling und Prozessmanagement (2011)
4. Gadatsch, A.: Grundkurs Geschäftsprozessmanagement, 6. Auflage, Wiesbaden (2010)

# Agile Process Management in an Industrial R&D Department

Marco Strauss and Siri Lang

ACHAT SOLUTIONS GmbH, Carl-Poellath-Str. 19, 86529 Schrobenhausen, Germany
{marco.strauss,siri.lang}@achat-solutions.de

**Abstract.** In a more and more dynamic world market with tougher competition and external, unpredictable risks, an integrated business process management is a key success factor. It is of high importance to be able to flexibly respond to continuously changing environmental requirements and thus ensure the essential agility. Qualitative and successful operational activities without defined processes are just feasible in micro organizations. The bigger an organization is the more important well-known and, in particular, documented processes become for the employees. Especially in large organizations with a variety of value-adding business processes, it is moreover of great importance to build up a consistent change management and stakeholder management, which work closely with the actual business process management for the successful execution of the processes or the goal-oriented structure of the actual business process management.

**Keywords:** Business process management, stakeholder management, project management, communication management, prototyping, development cycles, software system, process standard, workshop, interviews.

## 1 Introduction

### 1.1 Initial Situation and Project Objectives

Nowadays the composition of an engine is a complex process for a car manufacturer. Especially in the process of prototyping, when the variance of components is not yet foreseeable and therefore many flexible cycles of development take place, the documentation of the parts and components (i. e. the documentation of the engine) is a big challenge for engine manufacturers.

Within the scope of a company-wide improvement program in the area of interest a new software was introduced to significantly support the documentation of the engine composition. The software system was supposed to establish a fail-safe way to improve the access to information (which components are assembled in what prototype version) and ensure timely and demand-oriented ordering of components (Just in time). This software was supposed to provide an enormous gain of security as well as tremendous saving of time and costs.

To gain such benefits it is not sufficient only to develop and implement a software system. Firstly the prototyping or rather the process of engine composition has to get rethought and adjusted accordingly before, at a second step, the actual software system gets implemented.

In the setting we are talking about the first step was carried out only rudimentarily in the past. Also integration of employees as well as training of the new processes had not been carried out very systematically. The impact of the new software system's implementation (and therefore all accompanied process adjustments) was high, as it affected all R&D departments. Due to the fragmentary process adjustments and missing integration of employees, already at the start of the software project a big resistance against the introduction prevailed among employees. This attitude was amplified due to the fact that members of the project team had developed certain doubts they transferred into the departments.

Figure 1 shows possible consequences of changes on the attitude of an employee and thus on its motivation.

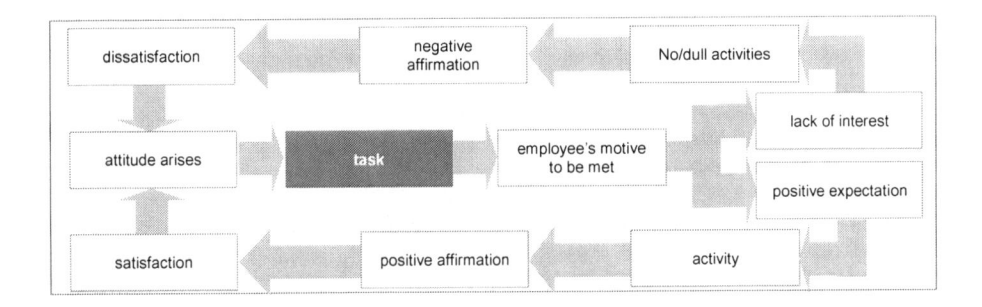

**Fig. 1.** Motives for attitude [1]

Objective of the project presented in this paper was to identify and document new processes, workflows and interfaces of tasks according to the use of the new software system and provide employees with adequate documentation and trainings. Additionally there was the challenge of integrating and involving affected employees to improve and stabilize their motivation and their interest to proactively take part during the process adjustment and later on. In the beginning of the project it also was necessary to reorganize project teams and structures to guarantee a most effective and safe project progress.

The introduction in section 1 of the article presents the initial situation, the prerequisites of the project and the customer requirements. In section 2 we describe the project phases and the methods applied for the single activities, while chapter 3 summarizes the major results. Cross-sectional management methods used in the project are dealt with in section 4. The article ends with some statements regarding the benefits for the customer in chapter 5 and a conclusion in section 6.

## 1.2 Project Prerequisites

At the time we took responsibility for the project as external BPM consultants, we found the following situation:

- A first rough main process was already defined but not applied consequently and not documented sufficiently.
- The rough main process did not meet the procedures of all involved departments.
- The rough main process has not been communicated or has been communicated just rudimentarily.
- The supporting software system was developed already in a first version and in use.
- The software system still had some bugs and did not include all requested functionality.
- The project organization was established and in place.
- General process trainings had taken place.

### 1.3 Customer Requirements

This means the project was already running and the development and introduction of a software system and the recognition of the need for process knowledge etc. were under way. As a consequence we had to meet requirements already set by the customer:

- The project organization was not allowed to be reorganized (punctually only).
- Both company sites had to be taken into account.
- All processes had to be described clearly, pragmatically and strikingly.
- Users should be provided with process knowledge in the form of a handbook.
- The scope ranged from the prototype stage of an engine until just before the production start.

## 2 Course of Action

The course of action used in the project followed our internal standard BEP (Beratungsprozess). Figure 2 illustrates the highest level of this consulting process of which the first five phases were executed during the project.

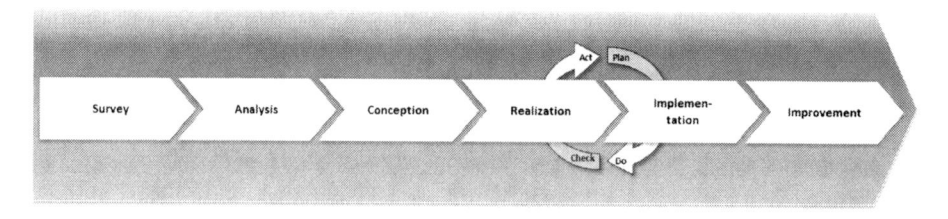

**Fig. 2.** Consulting process (BEP)

### 2.1 Survey and Analysis

Aim of the first and second phase was to clarify the project scope, to collect information from several sources, to evaluate their validity, to define an overall process standard on a major process level and to identify potential and opportunities for process improvement. The set of methods we applied was as follows.

## Sifting of Documents

At a first step, before the systematic census by individual and group interviews, process-related key documents (process and system descriptions, forms etc.) were identified, collected and briefly studied. On the one hand the relevant documents were identified by the use of a checklist, on the other hand, directly named and handed over by the project participants. The documents consisted of process and system descriptions with numerous pages/slides in Word and PowerPoint files.

First, the collected documents were logically sorted and thematically categorized and thus prepared for a more detailed analysis. Based on this rough inspection of documents an interview guideline was designed to interview the central knowledge sources and representatives of the divisions.

## Analysis of documents

In parallel to the steps already mentioned we analyzed the relevant documents, which only had been browsed through and categorized so far, in more detail.

Each document was analyzed following the "four eyes principle", meaning it was discussed by several people how up-to-date the content was, which links there were to other documents, how the content could be understood and evaluated and so on. The contents were cross-checked, chronically arranged, etc. The IT systems were allocated to the appropriate processes or rather process steps.

## Expert Interviews

As target persons for the expert interviews the key knowledge holders were identified, i. e. we deliberately chose two contact persons who would be able to answer to questions regarding the system and the processes.

Due to his organizational work and his role as project manager of a sub project the first expert had a very profound and deep understanding of the new software system, including its interfaces and functionalities, The second contact person directly experienced the historical process developments at operational work by his longtime affiliation to the organization and was therefore an expert in the procedural area.

## Group interviews

The information gathered so far we used as a basis for group interviews with representatives of ten operating divisions involved in the prototyping at both company sites. The discussions with these people led to an overview of the as-is process for each department, which represented their unique perspective (or mode of operation) on the process.

## Workshop

The sifting and analyzing of the documents and the interviews with the key knowledge holders and department representatives let us gain an overview of the subject and the present and prevailing problems. For instance the fact became obvious that, as a primary and fundamental problem, no consistent process standards were defined. This meant that on the one hand very different ideas existed about what a process should look like or how it should be described, and on the other hand it became clear that in the various departments there were very different ideas regarding the actual operational process flows, process steps and interfaces.

So we carried out a two-day workshop with the entire project team and people from the two company sites in order to establish a common understanding of process theory (process hierarchies, components of a process ...) among all stakeholders. Decisive, however, was the commitment to a consistent, superior process that should be formed as a consensus from all the individual ideas of the departments. These ideas and different perceptions of the process were all identified (15 variants), articulated and discussed. Finally all stakeholders agreed upon the description of a commonly developed, consistent as-is process and its associated sub processes.

## 2.2 Conception and Realization

The aim of the third and fourth phase was to make the findings from the analysis available and applicable for the organization by implementing process improvements.

As one of the outputs of this project, the customer required a handbook for the employees, which should support them in their daily business and documents the commitment to a common process and a common approach of the departments.

The customer also stressed that we should focus on the allover process orientation of the company, and confirm it. As "process orientation is, essentially, to know the needs of external and internal customers, to be able to implement them in the most efficient manner." [2] For a sound understanding and taking care of customer needs we made sure that all considerations and developments were presented and thoroughly discussed in the meetings of the project team and the steering board.

As a result the PowerPoint presentation of the main process and sub processes, the description of the individual tasks and the interactions within the system were made available to the staff via a portal on the intranet. During the realization phase it was given prominence to a distinctive and clear visualization in the developed project layout, making it easier for employees to orientate in the numerous process documents.

## 2.3 Implementation

The aim of stage five was to transfer the collected and documented process knowledge to the employees in order to make them live the process.

Providing a process description everybody had agreed upon on the intranet does not really mean to implement it. Getting people to live the new process requires additional effort, especially teaching them in comprehensive trainings.

By increasing the transparency of the overall processes and its interfaces, the trainings we organized helped to impart subject-specific knowledge, to increase employee's motivation to work according to the new processes by involving them and to increase the acceptance of the work of the departments involved (interfaces).

# 3 Results

Applying various methods as described in chapter 2 for carrying out the activities in the project phases led to the results summarized in the following sections.

## 3.1 Overall Process Standards

The main result of the project was the unique, standardized overall process with all its details. It is based on the common understanding and the commitment of all stakeholders in the R&D department, first of all the affected employees. By creating a uniform process standard the following advantages were created:

- The training of new employees was made easier.
- Responsibilities and areas of expertise are now clearly allocated.
- The cooperation between divisions, departments and individuals (interface) runs more transparent.
- The quality of the operations or the results became measurable for the first time.

### 3.2 Process Documentation and Training Materials

The developed process and training materials are characterized as follows:

- Creation of documents in PowerPoint format.
- Strong and clear visualization to ease orientation in the documents.
- Process documents applicable to look something up, or for self-study and for training purposes.
- Materials accessible through a portal on the intranet.
- Strong process hierarchies in the construction of the overall approach.
- Illustrated both from a process side and a system point of view.
- Descriptions focus on roles.

### 3.3 Platform for Systematic Storage

To provide process and training materials a central platform on the intranet was selected as an appropriate medium. It is characterized by:

- Use and intentional employment of the main process as a central element in orientation for all process and training materials.
- Structuring of all documents along the main process.
- Separation of process descriptions into small and manageable sub documents.

### 3.4 Acceptance of Change

The assurance of the short- and long-term acceptance and thus the motivation of the employees for really living the verified process were crucial to the project success. That acceptance was generated primarily by the following means:

- Ongoing supervision of the employees affected during the change.
- Documentation of individual problems and concerns.
- Demonstration of personal benefits.
- Execution of interviews and talks with focus on professional matters.
- Composition of a project team, including representatives from the departments (promoters).
- Focus on roles and areas of responsibility at the structuring of the process descriptions and training materials.

## 4 Cross-Sectional Management Methods

In chapter 2 we described methods used to support single tasks. Additionally various cross-sectional management methods were applied as follows.

## 4.1 Project Management

"A project is a temporary company, which is made to create a unique product, service or result." [3] These typical attributes were valid for our project too. We had around 3.000 people affected. As it was a running project with major management attention an outstanding project management was assumed to be a critical success factor. Therefore the company relied on the help of external experts in this field of activity. Those experienced project leaders built up a "right-sized" project management without overhead that could have slowed down the progress.

Due to the high number of project participant they not only needed to carefully plan, prepare, carry out and follow up the project meetings, but also to drive the project progress by managing the task accomplishment as well as open issues. These tasks were supported by a project management and project planning tool, based on Microsoft Excel, and well-known and accessible by all team members. In project management it is essential for the person in charge to constantly keep cost, quality, quantity and time under control. Figure 3 represents these four aspects of project controlling.

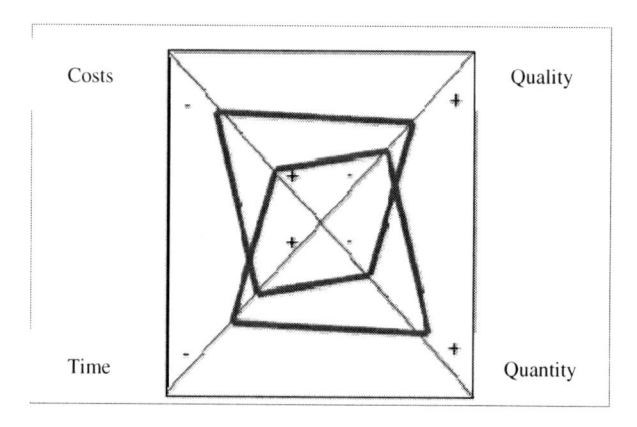

**Fig. 3.** The four aspects of project controlling [4]

## 4.2 Stakeholder Management

Stakeholder management is a very important discipline in projects, which show a cross-border characteristic and engage a very large number of people. As a matter of fact the importance of stakeholder management as a success factor increases with the number of participants/stakeholders involved. In our project we used a two-level approach in order to establish a stakeholder management which was effective and did bother the project participants as little as possible. At first interviews with the project team served to define target groups and their specific needs. The findings were documented in a specially designed Excel sheet. On level 2 they enabled the person in charge to continuously have an eye on the satisfaction of the identified stakeholders and take measures if necessary.

## 4.3 Change Management

Because of the initial situation, it was elementary for this project to build up the motivation of all project stakeholders and to keep it up. "If you want commitment you must offer sense. To effectively implement changes, the understanding, acceptance and commitment of staff is essential." [5] Thus, the participants were grouped in parties and individually supported during the change process. This was necessary as the lack of acceptance for the project and the resulting lack of motivation was recognized very early when we took responsibility. The phenomenon of poor motivation and a lack of commitment are found very often in projects directed by the management board. Figure 4 shows defense mechanisms, change management is trying to counteract.

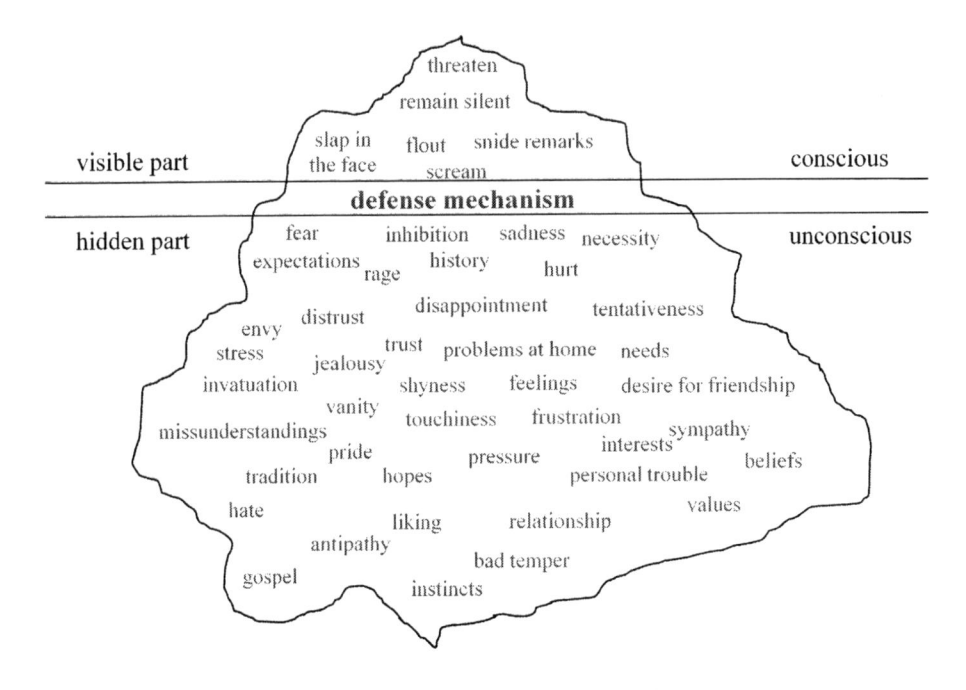

**Fig. 4.** Simplified iceberg model [6]

During the whole project period, an external change manager was available for the project participants (managers and employees) as a central point of contact. It was important to find a suitable person who had the necessary empathic intelligence to fill out this role. The change manager's task was to provide assistance, by always taking into account the individual needs of the participants. This role obviously could be identified as a success factor in the project.

## 4.4 Information and Communication Management

Information and communication management serves satisfying the information and communication needs of the stakeholders.

In our project we established a project marketing as a major element of the information and communication management.

Project marketing is dedicated "(...) to the discrepancy between conception and execution (...). Significant [here] is the employee's participation, which consists of the communication and integration of employees." [7]

For example, right at the beginning of the project a logo was designed and presented to the participants with the aim of increasing identification with the project, strengthening the external perception of the project and increasing its recognition factor.

Various project newsletters and a central project section in the customer's intranet served as electronic channels for information and communication around the project.

In order to communicate relevant information to the divisions team members, especially the promoters, also gave presentations in meetings on middle and top management level.

## 5 Value and Benefit for the Customer

The newly implemented system holds a central role at the customer's operations.

Thus it was a must to make the employees adapt the process and work along it using the functionality of the new software system. The improved process enabled all parties involved to do so.

By the early integration and participation of employees in the design of the process the acceptance of stakeholders was assured. This acceptance is fundamental for the success of process compliance, as only the employees can bring a process to live and establish it.

The following selection of participants' comments describes the improvements that have been achieved by the process change and show its positive perception:

- "Theory and practical trainings make the use of the system user-friendly."
- "The departments have been involved and are now well integrated."
- "Very good information policy."
- "The cooperation between the departments is much better now."

## 6 Conclusion

The project was set up and started as a part of a continuous improvement process (CIP) in the entire division. All intended project results were created and approved and the employees live the process and work successfully with the new system. Now it is time to pay special attention to sustainability and a documentation of lessons learned future projects can benefit from.

During the project we gained the following major insights:

- The breakdown of established patterns of thinking and the achievement of acceptance and motivation of the persons concerned is very costly and time consuming and can only be achieved through continuity and communication.
- The earlier stakeholders are involved and the more communication takes place, the better it is for the success of the project.

- To unify different views and depict them on a higher level, substantial technical knowledge and a lot of empathy is required.
- Essential for the users is to recognize their own role and personal added value and benefit.
- A good mutual understanding of the colleagues (interfaces) is created simply by overcoming prejudices and information barriers as well as through insight and knowledge of overall relationships.
- The success of a project depends very much on the quality of management and control and on a trustful relationship with stakeholders.

We suggest to introduce the role of a process coordinator. This person would be responsible for maintaining the processes and would serve the users as a central point of contact. If understood and practiced correctly, this role could ensure the sustainability of the improvements.

## References

1. Albs, N.: Wie man Mitarbeiter motiviert, Berlin (2005)
2. Staud, J.: Geschäftsprozessanalyse, Berlin (2001)
3. Rudnik, B.: Projektmanagement-Modell für Beratungsprojekte, Studienarbeit, Norderstedt (2009)
4. Hobel, B., Schütte, S.: Gabler Business-Wissen, Projektmanagement, Wiesbaden (2006)
5. Kraus, G., Becker-Kolle, C., Fischer, T.: Changemanagement, Berlin (2010)
6. Meditation am Rundbau, http://www.rght.de/mediation/Bilder/Eisberg.gif
7. Friedrich, D.: Projektmarketing, Saarbrücken (2005)

# Differences in Business Process Management between Global Players and Micro Enterprises – Experiences from Practice

Jörg Bindner[1] and Gunther Mayer-Leixner[2]

[1] Siemens AG, San-Carlos-Straße 7, 91058 Erlangen, Germany
`joerg.bindner@siemens.com`
[2] n:t:r-software, Egstedter Str. 5a, 55262 Heidesheim am Rhein, Germany
`gmayer-leixner@ntr-software.de`

**Abstract.** Based on the experiences of the authors the differences in managing processes between micro enterprises and global players are analyzed. Of course the result of this investigation also is a list of best practices and lessons learned which are common for managing business processes for all types and sizes of companies. These show entry points for subjects to deal with Business Process Management and therefore starting points for S-BPM practices.

**Keywords:** Communication, S-BPM, process management, subject, change management, micro enterprise, global player, team building, knowledge management, workflow management, process introduction.

## 1 Introduction

For many years now thinking and acting in processes is considered as one of the greatest chances for optimizing a company's operations. There are many ways how to do that. In theory every company should be able to find appropriate approaches from the rich palette of possibilities. This fact makes it very interesting, that not in all areas and sizes of enterprises thinking and operating in processes has been fully established or even established at all. Especially in small and micro enterprises, that means in companies with less than 50 (micro: 10) employees and with a turnover of less than 10 (micro: 2) Mio. €, the implementation of measures and methods of process management are not in all cases up to date.

This text is based on the experiences of two persons with very diverse own process experience treasure boxes. One author holds a PhD in Geography and worked in several smaller companies as a consultant for software- and IT-products. These products typically are correlated with graphical information systems. During the work as a consultant he saw many micro enterprises as customer, partner and supplier or even as employer. The other author brought his Master in Computer Science to business first as software developer, later as software project lead. Later, as head of global software development he developed the first software process world for a business unit of Siemens Healthcare. Then he moved to a consultancy department and saw many other Siemens businesses and "friends" (maybe even small or micro enterprises) of Siemens and their typical process management habits from the perspective of a global player and based on the experience as a global software development process owner.

The experiences and observations of these two biographies can now be compared in order to understand the differences in managing processes between micro enterprises and global players. Of course the result of this investigation should be a list of best practices and lessons learned which is common for managing business processes for all types and sizes of companies.

Section 2 describes the meaning of process management to companies of all sizes and specifics for micro enterprises and global players in practice. In Section 3 the changes which can be observed when process and workflow management are introduced to companies are described. Also specifics for micro enterprises and global players are elaborated. Section 4 gives an outlook where main pain points and success areas can be observed for micro enterprises and global players concerning BPM. Section 5 concludes on the common approaches which are to be considered when wanting to be successful. Section 6 summarizes and concludes this work.

## 2 The Meaning of Process Management to Companies

### 2.1 Observations Valid for All Companies

The understanding and motivation to do process management is very individual and maybe driven by business management fashion. In early phases of process management the target was to gain competitive advantages like certifications or adaptation to customer's requirements. But also this was the foundation for recognizing, that identification, analysis, modeling, documentation and publication of companies' as-is-processes opens the chance to optimize these processes. This optimization includes aspects like a process review from the perspective of many stakeholders, visualization of processes, optimization of process interfaces, tool oriented optimization, etc.

On the other hand earning these potentials requires investments and changes of existing structures. Before one can see any process description decisions need to be made on methods, process architecture, detail level, responsibilities, tools etc. These important decisions cannot be made without a deep knowledge. This means that either a qualification program or consultation by experienced people is required. Oh dear, again an investment...

From that perspective e.g., the Siemens Reference Process House (RPH) has been developed. This process framework, which can be seen in Figure 1, clearly identifies on level 1 the key processes for each Siemens business unit as "Customer Relationship Management (CRM)", "Supply Chain Management (SCM)" and "Product Lifecycle Management (PLM)" (highlighted) and also some "Management Processes" and "Support Processes". It also contains the structure of these processes and breaks them down in level 2 in specific sub processes. By that the Siemens RPH is the framework for training programs, for discussions on optimization and it is the source of ideas for process modifications or for the generation of new processes. By establishing this standard within the global player Siemens, all employees are able to change from one to another business unit and understand the general concept of processes easily.

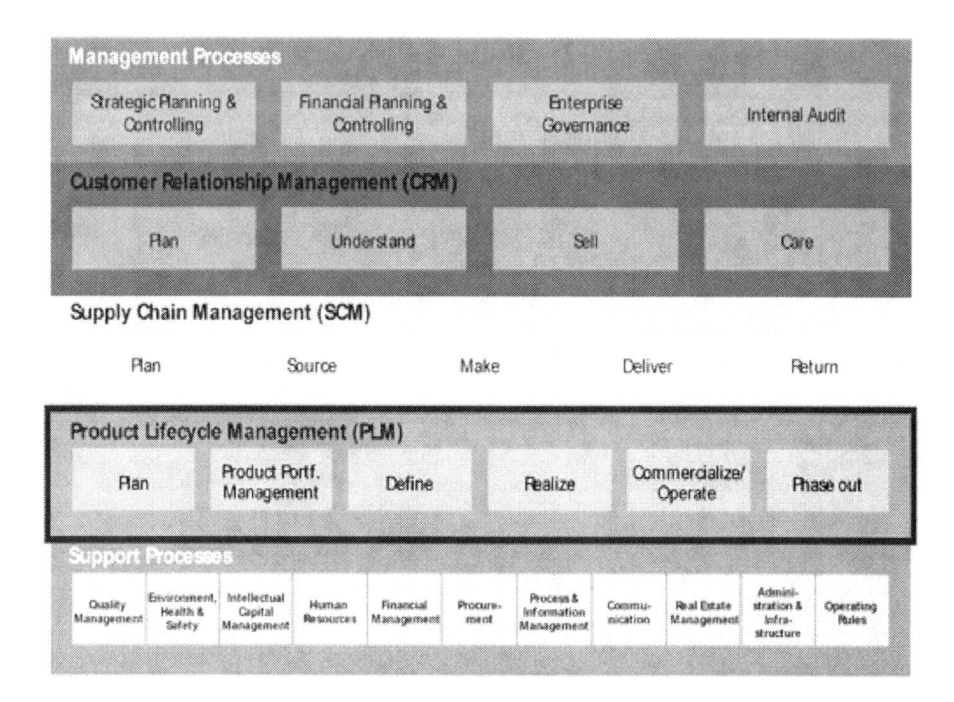

**Fig. 1.** Siemens Reference Process House [11]

Of course it is understandable, that definition of process promises improvements in internal structures. Managers and all employees have an improved basis for decisions, as they have transparency in structures, workflows etc. and therefore a better understanding of resource allocations and resource usage, of the value chain and quality issues. And it may show not expected progress within an organization.

An example for not expected effects in process management: A small enterprise has analyzed and documented a process for software introduction including import of data from legacy systems. The target primarily was to establish a common procedure and to collect best practices of experienced employees. No sooner said than done – the result was presented in an all employees meeting. And by that surprisingly a lot of interest became apparent. In many cases sales employees had to master challenges in explaining the software introduction and data import during sales events. Their knowledge was not structured, not official and not complete before. By learning and understanding the process, suddenly they had explainable and reliable structures and materials for performing their tasks with the customers in a real professional way. Process documentation by accident became a competitive advantage.

In spite of and in parallel to recognizable progress when working with processes in an enterprise these first activities (like identification of key processes, first process descriptions and graphical representation of processes) cannot yet be considered as real process management. In order to manage processes the process management cycle has to be performed entirely and repetitions have to be done. Only by performing this cycle, continuous improvements and adaptations can be initiated in order to ensure innovations, workflow improvements, implementation of new ideas and a good process climate. By that and by including all stakeholders, submarine process worlds can be avoided. Therefore in many cases the chances for optimization cannot be used. It is very critical and maybe even counterproductive, when a consultancy company does not walk the talk in the own organization.

Example: As a consultant one can see processes in many big global player enterprises which do not fulfill the above mentioned properties (this may also refer to the own organization!):

- There are too less resources for process maintenance, process improvements and training.
- Dedicated resources „manage processes" in part time (e.g. in less than 5 hrs. per week).

In consequence that means:

- Feedback from employees, that processes are misleading or contain bugs cannot be processed sufficiently.
- Documented processes are good and helpful, but not optimized for helping or identifying the key processes.
- Process management gets overtaken by itself.

The step from performing the process management cycle once to a continuous change is maybe the biggest step in process management. This requires that:

- Used traditions are changed on a sustained basis.
- Continuity in activities is replaced by continuous adaptations.

Continuous analysis, measurement, control, adaptation and optimization does not only refer to the levels of the process flow, but to all factors and structures which influence the process and are influenced by the process.

In that way fitting the new tasks into existing organizational structures of companies may be a real challenge: Managing processes has to be sorted into the line structure of a company, which is not possible in all cases, depending on the size of a company. In many cases central functions or departments are created (as can be seen in many bigger companies). Important tasks are facilitation of communication on processes, finalized projects, lessons learned, improvement potentials etc. in formal and informal ways.

In the context of this broad influence it can be seen, that management of processes is a key role and qualification in a company. Focus refers to internal processes. For selected industrial sectors' business, process modeling also may mean an additional or extended basis for the company's business model. In general this affects IT business (see also [9]), production oriented businesses (automotive, high technologies), but also consulting and service businesses.

## 2.2 Specifics for Micro Enterprises

It is strongly recommended for companies with neither enough competences nor enough experiences in process management for introducing process management to come back to professional support. This is the case for most of the micro enterprises. Details about this support differ from company to company. In extreme cases an external consultation triggers broad qualification together with the introduction project. Important is to find a way for sustainable measures. Again here the difference between "initiate new ways" and "live the new ways" has to be considered. The required financial equipment for this project has to be considered as investment. External consultants may help to avoid routine-blindness and silo mentality. Preconditions are an open communication and the recognition and usage of individual strengths (positive thinking). On the other hand external support may cause that after project closure the organization falls back into old structures and workflows. Therefore the hardening of open structures has to be a key focus in the process management introduction project.

Example: A privately owned IT company decides – surprisingly for the employees – to introduce processes and process management. The kick off for this activity is a 3 days introduction event for many of the employees, conducted by an external consultancy. Intended result should have been to generate clearness, motivation and an atmosphere of departure. But instead fear, tentativeness and excessive demands were recognizable. As a result the quick wins became unreachable – even worse: tasks have been distributed without reflection against the unchanged demands from daily business and the corresponding schedule. This especially has been valid within the management team. The external trainer was gone, not reachable. Follow up meetings, which have been promised and which should have been tracking the progress of the distributed tasks, were not conducted. Introduction of process management died of starvation in this case, and this was supported by the management team. The corresponding information about the official termination of these actions is still pending.

Especially in micro enterprises the initialization of changes very often comes from the management. This also refers to the introduction of process management. Management team of micro enterprises also very often is built solely by the owner of the company. The owner typically in the history of the company was the technical visionary, who is a brilliant technologist in his area, but not necessary a good manager or runner of his business. Source of good business decisions is a good gut feeling and working instincts. This builds hurdles: Process management and the targets of it are not well known and cannot be fully understood with all consequences. They are considered as modern business management stuff. In case the hurdle is conquered and the process introduction project is running, still during that project some nonlinear decisions can be observed. On the other hand in micro enterprises, which already today manage their processes, it can be recognized, that the required openness for communication and new ideas or leadership methods are available.

As already mentioned, introduction of process management requires significant effort, e.g., for analyzing and describing the as-is-processes and corresponding conventions. This not yet creates any value add for companies – but costs. For example, in [7] an investigation on the economic sense of introducing a development process can be found. For micro enterprises this means: patience, endurance and sensitivity are required, maybe even trust against external consultants. Especially the balance between today's cost and tomorrow's benefit needs to be tracked tightly. And the more employees are involved and cannot do their original tasks the more important is this task. A problem in this cost/benefit tracking is, that in micro enterprises the benefits by economy of scale effects is worse than in bigger companies.

Cost/benefit based decisions (including maybe wrong methods for savings, impatience etc.) make clear, that business process management in micro enterprises very strong is dominated by a top-down-approach. The special position of an owner-manager makes it easy to start, stop, change, reduce, expand etc. the process management introduction project or the process management approaches. In general the introduction process is jeopardized by too much top-down influence and therefore may be considered as additional tasks by the employees. And the result may extend the control of the management, increase the rules for employees and reduce flexibility for the individuals. As an example one can hear statements that the described processes are fixed for some (longer) time. Adaptations and investments are made more difficulty. Thus companies take the risk to reduce or lose their business agility (bottom-up activities, [12]).

## 2.3 Specifics for Global Players

In big global player companies process management is introduced broadly for a while. In addition to some of the above mentioned aspects an important target is to move competence about complex workflows with 100s of involved persons from the heads of individual experts into an asset of the company. This makes it trainable, controllable, optimizable etc. The possibility to set targets based on processes, maybe even based on a maturity model like the CMMI model stated in [5]. The possibility to manage parallel business units with standardized processes becomes reality. These examples show that process management generates key competences, economic value and generates growth opportunities. In addition global players very often act in regulated markets (medical business, rail business, etc.), where business process management is a must for any company in order to do business.

A big German global player for example some years ago after some effort for improving business processes did set a target to achieve in all software development departments a CMMI level of 3 within 3 years. The effect was, that broadly within the company the software development processes were improved significantly, no matter if the target could be fully achieved. Based on that first wave improvements were triggered also concerning product management, innovation management, manufacturing and service. In the second wave in a similar approach the entire product development departments were addressed. Finally as a result many very mature business process models have been established. With the third wave the top management wanted to achieve standardization between those mature business process models in terms of terminology, process architecture and process model. This managed improvement process did run for several years and should stand for best practice of business process management. Coming waves could address aspects like process automation or optimization of efficiency.

Another example is coming from a big enterprise, which makes revenue mainly with huge projects of a value of three- to four-digit million Euros. The example refers to project management procedures. There are many models, which show, how projects of any size and content can be managed successfully including best practice examples etc. Examples of these models can be the PMI handbook, Prince and Prince2. Additionally for IT projects one can find e.g. the Zachman framework. None of these frameworks is perfect and fits perfect to the task. These frameworks do not reflect all sizes of projects, all sizes of companies, all imaginable project complexities, all experience backgrounds the skills and specific needs of project team members and project manager etc. The do not sufficiently reflect the individuality of projects and project managers, what may require introduction of S-BPM paradigms A good project manager knows some of these mentioned models, at least those, which are relevant for the type of projects he does. Together with experience and personal skills like improvisation and the art of project management the project manager is more or less successful. In a big company, where a number of project types are relevant, based on these models and the experience of the extraordinary successful project managers an own project management process model can be worked out and established. This has been done in our example (also taking into consideration some aspects of S-BPM, e.g. specific communication needs).Based on this process model not only projects can be conducted, but also assessments, risk evaluations and consolidations, training programs etc. Finally project managers can be assigned to a wider variety of projects.

In practice very often process and department oriented silos are formed, if management does not consequently involve all persons, who are participating in the process. Even worse: sometimes management makes all efforts to introduce or optimize process management obsolete, e.g. by careless statements or giving bad examples. As soon as the process does not support the purpose of the enterprise, but vice versa the process must stand as reason (means excuse) for dedicated activities (means: passivity), something did go wrong.

Again an example from a consulting project: A very successful business unit of a bigger company needed to change management. A manager wanted to change his job, another retired etc. So at the end a significant portion of the top management was very new: CEO, CFO, CTO and head of product management. Before this change occurred, top management always had an eye on the running projects and the project teams knew that. Processes were developed with the purpose to support project management to keep the correct order of work and to make sure, nothing gets forgotten in the project plans. In case a relevant error became known, management made very clear, that this error is to be corrected as an effort of all. After this change in management occurred, a new style was established in the company. Team effort was replaced by clearly separated tasks. The process, which had been developed for a while, was not prepared to this style. Within a short time department silos had been developed. Problems and errors were not solved in a cooperative way, but errors were analyzed in an adversarial way. Right or wrong is no more important and cannot be finally decided. Important is, that this business unit lost significantly value during a short period of time and by that a negative pull was initiated: Important employees left the company, reorganizations, rumors about sale of the business unit, quality problems, loss of (important) customers, …

## 3 Process and Workflow Management Trigger Changes

### 3.1 General Considerations Valid for all Kinds of Companies

After having analyzed companies, which have introduced or are about to introduce process management, it is recognizable, that this fact results in many and various changes. Some of them are that apparent, that they – according to our opinion – very good can be recognized and described even by the majority of those involved. Those effects include:

- Intensive communication and cooperation in teams: Experience and improvement proposals are brought up and tracked much more intense by each individual employee. A critical aspect is to find and agree upon a common language.
- Optimization of workflows with the purpose of increased effectivity and efficiency can be initiated.
- New tasks, e.g. which support communication and implementation of improvements internally and externally can be identified.
- Active implementation of interface roles or functions for better coordination and optimization of interlinked task chains.

In addition also changes which are not so obvious can be found. Being not so obvious does not implicitly mean that they are less important:

- A first analysis of workflows normally focuses on technical competence and puts the technical expert into the limelight. As mentioned above, there are new tasks – in addition to that the function within the company and by that the employee gets new and in many cases more recognition and responsibility.
- A big focus is set on optimization. But optimization can have many facets. Not only things, which can be measured and subjectivitied are optimizations. But especially for cases, where top management drives or forces the process management activities, these measurable improvements are the only valid arguments. It is easily overlooked, that especially process optimizations have indirect effect chains. Process management opens new views, insights and are able to influence the orientation of a company.

What is this other than taking the most important aspects of S-BPM into consideration? All actors (subjects) should be active and involved in that process [8]. The type and intensity of changes are depending of the starting point and the vision connected to process management. Increased transparency first of all helps process analysts. And they are responsible to report and open improvement potentials, so that the business process management cycle can be initialized.

### 3.2 Specifics for Micro Enterprises

Let's start with an example: A company, which has been formed by merging multiple IT service companies located at multiple self-responsible sites, wants to standardize the processes, which are valid at the different locations. For that purpose workshops have been organized. These workshops start with a presentation of each of the different processes. This triggers discussions, which show after a short while, similar practices and tasks have different names and are supported by different tools or tool configurations. Having had this discussion opened the possibility to standardize wording and tools, where reasonable or necessary towards a common best practice. It also meant that understanding "the others" became easier and the company got into the situation to solve gaps at one site by temporary transfer of experts.

This example shows the bottom up approach for process management. The openness for a common success helped to initiate a successful common business process management. The company made sure, that the preconditions where good. So a critical issue is to provide good preconditions. In a good case the first measures already prove first successes by earning low hanging fruits and lead to a team spirit, to employees with openness to learn from each other. Further effects of a good start are:

- Individual strengths can be recognized and get used.
- Knowledge gets socialized.
- Team spirit gets increased, teamwork gets more dynamic.
- An Environment of trust gets built.

Very often we see a lot of topics, which are typical success factors of introducing business process management and process optimization.

The big uncertainty for the company is how the newly formed teams are placed in the company structures and how the teams interact. A big task for management is to build a supporting company structure with connected but not protected processes.

### 3.3 Specifics for Global Players

Introduction of business process management had many benefits for big companies and enables to solve very complex tasks with less people and cost or to solve these very complex tasks at all. It also opened possibilities of international value chains, which had not been imaginable before, although it may be still a challenge (for more details see [6].

But the introduction and optimization of processes especially in big companies goes along with the risk of reduced motivation, creativity, initiative of individual employees etc. Especially the definition of the size of the process group and the equipment of this group with power is very critical and a big challenge. A group, which is too small or too powerless in consequence means, that control is missing and in case of errors the buck is passed to the process group. A too big or too powerful process group results in ivory tower effects. Processes are specified or controlled to detail or process artifacts are tracked, because the process requires them, not because it makes economic sense to have them.

In big companies process optimizations focus on identification of inefficiencies because of lacks in strategy, competence, tools, technology, concept, documentation, organization or similar.

In a consulting project for example in a company in medical industry a focused efficiency analysis was made on meeting culture in the entire company. As a result an efficiency increase of 8 % could be worked out simply by optimizing the meeting structure.

Finally very often human factors and change management are overlooked. Introducing business process management or changing processes may be a tremendous change to the people involved. Ignoring good practices jeopardizes the entire success – respecting and making use of known concepts (like shown in [4], section 3) can be responsible for a success much better than expected.

## 4 Process Management – An Outlook

Nowadays there are big differences between how business process management is applied in micro enterprises and global players, especially in terms of experience and broadness of application; this refers to methodical broadness, to the way how tools are applied and to maturity level. Or in other words: Micro enterprises start applying process oriented management, make use of selected methods and apply typical tools (from the universal BPM toolbox) only in selected cases. For big companies the situation is much different, not only because the importance of business process management is much bigger. A more detailed comparison can be found in Table 1.

**Table 1.** Experienced gaps between micro enterprises and global players in terms of methods, tools, conventions of process management

| Methods, tools and conventions of process management | Micro enterprises Actual | Micro enterprises Required | Global Players Actual | Global Players Required |
|---|---|---|---|---|
| Knowledge about methods and tools of BPM | ☹☹ | ☺☺ | ☺ | ☺☺☺ |
| Knowledge about methods of process management | ☹☹ | ☺ | ☺ | ☺☺☺ |
| Knowledge about methods of team building | ☹ | ☺☺☺ | ☺☺ | ☺☺☺ |
| Knowledge about methods of change management | ☹☹ | ☺☺ | ☹ | ☺☺☺ |
| Knowledge about methods of knowledge management | ☹☹ | ☺ | ☹ | ☺☺ |
| Knowledge about application and integration of method competences | ☹☹ | ☺☺ | ☺ | ☺☺☺ |
| Knowledge about process modeling | ☹ | ☺ | ☺☺ | ☺☺ |
| Knowledge about tools of process management and workflow management | ☹ | ☺ | ☺ | ☺☺ |
| Availability of conventions and convention guideline | ☹ | ☹ | ☺☺ | ☺☺ |

It shows the differences between micro enterprises concerning those aspects of business process management, which have been considered as critical by the authors in their operative and consulting tasks. The 6-scale evaluation ranges from "☹☹☹", which means, that the discussed factor is not at all available respectively not at all required up to "☺☺☺", which means the opposite.

## 4.1 Specifics for Micro Enterprises

Management of processes and workflows more and more is becoming a central building block in companies. In the areas of communication, training, competence and knowledge management (according to [10]) and others, process management offers a broad fundament for improvements. Especially standardized processes get automatable and by that can be executed easier, faster and more deterministic. If standardization is the correct way depends on the process itself and how it is embedded in structures and operations of a company. In addition each improvement has to be evaluated and judged in the context of the type of business, business targets etc. Intelligent and empathic decisions have to be made on which kind of optimizations support best the company targets in terms of quality, image, employee satisfaction, speed, etc. Especially for micro enterprises it is not imaginable, that a full scale business process management will be made available in the companies. Very sensitive decisions need to be made about methods and tools which are reasonable in the context of the company. Target of selection should be to establish values and structures in the company in a way so that competences of each individual employee and of the entire company are available for continuous improvement of processes and structures. This strongly enables sustainable business success. The entrepreneur himself and many employees take over new roles:

- Hierarchy oriented leadership changes to coordination and teamwork.
- Ideas and innovations replace traditional procedures.
- (Key) processes are questioned and improved continuously.
- Transparency of decisions (ability to measure and judge based on facts) gets possible and can be used where required.

Process management and continuous optimization requires that all affected people can and want to involve themselves to the upcoming tasks of process improvement. It has to be clear, that process management requires new and extended competences from all involved, which typically extends the (technical oriented) role descriptions. This may cause feelings of "indisposition". In many cases innovations and continuous change are also source of worries, especially when change management methods are ignored.

The following example should illustrate a typical situation: A small IT-company refactored a software introduction process and defined new standards connected to that. An employee declined the proposal in a very resolute way with the argument, that these tasks are not possible to him with the proposed timeline. This reaction has been interpreted as a blocking position, as during the further discussion the continuous adaptations have been criticized. Furthermore the employee claimed to continue in the proven way. This also influenced the team.

## 4.2 Specifics for Global Players

In big companies there is a long tradition of business process management, in most cases in a top down approach and for many years. As this has been established, employees want to have influence on how the work is done. As this has been going on for a long time one can say, that the process authority – in good cases – moves to the employees. In consequence power and influence of managers is reduced, which also means, that they lose importance within the company. An example can be found in agile software development methods, which focus very strong on communication and autonomous teams. Precondition is, and this has been shown in several consulting projects, that the organization has achieved a certain process maturity before via process optimizations and inspection of process maturity by means of assessments.

A real consultancy project should stand as an example: We are looking into a company which develops, manufactures and distributes medical products. Traditionally this company applied a V-model based process (driven by regulatory requirements from e.g. FDA or TUEV) and achieved a CMMI maturity level of 3 with that process model. They wanted to move into the agile process world. The migration from a V-type process to an agile process could be mastered within a small number of iterations respectively within 4 months. After that product owner and scrum master had understood the process and were able to manage the project. And they managed the project instead of the management. The team took over responsibility for the product and was highly motivated to make the migration into an agile process model a success. It was the team, who drove this change and convinced management about the benefits. On the one hand there was a team, which worked in an agile model and was forced to make self-contained decisions about the product (of course within given borders). On the other hand there was a management team, which had to hand over a part of their decision power to the development team. This needed some discussions on higher levels and could not be established without conflicts – let's say "Management has to get used to it...!" And this hand over creates motivation and responsibility for each individual involved developer. Especially in medical environment this may also be very sensitive because of legal regulations. Details about this can be found in [1], [2], [3].

In parallel in big companies always there are intentions to standardize processes across departments, business segments, business units, corporate, locations, sub processes etc. in order to achieve the above mentioned targets related to business process management entirely. The increased transparency, cooperation and consistency promises increased manageability. In some parts, this probably is true. But on the other hand it is the intention of managers that the business runs. So the increased transparency, cooperation and consistency should never be the main argument to drive standardization – it should prepare to the next step: the full automation of standardized process across the whole concern without the need for manual media or format conversions. This opens the chance to eliminate table based submarine management processes, which is the real motivation for managers to standardize processes.

# 5 The (B)Right Way

During the long lasting experience in association with processes and process management in big companies in consulting projects as well as in micro enterprises the following set of lessons learned can be extracted as our collection of experience and best practices:

- ✓ Identification, description, analysis and improvement of process must consider actors, tools and environment and involve all parties (embedding the process in companies' workflows, role descriptions, resource planning etc.). S-BPM confirms this experience, as it puts the actors and involved parties into the focus as the subjects of business process management.
- ✓ Introduction of process management strictly must follow a strategy: pilot projects, KISS processes (KISS: keep it simple and stupid), made by humans for humans, usability including hedonic quality for supporting tools. In parts also S-BPM addresses these aspects of the strategy to introduce process management by focusing process management to the 5 major aspects, which are subject, message, send, receive and function.
- ✓ Process management needs time, first time to prepare the process management activities (e.g. prepare change management), then for making the process effective (e.g. analysis up to training), then for seeing the effects of the process (e.g. based on the operative process and the optimization cycles). Process management needs long-range. This may contradict with quick requirements for a certification, thinking in quarterly reports and similar effects. S-BPM also does not ignore the efforts for change management, training etc. Putting the subject into focus change management cannot be ignored.
- ✓ Process management requires dedicated competence and experience and therefore an own education and role.
- ✓ Processes must be controllable by the involved persons – they are the relevant subjects. It must be vivid and innovative concerning methods and content, e.g. by applying S-BPM paradigms. It must be actively supported by management, maybe even asked by management. Employees have to have influence on the processes. Traps are:
    - o Micro enterprises tend to keep things, which have been established a while ago with some effort
    - o Big companies tend to be fixed in terms of processes because of political issues or anxiety for errors
- ✓ Process management must not create (undesired) dependencies. In consequence this means that the target of getting less dependent of single key experts has to be taken serious. On the other hand the need of employees to be free in fulfilling their tasks should be respected. It is quite a challenge to keep these poles in balance.
- ✓ Process management and single processes must fulfill defined targets, be adjusted to company strategy, be focused (not overloaded with multiple purposes, e.g. certifications, operative tasks, protection, planning, excuses, training …) Process management for the purpose of process management is superficial and therefore obsolete in most cases. Important is to define a vision and reasoning, to derive ideas and to prioritize them. For every company – no matter if small or huge – the introduction of process management is unique and therefore to be handled as a project.
- ✓ Process management, standardization and automation have complex consequences, they define new tasks and roles, they automate and standardize. The biggest challenge is to get to the state for initializing the process management circle, which instantiates continuous change and adaptation. Therefore change management is a core aspect of process management.
- ✓ Communication, communication, as also mandatory in S-BPM (e.g. send, receive).

Many of these items make process management S-BPM and S-BPM answers them appropriately. According to the mentioned experience they are completely relevant to business process management. So maybe BPM and S-BPM need to address those not yet addressed aspects.

## 6 Summary and Conclusion

In order to earn as much as possible from the optimization potential it is not enough to select some tools from the universal and infinite business process management toolbox. Process management changes existing structures and activities significantly and it is indispensable to face the challenge of managing these changes. The influence of process management to structures and actions is different in terms of intensity and diversity. Aspects like business type and size of a company are critical influencing factors. The attitude of management towards (new) management methods forms more or less readiness for assigning resources to business process management. Taking this into consideration it should be clear, that big companies worked significantly more intensive and serious with business process management than micro enterprises. Therefore they have achieved also higher maturity levels than micro enterprises. In order to bring business process management to micro enterprises different approaches are required:

- Method competences need to be analyzed.
- Target settings need to be expressed clearly.
- Resource availability and quantity need to be clarified.
- Employees and people concerned have to be involved.
- Changes need to be managed, not only initiated.
- Changes must be made sustainable.
- Knowledge must be socialized.
- Values must be lived (openness, team work, trust, acceptance)
- Success and changes should be measureable.
- Success and benefit must be shared.

The project to introduce process management is a political project. Therefore a clear target definition is required for that project. Also required is to have a project manager and a project team with high social skills. Tools e.g. for analyzing and creating the processes in our experience very often have a too high significance in business process management: They are only tools! This too high significance leads to the issue that processes are built around the tool and therefore the above listed success factors are ignored or undervalued. This is not a new observation. In addition software for process management is considered as much too expensive and connected with too much effort for customizing especially for micro enterprises. For big companies the tools are too rigid and too inflexible. But the tools and the use of these tools did not change significantly over quite some time now.

From our perspective the negligence of social management skills (change management, knowledge management), the fixation on technical tools and the continuous disregard of complexity of holistic process management are the main reasons for the fact that this promising management method is not established broadly. So the tasks now are not easy:

- More focus on reality and complexity
- Less marketing for process management tools
- More invest in managing change and knowledge, which means to explain the possibilities, preconditions, efforts, risks and barriers of process management and its introduction (especially to technical oriented micro enterprise managers)

It is important to consider all the mentioned aspects for the planning of the process introduction or optimization project.

# References

1. Bindner, J., Hirschmann, C.: Agil in der Medizintechnik? Hand in Hand mit dem Qualitäts-management, Objekt-Spektrum Online, Themenheft Agility (2009), http://www.sigs-datacom.de/fileadmin/user_upload/zeitschriften/os/2009/Agility/bindner_hirschmann_OS_agility_09.pdf
2. Hirschmann, C.: Agiles Anforderungsmanagement in der Medizintechnik, Objekt-Spektrum Online, Themenheft Agility (2010), http://www.sigs-datacom.de/fileadmin/user_upload/zeitschriften/os/2010/Agility/hirschmann_OS_AGILITY_2010.pdf
3. Boehm, B., Turner, R.: Management challenges to implementing agile processes in traditional development organizations. IEEE Software (September/October 2005)
4. Claßen, M.: Change Management aktiv gestalten – Personalmanager als Architekten des Wandels. Luchterhand Verlag (2008)
5. Chrisis, M.B., Konrad, M., Shrum, S., Wesley, A.: CMMI – Guidelines for Process Integration and Product Improvement 2 edn. (2007)
6. Ebert, C., De Neve, P.: Surviving Global Software Development. IEEE Software (March/April 2001)
7. Erdogmus, H.: The economic impact of learning and flexibility on process decisions. IEEE Software (November/December 2005)
8. Fleischmann, A.: What is S-BPM? In: S-BPM One 2009 (2009), http://www.s-bpm-one.org/fileadmin/editor/downloads/2009/S-BPM-ONE-2009-07-Fleischmann.pdf
9. Hofmann, J., Schmidt, W. (eds.): Masterkurs IT-Management. Vieweg Verlag (2007)
10. Krcmar, H.: Informationsmanagement. Springer, Heidelberg (2005)
11. Siemens RPH2011: Siemens Reference Process House, taken on (March 14, 2011), http://www.it-production.com/index.php?seite=einzel_artikel_ansicht&id=27413
12. Yuliya, S., Gromoff, A.: Subject-Oriented Approach for Automation and Modeling of ITIL v3 Processes on Metasonic Suite. In: S-BPM One 2010 (2010), http://www.s-bpm-one.org/fileadmin/editor/downloads/2010/S-BPM-ONE-2010-12-Stavenko.pdf

# An Approach to Agility in Enterprise Innovation

Alexander Gromoff, Valery Chebotarev, Kristin Evina, and Yulia Stavenko

National Research University "Higher School of Economics", Kirpichnaya str. 33/5
105679 Moscow, Russian Federation
{agromov,kevina,vchebotarev,ystavenko}@hse.ru

**Abstract.** The midline results of a scientific survey of the definition of requirements for the development of an innovative ECM system are presented. These results were obtained during the second stage of a complex project carried out through Government Grant with participation of NRU and IT Corporation (Russia). The particular research is based on 3 scopes: 1) Enterprise Content Management (ECM) system as roofing, 2) umbellate Total Content Management system (TCM); 3) process-based enterprise innovation activity and subject-oriented approach to BPM.

**Keywords:** enterprise content, ECM, innovation, unstructured information, subject-oriented approach, business process management, S-BPM, communication network, contact net, networking.

## 1 Introduction

At the beginning of the twenty-first century the International Association for Information and Image Management (AIIM) formulated the concept of "enterprise content management" (ECM) [1]. In accordance with the AIIM concept ECM is an "umbellate" term which joins strategy, methods and means for collecting, searching, administering, storing, archiving and introducing enterprise content, from the intercommunications of staff, personnel and/or information systems.

In this scope 'content' means unstructured information created by humans and located on paper and in electronic documents, e-mails, messages, presentations, audio, video and image files etc. Usually, the amount of this unstructured information exceeds 80% of the meaningful content of the entire enterprise, where the rest is stored in structured data centers. Unfortunately, due to inefficient retrieval processes, this huge amount of information is rarely used in managing enterprise processes [2].

For this reason ECM R&D is one of the most rapidly growing sectors of the IT market (overcoming the traditional corporate sector) [3]. Referencing to the AIIM report in the near future actual improvements resulting from the ECM development and deployment will be cost reduction and efficiency growth in business processes. Afterwards, factors such as compliance management and reduction in "content chaos" will be realized, in other words, management of unstructured information. But surprisingly, such a serious part of enterprise activity in support of innovation activity is not mentioned in the AIIM report.

This particular work is dedicated to the study of definition of requirements for developing innovation support in the context of an ECM system, existing or planned for implementation. After this introduction we will clarify the meaning of innovation in our project. In section 3 we elaborate on how to set up an ECM system in order to support the innovation management process. Therefore, we look at this process from the subject-oriented point of view and apply S-BPM software to similar processes. In conclusion, the benefits the subject-oriented BPM approach delivers given the socio-psychological view on specific roles of subjects participating in innovation processes are summarized.

## 2 Models and Paradigms of Innovation Activity

Authors widely interpret the term 'innovation'. Our definition is based on [4], slightly modified:

*Innovation is an outcome of the process, where protectable results of intellectual activity are gained and used for developing patentable, worldwide acceptable products.*

Therefore, the process of creating innovation is called the innovation process. In order to understand other meaningful specifics of the term 'innovation', the next definition is introduced:

*Innovation is a market-driven unique implementation which leads to the qualitative growth of process or product efficiency.*

This definition reflects such important features of innovation as 'great market demand' and 'implementation'. Analyzing these two definitions four important attributes of innovation can be formulated:

- Innovation is the result of a process which dramatically increases efficiency of a main activity.
- Innovation is unique development with worldwide impact.
- Innovation accumulates intellectual property.
- Innovation has to be strongly in-demand by the market.

Any process innovation process is oriented towards particular objectives. Due to the above formulated attributes of innovation these goals should project the growth of economic efficiency, support intellectual creativity by the subjects of the innovation process, and should aim on satisfying certain market requirements and final users of the innovative product.

Hence, an enterprise which implements an innovation process has to think of questions such as: uncovering, developing and growing the key technologies within the enterprise; and instantly verifying and reconsidering its technological and intellectual potential. Answers to these questions could lie in several scopes:

- Consideration of internal processes of high maturity, namely, with established knowledge of process logic, internal risk, and quality control and management.

- Creation of expert competence centers, where knowledge can be accumulated, stored and distributed enterprise-wide. Experts in such centers should be linked cross-functionally, thus elaborating solutions for complex interdisciplinary problems.
- Implementation of a unified information field (UIF) support and management system, which becomes a basis for interdisciplinary links, deploying complex problems and external information environment, and monitoring of scientific and innovation trends.

Properly speaking, having chosen an innovative way of development an enterprise has to create a new structure for managing specialist staff, who are able to solve related problems and tasks. In this case it is possible to seriously consider knowledge economics or innovation economics, which could become an answer to the question 'when will we (Russia) start on the way towards innovation development'. The short answer is simple – when the corresponding conditions exists for:

- Instant improvement and management of internal processes and technologies.
- Generation and development of new knowledge of process logic and existing technologies.
- Specialists' desire for cross-functional experience and knowledge exchange.

One step towards the solution to the above issues, beyond financial investment, is the development and implementation of an innovation-oriented ECM platform. This platform must maintain and support the innovation process throughout its life-cycle. Consequently, requirements for this platform should depend on the organization of innovation development and on the methodology used for its realization, as well as on a number of social meaningful factors.

Nowadays two models of innovation process are known [6]:

- The first model describes a traditional organizational approach, which could be considered as linear innovation creativity process. Here, the predetermined sequence of actions is involved as integration of intellectual investments, innovation development, innovation implementation and improvement, and justification for the innovation or whatever applications it may have. This model has serious disadvantages such as a limitation of links between participants of the process and neglect of all good wills.
- The second model represents a newer approach and can be described as a nonlinear iterative innovation process. In this model multiple interdependent intellectual resources are involved at all stages of the process; in addition, parallel, iterative and quickly-modified process can be executed to meet rapidly changing business requirements. The model of multiple intellectual resources takes into account the diversity of these intellectual resources and creates conditions for their creative networking.

It is always necessary to consider methodological aspects that support the innovation process. There are two basic innovation implementation paradigms: the support of the innovations themselves, or the support of the intellectual resources that create them (i.e. the subjects of innovation activities) [6]. These paradigms have important differences, which affect the choice of methodology to be used for managing the innovation process.

*Paradigm 1: Innovation Support*

Features: focuses on the abstract subject and predicted situation, clearly regulated objectives and standards, normative model employment.

Attitude to subjects: domain knowledge, skills for the regulatory methods utilization and given scheme of the innovative process.

*Paradigm 2: Intellectual Resources Support (Subjects of Innovation Activities)*

Features: focuses on specific subjects, poorly regulated work, non-standard situations and descriptive models usage.

Attitude to subjects: procedural knowledge, skills for creating innovation in network structures, conditions for the subjects reflection.

## 3  Innovation Process Management from the Subject-Oriented Point of View

In order to build an innovative ECM system it is necessary to meet five requirements to the control system of the innovative process:

1. The innovation management system has to be self-organized to become vigorous, including networked structures, social networks and thus creating conditions for the diffusion of intellectual outputs.
2. High-level management has to be decentralized as a consequence of the self-organizing structure.
3. The system should be complex yet efficient. The variety of infrastructure elements and innovation activity subjects as well as interoperation between them leads to an additive effect, which is highly required in innovation process support.
4. To remain useful, the system has to offer its intellectual resources rationally offering outsourcing of the competences, thus, providing 'fresh stream' of the ideas, approaches, and solutions to the internal competences. It is necessary to maintain its existing resources, as well as to catalog new resources.
5. The system must operate on "natural selection" mechanisms. True competition and the selection of 'best of breed' are the key elements in building a self-improving and developing system.

Summarizing all five issues it is clear that the system must be able to support all subjects of the innovation process. The most reasonable way to develop such a system with the necessary capabilities is the application of the subject-oriented approach to the innovation process management, as in its way certain conditions can occur for the realization of process/network ad hoc social groups, and thereby an efficient process for obtaining and managing new knowledge.

The subject-oriented approach was developed by Metasonic AG (founded in 2004) and offers a platform for dynamic process-oriented applications which include modeling, validation and immediate execution of business processes [13] [14] [15].

The creation of Metasonic led to the emergence of a fundamentally new kind of business process management, namely, the Subject-Oriented Business Process Management (S-BPM). Immediate execution means that an executable application for workflow control is generated automatically from the description of business process models. Modeling, validation and implementation stages are integrated and automated.

According to the survey in [8] core advantages of the S-BPM for business process management include:

- Low cost, high quality, efficient automation of business processes;
- The ability to make quick adjustments and with immediate implementation;
- The ability to enforce active compliance management on all employees involved in business processes.

The technological advantages of S-BPM, as a platform for providing subjects with opportunities for creative and reflective work [9] [10] give it a decisive advantage.

The S-BPM system allows to:

- describe processes easily and rearrange models on-the-fly;
- imitate execution of process models in order to achieve synergy by comparing models with the colleagues using general creative potential;
- dynamically connect with new external, intellectual resources and/or processes performed by external subjects; execute processes exactly as modeled. This means that process users are always given real information about process runtimes, critical paths, and resource bottlenecks.

S-BPM refers to participants within a process as "subjects". Each subject in the process is defined, modeled and documented by the description of his/her individual actions. Here "subject" is considered not only as a resource, which is required to perform a specific action, but also as a rational person who possesses intelligence, creativity and reflection.

The S-BPM approach is supported by the Metasonic Suite. This platform consists of Metasonic Base, Metasonic Build, Metasonic Proof, and Metasonic Flow. Firstly, models are described in Metasonic Build, after that the completed models are validated with Metasonic Proof directly in a live enviroment and, finally, they are loaded on a server (Metasonic Base) as applications using Metasonic Flow.

Metasonic Build is the design component of Metasonic Suite; no additional programming is needed. The process participants can easily model their processes themselves using an intuitive user interface, and orchestrate the services they need for that purpose. They operate with five items: "subject", "message", "send", "receive" and "function". The last three items describe the subjects' states while performing the process.

Metasonic Build uses two types of models: the "subject interaction diagram" (communication flow) and the "subject behavior diagram" (internal behavior) [13]. The first model type is intended to describe the process of message exchange between subjects; the second one specifies the subjects' activities in the process by describing the subjects' states and transitions from one state to another.

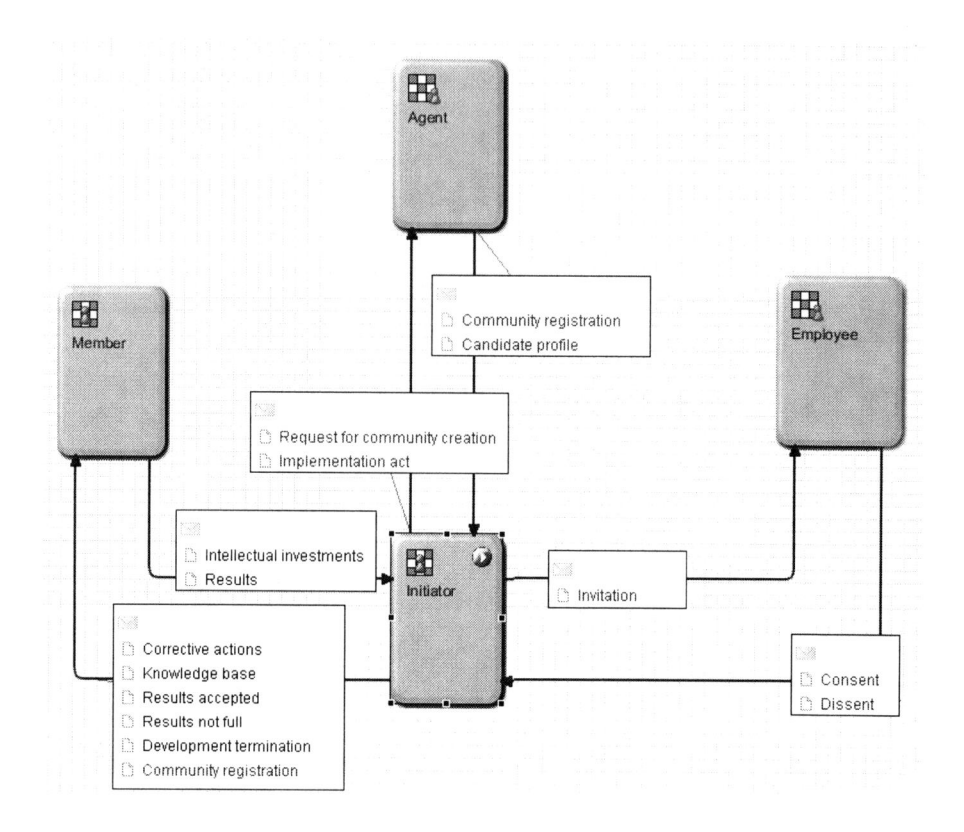

**Fig. 1.** Subject interaction diagram

Figure 1 shows an example for a subject interaction diagram in the innovation process. The subject "Initiator" sends the message "Request for community creation" to the subject "Agent" (this is not a man, but an element of an IT system). "Agent", who has staff profiles, sends two messages with his recommendations on potential investors of intellectual capital and their profiles back to the "Initiator".

Having examined the recommendations and profiles of candidates, the "Initiator" sends invitations to potential investors (subject "Employee") and, after receiving the consent, creates a new community for the innovation development. The formal establishment and registration of the community is operated by the "Agent". A potential investor becomes participant of the innovation process. The development of innovation begins after the collection of intellectual investments of the community.

Figure 2 shows the activity description of an innovation creation initiator (which has turned into the owner of the process). This model is the detailed decomposition of the subject "Initiator" in Figure 1. This model does not need difficult logic constructions and operators typical for notations of traditional modeling methodologies. All necessary decisions according to the logic of process performance are made by the subject who possesses a certain degree of freedom within the limits of the given process model.

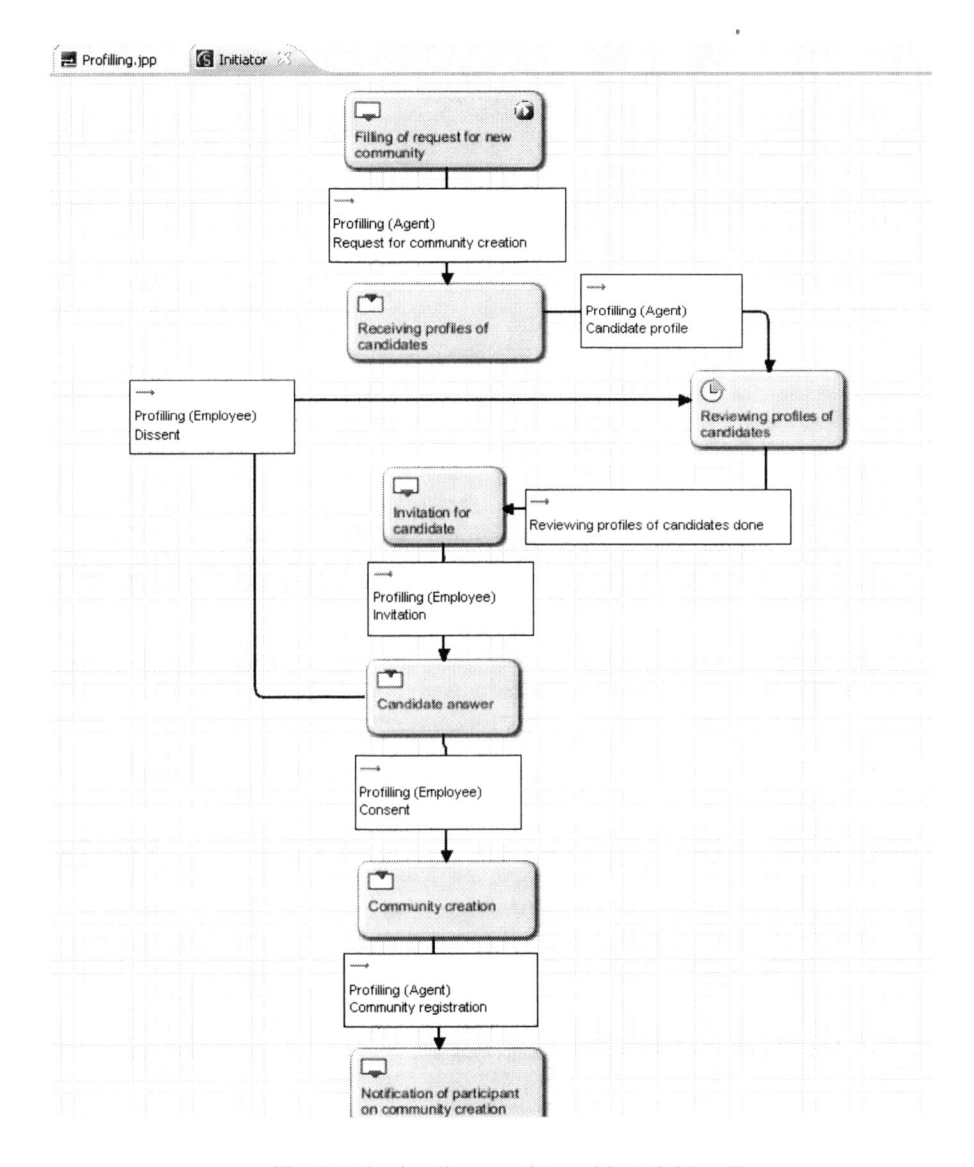

**Fig. 2.** Behavior diagram of the subject "Initiator"

If there is a necessity to increase or to narrow the degree of subjects' freedom, the subject itself could easily adjust the model respectively. For this purpose the real subject (the employee of the enterprise) needs to study only 5 (five) elements of modeling and several ways of their interconnections.

Then what comes after shaping models of these two types? Before answering this question, let us recall the traditional approach to modeling. For example, the methodology and tool system ARIS allows modeling on three of five levels (stages) of systems life-cycle development: Requirement Definition Level, Design Specification Level and Implementation Level. At the first stage models which define business requirements to the projected system are under construction. The Design Specification Level models are transpositions of business requirements to information technologies. The Specifications Level models derive from the Requirement Definition Level models. Finally, the Implementation Level models describe the concrete implementation of the system; they follow from the Design Specification Level models.

The subject-oriented approach allows an alternate scenario of development. In relation to life-cycle development the two models presented above are the requirement descriptions of the workflow control system. To turn simple models into executable applications without programming skills, it is necessary to fill models and elements (subjects, messages, conditions, transitions) with all necessary attributes and properties. The procedure will provide the generation of the high-grade application, including connections to other information systems, electronic documents flows, automatic steps etc. Thus, one and the same models created with the Metasonic Suite describe a process at all three levels. Modeling is kind of combined with programming and allows round-trip engineering [13].

After creating the models it is possible to jointly validate them in an interactive computer-based role play with all people involved. Once the validation result is positive the models are loaded onto the runtime server and are instantiated as copies of the process if the defined starting event takes place. As mentioned before, in the innovation process each participant should have a degree of freedom in decision making which stimulates creativity, reflection, and self-organization. If a modification of the process is needed, it is brought into the corresponding model by the actors themselves. Loading the new model onto the server again automatically updates the application. All existing copies of the process (initial and changed) remain as well as the information belonging to the different versions. This is very important to gather and generalize the experience of the innovation activity within the enterprise.

In the process of innovative creativity the most essential risk factor is the loss of information applicability. In order to solve its challenges, continuous aggregation of investigated information and selection of relevant information is required. Hence, a controlled system of workflows connected with other information services providing reliable, efficient access to relevant information from unstructured sources, along with coding services, preservation and access to structured information is necessary.

## 4 Conclusion

The described approach using the S-BPM platform enables operational connection of multiple services permitting access to unstructured information and along with various DBMS with access to data at the field level. Thus, access to unstructured information can be carried out via one query executed simultaneously in several services connected to the system at a time, such as, Yandex, Google, Exalead or Fast. Therefore, there is an auto-generation of system architecture of innovation process management which could be corrected and analyzed by a subject-matter expert group, responsible for processes of innovation development, as the solution matures.

It is worth nothing that the flexibility of the solution's architecture is the cardinal advantage, enabling innovative results in the optimal way. Morally, formulated in 1983 by V.A. Legasov [11], the concept of flexible production management on a universal information highway, is available today in the form of services on the information corporate bus (ICB).

The above description demonstrates that a high-grade innovation-focused ECM system can be designed only from the subject-oriented point of view to innovation process management. This approach has advantages not only to innovation processes, but also for all processes that demand flexibility, simplicity and speed of modification. The S-BPM implementation as part of an innovation ECM system gives enterprises a powerful tool for independent management of business processes and ECM system services.

The subject-oriented approach to innovation processes accounts for socio-psychological factors, which are integral to innovations development. The purpose of this article was not to provide a detailed description of socio-psychological factors; for this reason we present only general reasons and recommendations.

First of all, creativity is a rare human feature. It is worthwhile to include in the network of innovation communities only those employees who want to be and can be engaged in innovation development. It is a special "elite" network and its participants (subjects) should acknowledge certain ideological principles. Each employee who wishes to be engaged in the innovation process has to study and undertake certain common rules for all participants. Rezak's "Links decide all, Rules for positive networking" provides proven rules for the creation of these types of networks. [12]

Secondly, for effective performance of the innovation process it is necessary to consider psychological features of each subject and, accordingly, conducting additional research.

Finally, it is necessary to identify within unstructured information parts containing dramatic distortions, which were more or less consciously brought into the system by subjects. Not to do so turns the application of semi-structured information for enterprise governance problematic.

While creating innovation ECM systems it is indispensably to provide support for nonlinear innovation processes that take into account a variety of intellectual investment sources, interdependence and parallelism of development cycles of an innovation, and constant orientation on demand, thus providing agility to the holistic process.

Modern requirements of innovation ECM systems can be executed only with a focus on supporting innovation subject through the subject-oriented approach to innovation process management.

During the creation of innovation ECM system it is necessary to consider the essential impact of socio-psychological factors on the innovation process.

Generation of methodology for innovation activity in all phases of its development is necessary to realize the goal of the current government program on transition to innovative economics. The speed of innovations is directly proportional to the degree of intellectual resource integration within a single enterprise or a group of enterprises which have set out to achieve such an ambitious objective.

# References

1. State of the ECM industry (2011), http://www.aiim.org/pdfdocuments/ECM-State-of-Industry-2011.pdf
2. Litomin, A.: Transition to electronic documents and electronic content management, http://www.oraclepro.ru/events/spb2010
3. Forecast analysis: Enterprise Application Software Worldwide, 2009-2014, 3Q10 update, Gartner, http://www.gartner.com
4. Azgaldov, G., Kostin, A.: Intellectual property, innovation and qualimetry. Economy strategy 2(60), 162–164 (2008)
5. http://ru.wikipedia.org/wiki/%c8%ED%ED%EE%E2%E0%F6%E8%E8
6. Lepski, V.: Basics approach and ontology of subject-oriented scope of innovation development. Reflective process and management (2), 66–70 (2007)
7. Provintzev, P.: New requirements to innovation process management process. Reflective process and management (2), 5–28 (2007)
8. Active Compliance Management with subject-oriented Business Process Management. On the way to service-oriented business, S.A.R.I. (2009)
9. Gromoff, A., Chebotarev, V.: BPM Approach Evolution. Business Informatics (1) (2010)
10. Chebotarev, V., Borodina, D.: Specificity of S-BPM use. Business Informatics (2) (2010)
11. Legasov, V., Safonov, M.: Flexible production. Chemical industry (8), 470–477 (1985)
12. Rezak, D.: Links decide all, Rules for positive networking, p. 208 (2009)
13. Fleischmann, A., Schmidt, W., Stary, C., Obermeier, S., Börger, E.: Subjektorientiertes Prozessmanagement, München (2011)
14. Fleischmann, A.: What is S-BPM? In: Buchwald, H., Fleischmann, A., Seese, D., Stary, C. (eds.) S-BPM ONE 2009. CCIS, vol. 85, pp. 85–106. Springer, Heidelberg (2010)
15. Schmidt, W., Fleischmann, A., Gilbert, O.: Subjektorientiertes Geschäftsprozessmanagement. HMD – Praxis der Wirtschaftsinformatik, Heft 266, 52–62 (2009)

# Methods of Process Modeling in the Context of Civil Services by the Example of German Notaries

Barbara Handy, Max Dirndorfer, Josef Schneeberger, and Herbert Fischer

Hochschule Deggendorf
Edlmairstraße 6+8, 94469 Deggendorf, Germany
{barbara.handy,max.dirndorfer,josef.schneeberger,
herbert.fischer}@fh-deggendorf.de

**Abstract.** The project STERN aims to support German notaries to implement a secure electronic communication structure involving numerous governmental and private parties. Communication is an integral part of the business process in a notary's office and has to be handled economically, fast, easy, trustworthy, and secure. Therefore, a careful analysis of the notarial workflows is in order. A variety of process modeling techniques is explored to identify their suitability for distributed and communication intensive workflows. To identify the best modeling approach, evaluation criteria were established. Some typical tasks of the application domain were modeled with the different methods and finally presented to and discussed with notaries. The results of this study are presented and an outlook on the further course of the project is given.

**Keywords:** Electronic government, flow-oriented modeling, object-oriented modeling, subject-oriented modeling, notaries, Business Process Modeling.

## 1 Introduction

The project STERN[1] is a joint research project started in 2010 that tries to improve the electronic communication tasks of notaries. These communication needs are quite challenging, since they involve numerous and varying communication partners in sophisticated and elaborated workflows. Moreover, communication has to be secure and as easy to use as possible. The STERN project is a collaborative effort funded by the Bavarian Ministry of Research. The project partners are Hochschule Deggendorf, Bundesnotarkammer Berlin, and the software company Westernacher Products and Services.

The project goal is to facilitate and improve electronic communication for notaries. In order to improve our understanding of the communication processes we started out to model various typical workflows using multiple different modeling methodologies. Our goal is twofold. On the one hand we want to describe and visualize workflows for a better reconcilement with notaries on the other hand we are interested to evaluate

---

[1] STERN is an acronym for "Sichere Teilnahme am elektronischen Rechtsverkehr für Notare" i.e. "Secure Participation in electronic legal Transactions for Notaries".

the different modeling frameworks for our purposes. An adequate visualization and description of processes facilitates a common understanding and makes it easier to discuss relevant issues. This in turn is essential to optimize the respective processes for all stakeholders, to maximize acceptance and to lead to a lasting and shared success. Furthermore, an appropriate visualization of those processes is a good communication base between our users, the notaries, communication partners, and the programmers of interfaces and services.

Notaries run and represent a public office.[2] They perform the certification of legal transactions, the authentication of signatures, and similar tasks that require a maximum degree of trust. An official deed created by a notary is considered reliable and officially authorized. In Germany there are two forms of notaries. On the one hand there are full-time notaries who are operating their public office exclusively. On the other hand there are notaries who may be lawyers in addition [1]. Independently from the form of the notary the activities and responsibilities are identical.[3]

In a notary's office, the staff members are rarely experts in computer networking. Nevertheless, electronic communication has to be safe, confident, and easy to use. The software has to clearly exhibit appropriate communication partners and to indicate secure communication channels. Notaries have to communicate with a large variety of partners ranging from private and institutional clients, to register courts, land registry offices, municipal administrations, banks, and tax offices. Although, most of these relationships are still serviced using paper mail the situation will change dramatically in the near future. For example, since January 1, 2007 German notaries are forced by law to perform registrations at the commercial registry in an electronic way [2]. Further processes will follow in the near future. An example is the electronic register of wills which may be accessed exclusively by computer communication.

In a broader sense, our investigations may contribute to a better understanding of the communication needs in e-government. Electronic government processes are describing relations between public authorities and individuals, public authorities and enterprises, and among public authorities themselves. Easy to use and secure communication channels are a key factor in optimizing and efficiently running a public administration. These issues arise with federal administrative processes as well as provincial or municipal administrative services [3]. Consequently, an efficient communication is a key factor for successful e-government.

## 2 Process Modeling for Notaries

A notary may be considered as the central hub with many communication links in a star communication. He provides the knowledge to act legally compliant and neutrally with all the involved parties. In the STERN project, we selected some significant processes in the context of the notary's tasks to be visualized for different audiences. In particular, the visualization has to be easily comprehensive for notaries and the staff in the notary's office.

We have chosen three modeling techniques:

---

[2] In Germany, this is regulated by law – see §1 Bundesnotarordnung (BNotO).
[3] See: http://www.bnotk.de/Notar/Notariatsverfassungen/index.php for a description of the various types of notaries in Germany.

- Flow-oriented modeling – eEPC and BPMN
- Object-oriented modeling – activity diagram and use case diagram
- Subject-oriented modeling – S-BPM

The flow-oriented approach deals with the modeling of business processes. The model visualizes tasks and their procedural sequence which will be executed step by step. The steps in the processing logic are combined using logical symbols. Thus sequences, parallelism, choices, and iterations can be depicted.

Object-oriented modeling—represented by UML—is a standardized graphical modeling scheme to visualize complex technical systems. UML provides a wide range of standardized types of diagrams. Therefore, even complex systems may be modeled in a clearly arranged and comprehensible way. UML diagrams can be used in every phase of the systems design and they offer a feasible means for the communication between system analysts and business users.

Subject-oriented modeling is particularly suitable for the description of communication intensive business processes. Unlike object-oriented models S-BPM focuses on the subjects i.e. the participants respectively the actors of a process are in the central focus of attention. This does not mean that the approach neglects predicates and objects [4].

These three modeling paradigms are chosen for various reasons. eEPC, activity diagrams, and use-case diagrams have been used in several projects in our application domain before. Therefore, we want to compare these techniques to newer modeling methods: S-BPM in the area of subject-oriented modeling and BPMN for flow-oriented modeling, which has left beta in Version 2.0 in early 2011 [5]. These new techniques offer innovative approaches which have yet to prove their adequacy in our application domain.

## 2.1 Requirements on the Modeling Methods

The major challenge for modeling methods is to visualize the structure of notarial processes. The different tasks have to be placed and modeled in proper chronological order. Perceiving process models and interpreting them for task execution leaves room for individual interpretations and misconceptions. To avoid this as far as possible, Frank and van Laak [6] propose three kinds of requirements for modeling languages:

- *Formal requirements* are very important in order to check the models integrity or to do model transformations.
- *User-oriented requirements* relate to the comprehensibility of the models and their visualization with the aid of the proposed modeling concepts. The users are modelers and viewers of the models.
- *Use-oriented requirements* are requirements of the specific domain.

User- and use-oriented requirements may have contrary aims, e.g. it is possible that an easy to learn modeling technique does not offer all necessary concepts for a particular application domain. In our context, the formal requirements of a modeling method are currently neglected and will be considered at a later stage of the STERN project. We currently concentrate on the user, i.e. the notaries and their communication partners as

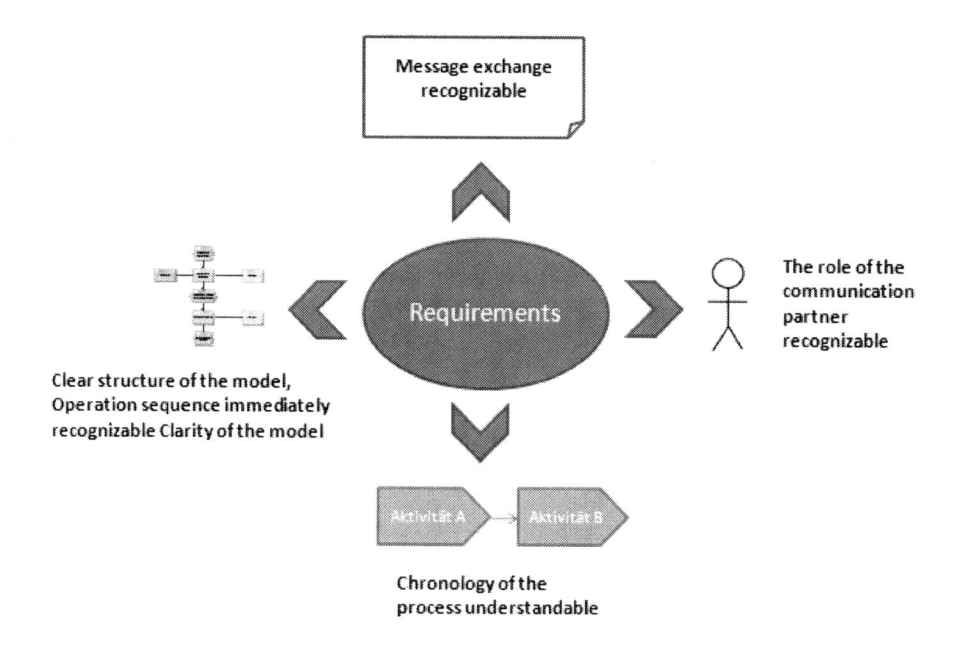

Fig. 1. Requirements on the modeling methods

well as the field of application, i.e. communication links and communication processes in the notary's context. Starting from these two principal requirements we defined more specific criteria depicted in Fig. 1 and described in more details in Table 1.

## 2.2 Evaluation Methodology

We evaluated the chosen modeling techniques according to the following scheme.

**Visualization of processes**
Different tasks from the notarial context were chosen to be modeled and visualized with the mentioned approaches. It was ensured that the tasks have comparable complexity.

**Evaluation with notaries**
The models respectively their workflow visualizations have been presented to five notaries. In an interview, the notaries were asked to read the process models step by step and to explain what they are seeing. Afterwards, a questionnaire (see Figure 2) with open and closed questions was filled out to inquire properties of the visualization model.

**Consolidation of results**
In a final step, the questionnaires were analyzed and the results of the five interviews were combined. The findings are the basis for the discussion in the following chapters.

**Table 1.** Requirement definition

| Requirement | Description |
|---|---|
| Message exchange | The communication of the notaries with different partners includes the exchange of documents and messages. The exchange of these messages should be visible in a model. |
| Role of the communication partners | The role of the communication partners in a process should be recognizable. The goal is to see at a glance who is talking to whom, who initiates the process, or ends it. The notary should be able to identify himself clearly in a variety of communication partners. |
| Process flow and timing | The timing of the process should be apparent. Both the procedural sequence of the process and the timing should be instantly recognizable.<br>In notaries, there are many interdependent process steps, i.e. to perform some activities pre-conditions have to be met. For example, before an entry at the Land Registry can be performed, all required documents have to be certified first. |
| Visualization of none sequential process steps | In the notary's office, a lot of the processes run in parallel at the same time. It is often not clear in which order steps have to be processed and, therefore, it is important that modeling methods offer solutions to visualize such situations. E.g., in some cases it is necessary to send different messages to different communication partners simultaneously and the message transfer does not require any particular ordering. The messages sent may trigger different sub-processes in turn and their order is not known when the process is started. |
| Understandability | The understandability of the model is one of the most important aspects. The model should be understood immediately and at the first glance without having any deeper instructions of the modeling approach. |
| Clear structure of models | A clear structure of the model is very significant. Despite the complexity of the processes, the structure of the model should be displayed clearly.<br>This aspect is very important because the stakeholders are no modeling specialists in general. Clearly structured models help to provide a quick overview. |

## 2.3 Methods of Modeling

### 2.3.1 eEPC (extended Event-driven Process Chain)

EPC is a frequently used process modeling technique that represents workflows as a graph with the following elements: events, functions, control flow, and logical symbols ("and", "or" and "xor"). EPC is a directed graph [7] and is read from top to

```
1.5. Wie verständlich* ist für Sie das BPMN-Modell?

    O sehr gut verständlich
    O gut verständlich
    O verständlich
    O schlecht verständlich
    O nicht verständlich

* Haben Sie das Modell auf den ersten Blick, sofort verstanden, ohne
Hilfestellung des Interviewers.
```

```
2.2.1 Wer sind die Beteiligten(Kommunikationspartner)?

2.2.2 Wer stößt den Vorgang an?
```

Fig. 2. Examples for open and closed questions about process models

bottom and reflects the temporal sequence. It is possible to extend EPC with elements from the organizational and data view (e. g. software modules, documents). In this case it is called eEPC – extended Event-driven Process Chain [8]. Figure 3 shows an example diagram from our application domain.

EPC as a modeling method offers several advantages. Standardized processes can be depicted easily and they are quite comprehensible even without a deeper knowledge of the technicalities. The disadvantages of this modeling technique are problems when illustrating complex workflows. In particular, there is no possibility to express the communication flow and even the role of communication partners is not visible. eEPCs are a tool very well suited for the communication between application specialists and an IT department. However, in our case some important aspects are not modeled appropriately. For example, the following questions cannot be answered by eEPCs: "What is the relationship of functions and relevant business data?" or "Should the transaction only be done with XNotar or is it also possible by web service?" Our findings are summarized in Table 2.

### 2.3.2 BPMN (Business Process Modeling Notation)

BPMN provides a graphical representation of business processes in a standardized and comprehensive notation for both, a business as well as a technical view. Basic elements of the BPMN are: flow objects, connecting object, artifacts, participants, and data. The focus of BPMN models are the sequence and the message flow as well as the exchanged messages and data. BPMN provides a powerful notation for modeling business processes and the diagrams are comprehensible to process modelers as well as process developers. The organizational structures are modeled in manageable pools and lanes. This allows representing even complex processes very clearly.

Methods of Process Modeling in the Context of Civil Services 287

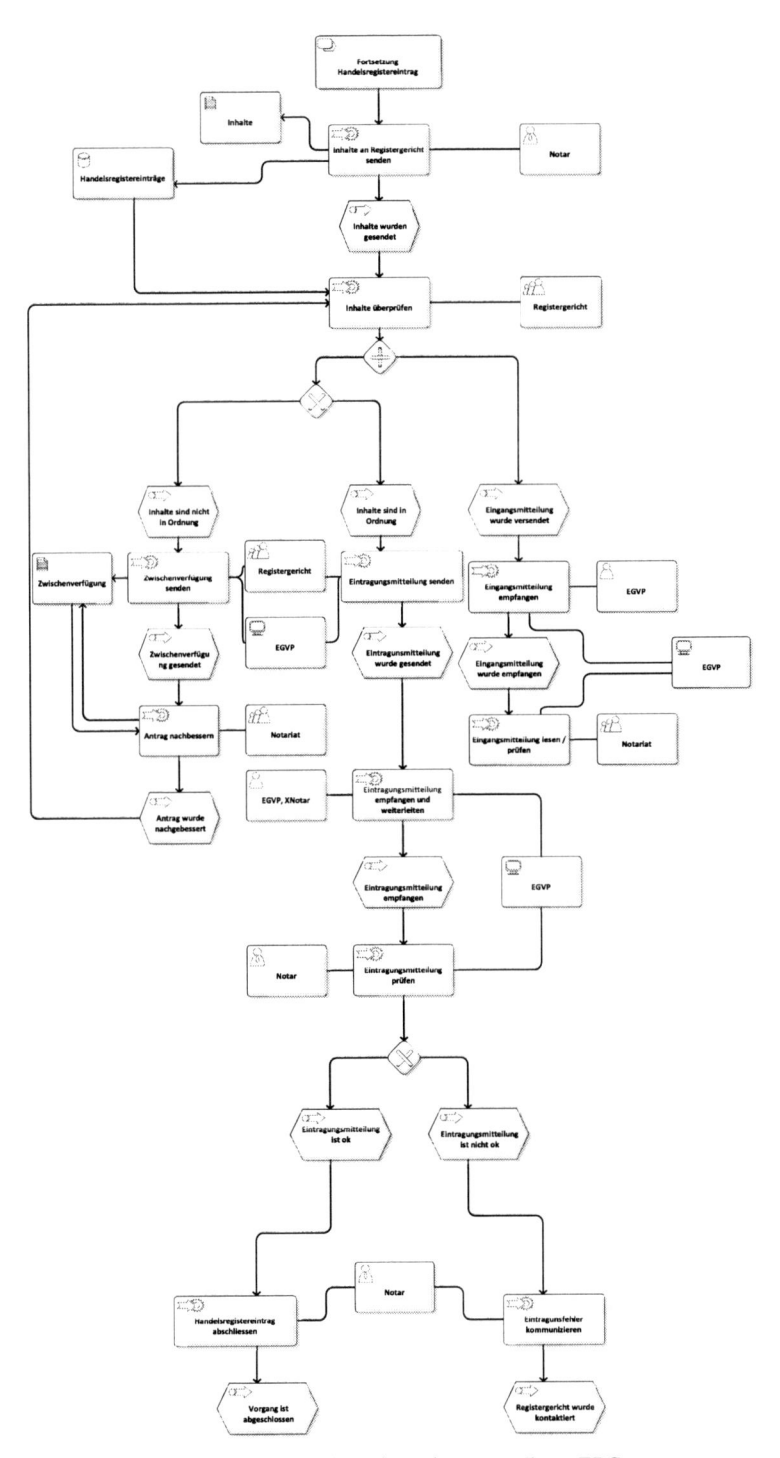

**Fig. 3.** Excerpt of "trade register entry" as eEPC

**Table 2.** eEPC evaluated based on our requirements

| Requirement | Description |
|---|---|
| Message exchange | The message exchange is not visible in EPC. This is possible in eEPC but it still does not provide an adequate visualization to describe communication flows between the different communication partners. |
| Role of the communication partners | The assignment of participants to individual process steps is possible in eEPC. However, the presentation of these assignments is far less elegant than the use of pools and lanes, which are not available in eEPC. |
| Process flow and timing | The sequence of the process steps is immediately recognizable. |
| Visualization of none sequential process steps | With the help of the logical "and" operator it is possible to depict parallel sequences of process steps. |
| Understandability | EPC is generally modeled with six basic symbols (function, event, control flow and three logical operators) which can be understood very quickly. |
| Clear structure of models | The model has a clear structure since it resembles a directed graph. Unfortunately, there are no means in EPC to visually structure more complex processes. |

**Table 3.** BPMN evaluated using the criteria

| Requirement | Description |
|---|---|
| Message exchange | The exchange of messages is poorly visualized in an Activity Diagram. It is not suitable to describe the communication flow of multiple communication partners. |
| Role of the communication partners | The roles of the participants can be seen immediately by the use of responsibility divisions. Like in BPMN there is the possibility to use pools to visualize the communication partners, however, there is no possibility to model the internal structure of a pool with lanes. |
| Process flow and timing | The activity diagram is a directed graph that is read vertically or horizontally. It reflects the temporal sequence. |
| Visualization of none sequential process steps | With the help of fork and join nodes parallel sequences can be modeled [12]. |
| Understandability | By the simplicity of the icons, an Activity Diagram can be understood very quickly. |
| Clear structure of models | The model has a clear structure based on a directed graph. It can be structured further by the use of the variety of elements. |

**Table 3.** (*Continued*)

| Requirement | Description |
|---|---|
| | Gateway enables the definition of rules such as a "2 out of 3" rule. Another interesting feature is the ad-hoc sub-process that involves several tasks which can be run in arbitrary order and as often as necessary. |
| Understandability | BPMN uses many symbols, but they can be quickly understood and comprehended. This is achieved inter alia through the division into five basic groups of symbols [10]. |
| Clear structure of models | The model has a clear structure based on the process flow. |

BPMN 2.0 offers three different diagram types, namely Collaboration Diagram, Choreography Diagram, and Conversation Diagram [9]. In our case, we only used collaboration diagrams. Our findings from the interviews with the notaries are summarized in Table 3 and an example diagram is shown in Figure 4.

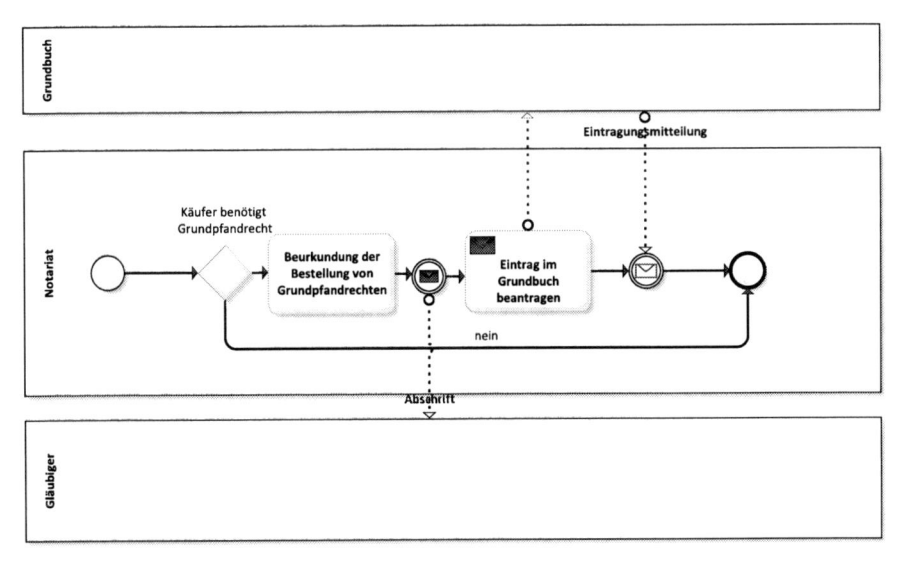

**Fig. 4.** "Registration of charges on real property" as BPMN diagram

### 2.3.3 Activity Diagrams

Activity diagrams visualize the temporal flow of processes and they are useful describing different levels of abstraction [11]. An activity diagram is a flow diagram illustrating task sequences similar to eEPC or BPMN. Like BPMN, activity diagrams offer the possibility to use pools and lanes for a better overview of the process. An activity diagram emphasizes the time flow of the processes considered. Even very complex sequences with exceptions, leaps, and loops can be modeled in a clear and comprehensible way. An example for an activity diagram is shown in Figure 5 and Table 4 summarizes our findings in the interviews with the notaries about Activity Diagrams.

290   B. Handy et al.

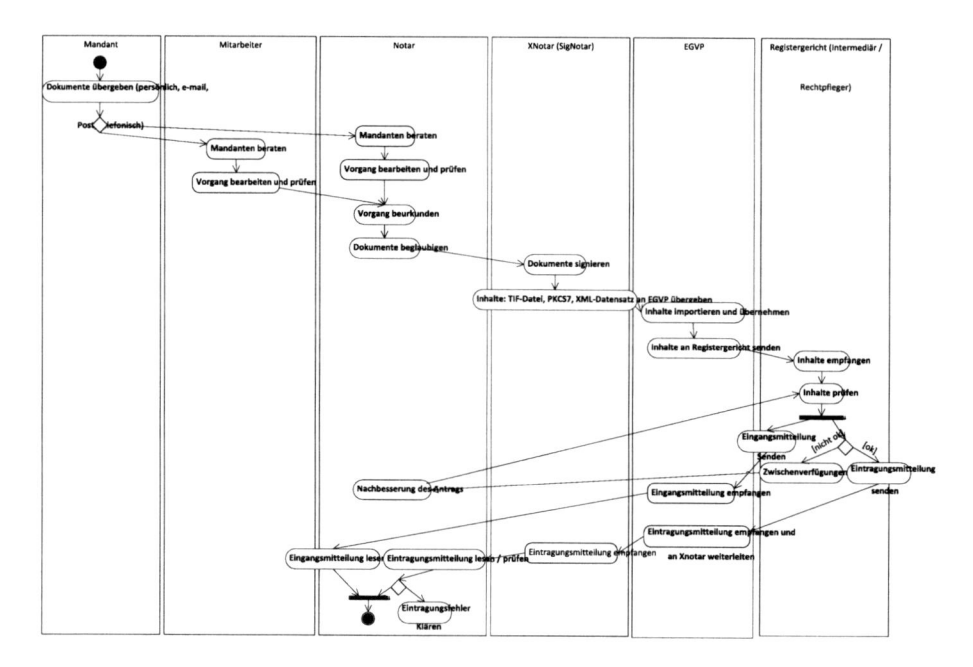

Fig. 5. Excerpt of "trade register entry" as Activity Diagram

Table 4. Activity Diagram evaluated using the criteria

| Requirement | Description |
| --- | --- |
| Message exchange | The exchange of messages is poorly visualized in an Activity Diagram. It is not suitable to describe the communication flow of multiple communication partners. |
| Role of the communication partners | The roles of the participants can be seen immediately by the use of responsibility divisions. Like in BPMN there is the possibility to use pools to visualize the communication partners, however, there is no possibility to model the internal structure of a pool with lanes. |
| Process flow and timing | The activity diagram is a directed graph that is read vertically or horizontally. It reflects the temporal sequence. |
| Visualization of none sequential process steps | With the help of fork and join nodes parallel sequences can be modeled [12]. |
| Understandability | By the simplicity of the icons, an Activity Diagram can be understood very quickly. |
| Clear structure of models | The model has a clear structure based on a directed graph. It can be structured further by the use of the variety of elements. |

### 2.3.4 Use Case Diagram

A Use Case Diagram (see Figure 6) describes the activities of the users with use cases and it consists of a small number of simple symbols. Its simplicity makes this diagram a good candidate for the communication between a client and a contractor.

Use Case Diagrams are very useful to provide an overview of the whole system at a high level of abstraction [13]. Use Case Diagrams do not illustrate behavior and task sequences, they only exhibit the links between the roles and the use cases. The temporal order of process steps and complex decision situations cannot be modeled. Use cases are a good means of communication to discuss professional and technical issues. Our findings with respect to notarial processes are summarized in Table 5.

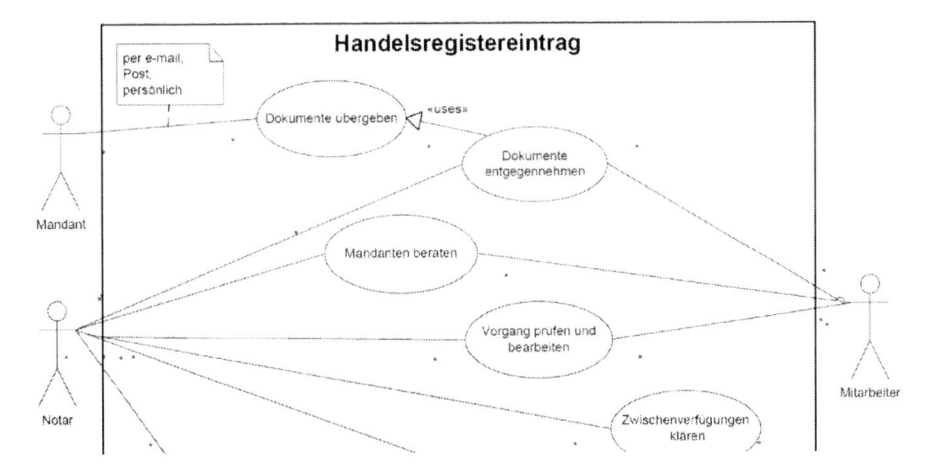

**Fig. 6.** Excerpt of "trade register entry" as Use Case Diagram

**Table 5.** Use Case Diagram evaluated using the project's criteria

| Requirement | Description |
| --- | --- |
| Message exchange | The message exchange is not modeled in a Use Case diagram. |
| Role of the communication partners | The roles of the communication partners are present in a Use Case diagram, however, they are hard to understand. Diagrams can be confusing if the number of use cases is large. |
| Process flow and timing | A task sequence or temporal sequences are not shown in the Use Case diagram by definition. |
| Visualization of none sequential process steps | Since no defined order is given no sequences are presented. |
| Understandability | Use Case diagrams are modeled with only 5 symbols. Therefore this approach is understood easily. |
| Clear structure of models | The model is moderately structured. This is heavily dependent on the extent of the described situation. |

### 2.3.5 S-BPM

S-BPM stands for "Subject-oriented Business Process Management". This is a new process description technique that was invented by Albert Fleischmann [17]. The aim of this method is to quickly and easily create dynamic business applications and to integrate them smoothly into an existing IT infrastructure [14]. The subject-oriented process description is done by three views or design levels [17] [15]:

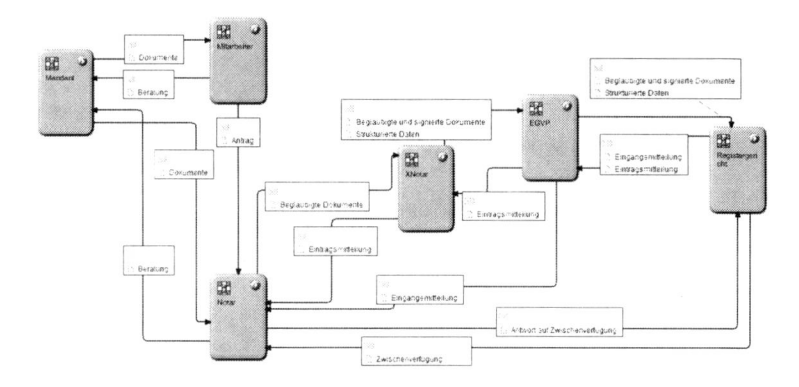

**Fig. 7.** SID for "trade register entry"

- The subject-interaction diagram (SID) depicts the subjects which are the entities involved in the process, their interactions and interfaces. Figure 7 shows an example SID.

- The subject-behavior diagram (SBD) models the behavior of the individual subjects and the dynamic requirements for the process description.

- Application of subjects: The individual process steps are resolved in working processes.

Unlike UML, in S-BPM no different types of charts are used. The three views rather show different aspects of the modeled process. Nevertheless, S-BPM uses similar concepts as the already discussed modeling methods. In particular, it relies on an adapted variant of activity diagrams. S-BPM describes the activities of the actor and shows which interactions (i.e. Messages) are needed for execution [17]. Furthermore, S-BPM emphasizes the fact that the process tasks need to communicate in order to synchronize for the common overall process goals [14].

The focus of S-BPM is the representation of message flow and communication between the subjects of a business process. By splitting into three different views, the model seems very well structured. Furthermore, the use of very few symbols facilitates the understandability of this modeling technique. Table 6 summarizes our evaluation of S-BPM with regard to our evaluation criteria.

**Table 6.** S-BPM evaluated using the project's criteria

| Requirement | Description |
|---|---|
| Message exchange | The exchange of messages is immediately visible in SID. Messages are sent between single subjects i.e. the actors. |
| Role of the communication partners | The roles of communication partners are easy to identify in S-BPM, however, they are difficult to see in SBD. |
| Process flow and timing | The timing of operation cannot be traced in the SID. Following the subject-oriented paradigm, even SBD shows only the time-sequence for each subject. A deeper analysis of the process flow is difficult especially in SID, since the temporal and logical sequences are not accented. |
| Visualization of none sequential process steps | In S-BPM different subjects can perform activities in parallel. However, a subject cannot run parallel activities. |
| Understandability | SID is comprehensible without any further explanation. In order to understand the relationships in SBD the viewer has to put himself into the current role's position. |
| Clear structure of models | The model has a clear structure. The process flow structures the models. The partitioning into different subjects is a convenient structuring element. |

**Table 7.** Comparison of modeling methods

| Modeling Method / Requirement | eEPC | BPMN | Use Case Diagram | Activity Diagram | S-BPM |
|---|---|---|---|---|---|
| Message exchange | o | ++ | -- | - | ++ |
| Role of the communication partners | o | ++ | o | ++ | + |
| Process flow and timing | ++ | ++ | - | ++ | o |
| Understandability | ++ | + | + | ++ | o |
| Clear structure of models | ++ | + | - | + | + |
| Legend: ++ = very good, + = good, o = satisfactory, - = adequate, -- = inadequate |||||| 

## 2.4 Comparison of Modeling Methods

In order to summarize our evaluation results, we introduced a simple rating scheme for the modeling approaches presented in the previous sections and our results inquired in our interviews with the notaries. Possible values for the fulfillment of a requirement ranges from "very good" to "inadequate". Obviously, this is quite coarse but it provides a quick rating (see Table 7). Our comparison has also been acknowledged by the notaries.

## 3 Conclusion

EPC puts the logical time-sequence of events in the foreground, has a clear structure and is understood very quickly. Additionally to the advantages of EPC, BPMN provides good means to visualize the message exchange and the role of the communication partners. Use Case diagrams are easy to understand, however, too superficial and only suitable as an overview of the required standards. Activity diagrams are an extension of use case diagrams and useful to visualize the sequence of business processes. They are similar to flow-oriented modeling approaches such as BPMN. S-BPM visualizes the behavior of the subjects respectively the actor and the messages exchanged between them. For the particular needs of the STERN project, BPMN seems to be the best choice. However, only the use- and user-oriented requirements have been considered so far.

S-BPM is well suited to visualize the exchange of messages between all the communication partners. The notation is easily comprehensible without further training. For the special needs in the STERN project, it would be desirable if it would be possible to show the temporal sequence of message exchange. By dividing the process into individual subjects, the communication partners can identify themselves with the models very well. But the overall flow of the process is not apparent at the first glance since each subject is shown separately. It would be helpful to integrate a visualization possibility that shows the interaction of the subjects together with the internal processes as a comprehensive overview. It also would be convenient if S-BPM would offer some support for none strict sequent process parts as shown in [16].

In the further progression of the STERN project not only the visualization of the processes is of importance but also more technical aspects, like computer-based workflow execution or model based testing. In the next step a detailed documentation of notary processes will be developed considering technical as well as business aspects. Thus the modeling techniques will be further evaluated. Our aim with the more elaborate documentation is to find clues for optimizing the processes and in particular user interfaces to control them in a easy and intelligible way.

## References

1. Neie, J.: Büropraxis und Büroorganisation. In: Bös, B., Leßniak, K., Strangmüller, H., Neie, J. (eds.) Praxishandbuch für Notarfachangestellte, pp. 1–87. RENO-Verlag, Berlin (2010)
2. Bettendorf, J.: Dienstordnung und Büro. In: Brambring, G., Jerschke, H.-U. (eds.) Beck'sches Notar-Handbuch, pp. 1665–1711. Beck Juristischer Verlag, München (2009)
3. Becker, J., Algermissen, L., Falk, T.: Prozessorientierte Verwaltungsmodernisierung: Prozessmanagement im Zeitalter von E-Government und New Public Management. Springer, Heidelberg (2009)
4. Schmidt, W., Fleischmann, A., Gilbert, O.: Subjektorientiertes Geschäftsprozessmanagement. HMD - Praxis der Wirtschaftsinformatik. HMD-Heft 266 (2009)
5. OMG eds: Business Process Model and Notation (BPMN), Version 2.0 (2011)
6. Frank, U., van Laak, B.L.: Anforderungen an Sprachen zur Modellierung von Geschäftsprozessen, Arbeitsberichte des Instituts für Wirtschafts- und Verwaltungsinformatik, Nr. 34. Fachbereich Informatik Universität Koblenz-Landau (2003)

7. Frink, D., Lassen, S., Luczak, H.: Grundlagen des Workflowmanagements in der Produktion. In: Becker, J., Luczak, H. (eds.) Workflowmanagement in der Produktionsplanung und -steuerung: Qualität und Effizienz in der Auftragsabwicklung steigern, pp. 1–71. Springer, Berlin (2003)
8. Freund, J., Götzer, K.: Vom Geschäftsprozess zum Workflow. Ein Leitfaden für die Praxis. Hanser Wirtschaft, München Wien (2008)
9. Allweyer, T.: BPMN 2.0 - Business Process Model and Notation: Einführung in den Standard für die Geschäftsprozessmodellierung. Books on Demand, Norderstedt (2009)
10. Freund, J., Rücker, B.: Praxishandbuch BPMN 2.0. Hanser Fachbuchverlag, München Wien (2010)
11. Partsch, H.A.: Requirements-Engineering systematisch. Springer, Berlin (2010)
12. Rupp, C., Queins, S., Zengler, B., Jackle, M., Hahn, J.: UML 2 glasklar. Praxiswissen für die UML-Modellierung. Hanser, München Wien (2007)
13. Steinpichler, D., Kargl, H.: Projektabwicklung mit UML und Enterprise Architect. SparxSystems Software, Wien (2010)
14. Metasonic: Was ist S-BPM?, http://www.metasonic.de/was-s-bpm (last access March 2011)
15. Fischer, H., Fleischmann, A., Obermeier, S.: Geschäftsprozesse realisieren - Ein praxisorientierter Leitfaden von der Strategie bis zur Implementierung. Vieweg+Teubner, Wiesbaden (2006)
16. Fleischmann, A.: What is S-BPM? In: Buchwald, H., Fleischmann, A., Seese, D., Stary, C. (eds.) S-BPM ONE 2009. CCIS, vol. 85, pp. 85–106. Springer, Heidelberg (2010)
17. Fleischmann, A., Schmidt, W., Stary, C., Obermeier, S., Börger, E.: Subjektorientiertes Prozessmanagement, München (2011)

# Business Process Management: A Survey among Small and Medium Sized Enterprises

Patrick Feldbacher, Peter Suppan, Christina Schweiger, and Robert Singer*

FH JOANNEUM – University of Applied Sciences,
Alte Poststraße 147, 8020 Graz, Austria
robert.singer@fh-joanneum.at

**Abstract.** The purpose of this research is to evaluate to which degree small and medium-sized enterprises (SMEs) use process management techniques and methods. The findings result from 20 interviews that were conducted in 11 small- and medium-sized enterprises in the manufacturing and service sector in Austria. The information retrieved from the interviews was used to rate the overall process management performance of the company. The underlying maturity model for this rating process is based on an adaption of Michael Hammers Process and Enterprise Maturity Model (PEMM). Service companies, in average, reached a higher maturity level than manufacturer did. Also companies that are active in the IT sector had a higher maturity level than companies from other industries. It turned out that there seems to be a strong connection between leadership and the maturity of business process management within the company. This article provides an insight into the process-related activities of small and medium enterprises in Austria. It is explained how business process management is relevant to SMEs.

## 1 Motivation

It seems that there is still no clear and agreed understanding of the terms business process (BP) and business process management (BPM)[1]. Depending on a personal point of view, BPM is an idea, a concept or a methodology and even more important there are different interested parties such as business management and administration, software developers and computer scientists [19]. Notwithstanding that this field is 20 years old we are confronted with an unclear and confusing situation and have to accept the fact, that "BPM is still in its infancy" as Hammer [9] has pointed out recently. Similarly, the assumption of vom Brocke [3]: "... the BPM community is still short of a publication that provides a consolidated understanding of the true scope and contents of a comprehensively defined business process management". Since van der Aalst et al. [1] wrote in 2003 "Although the practical relevance of BPM is undisputed, a clear definition of BPM and related acronyms are missing. Moreover, a clear scientific foundation is missing" nothing fundamentally has changed.

---

* Corresponding author.
[1] Interchangeably we will use the phrase process if we mean business process.

BPM has its roots in the process orientation trend of the 1990s. Michael Hammer and James Champy published the seminal book "Reengineering the Corporation" and described the radical redesign of business processes in companies [10]. They describe a business process as "... a collection of activities that take one or more kinds of input and create an output that is of value for the customer". Each product a company provides to the market is the outcome of a number of activities. Business process management is a method to manage and organize these activities and to improve the understanding of the given inter- and intra-relationships. BPM includes methods, techniques, and tools to support the design, enactment, management, and analysis of operational business processes.

Unquestionable BPM is tightly coupled with technology questions, e.g. such as business process management systems (BPMS). We think that before we seriously can study the requirements of IT Systems [18] we have to understand and agree on common standards and methods of BPM itself. From a business point of view, we follow Hammer [11] and others who define a business process as large-scale, truly end-to-end process focusing on high-leverage aspects of the organizations's operations to gain competitive advantage and far better results. We think enterprises are truly interested in this point.

It exists a number of studies in the field of business process management and process orientation. Kohlbacher [13], for example, reviewed 26 studies and came to the conclusion, that it would be interesting to examine the relationship between process orientation and organizational performance in details. Most studies lack this crucial aspect. Most studies report positive impact of process orientation on organizational performance. Kohlbacher proposes as plausible explanation a possible bias based on the fact, that positive aspects are more often published by the popular press than negative ones. Palmberg suggests in her work [17] that it would be interesting to explore the relationship between the functional and organizational perspective by using the framework of Hammer [8].

The purpose of this paper is to present the results of a qualitative research study about process management in small- and medium-sized enterprises. Small- and medium-sized enterprises make up a significant percentage of the total amount of enterprises in Austria. More than 60% of all Austrian employees are employed in small- and medium-sized enterprises in 2009 [16]. Although the percentage shows clearly that SMEs are an extraordinarily vital part of the economy, most studies about business process management focus on large enterprises. Only 20% to 45% of surveyed enterprises in recent European business process management studies were SMEs [12][6]. SMEs are defined as enterprises with up to two hundred and fifty employees[2].

The empirical study presented in this paper answers five research questions. The main idea was to clarify to which extend small- and medium-sized enterprises

---

[2] http://ec.europa.eu/enterprise/policies/sme/facts-figures-analysis/sme-definition/

use process management techniques. The research questions derived from this idea are:

- Does a link between company success and its process management maturity level exist?
- What process management maturity levels exist in small- and medium-sized enterprises?
- How will the influence of process management change within the companies in the next three to five years?
- How does process management develop within small- and medium-sized enterprises?

To answer these questions we interviewed representatives of 11 Austrian companies of the production and service sector. Based on the interviews we assigned for each company the adequate maturity level (16 dimensions; ranging from employee knowledge over process design to leadership). The underlying maturity model and the final results of the study will be presented in a later section.

In the next section we describe the research design and the methodology used in the empirical study. Afterwards we present a discussion and a summary of the results.

## 2 Research Methodology

The purpose of the study is to evaluate the extend of use of business process management techniques and their connection to business results in small- and medium-sized enterprises in Austria. To be able to compare the degree of business process management, a maturity model is used. As mentioned in the introduction, the data was collected from interviewing representatives of 11 Austrian companies. This section deals with how the data was collected, how the companies were selected and how the data was analyzed.

### 2.1 Mixed Methods

The study uses an empirical method called mixed methods. Figure 1 shows the structure of this method. "Mixed Methods aims at developing theories for praxis relevant knowledge, based on the combination of theory developing qualitative methods and quantitative techniques for data collection and analysis"[3] [2]. The method starts with qualitative research questions, represented by the square in figure 1. Based on the defined qualitative research questions data is collected and analyzed. The result of this analysis is the input for a consecutive quantitative data collection and analysis.

### 2.2 Purposeful Selection

In this empirical study as part of a selection strategy a recovery plan was defined to determine which organizations will be consulted. The sample includes a group of 11 companies from the manufacturing and service sector [4].

---

[3] Translated from German by authors.

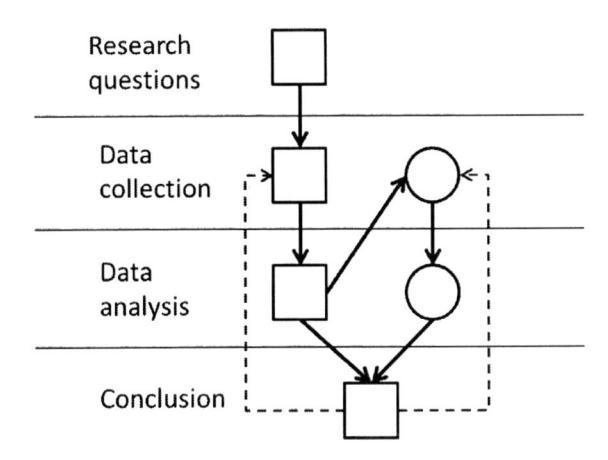

**Fig. 1.** Research process of *Mixed Methods*. Squares denote qualitative, circles denote quantitative research stages and actions.

The surveyed companies had to be in the integration phase, what means that they already have existing social and technical subsystems. In the integration phase, companies start to define their processes more accurate and more efficient [7]. They did not have explicitly to use or live process management. The aim was to investigate the maturity of business process management in SME and – if possible – the relationship of process management with business success. Since it is difficult to assess externally if a company does process management there was the assumption that a company is in the integration phase, or at least on the way to this phase, after eight years of existence. Thus, only companies that have existed for at least eight years were chosen for the survey. The companies were organized into three groups as shown in Table 1 and Figure 2. The sample size contained four[4] companies per group (group 1: 1-15 employees, group 2:16-60 employees, group 3: 61-250 employees). Two companies from the service sector and two companies from the production area were surveyed per group. One hypothesis defines that employees of higher authority see the process management of their company as more advanced, as employees of a lower level. To proof the accuracy of this hypothesis, two persons of each company were interviewed separately from each other - one person from the management level and one from the employee level [14].

In total, eleven companies of the production and service sector were interviewed. As mentioned above, it was regarded that the companies are in the integration phase. One company could not meet these requirements, because it was younger than seven years. However, the company was included in the study in order to gain experiences of a younger company too. Five of the surveyed companies were between seven and ten years, three were between ten and 20 years, and two have existed for more than 20 years (see Figure 3).

---
[4] We could not find a production company for the survey from the first group.

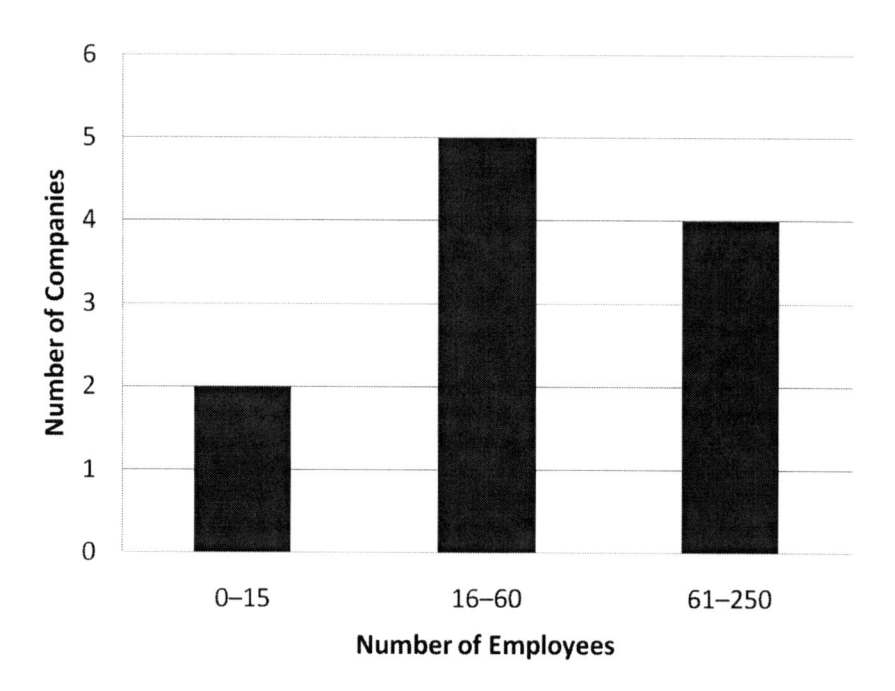

**Fig. 2.** Distribution of selected companies based on number of employees

**Table 1.** Classes and distribution of surveyed companies. DL1...DL7 denote the surveyed companies from service sector, P1...P4 denote the surveyed companies from the production sector.

| Number of Employees | Companies from Service Sector | Companies from Production Sector |
|---|---|---|
| 1–15 | DL1, DL2 | |
| 16–60 | DL3, DL4, DL5 | P1, P2 |
| 61–250 | DL6, DL7 | P3, P4 |

The legal form of the companies were predominantly (64%) companies with limited liability. The remaining companies were either corporations that were public limited companies, cooperatives or sole proprietorships. Figure 4 illustrates this distribution. The following list shows, in which sectors the surveyed companies were active:

**Service sector**

- Financial sector
- Insurance Industry
- Marketing, publishing and event agency
- IT and IT-consulting
- IT System Integrator

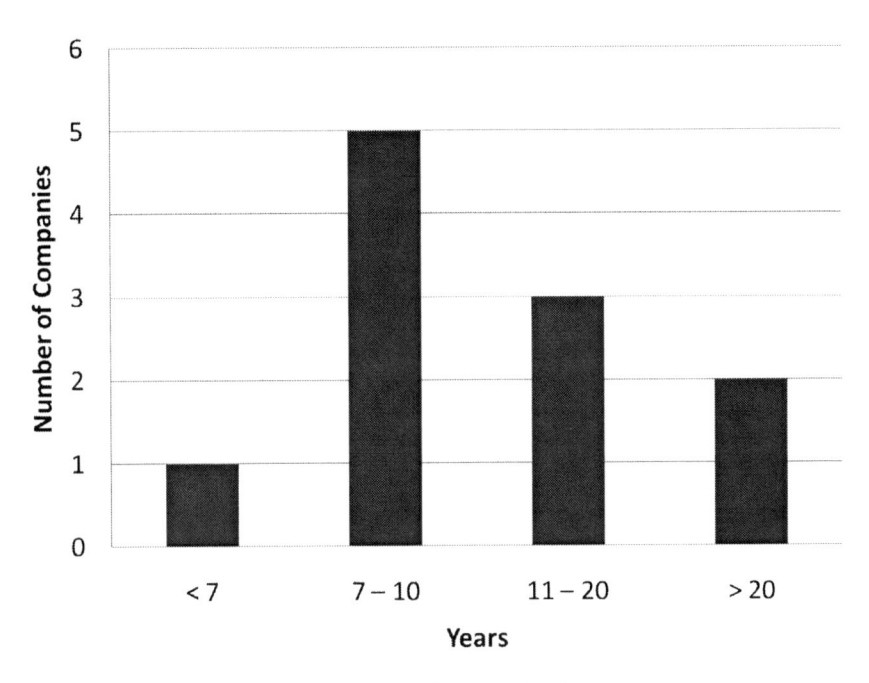

**Fig. 3.** Maturity of companies in years

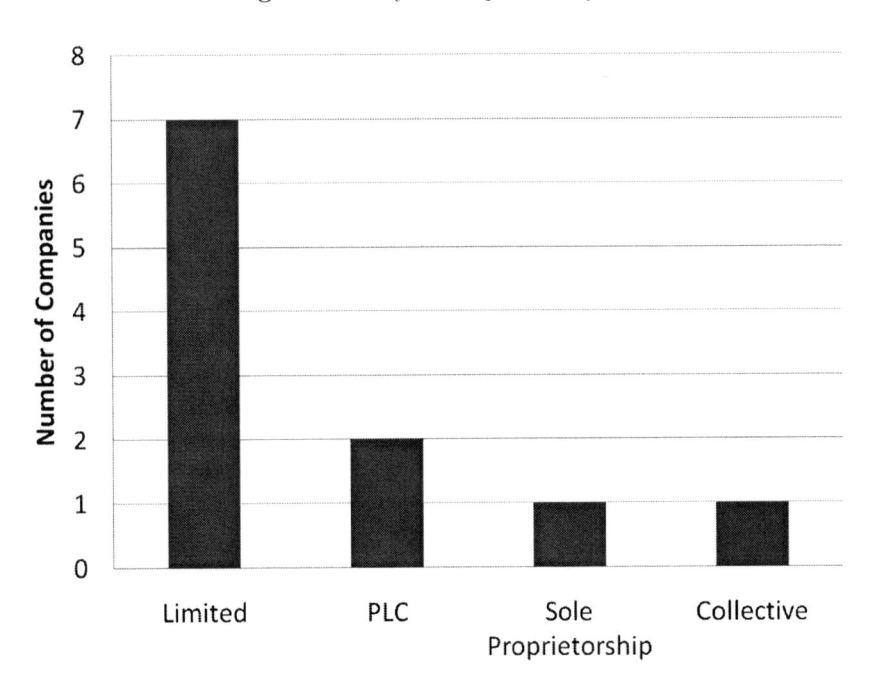

**Fig. 4.** Distribution of legal form of the surveyed companies

- Research, data processing, IT
- Telecommunications

**Production sector**

- Food production
- Apparatus engineering
- Steel & Metalworking
- Joinery & Commercial

### 2.3 Data Collection

Each company provided two employees: one from the management level and one from the classical staff-level. Care was taken to achieve a proper balance between management and staff level. Since it was not always possible to interview the director or manager of the company, a department or project manager was interviewed. Two persons per company were interviewed to represent different views on the topic of process management. If only one person had been questioned, this would have distorted the results, because it is assumed that a person is more likely to talk about the positive aspects of the topic. If there is the knowledge that a second person is interviewed, the person will try to answer truthfully. Then, if both statements are considered, the current conditions in the company can be estimated remarkably well. It was interesting how far, in some cases, the view on a company can differ. One example for this phenomenon: the companys profitability, compared to the sector, differs between the two interviewed persons from low to high. Nevertheless, by and large the answers regarding process management were mostly identical.

In the course of the study, interviews were conducted which constitute the main source of data. Before each interview, every organization was contacted and agreed to participate in the study. A qualitative case study generally relates to only a few cases, however, provides much and deep information. The target is to exemplify a holistic view of the topic [14]. Even a single interview can bring new observations and discoveries [4]. The interview was structured as an open discussion, to build an open relationship between the interviewer and the interviewee. As a result the interviewee is usually more accurate, reflective and honest on the subject [15]. The survey method was a problem-oriented interview. The researcher prepares himself or herself by studying literature about the subject. A theoretical concept is developed from relevant aspects of the problem area [14]. The interview is set up with open questions to create a discussion between two people. The interviewer allows the interviewee to speak as freely as possible [15]. The data was collected by using different techniques. Through a short questionnaire about the person and the company in general, the person was introduced slowly into the interview and was initiated in the subject of the interview. A guideline, which has emerged from preliminary consideration, guides the interviewer through the interview [14].

Most of the companies representatives did not know what process management is. Therefore, a simplified interview guideline was developed to be able to get as much information as possible from the interviews to be able to assign a maturity level.

### 2.4 Data Analysis

All interviews were recorded with a voice recorder and transliterated for analysis and interpretation. The collected data was evaluated immediately after the survey phase. The data collection and the data analysis was done in parallel. The collected data was analyzed using MAXQDA[5], a software for qualitative data analysis. During this data analysis, a code system was developed that allowed to connect answers from the interviews with codes that allow to answer the research questions. This procedure was done within a discussion of two researchers. Every code assignment was discussed until both researchers agreed on the right assignment. The qualitative results were evaluated and compared step by step. In doing so, the number of interviewed persons was not as relevant as the quality of the individual findings. Each case could characterize key points and draw attention to upcoming comparisons [4]. Two people were interviewed from each company. The answers of both persons first were considered separately and then compared [4]. After all interviews were completed and every interview was coded and analyzed every interview was coded again within the scope of new knowledge that derived from all the interviews and analyses. One company was not included in the final results because it has a unusually structure and, therefore, would have distorted the results.

## 3 Maturity Model

The maturity model used for comparing the companies process management systems is an adaption of Michael Hammers Process and Enterprise Maturity Model (PEMM)[6] [8][11]. The maturity model is based on the idea that companies need to ensure that their business processes become more mature. To make this happen, companies must develop two kinds of characteristics: "process enablers, which pertain to individual processes, and enterprise capabilities, which apply to entire organizations" [8].

Before choosing PEMM as a basis for the study, different maturity models, like CMMI, EFQM, and GPM were analyzed. PEMM fits most likely the needs of the study because it was easy to use and easy to adapt for the special needs of the study. For the study – and a following quantitative study – a model is needed which could also be used by a non process management professional. Most of the analyzed models use percentage ratings for evaluating a maturity level. This is neither suitable for use in an online questionnaire, nor it supports

---
[5] http://www.maxqda.com/
[6] The full PEMM model can be downloaded from http://www.hammerandco.com

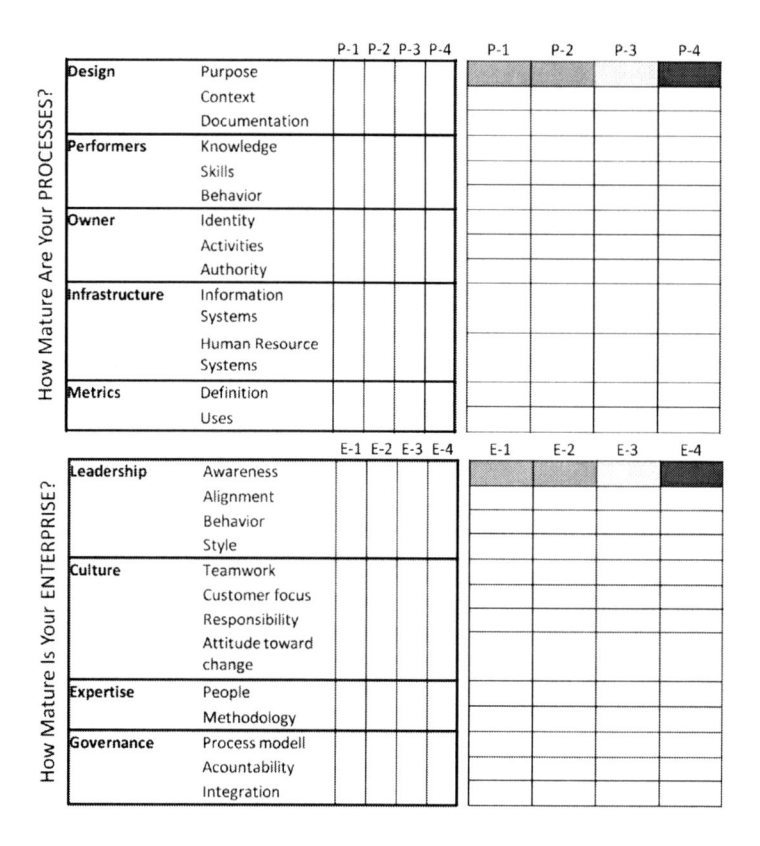

|  |  | P-1 P-2 P-3 P-4 | P-1 | P-2 | P-3 | P-4 |
|---|---|---|---|---|---|---|
| **Design** | Purpose | | | | | |
| | Context | | | | | |
| | Documentation | | | | | |
| **Performers** | Knowledge | | | | | |
| | Skills | | | | | |
| | Behavior | | | | | |
| **Owner** | Identity | | | | | |
| | Activities | | | | | |
| | Authority | | | | | |
| **Infrastructure** | Information Systems | | | | | |
| | Human Resource Systems | | | | | |
| **Metrics** | Definition | | | | | |
| | Uses | | | | | |

*How Mature Are Your PROCESSES?*

|  |  | E-1 E-2 E-3 E-4 | E-1 | E-2 | E-3 | E-4 |
|---|---|---|---|---|---|---|
| **Leadership** | Awareness | | | | | |
| | Alignment | | | | | |
| | Behavior | | | | | |
| | Style | | | | | |
| **Culture** | Teamwork | | | | | |
| | Customer focus | | | | | |
| | Responsibility | | | | | |
| | Attitude toward change | | | | | |
| **Expertise** | People | | | | | |
| | Methodology | | | | | |
| **Governance** | Process modell | | | | | |
| | Acountability | | | | | |
| | Integration | | | | | |

*How Mature Is Your ENTERPRISE?*

**Fig. 5.** A snapshot of the process dimension of the PEM-Model to assess process maturity. The right four collumns contain the assessment results: green means largely true, yellow means somewhat true and red indicates largely untrue. The columns denoted with P-1, P-2, P-3, and P-4 (respectively E-1...E-4) originally contain descriptive text to explain the maturity level. The first line is filled out for demonstration purposes.

an open discussion in the interviews. This are the reasons why Michael Hammers PEM-Model was chosen. Furthermore, it has a practical approach to the topic that helps to design the guideline for the interviews. There are even more maturity models, but all of them are rather sophisticated and are not easy to understand, to explain, and to use. A remarkably specific quality of PEMM is the consideration of dimensions related to enterprise capabilities which supports a more systemic view of organizations.

The PEMM is separated into two parts: an enterprise and a process part. Each part exists of categories, dimensions and strength levels. Figure 5 shows a schematic view of this model. Each box contains a description. When assessing a process the assessor decides for each box if it is largely true, somewhat true or if it is largely untrue. An example for such a box description from Michael Hammers PEMM would be Metric-Definition Strength Level 2: "The process has end-to-end process metrics derived from customer requirements" or for Governance-Process Model Strength Level 1: "The enterprise has identified some business processes". This straightforward concept fits perfectly for the study. However, the questions asked by Hammer showed up not to fit our needs.

In small- and medium-sized enterprises it is hard to apply Hammers model. None of the companies surveyed could achieve any of the maturity levels defined by Hammer. The PEMM perfectly fits for larger enterprises which already have a running process management system, but it lacks support for small- and medium-sized enterprises. The model was revised, due to the fact that most of the companies not even accomplished to achieve maturity level 1 when using the PEM-Model.

The adaption of the PEM-Model was based on the beforehand defined criteria the model has to meet (easy to use, support open discussion, support for online surveys). The interviews where based on this revised PEM-Model. While analyzing the data collected from the interviews the first time, it emerged, that the modified PEMM had to be adapted again, according to the results of the interviews. This adaption of the modified model can be seen as a refinement of PEMMs maturity level 1 for small and medium sized companies (it can be interpreted to spread maturity level 1 into five sublevels). The final maturity model can be seen as one result of this study because it emerged during the analysis of the data.

Like in Hammer's PEM-Model, the adapted model consists of various dimensions. Every dimension has five possible strength levels. The dimensions are categorized into three categories:

- Performer and Culture
- Leadership
- Process Management

In principle, the "sense" of the original dimensions remain the same, but we have compressed and combined them according to our findings. Figure 6 shows the dimensions of the adapted model. For each dimension each maturity level is defined in the model with one to three short and concise sentences. The person who uses the model for determining a companys strength level needs to choose the maturity level for each dimension that is most suitable for the company. Each box contains a short and concise description that helps the assessor to identify the right maturity level for a dimension. Examples for dimensions are process design, process documentation, structure, employee knowledge, customer orientation, or teamwork. An example for maturity level 3 within the dimension "responsibility" would be "Official process owners are defined and have authority to decide". The final result for each enterprise is a maturity level for every category. Based on the interview data for each company each dimension was evaluated and a maturity level was set. The average maturity level of the dimensions of a category determines the category's maturity level.

The adapted model uses a wide definition for the term process. This is because small- and medium-sized enterprises often do not use the term process. If the model uses a strict definition of the term process, almost every interviewed

|  |  | M0 | M1 | M2 | M3 | M4 |
|---|---|---|---|---|---|---|
| Performer and Culture | Knowledge |  |  |  |  |  |
|  | Behavior |  |  |  |  |  |
|  | Teamwork |  |  |  |  |  |
|  | Customer focus |  |  |  |  |  |
|  | Communication |  |  |  |  |  |
|  | Attitude toward change |  |  |  |  |  |
| Processes | Expertise |  |  |  |  |  |
|  | Infrastructure |  |  |  |  |  |
|  | Owner |  |  |  |  |  |
|  | Process Model |  |  |  |  |  |
|  | Metrics |  |  |  |  |  |
|  | Documentation |  |  |  |  |  |
|  | Context |  |  |  |  |  |
|  | Structure |  |  |  |  |  |
| Leadership | Awareness |  |  |  |  |  |
|  | Behavior |  |  |  |  |  |

**Fig. 6.** The dimensions of the adapted PEMM (without columns for assessment). The assessment concept remains the same. The columns denoted with M-0, M-1, M-2, M-3, and M-4 again contain descriptive text to explain the maturity level.

company would reach maturity level 0 in the adapted model. Therefore, for example, documentation of work instructions counts as process documentation. For this study the two interviewers assessed the companies together in a discussion. This method increased the quality of the outcome because two views on the companies where brought in together with the data from the interviews.

## 4 Findings

This section deals with the findings of the presented study. The research questions will be answered and some further findings will be presented. The section starts with an overview of the respondents and then goes deeper into the details of the research questions.

15% of the respondents were female, 85% were male. This could not be influenced because the companies themselves have selected their representatives. 55% of the respondents claimed "university" as their highest educational qualification. 35% have a school-leaving examination, that is an Austrian school graduation, which gives the person a general qualification for university entrance. The last 15% reported that they completed an apprenticeship. Figure 7 shows the distribution of the interview partner. The total number of interview partners was 20. This was because one company allowed only one person to attend the interview. Additionally, one company existed only out of two people and we only had the possibility to interview one of them.

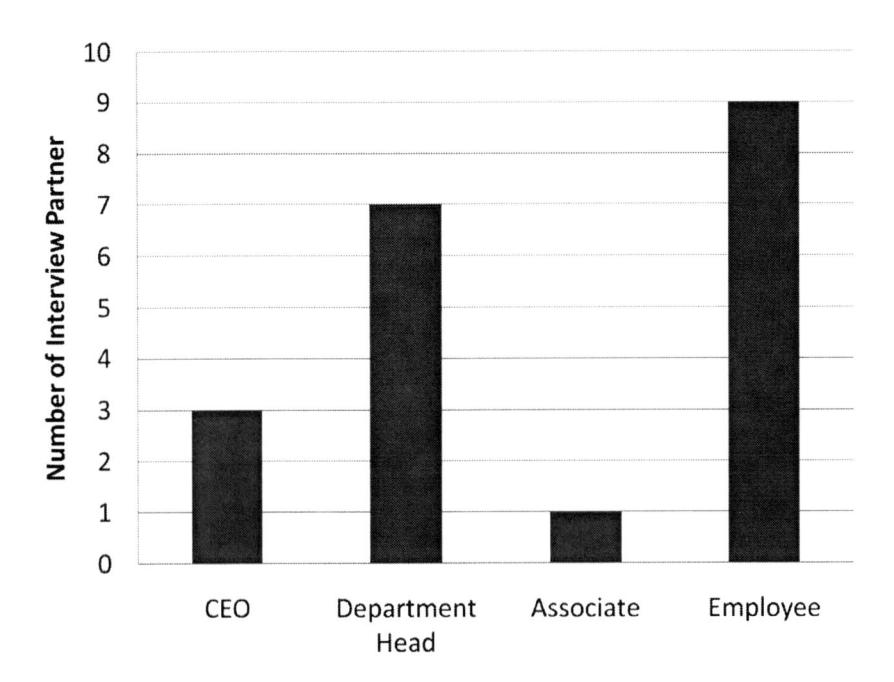

**Fig. 7.** Distribution of the interview partner. In each company one interviewee was from employee and one from management level.

An interesting and important aspect was that the surveyed small- and medium-sized enterprises do not have explicit process design or process documentation. However, especially service providers have defined workflows and work procedures. These were "accepted" as a type of process management. As mentioned before, for example, documentation of work instructions counts as process documentation. The employees know their working procedures and how their work affects other employees work, but mostly these procedures are not designed or documented. One interviewee said in this regard "... our company is more like a family, we do not document a lot, because everything is done orally"[7].

Figure 8 shows the distribution of the maturity levels, answering the research question, what process management maturity levels exist in small- and medium-sized enterprises. It can be seen that the Maturity Level of Employee and Culture always at least reaches level two in our model. Nevertheless, most of the surveyed small- and medium-sized enterprises neither use process management nor use their (workflow) documentations for optimizing their processes. Most companies use their documentations to train new employees. The employees often even do not know how their work affects the final product or the customer. This shows that there is a significant potential on the employee side for using process management concepts.

---

[7] Interviews were conducted in German; all quotes are translated by the authors.

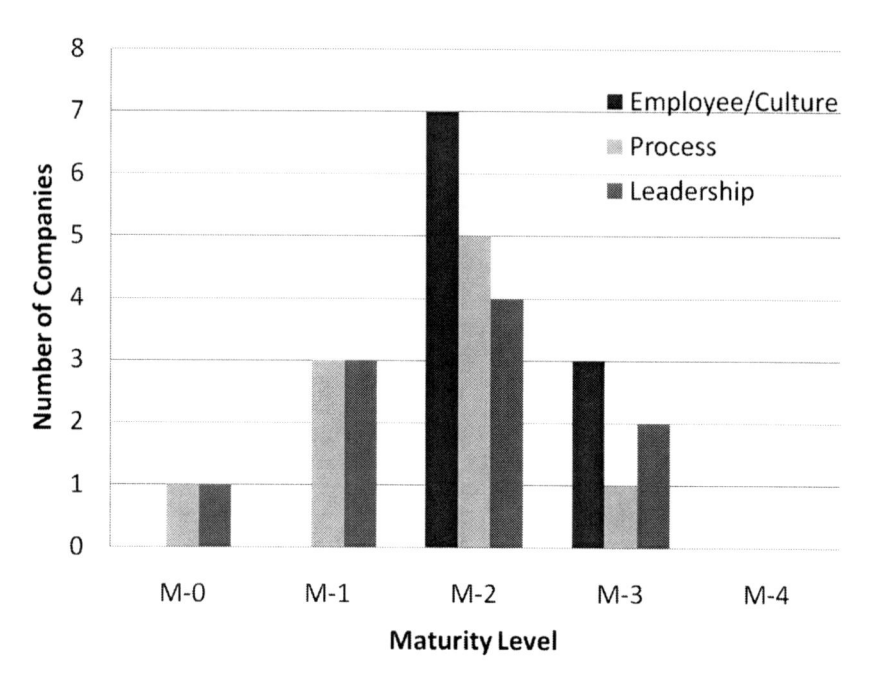

**Fig. 8.** Distribution of the maturity levels for the three dimensions of the adapted PEM-Model

The main research question was if there exists a connection between company success and process management maturity level. Our study was not able to find a clear answer on this question. Companies that think that they actually execute and live process management are convinced that the use of process management has a positive effect on their business success.

> I firmly believe that the use of process management can positively impact a company's success. If you filter out one single case or can avoid a mistake, you have probably already won. (interviewee).

On the one hand, it was not possible to find a connection between the success of a company and its usage of process management. Some companies which do not adopt process management are very successful. On the other hand, the only company with a high maturity level assessed itself as well profitable. In companies with maturity level M-1 and M-2 the opinions of the employees on the profitability of the company vary between average and high. The only company that assessed its profitability compared to the industry as low was a start-up.

Regarding the question how process management develops within small- and medium-sized enterprises it was hard to find convincing answers. Most companies started using process management techniques because they grew. They use methods like documenting workflows for training new employees or managing stand-ins. There was no clear answer at which company size (number of employees), companies start to document or use process management techniques.

However, it was obvious that the first technique every company used was documenting existing workflows or processes. It also turned out that there is a strong link between top management and the process management. Without support and promotion of the top management the development of process management would not be possible. The knowledge about business process management of the manager in companies of this size determines if process management will be used or not. It was also observed that higher education level and prior knowledge of the top management supports the commitment for process management.

The last research question was, how the influence of process management will change within the companies in the next three to five years. The interviewees saw the future regarding documentation, process and work nearly identical. They believed that it could be crucial in the future, but it is only strengthened as necessary or needed. Some argued that if the company grows, it will become more important, because the structures will be more complex and will not be manageable anymore. One interviewee mentioned that "... if there are relatively simple procedures then it is simple to manage them and you do not necessarily have to involve processes. But if it is as complex as in the automotive industry then processes are important." Another interviewee of a service company noted:

> We experienced within the company that there are problems and friction losses in our business. Sometimes you can save hours of unnecessary work i.e. for searches or asking for information, if you define areas well and create interfaces. The company actually works really well, but with our tremendous growth we have noticed that procedures are not defined and documented. For new employees, it was difficult to find out what their responsibilities are and how they are connected to other business areas.

Beside the research questions, other interesting aspects were found. Every surveyed company had a flat organizational structure. This is a fact Michael Hammer saw as something very important. During a reengineering process "organizational structure change - from hierarchical to flat" [10]. This shows that the structure of the surveyed companies supports process management. The question is why they do not use this potential.

Another noteworthy aspect that came up during the interviews was the topic of certifications. In the surveyed SMEs process or quality management certifications such as ISO (International Organization for Standardization) or EFQM (European Foundation for Quality Management) were not as relevant as previously thought. Certifications – such as the well known ISO9000 series – are normally based on an efficient business process management system. It is therefore pertinent to investigate this point during interviews. In the survey, only two companies (corresponds to 18 percentage) were able to provide an enterprise-wide certification. Another company had a certification in one department. All three companies have more than 70 employees. Figure 9 shows the distribution of the certifications in the surveyed companies.

Most of the statements in this regard were that a certification with such a company size (SME) would only make sense, if the customer or the industry

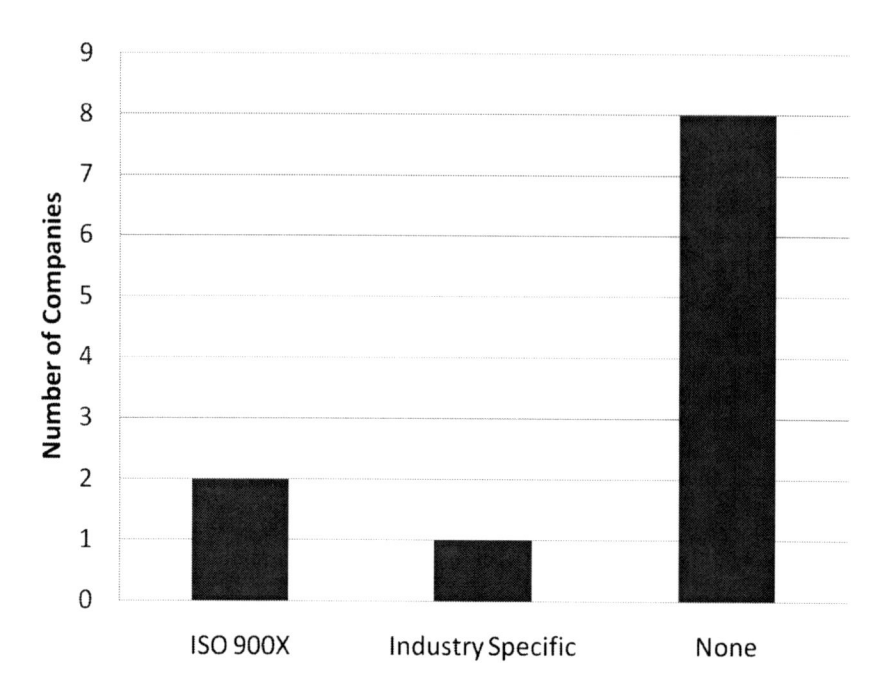

**Fig. 9.** Distribution of certifications among the surveyed companies

sector requires it. It would only add complexity and additional costs and would not bring any additional value to the company.

> I see no advantages in a certification at our company size. They are nice, but we wont benefit from them at the moment. You have to invest a lot of effort into them.

Another interviewee said, that "... certifications are not relevant to us. [...] they are not yet required." Therefore, most companies do not plan to achieve a certification. It should be noted, that the only company that is fully ISO 9001 certified, was also the only one to achieve maturity level 3 (which is still rather low compared with Hammers maturity model).

## 5 Discussion and Outlook

At first it was assumed that the more a company is technology-oriented, the higher is the process management maturity. This could not be clearly identified and confirmed. However, it clearly turned out that the more work is done in front of computers it is more likely that procedures are documented. In contrast, for example, an artisanal company rarely uses information technologies what results in the fact that process management has no meaning for this company.

Like presented in the findings, we had a closer look at the development of process management in companies. Therefore, we asked at what point companies started their process management programmes. Mostly it was specifically addressed to the connection between process management and the number of employees. Remarkably, the opinions differ a lot in this respect. One interviewee said, for example "... it makes sense as soon as more than two employees are present. [...] The more people the more detailed it should occur."

Another interviewee argued that "... in our case, we reached a certain limit with 60 to 70 employees where we realized that we need a more and better structured organization". Another statement refuted it completely: "Without [process management] you do not need to think about letting the company grow. Once you have a single employee it has to be clear what you expect from him or her". Based on these statements it can clearly be seen that the companies are divided. This is a topic that would be interesting for further studies: At what point of organizational maturity process management can help a company and when it is – probably – an unnecessary overhead.

Like mentioned in the research methodology section the presented study is based on the mixed methods research methodology. The study is the qualitative part of this work. Based on the results of this research a quantitative survey will be made among small- and medium-sized enterprises in the German-speaking part of Europe [5]. The main focus of this quantitative study will be the connection between process management and company success. Therefore, company representatives will fill out an online survey that includes questions about the success of the company and its process management. The process management again will be measured with the presented adaption of the PEM-Model. Furthermore, we hope to find significant differences between the different sectors to be able to better understand the impact of business process management on SME. The upcoming survey will also try to verify the results of the presented qualitative study.

We are anxious to see if process management will be increasingly important in the future or not and especially how SME deal with the topic of process management.

# References

[1] van der Aalst, W., ter Hofstede, A., Weske, M.: Business Process Management: A Survey. In: van der Aalst, W.M.P., ter Hofstede, A.H.M., Weske, M. (eds.) BPM 2003. LNCS, vol. 2678, pp. 1–12. Springer, Heidelberg (2003)
[2] Baumgarth, C., Eisend, M., Evanschitzky, H. (eds.): Empirische Mastertechniken: Eine anwendungsorientierte Einführung für die Marketing- und Managementforschung. Gabler (2009) (in German)
[3] vom Brocke, J., Roesemann, M.: Foreword. In: Handbook on Business Process Management, vol. 1, pp. vii–ix. Springer, Heidelberg (2010)
[4] Brüsemeister, T.: Qualitative Forschung - Ein Überblick, 2nd edn. Vs Verlag (2008) (in German)
[5] Feldbacher, P., Fleiß, J., Singer, R.: Business Process Management: A Survey Among Small - and Medium Sized Enterprises (to be published)

[6] Gadatsch, A.: Status Quo Prozessmanagement 2006 Kompetenzzentrum für Geschäftsprozessmanagement (2007) (in German)
[7] Glasl, F., Lievegoed, B.: Dynamische Unternehmensentwicklung, Grundlagen für nachhaltiges Change Management, 3rd edn. Freies Geistesleben (2004) (in German)
[8] Hammer, M.: The Process Audit. Harvard Business Review 4 (2007)
[9] Hammer, M.: What is Business Process Management? In: Handbook on Business Process Management, vol. 1, pp. 3–16. Springer, Heidelberg (2010)
[10] Hammer, M., Champy, J.: Reengineering the Corporation: A Manifesto for Business Revolution. Harper Business (1993)
[11] Hammer, M., Hershman, L.W.: Faster, cheaper, better. Crown Business (2010)
[12] Knuppertz, T., Schnägelberger, S.: Status Quo Prozessmanagement 2007/2008 Kompetenzzentrum für Prozessmanagement (2008) (in German)
[13] Kohlbacher, M.: The effects of process orientation: a literature review. Business Process Management Journal 16(1), 135–152 (2010)
[14] Lamnek, S.: Qualitative Sozialforschung - Methoden und Techniken. In: BeltzPVU, vol. 2 (1995) (in German)
[15] Mayring, P.: Einführung in die Qualitative Sozialforschung. In: BeltzPVU, 4th edn. (2001) (in German)
[16] Oschischnig, U.: Statistical Yearbook 2010. Austrian Chamber of Commerce (2010)
[17] Palmberg, K.: Experiences of implementing process management: a multiple-case study. Business Process Management Journal 16(1), 93–113 (2010)
[18] Patig, S., Casanova-Brito, V., Vögeli, B.: IT requirements of business process management in practice – an empirical study. In: Hull, R., Mendling, J., Tai, S. (eds.) BPM 2010. LNCS, vol. 6336, pp. 13–28. Springer, Heidelberg (2010)
[19] Weske, M.: Business Process Management: Concepts, Languages, Architectures. Springer, Heidelberg (2007)

# Author Index

Back, Gregor   48
Bastarz, Fritz   109
Bindner, Jörg   256
Bonaldi, David   98
Borgert, Stephan   190

Chebotarev, Valery   271

Daniel, Klaus   48
Dirndorfer, Max   281

Evina, Kristin   271

Feldbacher, Patrick   296
Ferschl, Michael   139
Fischer, Herbert   281
Fleischmann, Albert   175

Gerhardt, Eduard   155
Gromoff, Alexander   271

Halek, Patrick   109
Handy, Barbara   281
Heininger, Richard   175
Herrmann, Christian   80
Hilgarth, Bernd   34
Hirayama, Takeshi   215
Hosaka, Sadao   215
Hufgard, Andreas   155

Kawai, Hiroyuki   215
Komiyama, Shota   215
Kröckel, Johannes   34
Kurz, Matthias   80, 139

Lang, Siri   246
Lindner, Hans-Günter   126

Mayer-Leixner, Gunther   256
Meyer, Nils   175
Mühlhäuser, Max   190

Nakamura, Minoru   215
Nakamura, Shinji   215
Neubauer, Matthias   65

Oppl, Stefan   16

Pinter, Eva   98

Radmayr, Markus   175
Reichelt, Dominik   139
Reinheimer, Stefan   115
Rothschädl, Thomas   175

Schaller, Thomas   139
Schneeberger, Josef   281
Schweiger, Christina   296
Singer, Robert   296
Stary, Christian   3, 65
Stavenko, Yulia   271
Steinmetz, Joachim   190
Strauss, Marco   246
Suppan, Peter   296

Tan, Toshihiro   215
Totter, Alexandra   98
Turinsky, Martin   232

Yuki, Katsuhiro   215